Paddington

A History

Greg Young, Editor
The Paddington Society

16pt

Copyright Page from the Original Book

A NewSouth book

Published by
NewSouth Publishing
University of New South Wales Press Ltd
University of New South Wales
Sydney NSW 2052
AUSTRALIA
newsouthpublishing.com

Published in association with The Paddington Society.
www.paddingtonsociety.org.au

© Copyright in compilation, The Paddington Society
and Greg Young 2019
First published 2019

10 9 8 7 6 5 4 3 2 1

This book is copyright. Apart from any fair dealing for the purpose of private study, research, criticism or review, as permitted under the Copyright Act, no part of this book may be reproduced by any process without written permission. Inquiries should be addressed to the publisher.

 A catalogue record for this book is available from the National Library of Australia

Design Tonto Design
Cover image The commanding view of Paddington and the city from atop the Royal Hotel. *Simon Wood Photography, 2017*
Endpapers (hardback edition) Jacarandas beside Victoria Barracks, defining the edge of Oxford Street. *Simon Wood Photography, 2017*
Printer Everbest

All reasonable efforts were taken to obtain permission to use copyright material reproduced in this book, but in some cases copyright could not be traced. The publisher welcomes information in this regard.

This book is printed on paper using fibre supplied from plantation or sustainably managed forests.

TABLE OF CONTENTS

Preface	ii
Acknowledgments	v
Notes on authors	xii
Paddington: An introduction	xxi
Chapter 1: Aboriginal Paddington	1
Chapter 2: Mapping Paddington	42
Chapter 3: Ever-changing Paddington	77
Chapter 4: Early Paddington	164
Chapter 5: The Victorian suburb	220
Chapter 6: Gentrification	295
Chapter 7: Conserving Paddington	326
Chapter 8: Bohemian Paddington	389
Chapter 9: Creative Paddington	430
Chapter 10: Changing landscapes	493
Chapter 11: Survival	544
Appendix: The Paddington Terrace House: 1840–1910	575
Endnotes by chapter	596
Select bibliography	695
Index	705

This book is an initiative of The Paddington Society to celebrate the 50th anniversary of its formation in 1964.

Preface

The story of Sydney's Paddington has intrigued residents, visitors and professionals for a considerable time. Members of The Paddington Society committee have grappled with its special qualities for over 50 years in an endeavour to understand and explain the complex overlay of events which gave rise to the delightful place we see today. Without knowledge of the past, it is difficult to fully value a place and to recognise what is needed to conserve its special qualities.

The challenges have changed. Now that Paddington is highly prized, there are many who want to introduce values that don't fit, and to stretch the boundaries of reasonable development in a conservation area.

We hope that this book will serve to inform not only those who seek to live here but also the authorities who control compliance, traffic and services, and to provide to all involved in Paddington's evolution a benchmark for what is reasonable to change and what must be carefully conserved. For they all play a part in continuing the spirit of the place and ensuring that the legacy continues for further generations.

This book has been in the making for over four years, made possible by generous bequests and donations, and by the untiring efforts of The Paddington Society History Committee who held the process together with enthusiasm over the long journey from inception. We are fortunate to have had the ongoing assistance and insights from the editor Dr Greg Young, who made a significant contribution to shaping the book concept, and balanced our desire for a definitive physical history of the place with a need to make the story sociologically relevant and interesting to today's informed readers.

Contributing authors are well known for their special interests and we are indebted to each and every one of them for bringing their particular talents and skills to focus on Paddington.

We believe that this book will set new standards in terms of urban history, and we hope it will bring a better appreciation of the importance of the place now and into the future. We hope that you enjoy the discoveries within these pages.

Will Mrongovius
President
The Paddington Society

Acknowledgments

The Paddington Society History Committee

The Paddington Society would like to acknowledge the generosity of numerous donors who enabled the vision for the book to be realised: we extend to each of them our deep appreciation.

The Society acknowledges the generous bequest from the Estate of Kathleen Hooke, a long-term Paddington resident and member of The Paddington Society. The bequest provided the seed funding and impetus to create the book in her honour. Many generous donations were also made by other Paddington residents and Society members; these major donors are listed separately.

The project was supported in its early stages by the Create NSW Cultural Grants Program, a devolved funding program administered by the Royal Australian Historical Society on behalf of the NSW Government. This took the form of a grant which facilitated exhaustive research of manuscripts, maps, paintings and photos of early Paddington, as a resource for the future. The research was skilfully carried out by Louise Prowse, to whom we are deeply indebted.

Our thanks go to Woollahra Municipal Council for a substantial grant, through their Community and Cultural Grants Program, to assist with digital image and copyright charges for selected imagery for the book. We are grateful for the assistance of Dr Paul Ashton in managing the image permission process, and to Liz Cranfield of Conybeare Morrison for assisting the Committee with the graphic visualisation of the project.

We also thank the City of Sydney for a very generous grant under the Cultural and Creative Grants and Sponsorship Program, which went a long way towards making publication of the book possible.

Others in our debt are the librarians and archivists who generously gave of their time to assist with sourcing graphic material, as well as those who gave their time freely to read the early chapters and provide useful commentary.

The Society has been fortunate to have the interest and support of NewSouth Publishing and, in particular, publisher Elspeth Menzies, whose interest and chapter comments contributed significantly to the book.

THE COMMITTEE:
Linda Gosling (Chair)
Robyn Attuell
Esther Hayter
Krystyna Luczak
Bill Morrison
John Richardson
Minty Smyth

The Editor

Many factors come together in producing a history involving the talents of a diverse cross-section of historical specialists, more than a dozen in all, and of The Paddington Society, one of the country's leading urban conservation groups. The challenge was to shape a book to bring these interests together based on a balanced and up-to-date historical vision. To this end I developed an initial collaborative book concept, advised on the selection of talented authors and provided them with chapter briefs. A full-day authors' workshop aligned the book's approaches and themes. The writing process itself included comments on each draft chapter from other members of the writing team, The Paddington Society History Committee and the publisher. The result is, I believe, a robust book that presents a series of chapter 'windows' onto the suburb's history that can be dipped into individually or read together as an integrated narrative.

My thanks are due to the authors for their perseverance in a lengthy and demanding process and to Dr Paul Ashton for advising on illustrations and editing.

I acknowledge the foresight of NewSouth Publishing in taking on the book and am grateful to the publisher Elspeth Menzies for comments on draft chapters and to Emma Hutchinson for smooth coordination of the project. Finally, my thanks go to The Paddington Society History Committee for its engagement at all stages in the process.

Dr Greg Young
Adjunct Professor
University of Technology Sydney

Major Sponsors

City of Sydney
Woollahra Municipal Council
Royal Australian Historical Society (RAHS)/NSW Government

Major Donors

Kathleen Hooke (bequest)
Greta Archbold
Robyn Attuell and Bruce Druery
John and Anne Fraser
James and Leonie Furber
Esther Hayter
Theresa Jacques, Aaron and Samuel Todd
Alan and Barbara Marshall
Moran Arts Foundation
The Moran Family
Bill and Elizabeth Morrison
Will Mrongovius and Diane Davies
Peter Poland (in memory of June Poland)
John and Virginia Richardson
Leo Schofield
Minty Smyth
Graham Stewart and Suzy Rea

Philip Thalis
Kay Vernon
Francis Walsh
Woollahra History and Heritage Society

Notes on authors

Dr Helen Armstrong

Dr Helen Armstrong has been an academic landscape architect since the late 1970s and set up the UNSW Cultural Landscape Research Unit with Craig Burton which documented numerous Australian cultural environments and their resultant landscapes. In the 1990s she explored migrant heritage places, published as *Migrant Place-making in Australia.* A long interest in peri-urban landscapes culminated in her book, *Marginal Landscapes.* She became the inaugural professor of Landscape Architecture at Queensland University of Technology (QUT) in 1997 and is currently emeritus-professor at QUT.

Dr Paul Ashton

Dr Paul Ashton is adjunct professor at Macquarie University, the University of Canberra and the University of Technology Sydney where, in 1999, he co-established the Australian Centre for

Public History. Co-editor and founder of the journal *Public History Review,* his numerous publications include *Public History and Heritage Today,* which he co-edited with Hilda Kean, and *Once Upon a Time: Australian writers on using the past,* co-edited with Anna Clark and Robert Crawford.

Robert Brown

Robert Brown is a founding director of Casey Brown Architecture. He has a Masters of Advanced Architectural Design from Columbia University and a UNSW architectural honours degree on the Paddington terrace. The first Australian to receive a UK SPAB Lethaby Travelling Scholarship for historic building repair, his practice has won the AIA Lachlan Macquarie and Francis Greenway awards, the Canberra Medallion and the RIBA World Wide Award for Architecture. Robert is currently a studio master in the Master of Architecture degree, UNSW.

Sheridan Burke

Sheridan Burke is a heritage consultant and an expert in modern heritage. She specialises in planning for the conservation, interpretation and management of historic places locally and internationally, ranging from Australian suburbs to monitoring missions for UNESCO World Heritage Sites and heritage management training with the Getty Conservation Institute. She is president of the ICOMOS Advisory Committee and its Twentieth Century Heritage International Scientific Committee, an adjunct professor, University of Canberra and an expert member of the Sydney Opera House Conservation Council.

Robert Griffin

Robert Griffin is a heritage consultant with expertise in the architectural history of Sydney. He has lectured and published widely on the history and design of Sydney houses, on historic interiors and the conservation of historic buildings. Robert has also curated exhibitions on Australian colonial architecture, social history and decorative arts and has been responsible for the conservation and interpretation of some of Sydney's most significant sites including Elizabeth Bay House, Government House, Sydney and The Sydney Mint.

Sandra Hall

Sandra Hall is a film critic for the *Sydney Morning Herald.* She is also the author of two novels, *Beyond the Break* and *A Thousand Small Wishes,* as well as *Tabloid Man,* a biography of the press tycoon, Ezra Norton, and two books on the history of Australian television: *Supertoy: 20 years of Australian television* and *Turning On: Turning Off: Australian television in the eighties.* In 1994, she won the Pascall Prize for film criticism.

Dr Paul Irish

Dr Paul Irish is a historian and archaeologist with heritage consultancy MDCA, and has a longstanding interest in the Aboriginal history of Sydney. He has recently published the book *Hidden in Plain View: The Aboriginal people of coastal Sydney* and regularly holds public talks. As the recipient of the 2015 NSW History Fellowship he prepared the touring exhibition *This Is Where They Travelled: Historical Aboriginal lives in Sydney* in collaboration with researchers from the La Perouse Aboriginal community.

Dr Peter McNeil

Dr Peter McNeil is distinguished professor of Design History at the University of Technology Sydney and Finland distinguished professor at Aalto University. An award-winning author, he is a fellow of the Australian Academy of the Humanities where he is section head for the Arts. He publishes and lectures internationally across design, fashion, textiles, interiors, architecture and the urban condition. His publications on Sydney designers circa 1920–30 have been widely reprinted. He has lived happily in or beside Paddington for 25 years.

Bill Morrison

Bill Morrison is an architect and urban designer and director of Conybeare Morrison Architects and Context Landscape Design. He has lived in Paddington for over 40 years and has served on The Paddington Society Committee in excess of 25 years, recently being awarded life membership for his contribution to the conservation of Paddington and work on the public domain. Bill's interest in the urban morphology of cities gave rise to detailed studies of Paddington, including the original mapping sequence in this book.

Dr Peter Spearritt

Dr Peter Spearritt's *The Sydney Harbour Bridge: A life,* is now in its third edition. His *Sydney's Century: A history,* won the NSW Premier's prize in 2000. He has written *Australian Dictionary of Biography* entries on many of Sydney's identities, from JJC Bradfield and LJ Hooker to the cartoonist Emile Mercier. He is co-author of *Electrifying*

Sydney and *Holiday Business: Tourism in Australia since 1870.* His book *Where History Happened,* an account of revealing places and events around Australia, will be published by the National Library of Australia in 2018.

Sharon Veale

Sharon Veale is a public historian and urban planner with over 20 years' experience in cultural heritage management. She is chief executive of GML Heritage, a multidisciplinary heritage consultancy with Sydney, Melbourne and Canberra offices. She teaches heritage planning at UNSW, is a member of the National Parks and Wildlife Service Advisory Council and the Sydney Living Museums Board of Trustees. She is on the editorial committee for *Historic Environment* and a full member of Australia ICOMOS and the Planning Institute of Australia.

Garry Wotherspoon

Garry Wotherspoon is a Sydney-based writer, a former academic and former NSW history fellow. His books include *Sydney's Transport: Studies in urban history*, and *Being Different: Nine gay men remember*. His *The Sydney Mechanics' School of Arts: A history* was shortlisted for the NSW Premier's History Awards, and his *Gay Sydney: A history* was shortlisted for the Queensland Literary Awards. He was awarded Australia's Centenary of Federation Medal for his work as an academic, researcher and human rights activist.

Dr Greg Young

Dr Greg Young, editor, is adjunct professor, University of Technology Sydney. He is a historian and planner distinguished internationally as a cultural theorist and strategist. The author of *Reshaping Planning with Culture, The Culturisation of Planning* and principal editor of *The Routledge Research Companion to Planning and Culture,* he was the NSW Heritage Council's first historian and advocate, the inaugural NSW Premier's Max Kelly Scholar to Venice, Italy and the first Australian planner awarded a US Getty

Scholarship. <wikipedia.org/wiki/Greg_Young_(planner)>.

Paddington: An introduction

Greg Young

On a sunny winter's day in 1969,[1] at a demonstration of up to 2000 strong, Paddington and Woollahra residents marched down the elegant Jersey Road that divided the two suburbs, verandahs on either side garlanded with wreaths and swags of black crepe. Wearing funeral colours – some in black aprons to collect donations – they had turned out to protest stubborn government road-widening and demolition proposals with the same flair for publicity shown by the great New York pioneer of urban activism, Jane Jacobs. The media savvy campaign, devised by high-octane adman and journalist Leo Schofield, won the day and the proposals were ultimately dropped, but other factors that underlay the protest also made their contribution to saving Paddington.

The arrival of European migrants in the 1950s began the area's revival from the social and economic ravages of the Great Depression. This paved the way for the middle-class 'new urbanites' who guided the suburb across the early 1960s minefield of modernist planning proposals that could have wiped it from the map. Now a chic and cherished urban village, Paddington is revealing its once hidden Indigenous history – highlighted in this book – even as it faces up to new and more subtle threats to the integrity of its heritage landscape.

Paddington, in the Eastern Suburbs of Sydney, holds a firm place in Australia's national imagination as the model of a fashionable heritage suburb, mirrored around the globe by other legendary quarters such as Chelsea in London, the Left Bank in Paris and Greenwich Village in New York. Paddington is recognised as one of the largest concentrations of intact Victorian terrace housing in the world and is a microcosm of inner-suburban life, and trends in development, from Sydney's earliest times. Forming a mosaic of random angles and grids, the suburb lines two natural amphitheatres divided by the Oxford Street ridge. Aerial views indicate a circular pocket of 150 hectares nestled in the topography of an ancient river valley, the home of some 13,000 residents according to the latest census.[2]

By 1890, 3800 houses had been constructed in the area and the final shape of the municipality was apparent.[3] Residents were a more or less equal number of locals and foreign born from a mix of classes dominated by the 'upper working' and 'lower middle class', with 'a sprinkling of professional men'.[4] This was the scene for a thriving residential and commercial community throughout the late 19th century with good connections to the city as transport evolved from horsebus to tram. The Great Depression was a blow to a suburb already on the slide by the early 20th century, but the Paddington community practised mutual aid, and took pride in itself. With the arrival of gentrification in the 1960s, Paddington's celebrity terraces and their newly leafy surrounds came to define the village. The area emerged as a byword for inner-city gentrification and a symbol of the new metropolitan Sydney, along with the Opera House, Harbour Bridge and the city's birthplace in The Rocks.

A 'built oasis', Paddington is bounded by housing to the east and west, and by green spaces to the north – Rushcutters Bay Park, Trumper Park and Trumper Oval – and to the south – Moore and Centennial Parks. The overall consistency of this mosaic of streets, porous lanes, terrace rows, pubs and corner shops – offset by an intricate diversity of shape, size and ornamentation – is a pedestrian's delight.

Figure I.1: The Paddington pocket. Seen today from Sydney Harbour, Paddington is visible as a contained village, separate from its surrounds and with a strong relationship to Rushcutters Bay. Airviewonline.com

Figure I.2: Built oasis. An abundance of vegetation, with Underwood Street (diagonal on right), Elizabeth Street (with mansion terrace facades in centre) and Grand National Hotel on corner. Sydney Images.

Presenting Paddington

The first major history of Paddington was written in 1978 by historian Max Kelly. In his book *Paddock Full of*

Houses: Paddington 1840–1890, Kelly argued that the area's history could one day be written as the life of three, four or more suburbs.[5] The intervening years have added still more layers and new themes and this book covers Paddington's history as the story of a complex evolution up to the current phase of hyper-gentrification. At the same time, the book acknowledges the emergence of new and different historical perspectives, heritage values and community needs. As a result, the reader will find here current topics such as Indigenous, creative and landscape history, as well as Paddington's future prospects, including its conservation in a world city subject to globalised trends in property, media and employment.

These changes in perspectives and needs are not neutral, however, and demand re-thinking. For example, the rise of Indigenous history presents an opportunity to tell in a suburban setting a pre- and post-contact Aboriginal history in a seamless way. The transformative impact of migration in two separate centuries – the 19th and 20th – are also central to the story. In the 19th century, Scots, Irish and English migrants built Paddington as Sydney's first commuter suburb; following World War 2, so-called New Australians saved it from blight.

Figure I.3: A grand, consistent terrace row, 5–11 Heeley Street. On the left the home of Max Kelly, Paddington historian and first president of the pioneering Sydney History Group, 1975. Simon Wood Photography, 2017.

The arrival of university students, bohemians and middle-class gentrifiers expanded the pattern of cultural and lifestyle diversity that characterised the

1950s, 1960s and 1970s. These groups also created a wave of support for urban conservation and new planning measures that swept through the decades of the last century and into our own, only to lose much of their energy at that very point. In governance, a more mercantile approach to heritage as an asset emerged, one that expressed the broader neo-liberal economic climate that for the past three decades has influenced governments and corporations worldwide. As a globalised heritage area at an international price point, Paddington has faced pressures to develop and upscale at the expense of its traditional urban character. Ironically, at the same time, Australia's exceptional population growth in OECD terms,[6] coupled with Sydney's role as a magnet for urban migration, has meant that urban issues have achieved greater importance on the national and city agendas.

Architects and planners have also increasingly recognised the terrace house as embodying a form of sustainability wisdom, an inspirational 'tube for urban living',[7] able to serve as an architectural and planning model for Sydney in more densely populated times. Yet while urban issues rose in importance in the 1970s, since then the high tide of urban history has retreated with fashion in historical research moving to other fields. The downplaying of urban history, however, limits the development of fresh insights into heritage and its conservation.

The digital revolution and the proliferation of social media have also undercut historical and book cultures. This poses the question of how best to convey the 'up and down' cycles of Paddington's history as well as its architectural and landscape attributes, especially for millennial readers upon whom responsibility for the suburb's conservation will come to rest. Fortunately, remarkable graphic resources are available to help tell Paddington's story to the generations of a predominantly 'visual age'. This book represents some of the best of Paddington's iconography, including the physical growth of the suburb mapped over time. Its diverse chapters and thematic richness illuminate the area's complex built and social evolution, while honouring its Indigenous history and eye-opening story of cultural diversity to which migrants, artists, writers, students, sexual minorities and creative professionals of all types contributed.

Paddington may also be viewed as a place where the riches of history, heritage and landscape are seen as sideshows – and also inducements – to property speculation and upscaling. Alternatively, this bounty may be seen from the perspective of artists, writers and poets, and much of the community, as a source of inspiration.

Since the 1960s, partly through the impact of television, film, newspapers, magazines and advertising, Paddington has carved out a symbolic territory many times the size of its geographical area. The lives of prominent residents including legendary artists along with public figures influential in the broader creative industries, have provided colourful grist to the media's mill. In addition, numerous documentaries have contributed to the image of the suburb including the 1962 ABC's *Four Corners* program 'Paddington Gentrification', and fictionalised dramas such as the 1970s landmark television series *Number 96.* This soap opera was closely identified with Paddington, not least for the presence of 'Don', a sympathetic gay character played by Joe Hasham (sometimes claimed as the first such character openly portrayed on television on a regular basis worldwide).[8]

In this context, Paddington won a nameless publicity contest and its fortunes continued to revive. Oxford Street, the once charmed high street, and the famous Paddington Markets became part of a general creative and cultural hub, an urban village that attracted widespread national media attention and some of the highest visitor numbers in Sydney. Yet Paddington was not always of interest Australia-wide. In the 1940s and 1950s Paddington was disparaged and officially designated a slum. The 'bright new vision for Sydney'[9] of the 1948 *County of Cumberland Planning Scheme* described Paddington 'as requiring replacement, either immediately or within twenty-five years'.[10]

The combination of the discovery of the suburb by migrants after World War 2 and the arrival of a new kind of sensitivity to heritage and a broader conservation sensibility saved Paddington from the fate proposed by politicians and planners. The running planning battles for Paddington are documented in this book and while the Sydney conservation tide may have receded with the new millennium, Paddington is nevertheless nowadays recognised as of enduring importance comparable to other heritage gems from around the globe.

People and personalities

The Indigenous land on which Paddington sits is Cadi land, home to the Cadigal people. Here Aboriginal life evolved over a period of many thousands of years in an area known as 'Kogerah'. But Aboriginal people have also played a part at every stage in the history of Paddington as valuable new research in this book shows. In the 19th century Indigenous people lived alongside local settlers and in the 20th century remained in Paddington. Aboriginal organisations also created new links to the suburb thereafter and Indigenous residents form part of the contemporary urban village.

The suburb of Paddington was built in a number of major stages to produce an open-air museum still clearly visible today.[11] The first stage began with European settlement up until the period around 1840 and included the making of the first land grants to leading emancipists and prominent officials who built graceful mansions and led privileged family lives on their estates. The pattern of the estates themselves shaped later subdivision of the suburb, often in serendipitous ways.

In spite of unpromising sandy terrain on the ridge, the location of the early strategic communication route to the Pacific Ocean at South Head and the construction of Victoria Barracks in the 1840s, triggered the development of a number of small cottages. Many of these survive today to form the nucleus of what became known as Paddington village. The second stage is represented by the creation of the colonial rural village and later municipality between 1840 and 1870. Following the gold rushes in the 1850s, demand for housing in Paddington and other Sydney areas skyrocketed as Sydney's population boomed. From the late 1860s, the early estates were subdivided and a frenzy of terrace building ensued. Shops, pubs, transport and suppliers of all kinds followed, along with schools, churches and community associations.

By 1891 Paddington was home to almost 19,000 residents.[12] In this guise Paddington flourished until after World War 1 when the tide of fashion turned against the terrace house, and those residents who could, left for quarter-acre blocks in the suburbs. With a sharp downhill slide, Paddington wound up as a 'slum suburb', facing the grim realities of the Great Depression. Following World War 2 and Paddington's amalgamation into the City of Sydney in 1948, proposals for slum clearance and remodelling were put forward. In spite of modernist planning proposals such as these to, as it were, clean the urban slate, in fact Paddington began to revive. Thanks to the arrival of 'New Australians' seeking cheap rents and jobs nearby to the south, in company with university students and hippies, the area reinvented itself. Young professionals also arrived, and with 'cultural practitioners' (dubbed so by author and critic, Clive James), gentrification was soon in full swing. None of this prevented the Department of Main Roads proposing a series of expressways around and through Paddington that would have swallowed the suburb. In response to these proposals the Paddington Society was formed in 1964 as one of Sydney's first resident action groups.

The Society embraced many remarkable members, including two of its founders, the poet and broadcaster John Thompson and his writer partner Patricia Thompson. In her memoir *Accidental Chords,* Patricia describes herself and her husband as 'prigs about the public interest and the common weal'.[13] Fortunately they were not alone and the Society went on to win the campaign known as the 'Battle for Paddington'. There were however many battles in the extended campaign to introduce and refine conservation planning measures. The Society approached these with acumen and utilised professional studies and submissions based on international evidence. This facilitated the introduction in 1971 of the City of Sydney and Woollahra Planning Schemes, which were the first positive legal measures for urban conservation in Paddington. In 1979 Paddington also became the first conservation area listed by the prominent voluntary conservation body, the National Trust of Australia (NSW), and in 1980 it was listed on the – now defunct – Commonwealth Register of the National Estate.

Paddington in the early phase of its gentrification in the 1960s and 1970s was a significantly bohemian place, crowded, noisy and colourful. It was a suburb variously called home by likes of TV personality Jeannie Little, designer Florence Broadhurst and rock star and lead singer of INXS, Michael Hutchence. Pubs thrived with bands and customers spilling onto the streets, while terraces were party houses at the ready with candles in bottles, paper lampshades and beanbags. And for many it was said not to be a party unless the police arrived. This early period of gentrification was characterised by mixed incomes and employment but the upward spiral of the trend in the 1980s meant that by the 1990s the suburb was consistently transformed. Since then, a subsequent phase of hyper-gentrification has come to prevail with almost 20 per cent of residents now employed in the finance industry.[14] With hyper-gentrification, terraces become more like casino chips. Behind the facade, the interior layout and architectural detail fall prey to removal, or in the case of the amalgamation of adjacent houses are opened to a double width. In these cases, the past stops at the front door. The reduction in support for urban history and the conservation ethos, along with the growth of entrepreneurial approaches to heritage as wealth creation, suggest that the values of the early gentrifiers are now under disruption.

In spite of this, Paddington as a place of complex urban character and visual detail endures. The original 'street-making discipline' of the suburb is conserved and in the hands of adept architects, 19th century terraces have been flooded with light and space.[15] The many lives of Paddington can be read in the layers of its cultural landscape and long-term familiarity deepens understanding. The more you observe an aesthetic object the more of its properties you come to absorb[16] and this is as true for a heritage suburb as for a conventional work of art.

Overlaying the buildings and their ornate details and the intricate pattern of streets, laneways and vistas is a picturesque landscape, gentrified through the widespread planting of colourful jacaranda trees, creepers and scented plants. The flamboyance of the larrikin landscaping of the early gentrifiers is now being tamed in the public domain: the large trees and large dogs of the 1970s and 1980s have shrunk to the small trees and small dogs of the present-day embourgeoisement. The landscape story is a continuum taking in Aboriginal occupation before and after the ancient flooding of Sydney Harbour and the several stages that characterise the building of the European settlement.

Communities

In the words of the architectural writer Robert Harbison, cities and suburbs thrive by remembering the 'pungent compost of past lives'.[17] Paddington is no exception with a remarkable and lively history of social and cultural diversity. Aboriginal people have been part of the life of Paddington throughout its built history. In the 19th century the Rushcutters Bay flats were leased to Chinese market gardeners who dominated the supply of fresh vegetables to Sydney until they were driven out by racist sentiment and a campaign against them in the period 1900 to 1910.[18] The mass migration of 'New Australians' in the 1950s led to Greeks, Italians, Portuguese and Eastern Europeans settling in Paddington, while the Jewish contribution to Paddington was considerable in the 19th century.[19] Gay men (in particular) and gay women also came to Paddington as gentrifiers and to access favoured venues and the Paddington markets. Creative artists of all stripes were inspired by and resided in Paddington and the strong local presence of creative industries made their synergistic existence felt.

A place in history

Why do some histories stand the test of time and others do not? In Paddington's case Max Kelly's history (1978) was based on an innovative use of sources, 'not only on rate-books but on tram tickets and old architraves'[20] and employed compelling illustrations, even in black and white. Kelly was also a lightning rod for the environmental and conservation consciousness of his time. As a resident in London in the swinging '60s while enrolled at the London School of Economics, Kelly immersed himself in the life and architecture of Rome and London and was exposed to the flourishing of British cultural studies. As a moonlighting model for cigarettes, famously on motorway billboards, he was perhaps the perfect subject for the new discipline. In Sydney, this liberal communitarian became the admired first president of the Sydney History Group, a group of urban historians and heritage activists founded in 1975.[21]

While all histories draw on earlier work, it is also universally true that every generation writes history in its own way to serve its own needs. Also the ability to see the past in the present is a form of understanding, and is important because as Winston Churchill recognised, 'we make the city and the city makes us'. The green bans in 1970s Sydney and the work of historians, architects and activists in suburban societies such as the Paddington Society reflected this. Entwined with these activities were government policies, legislation and regulation at every tier. In spite of these advances, this book notes the weakening of heritage protection in the current century. Even so, Paddington is the concrete outcome of environmental agitation and protective conservation measures that began in the 1960s. The planning victories of the period were real, although their story is a piecemeal one as progress edged forward in the 1970s. A number of heritage development control plans were adopted by the two responsible councils – Woollahra City Council and the City of Sydney – and shone a light on the fine grain of the suburb to indicate appropriate new building forms, materials, colours and landscaping.

Figure I.4: Max Kelly, historian and 'Renaissance man'. Pictured on steps of the State Library of New South Wales, 1995. Courtesy of Tony Fragar.

My Paddington

One of Australia's most influential historians Bernard Smith singled out the painter Sali Herman (1898–1993) as the first person to see the Australian suburb in art and to depict it as a personal environment.[22] Margaret Olley complemented Herman's work in her much-loved domestic paintings in which the personal interior of her terrace and studio were portrayed as a 'living canvas'. At her home she received and entertained *tout le monde* and through the magic of 'Olley Land' transcended Paddington's material limits.

In my case, a knowledge of Paddington came to me from many directions.

The 'deep walking'[23] of the flâneur, in the words of the playwright Louis Nowra, was a key source along with the power of Sali Herman's paintings and various histories and novels, plus memories of neighbours and others. Additionally, a simple but eye-opening description from an architect – Alec Tzannes – who described the suburb to me in the late 1970s as 'the Paddington Hill', nestled like a Greek village in its landform. In common with many in the 1970s, I began to create a home by renovating a dilapidated terrace with a bathroom in a lean-to at the rear and a lavatory in its original position on the old privy lane. I painted the balcony sitting-room white, sanded and polished the honey-coloured timber floors and under-furnished the rooms. Returning home of an evening from a position in the NSW government, I was always eager to get on with the job. While watching the neighbourhood from my cast-iron balcony, entertaining friends there and walking and cycling the streets and lanes, I absorbed more and more of the suburb as my interest spread in ever-widening circles of attention.

Figure I.5: Paddington as a personal environment. Sali Herman, The Women of Paddington, 1950. © Sali Herman/Licensed by Viscopy, 2017. Image courtesy of Deutscher and Hackett, Sydney.

Figure I.6: Olley Land, Margaret Olley, The Yellow Room, 1989. Courtesy of the Estate of the Artist and Philip Bacon Galleries, Brisbane.

Throughout the 1980s and 1990s I became acquainted with the diversity of residents in the neighbourhood, including old timers who had lived in Paddington as a slum and knew the illegal betting and sly grog shops. The eclectic residential mosaic surrounding me told the tale. Within 50 metres of my door were three distinctive households. To the south lived lifetime residents Olive Isdale (1923–2016) and her third husband Victor who had once delivered

Paddington its ice along with chilled sly grog.[24] Into her 90s, Olive continued to sing *On the Street Where You Live* as the culmination of the neighbourhood Christmas Party. To the west lived Slasher with a reputation surviving from the Sydney razor gangs of the 1920s. On the north were the Krygers,[25] prominent divorcees who went into hiding from the Establishment's gaze in Paddington – still possible in the 1960s – and stayed on as public benefactors and suzerains of a property row. As experience has taught me, the ability to see the past in the present is especially poignant when viewed at close quarters through communities, friends and neighbours.

Book outline

Developed mainly in chronological sequence, this book canvasses many fields including Indigenous history, cartography, landscape analysis, social, architectural, design and transport history and the sociological understanding of creativity and its networks at a suburban level.

Figure I.7: The watcher on the cast iron balcony. Greg Young and self-renovated terrace, Paddington, 1979. Photo: Sheridan Burke.

The book begins with a chapter by Paul Irish 'Aboriginal Paddington' which describes the area seamlessly as an evolving Indigenous home before and after the effects of the global ice age, throughout the 18th, 19th and 20th centuries and with Aboriginal connection current today.

The underlying topographical structure of Paddington is shown by Bill Morrison in 'Mapping Paddington' to have shaped a serendipitous history illustrated through original retro-maps revealing snapshots of Paddington 'taken' at key points in its developmental history.

The general history of the suburb is portrayed as a chequered story in 'Ever-changing Paddington' by Garry Wotherspoon and Paul Ashton. The account encompasses Georgian land grants and estates, Victorian mid and later 19th-century mass terracing, the ravages of the Great Depression and ultimately gentrification.

A special focus on Paddington's often forgotten early 19th-century development is provided by Robert Griffin in 'Early Paddington'. The chapter demonstrates that much of the evidence of Paddington's early grants and gentry estates survives in street names and layouts and in landscape elements and small terraces that remain as contributors to Paddington's charisma.

The Georgian gentry estates were followed by the swelling of Sydney's population and a period of Victorian subdivision and feverish terrace building that created today's street patterns and predominant architectural character. This pattern is described and illustrated with significant graphics in the chapter 'The Victorian Suburb' by Robert Griffin and Robert Brown.

In 'Gentrification' the story of the cumulative social, economic and cultural changes that Paddington experienced from the 1960s is described by Sharon Veale and Peter McNeil. This period began with the arrival of university students, migrants, artists and new urbanites who constituted its first phase and led eventually to more recent transformations in demography, tastes and incomes. This includes the rise and media publicity surrounding creative individuals and innovative businesses that fuelled the Oxford Street retail boom – until its demise – and the supplanting of the first phase of migrant revival and bohemian gentrification by current wealth and property speculation.

The conservation of Paddington in the period following World War 2 is the subject of a finely detailed account

'Conserving Paddington' by Sheridan Burke which describes the planning measures of the period, the role of major players such as the Paddington Society, national and international influences on planning and development controls and the significance of cultural themes[26] and future conservation models.

Colourful residents and the bohemian figures and artistic tribes of the gentrification period are evoked in 'Bohemian Paddington' by Sandra Hall including the creative individuals and businesses, tastemakers and trendsetters that set Paddington on its contemporary course.

Paddington's association with the arts in Sydney in the 19th and 20th centuries ranged across literature, art, music, design and creative businesses along with bohemian and artistic networks that overlay the suburb. This pattern and its important 19th century backstory pre-date the arts hub of the 1960s and are evocatively described by Peter McNeil in 'Creative Paddington'.

Paddington is also a significant and revealing landscape. The continuum of landscape changes in the area involved not only the Europeanised ridge and uplands but also the quarries, waterways, recreation areas, gardens and streetscapes of the public domain. These features shifted in appreciation and aesthetic assessment – at times completing a full circle in evaluation – as charted by Helen Armstrong in 'Changing landscapes'.

The last chapter in the book is a shrewd account, located in a national context, of Paddington's remarkable survival and its fame. Peter Spearritt in his chapter 'Survival' also gives a heads up on the specific geographical, developmental and even geological advantages that give Paddington a lasting edge.

The book concludes with brief notes on the nature of the British and the distinctive Sydney terrace in the essay 'The Paddington terrace house: 1840—1910'. The form of the terrace house and its features are concisely described and illustrated with elegant line drawings based on meticulous architectural research.

Suburb of the future

The historian and art critic Robert Hughes remarked in *The Shock of the New* – his groundbreaking 1980s television series – that the real estate agents of Paddington owe a debt of gratitude to the painter Sali Herman, one of the first to see beauty behind the peeling paint of Paddington's terraces.[27] In the 2010s much of this 'debt' is owed to the media, as it seeks to exalt the capture of property value. Australian reality television programs, based on competition between 'fixer-uppers' and ubiquitous global property programs have had the effect of aggrandising renovation, development and real estate. A global narrative has gripped the public imagination and created a fascination with property speculation.[28] But this is not without consequences. As in other hotspots in global cities, Paddington's heritage undergoes a subtle metamorphosis as special or distinctive historical and architectural features are transformed into monetary value.

If an increasing part of the appeal of a heritage suburb is pecuniary, however, it is less likely to be perceived as historical. In this way the past is drained, along with the future, and Paddington walks a tightrope.

Yet the social and economic churning of modern suburbs and cities always produces regrets. In the 1980s, residents left Paddington because they felt it had lost its bohemian spirit,[29] while others were driven out by rising rents. In the face of such change, it may be time to remember Marjorie Barnard and Flora Eldershaw's classic Sydney novel from the 1940s, *Tomorrow and Tomorrow and Tomorrow,* which described a national contradiction. The writers claimed that Australians had worked the land with courage and endurance but stood to compromise this 'with greed and lack of forethought'.[30] A salutary conclusion that inspires us to reflect on the work of a third century, the 21st, in building and saving the national treasure that is Paddington.

Chapter 1
Aboriginal Paddington

Paul Irish

* Aboriginal and Torres Strait Islander readers are warned that this chapter contains images and descriptions of deceased persons. We advise reading and viewing with caution and apologise for any distress unintentionally caused by the inclusion of this material.

When Europeans first arrived in the area we know today as Paddington, they saw several creeks winding their way through the scrub of what was later called the Lacrozia Valley towards the mudflats of Rushcutters Bay and into Sydney Harbour. Aboriginal people had known the Paddington area for much longer; since before the bay they knew as Kogerah or the harbour even existed. They had witnessed their creation and the evolution of the local landscape.

Twenty thousand years ago the Paddington area was bound up in a global ice age. Though there were no glaciers in Sydney, the climate was cooler and sea levels were much lower. The harbour headlands looked down over a forested valley to a river that meandered its way along what is now Sydney Harbour to the ocean many kilometres east of today's coast.[1] Rushcutters Creek flowed down into that river between the ridges of Darling Point and Darlinghurst, passing between the hilltops of Clark Island and Garden Island along the way (see Figures 1.1 and 1.2).

Figure 1.1: Distant View of Sydney and the Harbour, Captain Piper's Naval Villa at Eliza Point on the Left, in the Foreground a Family of Aborigines, by Joseph Lycett in 1817 shows a view up Sydney Harbour towards Circular Quay from Vaucluse. During the last ice age, Rushcutters Creek was one of many that flowed into a deep valley that was later flooded by rising seas to become Sydney Harbour. Garden Island (pictured far centre) was a hill joined to the mainland to the west of Rushcutters Creek. National Library of Australia.

We do not know much about how Aboriginal people lived in this ancient landscape, but we know they were there. Archaeological remains elsewhere in the Sydney region show this, but much of the evidence closest to Paddington now sits beneath the waves. Around 18,000 years ago the sea began to rise as ice sheets elsewhere in the world began to melt. Over the next 10,000 years, hundreds of generations of coastal Sydney people watched the water slowly encroach across the coastal plain to fill the valley of Sydney Harbour. The rising waters consumed up to two metres of shoreline each year and may have caused the realignment of some coastal groups as their lands were flooded. But the end result was the creation of a harbour and bays that teemed with fish and shellfish; a fishing paradise that Aboriginal people expertly exploited.[2]

Living in Kogerah

For the last few thousand years, Paddington and Rushcutters Bay looked more or less as they did when the first

Europeans arrived. We tend to view how Aboriginal people used this landscape through the rich record of pictures and words created by these wide-eyed strangers, but their snapshots have given us a misleading sense that this way of life was unchanging. Archaeological records tell another story, showing how Aboriginal people honed their toolkit to exploit the harbour's resources; for example, adding shell fish hooks around a thousand years ago to the fishing spears they used.[3] We do not have any archaeological evidence from Paddington or the surrounding suburbs because much was destroyed by urban development long before anyone thought to look (though some things may yet be discovered in parks or backyards). However the rich archaeological and historical record of the harbour allows us to recreate something of how Aboriginal people used Kogerah – as they called Rushcutters Bay – and its Paddington hinterland in the centuries before Europeans arrived.[4]

Sydney's Aboriginal people were divided into clan groups of 25 to 60 people, who traced their lineage through their fathers back to a common ancestor, shared totems and had primary rights to their clan estate. The estate that covered Paddington was known as *Cadi,* and extended west along the southern side of the harbour to around Darling Harbour, and covered most of today's Eastern Suburbs. The clan with rights to that estate were known as the *Cadigal,* meaning the people of Cadi, but their social and cultural world extended far beyond this relatively small area. Women married outside the clan, binding the Cadigal to neighbouring clans such as the Wanngal to the west along the Parramatta River and the Gameygal to the south around Botany Bay, and also to groups much further afield. Clans held ancestral identity, but on a daily basis Aboriginal people lived in what we call bands, comprising the men and unmarried women from the clan and women married in from other clans. Sometimes they lived as a large group, while at other times they fragmented into smaller family units.[5] Aboriginal people were custodians of their clan lands, but also had links to other areas through the clans of their spouses, parents and grandparents and through life events that occurred in different places (such as births, deaths and marriages). In this way, the Aboriginal people who lived around Paddington were linked to areas far beyond the Cadi estate, and they travelled around other coastal clan estates to maintain these links, sometimes beyond Sydney.[6]

Figure 1.2: The Cascade (or the waterfall), by G Roberts from Views mainly of the Eastern Suburbs of Sydney, 1859–1863, shows one of several freshwater streams that flowed into Rushcutters Bay. During the last ice age, the upper catchment creeks were relatively similar

to their present course. State Library of New South Wales.

The clans fished their way around the harbour by day, often in flotillas of bark canoes, and sometimes continued fishing into the night by torchlight. Women used canoes as mobile fishing factories, gathering shellfish from the shallows, opening them over small fires on clay pads in the canoe, spraying the chewed meat into the water as burley, and luring fish back onto the same fires via their pearly shell fish hooks – often nursing babies as they went (see Figure 1.3).[7] Men mainly fished with pronged spears, wielded with great dexterity from rocky headlands, from canoes or standing in the water off the beach (see Figure 1.4). From historical records and the archaeological evidence of coastal campsites known as shell middens, we know that they consumed a wide range of seafood, including oysters, cockles and other shellfish, as well as a modern angler's dream of a broad diversity of fish species.

Though fishing was a central part of Cadigal life, they also used the hinterland areas upstream along Rushcutters Creek, and further to the south over the ridge of today's Oxford Street, where an extensive wetland system drained into Botany Bay. Swamps across this landscape teemed with waterbirds, fish, eels, and tortoises while the surrounding scrub on both sides of the ridge contained a range of animals such as kangaroos, possums, lizards and snakes and a range of plant foods including fruits and berries, tubers, seeds and nectar.[8] These provided Aboriginal people with sustenance as well as raw materials such as sinew for thread, shell for fish hooks and cutting tools and fibre for fishing lines. What they could not gather locally, such as stone for spear points and axes, was obtained through trade extending across the Sydney region and beyond.[9]

Aboriginal people lived in sandstone overhangs and bark shelters around the harbour and its hinterland, often near freshwater streams, swamps or springs. They stayed in these camps for varying lengths of time, moving according to a complex and shifting calendar of family obligations, food availability and ceremonial duties. In the 1790s we know that male initiations were carried out in what is now the Royal Botanic Gardens and ritual 'payback' combats were fought at Rose Bay, though we do not know if these areas had always been used for this purpose. The presence of engraved images on the sandstone of the Eastern Suburbs also suggests that many other places held deep cultural significance to Aboriginal people.

As early Europeans noted, Aboriginal people maintained a network of pathways across the Eastern Suburbs, often following ridges and spurs but also crossing creek valleys. Some early colonial roads were based on existing Aboriginal tracks or used routes shown by Aboriginal guides, but the link was not always so direct, as Europeans were also motivated by a desire to find the easiest path through the landscape. Some pathways continued to be used as foot tracks by early Europeans, who retained the Aboriginal term *'maroo'* (or *muru*). One of these *maroo* went from the ridge of Oxford Street at

Darlinghurst Gaol down through Darlinghurst to Rushcutters Bay, crossing Rushcutters Creek around Bayswater Road.[10]

Figure 1.3: Watercolour illustration of a group of Aborigines fishing ca 1790s, attributed to PG King. State Library of New South Wales, Banks Papers Series 36a, image 5.

Figure 1.4: View from the Government Domain, Sydney, by Charles Rodius in 1833 from his

Views of Sydney and Parramatta, showing Aboriginal people fishing in Woolloomooloo Bay near Paddington. State Library of New South Wales, PXA 997 f.2.

Impact of the colony

From an Aboriginal perspective, the arrival of Europeans in January 1788 was a flagrant unauthorised occupation of a portion of the Cadi estate at Sydney Cove. As convicts and colonists explored and gathered food and resources around the harbour, they soon came into contact and conflict with Aboriginal people. The local mythology of Rushcutters Bay links the origins of its name to the first documented killings of Europeans in Sydney by Aboriginal people in May 1788, when two convicts were speared and clubbed to death while gathering reeds for thatching roofs. The story was first told by long-term Paddington resident Obed West (1807–1891), and although the bay was a place of reed gathering and unrecorded violent incidents may well have happened there, this attack did not. Contemporary accounts show that it took place 'up the harbour' (west of Sydney Cove), and there is no evidence to link it, or another similar attack several months before, to Rushcutters Bay.[11]

Violent encounters, the relentless theft of Aboriginal implements, and the expanding and unsanctioned use of Aboriginal lands and resources were an unprecedented assault on the lives of the Cadigal and neighbouring clans, but worse was soon to come. In April 1789, a smallpox epidemic swept rapidly around the harbour like a tsunami of death, killing hundreds of Aboriginal adults and children. There were few survivors of the Cadigal, not enough even to bury the dead.[12] The impact was catastrophic, shattering families and breaking social structures. Many have linked this devastation to a broader colonial fable that Aboriginal people were being forced to the margins of Sydney in subsequent decades, eking out a desperate existence on its fringes. The reality though, was very different.[13]

The surviving coastal Sydney people regrouped. They formed new bands along old lines, drawing on their extended family connections up and down the coast. The people who continued to live around the Eastern Suburbs included the surviving Cadigal men and women, and others linked to the area through parents, grandparents, marriage or life events. Their cycle of movements became wider than before to take in these new far flung connections, but they still lived at times in Sydney. By the early 19th century these regrouped bands were known to Europeans as the Sydney tribe, Botany tribe, Liverpool tribe and so on, reflecting their affiliation with particular areas (but masking their complex and further reaching connections). They were far fewer in number than before. There were around 50 to 100 people living around the harbour and Botany Bay throughout the 19th century, rarely in groups of more than about 20 in any one place at a time; but they were still there.[14]

From the 1810s, Governor Lachlan Macquarie developed a series of initiatives to try to Europeanise the survivors and persuade them to abandon their cycles of movement. In 1815 he tried to entice a group led by early colonial Aboriginal identity Bungaree (1770s–1830) who were living on the northern side of the harbour to settle into a life of farming and fishing by giving them land and a boat at Georges Head.[15] Although this was fairly unsuccessful, Macquarie tried again a few years later on the southern side of the harbour with the 'Sydney tribe'. In 1820 he and his family rowed from Sydney town to Elizabeth Bay with three boats full of local Aboriginal people to select a site for an Aboriginal village, which is partly contained in today's Beare Park (Elizabeth Bay).[16] The choice of this bay (known to Aboriginal people as Gurrajin) was not random. Europeans acknowledged that it was 'a place much frequented and delighted in by the Sydney blacks, to a family of whom indeed it belonged', and a number of historically documented burials in the area also demonstrate this.[17] As the illustration of the Aboriginal fishing village (Figure 1.5) shows, the village (referred to as Elizabeth Town or Blacktown) consisted of a number of timber huts along the shore, and it was supplied with a fishing boat and tackle.

The fluctuating population of up to several dozen people at Elizabeth Town, were locally connected, including a later leader of the Sydney tribe Thomas Tamara (1800s–60s) and Botany Bay man Mahroot (1790s–1850), whose father had been buried up the road at Rushcutters Bay several years before.[18] Macquarie had hoped that they would settle into a life of fishing and farming, but the idea of staying in one place did not fit with the Aboriginal imperative to maintain their family connections through movement.[19] Consequently, within a few years the village was abandoned, and was soon after taken over by colonial secretary Alexander Macleay as part of his Elizabeth Bay estate. As colonial secretary, Macleay attended the annual feasts held throughout the 1820s for Aboriginal people in Parramatta, where he met people like Bungaree. In 1830, when Bungaree became ill, Macleay arranged for him to be admitted to the General Hospital on Macquarie Street, but he died soon afterwards at Garden Island and was buried at Rose Bay near his first wife Matora (1770s–c 1828).[20] Few Aboriginal people appear to have used the Elizabeth Bay area after this time, but they did not abandon the harbour. Instead they lived in a number of autonomous Aboriginal settlements across the Eastern Suburbs, some of which remained occupied throughout the 19th century.

Figure 1.5: Elizabeth Bay, Sydney/With the bark Huts for the Natives, by E Mason (1821–23) from his Views of Sydney and Surrounding District. State Library of New South Wales, PXC 459, f.42.

Co-existing

Since the earliest days of the colony, Aboriginal people had come to know who was who among Europeans. Sometimes friendships formed, particularly between some Aboriginal children and the first generation of locally born children of convicts. By the 1830s and 1840s, those European children were adults, and some had become the wealthy and influential owners of large estates which nestled in the bushland of the Eastern Suburbs. They were still in contact with local Aboriginal people and were sympathetic to their desire to continue living around the harbour. Aboriginal people found that they could continue to set up camp on these estates, or on public lands.[21] At different times throughout the 19th century, Aboriginal settlements existed in most of the bays of the Eastern Suburbs.[22]

This pattern can be seen in Paddington through the Aboriginal use of the Barcom Glen property on the western slopes of Rushcutters Creek (see Figure 1.6). Barcom Glen was owned by convict Thomas West, whose son Obed West (1807–91) managed and lived on the property throughout most of his life, and wrote in his later years about his relationships with local Aboriginal people. As a child he had played with Aboriginal children, picking up some local language and learning about bush foods. He observed Rushcutters Bay as women fished with hook and line and men with their pronged spears.[23] Based on his enduring relationships with local people, Barcom Glen became one of several places in the area where Aboriginal people lived in the mid-19th century, though we know little more about it.

We have more information about another Aboriginal settlement that existed throughout the 19th century downstream from Barcom Glen on public lands at Rushcutters Bay.[24] Records show that it was in use from the 1850s (probably much earlier), and had a variable population of a few people to dozens on occasion. It shifted location around Rushcutters Bay and Edgecliff at different times, but one of the more popular sites was on the eastern side of the creek to the north of the New South Head Road tollgate in what is now Rushcutters Bay Park (see Figures 1.7 and 1.8). In the 1890s Aboriginal people at the settlement lived in several shelters they had constructed from wooden slabs and iron sheeting, clustered around a central campfire, but other types of shelter were probably also used.[25] Residents caught fish and gathered shellfish, exchanged some of their catch with visiting Aboriginal kin for birds and honey, and made and sold shell encrusted ornaments and wooden implements in Sydney to obtain the other things they needed. Women from the settlement also hailed passing traffic to ask for money or gifts for their children.

The Rushcutters Bay settlement was not a randomly selected place, but one which continued to have meaning to Aboriginal people, despite the encroaching roads and houses. Ceremonies continued to take place there until at least the 1870s, and it was part of a network of settlements around Sydney Harbour and Botany Bay. Most of the people who lived there were linked to the area. They included Jack Harris (1810s–63), whose connections were known and recognised by Europeans in Sydney. If he was ever hassled, he was renowned for his emphatic response 'this is my country'.[26] Like one of his contemporaries William Warrell (1790s–1863), who lived down the road at Rose Bay from the late-1840s, Harris was regarded as one of the 'last of his tribe', and when both men died within a few months of each other in 1863, it was assumed that 'authentic' Aboriginal Sydney died within them.[27] This overlooks the many other Aboriginal people who continued to live at places like Rushcutters Bay and Rose Bay and were connected to Sydney, but also had more diverse links that took them on broader rounds of movement across coastal Sydney and up and down the coast.

The enduring presence of a settlement like Rushcutters Bay among suburban Sydney challenges the assumption that Aboriginal people were automatically pushed out of the way by the growth of the city. Their presence was accepted by local residents, despite some clashes with local youths, and there are no known records prior to the end of the 19th century of attempts by locals or government officials to move them away. In part, this was enabled by the lack of interest by government in local Aboriginal affairs throughout most of the 19th century. Aboriginal and European Sydneysiders were more or less left to work things out for themselves, and a number of those Sydneysiders across the Eastern Suburbs such as Obed West at Paddington and Daniel Cooper, WC Wentworth and others further east around Rose Bay and Vaucluse, were sympathetic to the Aboriginal desire to continue to fish and hunt across their properties and the water reserves and commons. In the late 1880s for example, when a group of local teenagers visited an Aboriginal family who were living in gunyahs and a tent at Centennial Park in the late 1880s, they joined them playing cards around the campfire and noted that the group's tent had been donated by another sympathetic Sydneysider Richard Hill.[28] Aboriginal people were still camping at Moore Park in the 1890s.[29]

Figure 1.6: Barcom Glen house in the 19th century, when Aboriginal people were living on the property. Artist Unknown. Frontispiece in EW Marriott, Thomas West of Barcom Glen, Barcom Press, Sydney, 1982.

Figure 1.7: Horse and cart at the tollgate, New South Head Road, Rushcutters Bay, American & Australasian Photographic Company 1870–75. The photo looks east along New South Head Road past the tollgate and cottage. The Rushcutters Bay Aboriginal settlement was somewhere behind the cottage. State Library of New South Wales, ON 4 Box 13 No 38.

We should be careful though not to blindly laud this as an era of racial tolerance, or to assume that all Aboriginal people were well-treated. Life was still very tough. Aboriginal people continued to die young of preventable diseases, they were attacked and harassed by some Europeans, and most had few opportunities for work due to a lack of European education. Their lands had been taken without consent, and though they retained access to some areas, it was a far cry from the unfettered movement enjoyed by their parents and grandparents. Their continued access to the harbour was also dependent on factors largely out of their control, and these began to unravel towards the end of the 19th century.

Taking over

In the closing decades of the 19th century the rise of government and religious intervention in Aboriginal affairs combined to cause most Aboriginal people to leave their long-standing settlements around the harbour, and Paddington was bound up in these developments. In the late 1870s, missionaries became actively involved in Aboriginal welfare at several locations in regional New South Wales after decades of inaction. Through their Aborigines Protection Association, they lobbied politicians and other influential

Sydneysiders to support their work, providing practical and religious assistance to any Aboriginal people in need through their missions and on the streets of Sydney. The result was that parliament began to consider ways to engage with Aboriginal welfare (having had no official policy in this area for nearly half a century).[30]

Member of parliament George Thornton (1819–1901) proved pivotal to how this unfolded. In the 1850s Thornton had assisted with the annual distribution of government blankets to Aboriginal people in Sydney, and he was often visited by them at his Darling Point home in the 1860s and 1870s.[31] But he was increasingly of the view that Aboriginal people should only be given assistance in their home district, and because he believed there were no local Sydney people, he felt that Aboriginal people should be discouraged from entering Sydney. By 1881 Thornton could see that the government was primed to establish an official approach to the distribution of Aboriginal welfare, and he did not want it to be the indiscriminate charity advocated by the

Aborigines Protection Association. He used the presence of a group of Aboriginal people living in the government boatshed at Circular Quay and receiving government rations, to press the case to establish himself as the government's official 'Protector of Aborigines'. Thornton portrayed the boatshed residents as being from outside of Sydney and therefore as having no reason to be there other than to receive government charity, but in reality most were locally connected people. They included residents of the Rushcutters Bay camp who had shifted there for a few weeks to visit the city and sell their shell encrusted ornaments.[32]

Thornton's lobbying caused the government to close the boatshed settlement down in 1881 and make the La Perouse Aboriginal fishing settlement, quite some distance from town, the main place where its assistance could be obtained. He was also made the first NSW Protector of Aborigines in 1881, a role which was expanded in 1883 to become the Aborigines Protection Board (not to be confused with the missionary based Aborigines Protection Association). The board was initially a small group of volunteers who met once a week to approve requests for government assistance and had no legal powers over Aboriginal people. It did not try to shut other settlements down and as a result Rushcutters Bay continued to be frequented by Aboriginal people.

Figure 1.8: Looking from creek in Rushcutters Bay (later in the Park) to Darling Point with St Mark's Church (upper right), American & Australasian Photographic Company 1870–75, shows the creek and mudlfats at a time when Aboriginal people were still fishing and living nearby. State Library of New South Wales, ON 4 Box 56 No 253.

By the 1890s though, the board and police were monitoring Aboriginal people and the public were increasingly aware that there was now an organisation to contact if they were concerned about the presence of Aboriginal people in their neighbourhood, and that there was a conveniently out of the way place (La Perouse) where they could be sent.[33] It was in this context that the first recorded complaint was made about the Rushcutters Bay settlement in 1895. Police came to try to move Aboriginal people away but they refused, and nothing more was done.[34]

Records show that this settlement was used for several more years, but at the same time another key development was unfolding in the home of Harriet Baker (1860–1951) in Paddington that would eventually lead to its closure. Harriet was governess to the children of the Mona Estate at Darling Point, next to the Rushcutters Bay Aboriginal settlement, and residents would sometimes camp in the property's stone coach house.[35] She was also involved in the evangelical Christian Endeavour movement, which had established a mission church at La Perouse together with some of the Aboriginal people there. In a time of increasing police and public scrutiny, and when recent land reclamation had destroyed the adjacent wetlands, it seems that these people helped Harriet to persuade the Aboriginal residents at Rushcutters Bay to move to La Perouse, and by 1900, one of the last settlements around the harbour had been abandoned.

This final takeover of harbour lands was accompanied by an appropriation of Aboriginal knowledge. Well into the 20th century, Aboriginal people at La Perouse retained knowledge of former settlements like Rushcutters Bay, and the cross-cultural relationships that sustained them, but these memories did not find their way into history books.[36] In the mid-19th century, Europeans interested in Aboriginal culture obtained information directly from Aboriginal people. Paddington resident Reverend William Ridley (1819–78) for example, wrote a number of papers on different Aboriginal languages around New South Wales in the 1870s, based on personal research.[37] But as the century drew to a close, it was believed that the surviving Aboriginal people around Sydney had lost their 'authenticity' and retained no traditional knowledge. Instead, interested Europeans took over as the 'experts' in local language and culture (at least in the eyes of other Europeans).[38] In the 1890s, while living on Leinster Street in Paddington, William Campbell asked local European residents where to find rock engravings as he compiled a detailed book on the subject, but did not think to ask the Aboriginal residents of the Rushcutters Bay settlement just down the hill what they knew.[39] In any case, people like Campbell were not interested in the contemporary history of Aboriginal people, but in the 'authentic' traces of their former lives, ensuring that the history of Aboriginal endurance across the Eastern Suburbs remained hidden until relatively recently.

View from the inside

The abandonment of the Rushcutters Bay settlement by 1900 appears to have ended the era of locally connected Aboriginal people living independently in the Paddington area and across the Eastern Suburbs. There were still Aboriginal people living in Paddington after this time, but they were mainly individuals living in European houses, and most were not locals. Since the late 19th century, Aboriginal people had been entering Sydney in increasing numbers from areas far afield. Some moved to nearby Woolloomooloo and Darlinghurst, but we know little about their lives.[40] The majority of Aboriginal people who lived in Paddington in this period though were not migrants, but instead were bound up in the world of child apprenticeship and domestic service.

From the mid-19th century (and probably earlier) Aboriginal children had been working as domestic servants in Paddington. Most were from outside of Sydney and had been taken in or abducted from the violence of the frontier. From the occasional historical fragments that have survived, it is clear that their lives were often hard and short. Lucy from Queensland for example was taken as an infant (her parents were apparently still alive) into a European household in Queensland in the 1870s, and by the age of eight had moved with the family to Sydney. She ran away and for several years was in and out of emergency care after being placed with others who abused her, before being assigned to a Mrs Kernaghan of Paddington in 1886. By the following year she had been moved again, this time to the Maloga Aboriginal Mission on the Murray River where she grew sick and died at just 17 years of age.[41] Around the same time another Aboriginal servant in Paddington, a 12-year-old boy named Mogal absconded, hopefully into better circumstances.[42]

Paddington was not just the occasional end point for apprenticed domestic servants, but was central to the system through the child welfare operations at Ormond House, the former residence of early Paddington identity and gin distiller Robert Cooper (Figure 1.9). Since the early years of the colony, Sydney's poor and orphaned children had been placed in training schools and other institutions, and in the 1850s Ormond House functioned as a destitute children's asylum. Aboriginal children were most likely among the hundreds housed there before a new and larger asylum was built at Randwick in 1858. By the 1880s the government approach to child welfare shifted away from these institutions to a 'boarding out' (foster care) system administered by the State Children's Relief Board. Ormond House came into use once more as the central processing point for destitute children before they were sent into private care.[43] Aboriginal children were among the many who passed through Ormond House each month. When 15-year-old Herbert was apprehended by police after absconding from his 'guardian' at Redfern in 1891 for example, he was sent to Ormond House.[44]

In the late 19th century, there was no specific or different welfare policy for Aboriginal children, but they were often sent to the Maloga and Warengesda missions in western New South Wales. In the early 20th century, the Aborigines Protection Board instigated a child removal policy on an industrial scale after the passage of laws in 1909 and 1915 giving it widespread powers over Aboriginal people. Aboriginal girls and boys homes were set up at Cootamundra and Kinchela respectively, where children were trained to serve as domestic servants and farm hands. By the 1920s, hundreds of Aboriginal girls, some as young as 12, were working as domestic servants across Sydney, and this almost certainly included Paddington.[45] Though most Aboriginal domestic servants in Paddington would have been girls from outside the area, at least one had local connections. Lena Bungary (c 1907–1968) was from the La Perouse Aboriginal Mission but from the 1930s until her death she worked for, and often lived with, the Stephen family at Paddington. Elders from La Perouse recalled visiting Lena at the house on Jersey Road, and this remains a recognised link to the Paddington area in the community.[46]

Figure 1.9: Ormond House in 1895, when it was used by the State Children's Relief Board. The Paddington Society Archives.

Post-war years

In the decades following World War 2 Aboriginal people migrated into Sydney from country areas in large numbers, and many gravitated to places like Redfern, where an Aboriginal community had been forming for several decades.[47] Paddington did not have a pre-existing community to draw people in and consequently, while some did come to live there, it was not a focal point or community hub for Aboriginal people.[48] This was no doubt also due in part to the gentrification of the suburb, and a lack of social housing that saw an Aboriginal community develop for example in nearby Woolloomooloo. For this reason, the post-war Aboriginal history of Paddington is more notable for events that have linked the area to broader developments in Sydney and elsewhere.

Figure 1.10: Aboriginal debutantes at Paddington Town Hall in 1966. Dawn Magazine, May 1966, 15(5), p 5.

From the 1960s, Aboriginal people in Sydney began to set up services to meet their particular needs. The Foundation for Aboriginal Affairs was the first and most influential, offering employment, housing and education services to Aboriginal people at its George Street Sydney premises from 1964. It also organised events such as dances, both as social occasions and as fundraising for the foundation's other activities.[49] In 1966 the foundation decided to host the first Aboriginal debutante ball in Sydney as a way to foster pride among young women and their families, and Paddington Town Hall was chosen as the venue. At this time, the hall was a well-used social venue in Sydney, and was managed by the City of Sydney Council, which included councillors supportive of the foundation's activities. The ball took place on Friday 1 April and involved the presentation of seven young Aboriginal women to the NSW chief secretary, amid a crowd of 200 Aboriginal people and another 100 non-Aboriginal attendees (Figure 1.10).[50] It was a great success and was run again two years later, this time at Sydney Town Hall and in the presence of Prime Minister John Gorton.[51] During the mid-1960s a growing Aboriginal civil rights movement sought to highlight the deplorable conditions in which many Aboriginal people still lived. One of the first Aboriginal students at the University of Sydney, Charles Perkins (1936–2000), helped form the group 'Student Action for Aborigines' in 1964. The most famous action of the group was its 'Freedom Ride' bus tour of regional New South Wales in 1965, which brought the racism and segregation of country towns to public attention.[52] In preparation for the Freedom Ride, the group held fundraising events, which included a folk concert at Paddington Town Hall the month before. The concert featured an Aboriginal folk singer Jenny Bush, who was originally from Darwin and was working as a nurse at Marrickville Hospital alongside her twin sister.[53]

As explored in Chapter 9 the suburb has been a major centre for Sydney's art galleries since the 1960s. In 1976, Hogarth Galleries was at the forefront of promoting Aboriginal art as a modern and collectable art form, and since the 1980s the gallery along with Cooee Art Gallery and a number of others have hosted exhibitions of many Aboriginal artists from across Australia, including contemporary urban Aboriginal artists.[54] Through these exhibitions many Aboriginal artists and their families have come to visit Paddington, while many non-Aboriginal residents and visitors have caught a glimpse into the richness of Aboriginal Australia.

In a similar way, Paddington's Aboriginal history points to many broader Aboriginal themes. The ongoing local Aboriginal presence throughout the 19th century shows the tenacity and adaptability of Aboriginal people in the midst of a colonial city, while later developments link the area to a much broader story of administrative brutality and indifference, and the counter-efforts of Aboriginal people to break free of government control and manage their own destinies. There have been Aboriginal people present in Paddington throughout its European history. In recent decades the suburb has had a fluctuating Aboriginal population of up to several dozen people according to census figures, and these people, along with future residents and visitors will write the next chapters in Paddington's Aboriginal history.[55]

Chapter 2
Mapping Paddington

Bill Morrison

What gives Paddington its special qualities? Is it the houses, with their pitched roofs and chimneys, the balconies and the iron lace, the detail and the decoration, the stepping and the unlimited variation on a theme? How is that different to Surry Hills, Glebe or Newtown, all built roughly around the same time and deploying similar architectural typologies? Max Kelly put his finger on it most succinctly:

> ...the streets [of Paddington] have a vitality and a spontaneity ... determined, not by the dictates of logic or ease of construction but by the boundaries of early land grants ... that decided the complex and aesthetically pleasing street pattern.[1]

Kelly was referring to the 'intricate, close-grained and diverse' street pattern of Paddington. This was the result of early, rather ad hoc, land grants and the subsequent gentry grants, which formed a random pattern along Glenmore Road. Every boundary line, no matter its bearing, no matter its beginning, irrespective of topography, left its imprint and set the ground rules for what was to come. As a result, what we see in Paddington is a fluke of history, the accretion of layers over time. Paddington can never be repeated.

New maps of the old

This chapter sets about reading between the lines, unfolding the story of Paddington through a series of specially prepared maps showing the development of the place at key intervals in its history. Early Paddington underwent very little comprehensive mapping; those fragments that do exist require assembling, interrogating and reinterpreting to provide a fuller understanding of the place and the influences that made it. No rules or plans guided its creation; it developed rather, via a series of unrelated events, each of which influenced the next and resulted in what others have called an accidental suburb. Whether accidental or not it was a supreme example of *laissez-faire* giving rise to a unique environment and one which continues to attract people to its urban lifestyle.

The influence of urban form by gestures of the past is not unique to Paddington and can be seen in most cities that emerged before the modern-day process of planning took hold. It is, however, as much as anything these elusive almost invisible qualities formed by the boundaries of early land grants, which have, in their own way, created Paddington. This 'aesthetically pleasing' environment has over the years attracted creatives of all kinds to Paddington and generated the force that ultimately saved it from destruction. To many, the underlying patterns that brought about this endlessly fascinating place are unknown or at least invisible. Perhaps what draws people to its beguiling charm is unclear. One can live a lifetime in Paddington and never tire of the unfolding appeal of the streets, the rows of houses, the ups and downs, the twists and turns, the repetition and the variety. And, contrarily, this product of fate, this palimpsest, displays many of the environmental attributes that are now being mandated by governments to achieve sustainable development.

Early mapping

From the arrival of the First Fleet in 1788, land surveying and nautical mapping were an integral part of the settlement and development of the colony to establish both water depths for shipping and berthing and an understanding of landforms for the laying out of the township. Mapping the shoreline of Port Jackson commenced only days after arrival; establishing navigation channels in the harbour. This remarkable feat was carried out by naval officers Captain John Hunter and Lieutenant William Bradley aboard HMS *Sirius,* largely from the water but with some landings to verify bearings. The exercise, which was completed in nine days, extended from the Heads to Homebush along both sides of the harbour and gave rise to familiar place names such as Bradleys Head and Hunters Hill. The earliest map gave definition to the shoreline of Rushcutters Bay and the land to become known as Paddington.

However, the responsibility for the surveying of land and property was the realm of the surveyor general, most often a military appointment. Augustus Alt arrived with the First Fleet on board the transport ship the *Prince of Wales,* holding the position of surveyor of lands. Under Governor Arthur Phillip's instruction, Alt set out the basic layout of the township of Sydney – originally named Albion by Phillip – a structure of roads and property boundaries which largely persist to this day. The surveyor general's job was not only to lay out the land, but to measure and determine land grants for settlers who were considered by the governor to be worthy of reward for their efforts in establishing the penal colony. Early surveyors general included Alt (1788–1803), Charles Grimes (1803–11) and John Oxley (1812–28). By 1828 Major Thomas Mitchell was appointed surveyor general and took charge of survey activities until 1855.

The pivotal landmark

While in earlier times palaces and cathedrals took precedence in exerting influence and power over the community, Paddington was to receive a landmark of a different kind. This marked a pivotal point for the penal colony. Set on the ridge of Woolloomooloo Heights, adjacent to Old South Head Road, Darlinghurst Gaol, constructed from 1822, was to form an urban reference point not only for the growth of the township, but for the development of unexploited areas beyond. Commanding views from all directions, the gaol stood as a potent symbol of judicial authority over the people of the colony with public displays of hangings visible from the town. This landmark stood strongly as a moral and physical reference point throughout the development phases of Paddington and became the anchor for a major urban node in the form of today's Taylor Square.

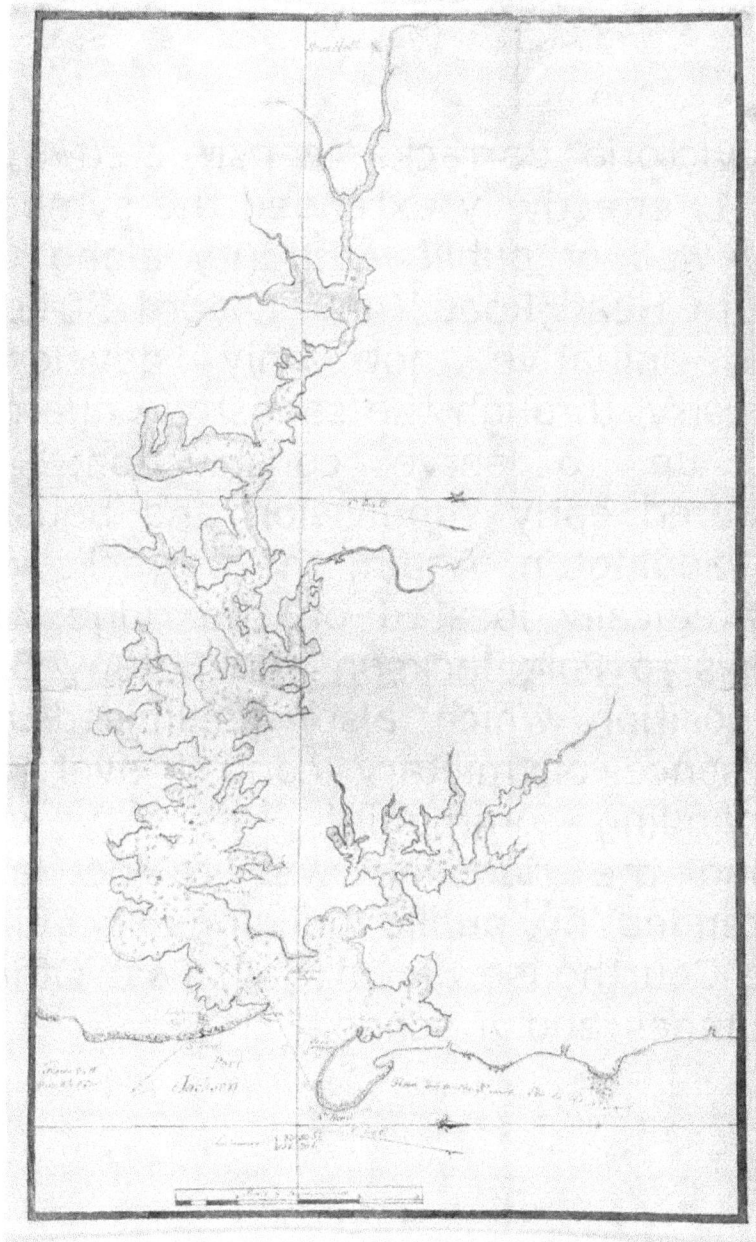

Figure 2.1: The shoreline of Port Jackson mapped by John Hunter and William Bradley in 1788, the first definition of the shoreline of

Rushcutters Bay. State Library of New South Wales.

Victoria Barracks, constructed from 1841, effectively extended the symbolic city wall of public authority along Old South Head Road (now Oxford Street). This initiative not only developed industry, through the sandstone quarries set up to serve construction, but fostered early subdivision and housing in Paddington. Again, the barracks was strategically located on the ridge with views to Port Jackson and Botany Bay, a position which also maximised the presence of military control over the expanding community. This 'city wall' along the ridgeline was to be later extended by public buildings including the Courthouse, Town Hall, Post Office, churches and a school.[2]

Figure 2.2: Darlinghurst Gaol and Courthouse c 1840, by Frederick Garling with views looking across and beyond Woolloomooloo to Sydney Town. State Library of New South Wales.

Beyond the horizon

The township in Sydney Cove was laid out fairly early in the colony, with tracks that were to become roads and streets allowing the take-up of land in a relatively ordered manner, but Paddington was a different scene. The area that was to become Paddington was relatively remote from the town in those days, an inaccessible mix of bushland, sandhills and swamps.[3] Few early settlers would have been aware of this tract, the home of many Aboriginal people, especially since the main views of the area were those from the harbour and from Old South Head Road. From the township, views were hidden by the skyline of Woolloomooloo Heights. To reach the area required a journey along Old South Head Road around the extensive farmland area of Edward Riley and past the emerging hillside of mansions looking west over the Woolloomooloo valley and, later, the gaol. Perhaps it was due to this remoteness and invisibility that Governor Lachlan Macquarie saw it as an area suitable for service industries that could support the growing township. As a result, early land grants were made for water mills, a thatch roof industry and a distillery. Paddington was to start its life as a quasi-industrial estate. (See Chapter 4.)

Figure 2.3: From Hyde Park to Darlinghurst Gaol 1842, by John Rae, showing Hyde Park, Museum, Darlinghurst Gaol, Sydney Grammar School, Burdekin's and Lyon's terraces. Dixson Galleries, State Library of New South Wales.

Early land grants

Over 200 acres (80 ha) of land were granted by the Crown between 1810 and 1822 for the purpose of developing service industries in the Paddington basin. The determining factor was to maximise natural resources for each intended use; milling, thatching and distilling. Thomas West's grant was located to take advantage of the

Rushcutters Creek on the western side; William Thomas's occupied a frontage to the bay and extended across the swamplands; and Robert Cooper, James Underwood and Francis Forbes' land, anchored by Old South Head Road and Point Piper Road, stretched to take in the low-lying streams to the east of the basin. On the south side of Old South Head Road, a grant to Charles Gordon was also established in the open 1000-acre (404-ha) landscape of the Sydney Common. As a symptom of the prevailing abundance of space, each grant took its own form in an ad hoc way without any overall binding structure. Access to some allotments was extremely limited. It was undoubtedly convenient, but in reality a carve-up into industrial farmlets without any reference to the broader context and with no regard for the leftover spaces between (the missing middle). However uncoordinated, the boundaries of these grants were to leave an imprint which would be reflected throughout the area's future development.

Often the extent of a grant was not altogether clear or accurate. Boundaries were uncertain, as track alignments moved over time and fencing did not reflect the survey line on plan. Natural features such as trees and rocks were used to take bearings. A swamp mahogany tree formed the north-westernmost alignment for Thomas West's property Barcom Glen and a shoreline rock provided the bearing point for the eastern boundary of Thomas's waterfront grant. The lack of precision over this process is borne out in the case of Thomas West, where the title to the land and its actual extent was only confirmed after several extended court battles many years later. (See Chapter 4.)[4]

Glenmore Road and gentry estates

Cooper, Underwood and Forbes' grant was the exception. It had good access potential with extensive frontages to the tracks of Old South Head Road and Point Piper Road. However, the tracks were located on high ground, too high to serve the distillery, sited to allow the distilling process to benefit from the fresh water streams and ponds in the low-lying areas. Fortuitously this required the development of Glenmore Road, foreshadowing the next phase of land grants for the wealthy administrators of the colony.

Given the continuous extent of land grants on adjacent allotments to the east – such as that of John Piper, as well as Benson, Brian and Bradley – it is curious that this slot of land between West's grant, Thomas' grant and Cooper, Underwood and Forbes' grant, was left unallocated. A plan may have existed to allow access to the distillery. Or perhaps this was yet another accident of fate. Either way Glenmore Road emerged and found its own way across the terrain and set in motion a collision of allotments, spaces and people that were to cast the mould for the future village.

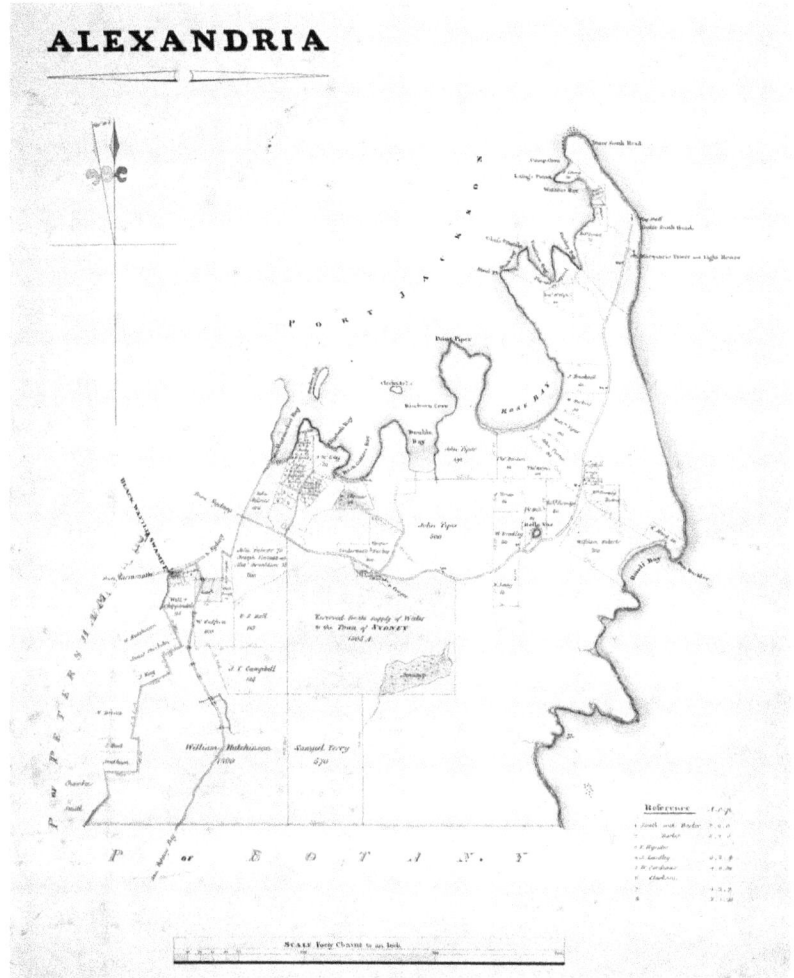

Figure 2.4: Parish of Alexandria, County of Cumberland Map, showing 40-acre grant to Thomas 1817 and the 100-acre grant to Cooper, Underwood and Forbes 1823. State Library of New South Wales.

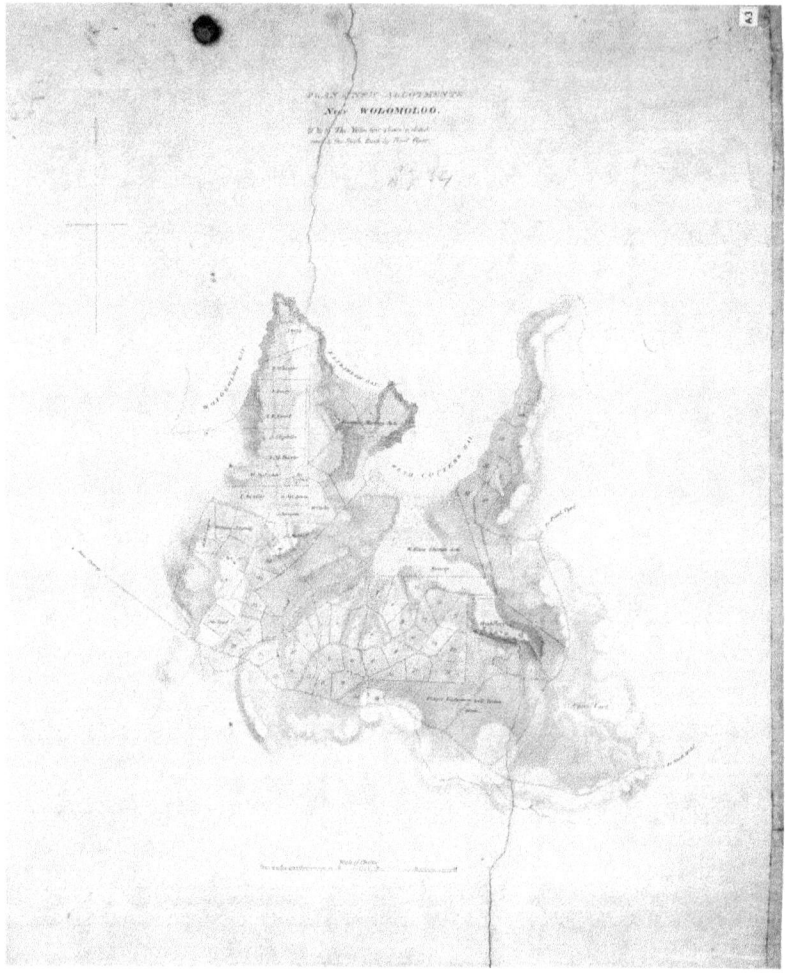

Figure 2.5: Rush Cutters Bay and Paddington showing the Gaol, allotments along Woolloomooloo Heights, swampland, and associated land grants along Glenmore Road, HF White 1828. State Records Map 5462. Reproduced with the permission of the Office of the Registrar General, a unit of the Department of Finance, Services and Innovation

Once access was available there was no reason not to offer this next phase of land grants; property ownership was to transform the valley. Grants, varying in size from 4 to 8 acres (1.6–3 ha), largely with frontages to Glenmore Road, were random in form, with angled boundaries driven by the twisting nature of the road and reflecting the undulating topography. Ideal for their purpose, they brought about the era of gentry villas and estates, as a stately form of residence for worthy citizens.

Subdivision and redevelopment

What followed between 1870 and 1900 was the progressive subdivision and development of each estate as it came time for each landowner to move on. Once subdivision began the die was cast and it was only a matter of time before most estates embraced the housing and economic boom that peaked in the late 1880s. In contrast to earlier development, each estate was planned within its boundaries, to maximise dwelling numbers and create an efficient system of streets. But again no overall plan existed; so each estate sought to reconcile its pattern of streets with those of adjacent estates that had been established earlier. Row after row of terraces emerged in the open landscape of Paddington, sometimes along the contour, sometimes against, as all but a few villas were demolished. In all of this change, the property boundaries of original land grants and secondary land grants remained. The random form of Paddington continues to this day.

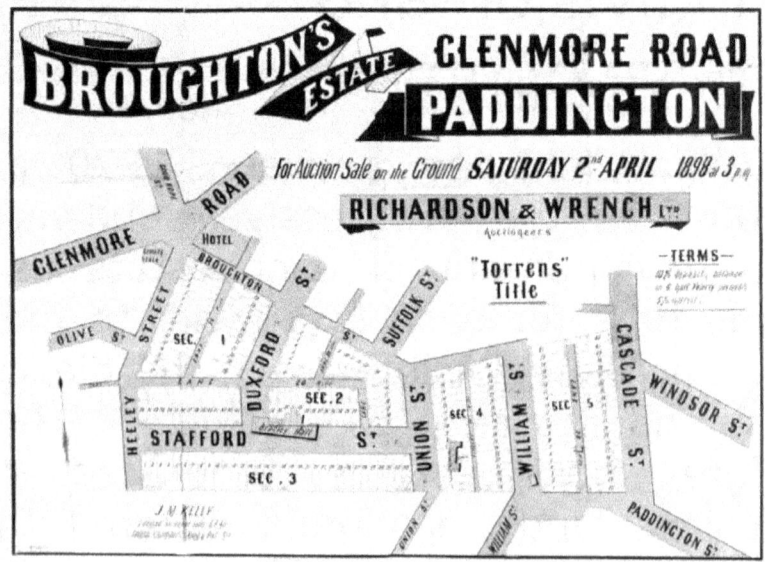

Figure 2.6: Auction notice for the Broughton Estate, 1898, showing Thomas Broughton's Bradley Hall and the subdivision pattern. This was one of the last of the gentry estates to be subdivided. National Library of Australia.

Retro-mapping

To reveal the mysteries of Paddington's development a series of comparative retro-maps have been prepared at varying periods using available historical maps set against current day digital mapping. These maps, drawn in a freehand style, have a reasonably high level of accuracy. The matching scale and graphic style of each map allows direct comparison, one to the other, so that the evolution is clearly visible.

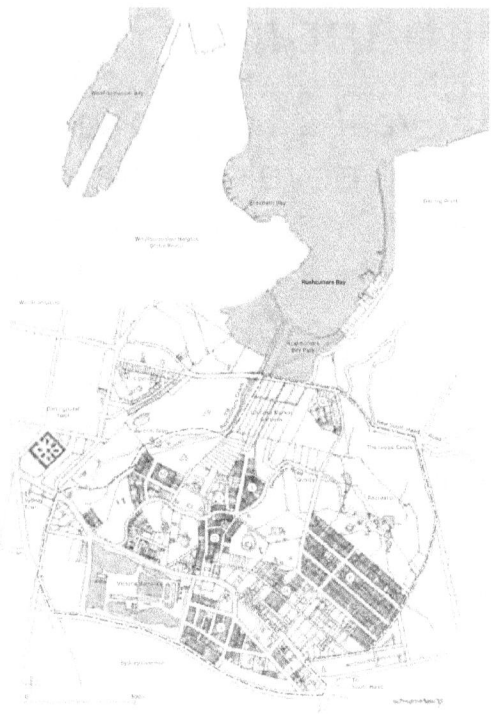

Figure 2.7: Example of Retro-mapping. Estate Subdivision 1870–90. © W Morrison 2017.

The area covered extends from Darlinghurst to the west, Darling Point, Edgecliff and Woollahra to the east and south to the sports grounds of Moore Park. To the north the early maps embrace Rushcutters Bay as an integral part of the Paddington environment and a significant focus for the Aboriginal community as well as the early settlers. The bay truly belonged to Paddington through those early times. Reference points include the gaol, the barracks and the bay with Oxford Street extending east–west across the lower section of each map.

These maps give a fresh perspective on Paddington, a snapshot representation at various times which depict key stages of development: from an interpretation of the found landscape at the time of European settlement; through the early days of land grants; the development of Glenmore Road and the subsequent land grants to colonial administrators; the development of gentry villas and their subsequent subdivision; to the built-up village of today.

The layered exploded axonometric projection of these maps serves to illustrate the influence of early boundaries through each historic phase and their persistence in the final form of Paddington. They can be seen in real life by the astute observer walking the streets. The maps are also presented individually to provide greater insight into the detail of each era. This focus on mapping tells its own story of the evolution of the place and portrays another level of understanding of the village we call Paddington.

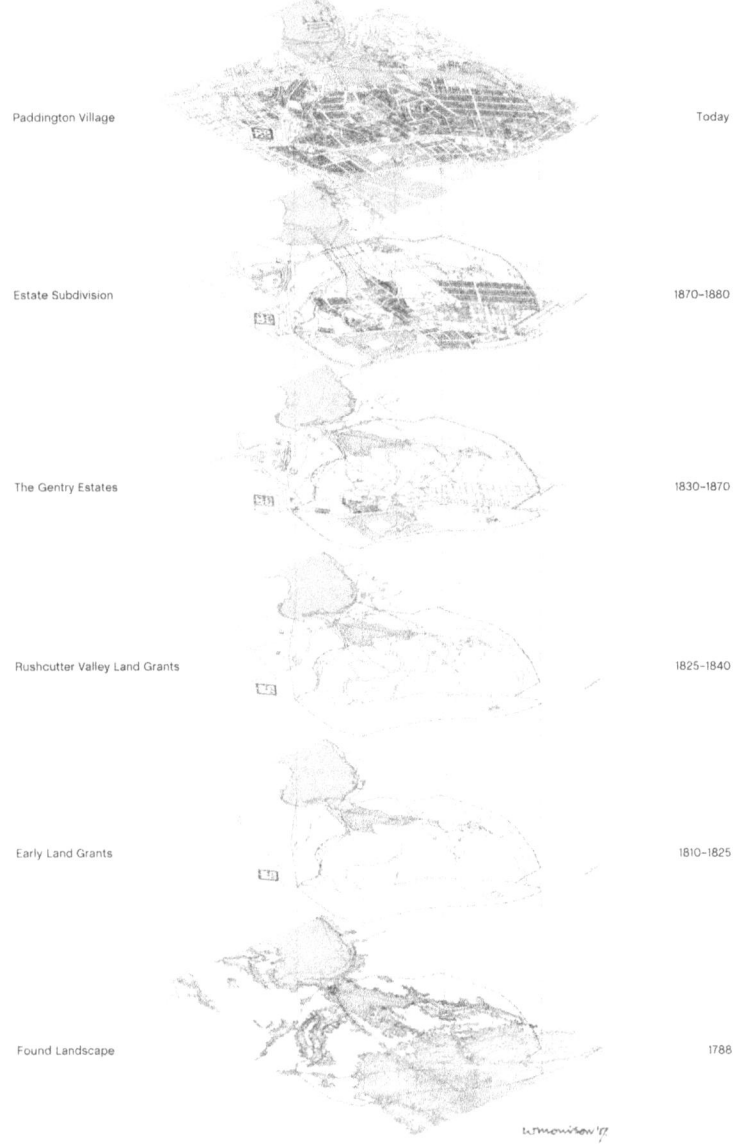

Figure 2.8: The underlying structure of Paddington. Exploded view showing the evolution of Paddington and the influence of early land grants. © W Morrison 2017.

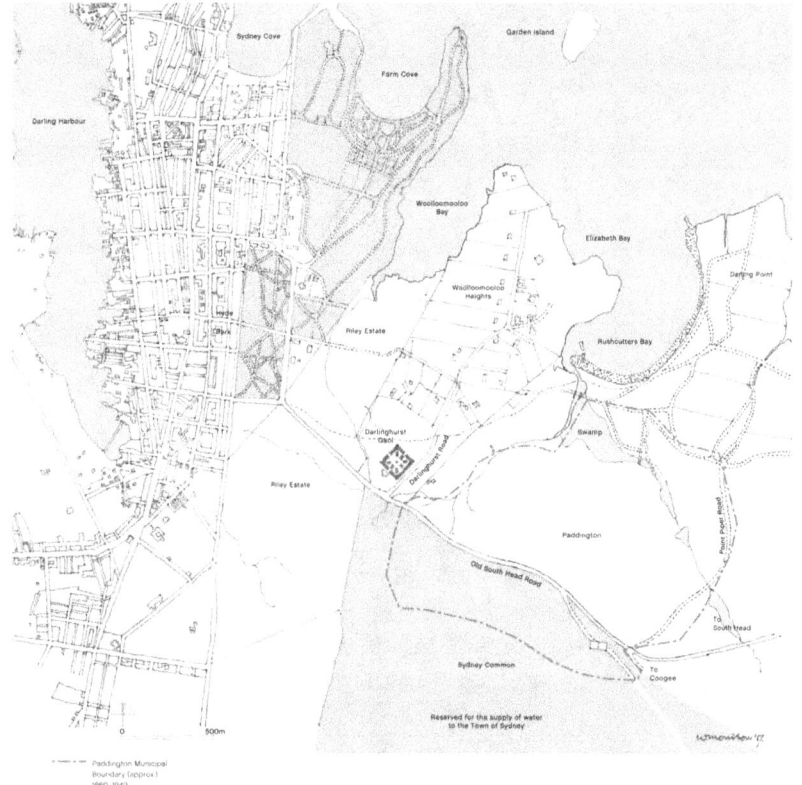

Figure 2.9: Paddington in context. Shows Paddington, situated 3 kilometres from the city across the Darlinghurst ridge and the Woolloomooloo valley. Before construction of William Street in 1832, Woolloomooloo Heights (now Potts Point) was accessed from Old South Head Road (Oxford Street) and Darlinghurst Road. Paddington was inaccessible other than on foot or by boat. William Street, the vision of Surveyor General Thomas Mitchell, opened up access to the east, through the extensive farmland of Riley, and led to the development of New South Head Road across the waterfront of Paddington. © W Morrison 2017.

Figure 2.10: Found landscape 1788. An interpretation of the landscape of Rushcutters Bay and Paddington, as may have been found by European settlers in 1788, typical of the landscape along the south-eastern shore of Port Jackson. It comprised woodland on sandstone along the lower slopes, and heath and scrub on

sandstone on the higher slopes. On the valley floor, fed by freshwater streams, were a series of low-lying marshy swamps. The original Aboriginal tracks (maroo) are shown: one on the ridgeline which became Old South Head Road (Oxford Street), and one leading down from Darlinghurst to the line of what was to become New South Head Road. The open heath landscape extended south from the Old South Head Road ridge toward Botany Bay and included the swampy land (now known as Lachlan Swamps). © W Morrison 2017.

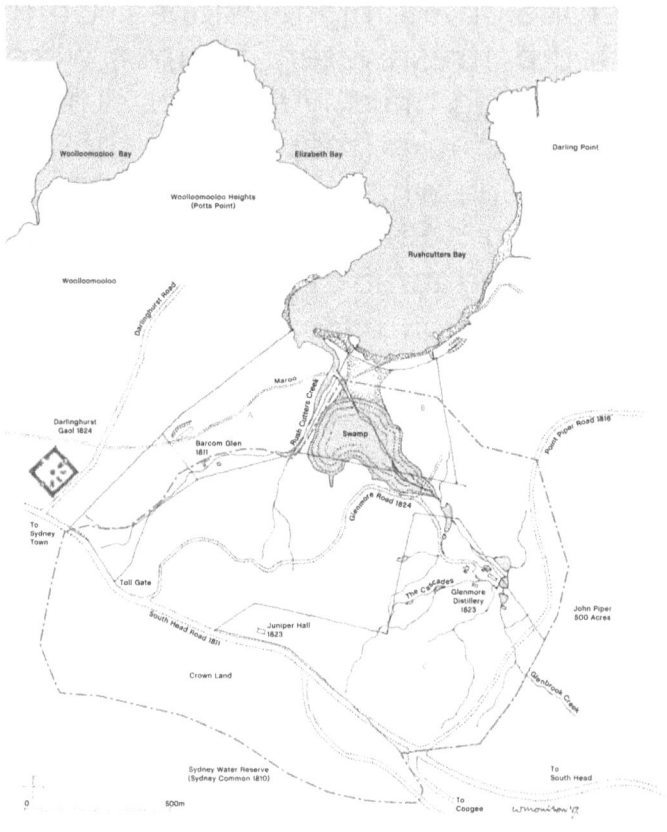

A Thomas West 1811 (71 Acres)
B William Thomas 1817 (40 Acres)
C Cooper, Underwood & Forbes 1823 (100 Acres)

Figure 2.11: Early land grants 1810–25. Shows the first land grants to Thomas West (71 acres), William Thomas (40 acres) and Cooper, Underwood and Forbes (100 acres). Thomas West's land was promised in 1810 to set up a watermill on the isolated Darlinghurst slopes, drawing water from the nearby Rush Cutter's Creek. William Thomas's land was at the mouth to the bay occupying largely swampy lowlands and provided roofing thatch for houses. Cooper, Underwood and Forbes' grant was for a distillery to serve the fledgling colony. A new road was formed across the broken terrain of the valley to more easily serve the low-lying distillery. Once in place, Glenmore Road opened up the valley for a number of land grants to worthy gentlemen of the colony. © W Morrison 2017.

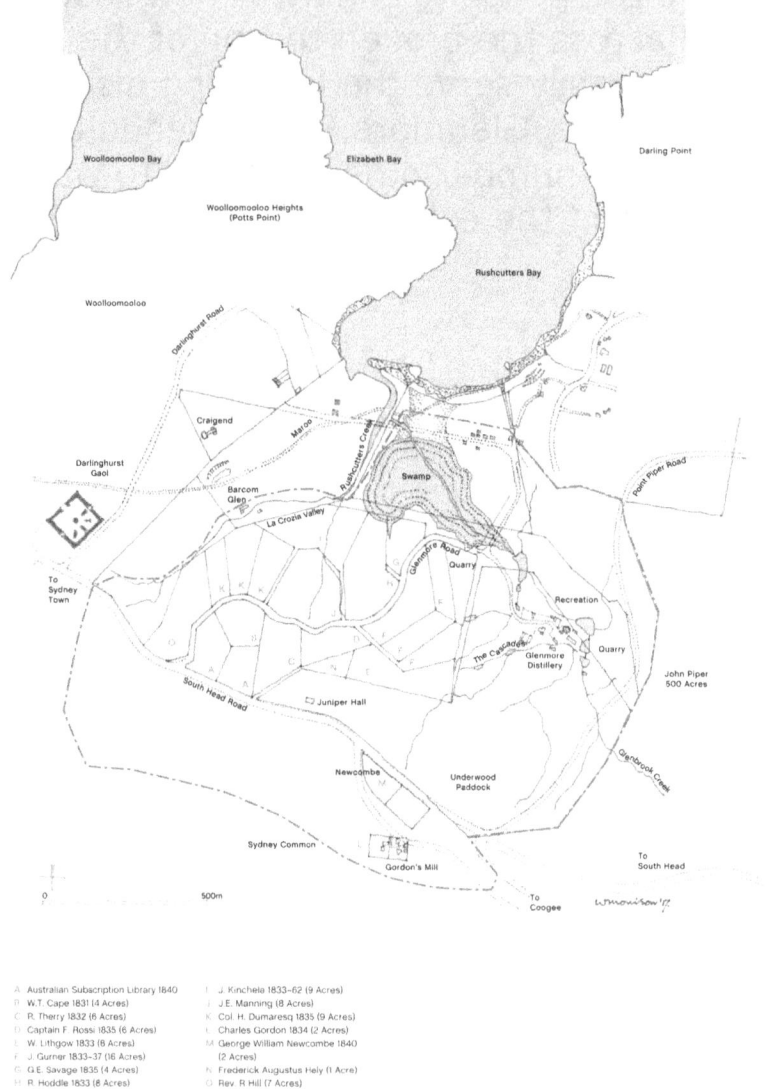

A Australian Subscription Library 1840
B W.T. Cape 1831 (4 Acres)
C R. Therry 1832 (6 Acres)
D Captain F. Rossi 1835 (6 Acres)
E W. Lithgow 1833 (8 Acres)
F J. Gurner 1833–37 (16 Acres)
G G.E. Savage 1835 (4 Acres)
H R. Hoddle 1833 (8 Acres)
I J. Kinchela 1833–62 (9 Acres)
J J.E. Manning (8 Acres)
K Col. H. Dumaresq 1835 (9 Acres)
L Charles Gordon 1834 (2 Acres)
M George William Newcombe 1840 (2 Acres)
N Frederick Augustus Hely (1 Acre)
O Rev. R Hill (7 Acres)

Figure 2.12: Rushcutter Valley Land Grants 1825–40. Between 1830 and 1840, almost 20 irregularly shaped land allotments were granted, the majority from 4 to 8 acres, with access from Glenmore Road. The irregular shape of the grants was to have a lasting effect upon the form of Paddington. There were also two reserves for quarries and a reserve for recreation. To the south of Old South Head Road, set amid the Sydney Common was the grant to Charles Gordon, set aside for establishing a mill in 1834, and a separate grant to George Newcombe in 1840. © W Morrison 2017.

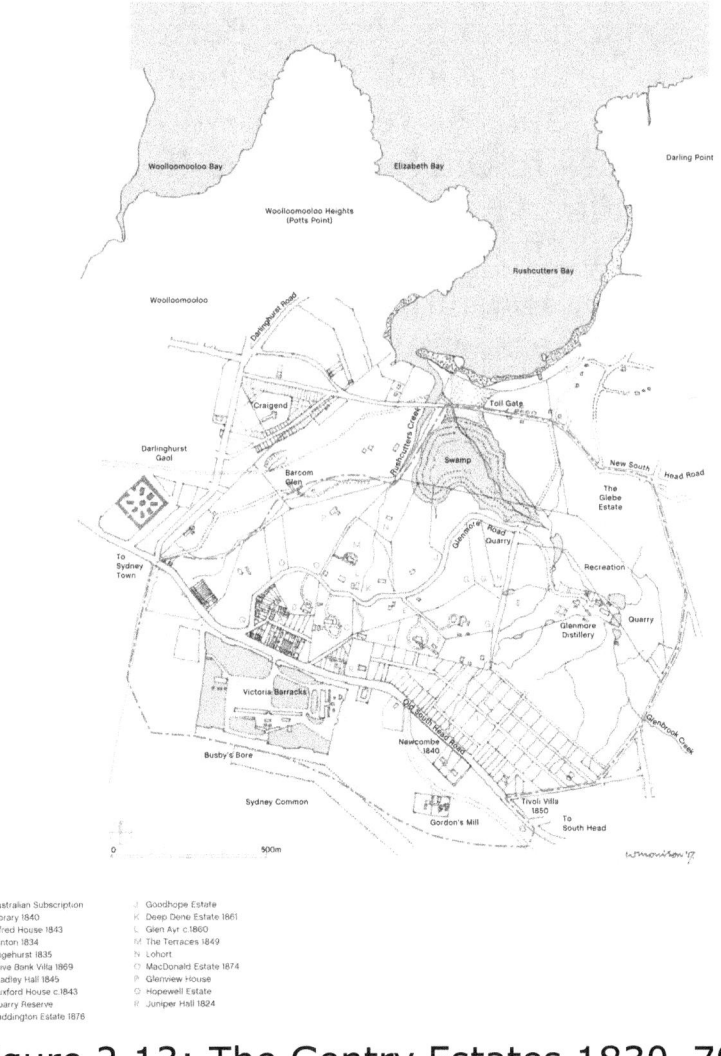

Figure 2.13: The Gentry Estates 1830–70. Between 1830 and 1870 substantial stone villas

were established along Glenmore Road with stabling facilities and formal gardens; they offered an attractive lifestyle with access to the city via Old South Head Road. At the same time subdivision into larger lots commenced on the first six acres of the Underwood Estate, and the Australian Subscription Library land was subdivided into smaller allotments to service the construction of Victoria Barracks. To the south a number of institutions including schools, churches, and the reservoir were sited with frontages to Old South Head Road. Villas included Elfred Estate, Flinton, Olive Bank Villa, Juniper Hall, Bradley Hall, Duxford, Goodhope, Deep Dene, The Terraces, Glenview Estate and others. © W. Morrison 2017

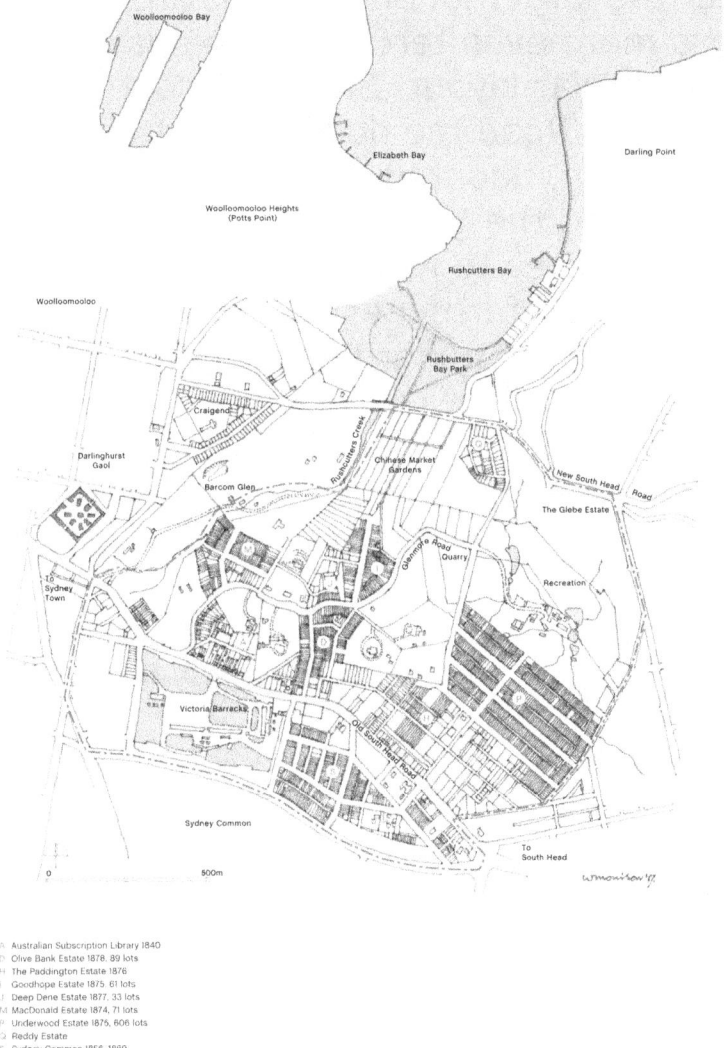

A Australian Subscription Library 1840
D Olive Bank Estate 1878. 89 lots
H The Paddington Estate 1876
I Goodhope Estate 1875. 61 lots
J Deep Dene Estate 1877. 33 lots
M MacDonald Estate 1874. 71 lots
P Underwood Estate 1875. 606 lots
Q Reddy Estate
S Sydney Common 1856-1889

Figure 2.14: Estate subdivision 1870–80. By the mid 1870s subdivision of the estates commenced and continued to the end of the century. The varied shape of these land grants fronting Glenmore Road gave rise to a haphazard form of development as each estate sought to maximise its dwelling numbers. There was no 'plan' and this in itself created much of Paddington's charm. To the east of Cascade

Street the larger landholding of Underwood – across more even terrain – gave rise to a far more regular layout. Similarly, south of Old South Head Road the development of parts of the Common, adopted a more regular pattern incorporating the grant to Charles Gordon and infilling the area to Moore Park Road. Between 1880 and 1900 further estates were subdivided including: 1885 Duxford Estate 146 lots, 1886 Underwood Estate (4) 214 lots, 1891 Elfred Estate 82 lots, 1893 Lawson's Estate 26 lots, 1898 Broughton Estate 132 lots. © W Morrison 2017.

Figure 2.15: Paddington village today. This map shows Paddington as a densely developed urban village, through the gradual subdivision of the gentry estates. The unique pattern is a combination of topography, land grants, and road alignments. Of the gentry villas only Olive Bank Villa, The Terraces, Juniper Hall and part of Engehurst remain. © W Morrison 2017.

Figure 2.16: Aerial photo 2013. Paddington today showing dense urban build up and irregular urban pattern, set within surrounding areas of Darlinghurst, Woolloomooloo, Woollahra and Darling Point. Spatial Services, NSW Department of Finance, Services & Innovation.

Chapter 3

Ever-changing Paddington

Garry Wotherspoon and Paul Ashton

What we now know as Paddington has a long, ever-changing and chequered history. It is now one of Sydney's more iconic and emblematic places, and one of the biggest and most intact Victorian suburbs anywhere in the world.[1] Its existence today is largely due to efforts by its residents to fight off those who have tried to destroy it; state and council bureaucrats, indifferent property owners, the Department of Main Roads, and developers. A tale of struggle. But also one of hope.

Early Paddington

Paddington began in the early 1840s, with the construction of the Victoria Barracks. But its European antecedents lie many decades earlier, with the construction of a road from the township at Sydney Cove to the South Head, where a signal station had been built at a high point visible from the town. This track – often referred to locally as the *maroo* – followed existing paths that had long been established by Aborigines. Captain John Hunter's map of the settlement in 1791 showed just such a track.[2] Work in 1803 and then later in 1811 led to improvements in the quality of this strategic South Head Road, particularly at a time when Britain was at war with France and the French had an ongoing presence in the south-west Pacific area. The road's surface was improved by Major George Druitt in 1820, and it was renamed the Old South Head Road (now Oxford Street) after construction of a new road to the South Head (New South Head Road) along the harbour foreshore was begun in 1831.

While its initial purpose was clearly functional, it also became the access road to some of the imposing villas being built by the colonial gentry.[3] A number of the colony's elite had begun to take up grants in the area accessed by this road, and between 1819 and 1840 a belt of villas sprang up to the east of Sydney Town. But not all grants in the area were for such grandiose purposes. The first, closer to the South Head Road, of 100 acres (40 ha), was made to Robert Cooper, James Underwood and Francis Ewen Forbes. Early in 1824 they commenced work on the Sydney Distillery, located at the eastern end of what is now Glenmore Road, between the South Head Road and Rushcutters Bay.[4] But the distillery partnership soon broke up. Underwood bought out Forbes's share for £6200, and then bought out Cooper, with whom he had quarrelled, for a further £1600. By July 1824, the works, which included eight vats and a large granary, were ready for business.

In 1825 Cooper built his mansion, Juniper Hall (a somewhat cheeky reference to what the distillery was producing – gin, made in part from juniper berries) on the South Head Road ridge. Underwood built his house on Glenmore Road, between today's Soudan Lane and the former distillery.[5] Cooper and Underwood in the late 1830s battled in the courts over both Juniper Hall and the 100 acres. Cooper kept his house and the 3 acres (1.2 ha) on which it stood, while Underwood received the remaining 97 acres (39 ha).[6]

The name 'Paddington' first appeared in October 1839, when Underwood subdivided 50 of his 97-acre grant. He called his subdivision the Paddington Estate, after the London borough of that name, and it covered the land from the Old South Head Road down to present day Paddington Street. The only prominent feature on the other side of the Old South Head Road was the Post Mill, run by the Gordon family, grinding wheat from the early 1830s.[7]

However, the good economic times the colony was experiencing, built on the pastoral industry and the South Pacific maritime trade, were not to last. The 1840s was a tumultuous decade that, while it saw the formal end of convict transportation in 1840, also experienced a major depression in the following years. And while that economic slump slowed the colony's growth, other developments were to have a beneficial effect in the Paddington area. Governor Bourke's decision to move the military barracks, which housed those 'licentious' soldiers of the New South Wales Corps[8] from Wynyard Square, kick-started Paddington's development, changing it from a quasi-rural place to an increasingly urban space.

The new site chosen for the barracks was located 'two miles distant' from Hyde Park along the South Head Road.[9] Strategically, it had views out to both the entrance to Botany Bay and across to the Heads at the entrance to Port Jackson. The barracks were designed by Lieutenant-Colonel George Barney, the first colonial engineer, and the commencement of construction in 1841 saw a village of sorts begin to emerge. Much of it was around the cottages built for the many artisans – stonemasons, quarrymen, carpenters and their labourers – working on both the construction of the barracks and the dwellings of the small community that grew up to supply goods and services to them and to the military establishment.[10] Some of the skilled stonemasons working on the barracks were Quebecois political prisoners, transported from Canada as punishment for their involvement in an aborted insurrection in 1836.[11] When Barney returned to Britain in 1844, the work was taken over by Major James Gordon, and the barracks was finally completed in 1848.[12]

Figure 3.1: The Old South Head Road above Rushcutters Bay, looking towards Paddington c 1842, Frederick Garling. State Library of New South Wales, a128221/V/22 (ML)

Figure 3.2: The Barracks and Paddington Village, Oxford St looking east, 1844, George Roberts' watercolour showing toll gates at

centre, village to the left and barracks to the right. State Library of New South Wales. SLDP PX52.

Early subdivisions

An early beneficiary of this shift of the New South Wales Corps was the Australian Subscription Library, founded in 1826 and located in Bent Street, Sydney.[13] It had been granted a parcel of land off the South Head Road to help support it, and when the barracks were to be built opposite this plot of land, its value increased immensely. The Library committee subdivided its 8-acre (3-ha) holding and offered it at auction as 'The Australian Subscription Library Estate'.[14] The sale of this land in May 1840 brought an excellent return, 'the sum of £3384, proceeds from the sale of the allotments in Rushcutters Bay'.[15] This was a forerunner of the many subdivisions that would reshape the district by the end of the century. One minor discontent – the toll-bars on the South Head Road at the beginning of Glenmore Road – caused consternation: 'It was a particularly unpopular toll, as everyone travelling to and from the barracks had to pay, and all produce, etc. supplied to the barracks was dearer because of the extra toll fees the vendors paid.'[16]

The subdivision of this estate formed the nucleus of what became known as the Paddington village. Gipps Street, one of the oldest in Paddington, was at its centre, while it was bounded by Spring and Prospect streets. A group of some of these quaint cottages and terraces from the mid-19th century have survived into the 21st century.

Before 1860, although there had been some 'industry' in the area – including wool washing, lime pits, water mills and quarries[17] – much of Paddington looked as it always had: 'a rugged country, perhaps the most wild looking place around Sydney; barren sandhills with patches of scrub, hills and hollows galore with much low lying flat and swamp'.[18] Scattered throughout were the houses built earlier by Underwood and Cooper, some development along the Old South Head Road, and those villas built for the colonial gentry on the slopes of the

'Rushcutters Valley'. Many of the latter belonged to members of the colony's legal profession or mercantile class,[19] often with frontages onto the 'new road in the Valley of Rushcutter' (subsequently Glenmore Road).[20] Ironically, Underwood was the only substantial landowner in the area to not have some form of 'grand establishment' there; no mansion, stables, servants or servants' quarters.[21] But this veritable tranquillity was about to change quite dramatically, and by the end of the century, Paddington had largely become the suburb the world would know today.

From village to suburb

The gold rushes from the early 1850s saw tens of thousands of immigrants come to the diggings in the colony. Not all enjoyed success, and many left the goldfields disgruntled. While some were encouraged to settle on small farms in 'the outback' – with the *Land Acts* of the early 1860s opening up crown lands for purchase or lease – many returned to Sydney to seek work in the various industries there. The city's population, which was a mere 39,000 in 1851, grew rapidly, to 56,000 in 1861 and to around 200,000 by 1871. By 1881 the population had grown to 221,000, and in 1891 greater Sydney had a population of 383,000.[22] Population growth of this kind ensured a long economic boom for Sydney, especially in the city's building and service industries, and particularly to meet a need for housing.

Paddington experienced the effects of this population influx. Whereas in 1840 its population was a mere few hundred, this had grown to nearly 1400 by 1851 with the completion of 'Barney's Barracks', as they were called. And from then on, it grew rapidly. In 1861 Paddington was home to 2692 persons living in 531 houses; by 1891 the population was not far short of 19,000, living in 3800 houses.[23] In the same period, Sydney's metropolitan suburban population had similarly jumped from 39,000 to over 275,600 (representing around a quarter of the colony's population).[24]

Initially, the Old South Head Road came to be seen as a good business prospect to catch the passing trade *en route* to the Belle Vue Hill and the South Head lookout, and more land was released there. Added to this was local population growth, and

Figure 3.3: Paddington in the 1870s. View from Darlinghurst near Barcom Glen, showing the villas of the Rushcutters Valley on the north-facing slopes, set within their surrounding grounds and surviving native vegetation. State Library of New South Wales, SPF7/12.

the village soon began to boast stores, produce merchants, water carriers, wheelwrights, blacksmiths, turnkeys, dairymen, a baker, a local midwife, and being close to the barracks, the inevitable house of ill-repute.[25]

Down on the harbour shore were the flats, literally a swamp that abounded with rushes, which were collected by the first European settlers, hence the name Rushcutters Bay. But from the 1830s the area was increasingly used for market gardens,[26] to feed the burgeoning population of Sydney. Originally worked by the Ridley family, the market gardens were then leased to Chinese gardeners who continued the industry there until well into the 1880s.[27]

Despite various streams that ran through Paddington – part of the reason that the original gin distillery was built there – most residents had to rely on water from 'the erratic but invaluable water vendor', Michael Vestor, who in 1868 would bring water to the door for a charge of half a penny per bucket.[28]

Figure 3.4: Jane Beard's Paddington Inn on the South Head Road. Penned on the image, 'Paddington from the West 1859'. George Roberts, Oxford Street looking east. City of Sydney Civic Collection 1988.785.

As historian and one-time resident Max Kelly noted in his history of 19th-century Paddington, between 1860 and 1890 an average of five new houses were constructed every fortnight. This not only demonstrated a vast capital outlay but also an ongoing need for both skilled and unskilled labour. It also generated demand for such diverse products as new bricks, window glass, slates, floor boarding, roofing iron, fireplaces, tin and plaster mouldings, and also for chairs and tables, saucepans, mangles, beds and bedding, carpets and wardrobes and bathroom fittings. This growth in Paddington was able to take advantage of the increasing industrialisation of production processes. Prior to the 1870s in Australia, for example, bricks were made by hand and brick-making was essentially a cottage industry. Mass production of bricks rapidly expanded in the last decades of the 19th century,[29] and Paddington's built environment, once characterised by grand sandstone, was to become dominated by bricks and mortar.

There was also a growing need for professionals, from doctors and dentists to barbers and tailors.[30] And with many young families among the new residents, schools were some of the first facilities to appear.[31] Paddington Public School was opened on Old South Head Road on 5 May 1856, as a model school. The local Catholic children were served by a small school built in 1866 on Old South Head Road, also used as a place of worship. In 1883, to relieve pressure on the Paddington Public School, the Glenmore Road Public

School was built. Designed by architects Blackman and Parkes in Italianate style, its location catered well for those children living on the Rushcutters Valley slopes. It included a master's cottage, and in 1902 an infants' school was added.[32] Also appearing were the various denominations of the Christian churches, to soothe the souls of their parishioners. Catering for the area's Presbyterians, the gothic-style St John's Presbyterian Church was built in 1859, while the first building, the old manse, had been built back in 1845, reputedly using surplus stone from the construction of the nearby Victoria Barracks.[33]

The Garrison Anglican Church was built on the corner of South Head and Oatley roads in 1857. It was there until the Water Board decided to resume the land for a raised reservoir, and the church moved further east, to the corner of Old South Head Road and Moore Park Road, becoming St Matthias' Church, opening there in May 1861.[34] For those Anglicans living in the Rushcutters Valley, St George's in Glenmore Road at Five Ways was opened in 1889, although the final building was only completed in 1897.[35]

For the local Catholic population, the St Francis of Assisi church was erected next door to the old school-church. Its foundation stone was blessed and laid on 23 March 1889, on what was now known as Oxford Street. Cardinal Moran officially opened the new church on Sunday, 22 June 1890.[36] But the Greeks had to wait nearly another 40 years before they had a local church. After a schism in Sydney's Greek community in the 1920s, St Sophia's Greek Orthodox Church was built in Napier Street, opening in September 1927.[37] These churches and schools played an important role in helping develop a sense of identity for Paddington's various communities.

While Paddington was to remain a 'walking city' for its poorest inhabitants, it was essentially a dormitory suburb and most of its residents needed to travel to work. Changes in transportation were critical for Paddington's growth; developments in 'mass transport' partially helped foster the growth of businesses on the Old South Head Road and the development of a suburb around it. Initially this consisted of horse-buses, starting in the 1850s with Richard Palmer's *Alpha* and *Omega,* and McClutchy's more opulent *Thistle,* 'with carpet covered cushions and door window'.[38] Many horse-buses were gaily painted and had distinctive names: *The Cricketer, The Lottery, Hit or Miss, The Florence, The Violet* and *The Beeswing* being prominent,[39] as was the *Eclipse.*[40]

Stories about the 'Paddington omnibus' and its adventures abound. English visitor John Askew recounted that while in Sydney he went by horsebus to the Paddington Inn, on the corner of Old South Head Road and William Street. It was run by Jane Beard,

> a handsome widow, about 25 years of age, rather stout, and with such a pretty English face, that I thought she was well worth going two miles to see, and paying 6d for the jaunt into the bargain.[41]

Figure 3.5: View of Paddington looking south-east from 'Hilton', residence of John Rae, Liverpool Street, Darlinghurst, c 1880s, with Paddington terraces in background and the Victoria Barracks on the horizon. State Library of New South Wales, SPF/558.

Other omnibus services followed, as locals petitioned for improved services,[42] and by 1870 Paddington had three bus routes: along Oxford Street, South Head Road and Glenmore Road, operated by the Waverley and Woollahra United Omnibus Company. Passengers could travel to Macquarie Place and Railway Square. The horse-bus system reached its zenith in the late 1880s. Horse-drawn cabs provided another alternative mode of transport.

With the local population growing, and more people travelling along the Old South Head Road on the omnibus, more taverns opened. These were also well patronised by the soldiers from the barracks, many young men without family ties:

> Pubs and taverns – with their lively atmosphere, the music of the accordion and fife, streetwise barmaids and a spot of betting on the side – thrived a few paces down the road from newly-built churches and schools.[43]

Such was the demand for beer that in 1857 Yorkshireman Joseph Marshall opened his brewery on Oxford Street near the corner of South Dowling Street. Marshall's Brewery soon became one of the largest in Sydney, winning a gold medal for its ale at the Sydney International Exhibition in 1880.[44]

Figure 3.6: Tram and coach on Oxford Street, Paddington, 1911, looking west from near intersection with Jersey Road. Old Sydney Album, personal postcard collection of David Critchley.

As more people settled in the area, new businesses opened on the Old South Head Road to the east of the barracks, mainly light industry and retail. Over the years there appeared Hyde & Co General Carriers, Davis & Co Tailors and Mercers, Mr Eames the Chemist, Richardson the watchmaker, various produce merchants, butchers' shops and general stores. Further up were boot-sellers, a baker and pastry cook, a milliner, and Harry Havenhand the tobacconist. Nearby streets also benefited: Newcombe Street had HG Foster's Bicycles manufacturer and shop; Stewart Street had Olding's Carriage Makers, who made ambulances and wagons for the Boer War campaign; and just by Elizabeth Street was Falkingham's leather grinders and boot-makers, while nearby was Twigg's furniture factory. And close to Victoria Place was Cook's Paddock, the overnight resting place for delivery horses for the James Cook Bakery at 32–38 Victoria Street. The bakery was famous throughout Sydney; it had 186 attention-getting carts shaped like huge 'High-Top' loaves of bread.[45] Down at the other end of Paddington, Kinsela's undertakers were in Greens Road opposite the barracks by 1870.[46] Such was the development of a local 'high street' along the Old South Head Road that the section between Boundary Street and Jersey Road had been renamed as Oxford Street by the council in 1885, both to reflect its upgraded status and to bring it into line with the already renamed lower section from Hyde Park.

Over time, there had emerged a clear class distinction in the mix of residents, reflected in their geographical dispersal. The working-class population, involved in day-to-day activities in their trades – carpenters, stonemasons, builders, blacksmiths, plasterers, fencers, coachbuilders, as well as food and retail service providers – either for locals or for the gentry in the 'Rushcutters Valley', were located largely on or near the Old South Head Road. That small group of 'gentlemen' – those professional men, lawyers and merchants and their families – lived in their imposing villas on their estates overlooking the harbour.

Municipal incorporation

Such was the suburb's development and population growth that it gained incorporation as a municipality in 1860. A petition to the governor for the creation of a Municipality of Paddington had been signed by 172 local residents in 1859; it was one of the first local areas to demand incorporation under the 1858 *Municipalities Act,* along with

Glebe, Parramatta, Randwick, Waterloo and Waverley. While the colonial government was primarily seeking to pass the bulk of the costs of suburban development onto local ratepayers, Paddington residents wished to take control of shaping their own environment.[47] The incorporation occurred on 17 April 1860,[48] and the first meeting of the Paddington Council was held at the Paddington Inn on 25 May 1860, with William Perry elected the first chairman.[49]

Nine years later, this desire to retain control was again demonstrated in strong local opposition to a move to incorporate Paddington into the City of Sydney. A Parliamentary Select Committee established to look into the matter 'concluded that amalgamation with the city was not in Paddington's interests'.[50] And it was a municipality with one very unusual feature: by the late 1860s, a good half of its total land area was still in the hands of the 'Valley's' few wealthy residents.[51] But change was in the air. From the late 1860s, and for a variety of reasons, many of the old estates were broken up, being subdivided and sold off, and what occurred was a massive infill of housing on the slopes of Paddington, one of the earliest centres of the building boom in terrace housing. But it meant that, of the many early 19th-century gentlemen's estates in the area, only the first to be built, Juniper Hall, The Terraces built in the 1840s, and the last, Olive Bank, built for John Ely Begg in 1869, survive today.

Figure 3.7: Tram on the Barcom Avenue viaduct, later known as the Burton Street viaduct and Cutler footway, looking east across Paddington terraces, c 1959. The line passed along Glenmore Road, Gurner and Hargrave Streets towards Woollahra and Bondi. It was finally closed in 1959, replaced by buses. Photo: J Fawl.

Much of the building activity in late 19th century Paddington was the work of 'spec' builders, who financed the construction of each new house from the sale of the last. Such was the ongoing process of building that for much of this period 'Paddington would have been a noisy, sometimes chaotic and muddy construction zone.'[52]

Among the rows of terraces being built on the slopes were some welcome providores. Down on Gurner Street was Mr OA Morcombe's quite stylish grocery store, touted as 'The Oldest Established Grocery Store in the District', where

> Mr Morcombe and his assistants wore long white aprons and straw boaters. There were no ready-packaged goods. Everything was weighed out on old-fashioned scales. There was loaf sugar, lump sugar, demerara sugar, and delicious halves of crystallized lemons and oranges with a fragrant deposit of citron scented candy in their hearts...[53]

Now responsible for paying for its own infrastructure, the speed of the suburb's growth required Paddington Council to arrange for a loan of £50,000 to allow for 20-odd miles (32 kilometres) of roadway – aligned, curbed and guttered – to be built.[54] This was partly necessitated by constant wrangling with authorities over who was responsible for road maintenance, particularly the suburb's major roads.[55] But such investment meant that by the turn of the century, 'Paddington was one of the largest and most flourishing municipalities around Sydney.'[56] As Kelly notes, 'In 1850 Paddington had been a village, remote from the life of the newly incorporated City of Sydney. Forty years and thousands of decisions later, it had become a suburb in every sense of the word.'[57]

Unlike most of the similarly new suburbs of the 1860s and 1870s, Paddington, with its barren and hilly terrain, had no heavy industry or large factories; many of the residents depended for their livelihood on jobs that mostly lay outside their suburb.[58] So even though Paddington did not start out as a dormitory suburb to the city, proximity to the city made it Sydney's first commuter suburb, and further transport innovations played an important role in this. Steam trams came first, early in 1881, commencing services through Paddington from Darlinghurst to Ocean Street Woollahra, along Glenmore, Gurner and Hargrave streets, along Moncur and Queen streets Woollahra, and to and from Circular Quay via Elizabeth and Park streets.[59] The Oxford Street line soon became the busiest in Sydney, carrying over 50,000 passengers a week. This led to a gradual decline in the old horse-bus services, which ended around 1889.[60]

Then in 1894 a cable tram network was built along the New South Head Road,[61] and while the rugged topography of the area sloping down from Oxford Street initially made it impossible for any trams to manage the gradients there, eventually, in February 1909, a new line through the Rushcutters Valley was finally opened, using the new electric technology.[62] Thus by the end of the first decade of the 20th century, Paddington was now well served by public transport, making commuting to the city quite easy.

The latter half of the 19th century also saw the construction of several imposing public buildings in the area. The first was the reservoir to hold water for the suburbs lower down; being at the height of the ridge made it an ideal location. Previously, Busby's Bore, constructed in the 1830s, had carried water from the Lachlan Swamps to Sydney Town, but growing demand and the gradual pollution of the swamps required a more permanent and practical solution.[63] Work on the Paddington Reservoir commenced in 1864, although it was not completed until 1866. It was enlarged 10 years later, to a holding capacity of two million gallons. The reservoir operated until 1897, when the higher Centennial Park Reservoir was commissioned.

Figure 3.8: Re-laying tram lines in Glenmore Road outside Royal Hotel at Fiveways, c 1920. Photo: J Fawl.

Figure 3.9: Paddington Town Hall, Oxford Street, c 1900s. Woollahra Libraries Local History Collection.

By 1890, Paddington's remarkable growth had led it to become Sydney's second wealthiest suburb, Balmain being the richest. To mark this achievement, Paddington aldermen decided in that year to build a 'splendid Council Chamber, in keeping with the requirements and worthy of so important and progressive a Borough as Paddington'.[64] As the suburb had grown and become more prosperous in the 1880s, the present site was purchased, and Premier Sir Henry Parkes laid the foundation stone in 1890. Built at a cost of £15,000 and opening in 1891, it replaced the first council venue built in 1866 opposite and further down Oxford Street. Only 29 invitations had been sent out on the occasion of the first opening, including 19 to Rushcutters Valley gentry and five to members of parliament.[65] But for the 1890 ceremony, thousands of locals and many dignitaries and other visitors attended, and not unexpectedly, some of Parkes's long speech was to draw cynical responses from parts of this crowd.[66] The 32-metre clock tower was added in 1905.[67] Other important manifestations of Paddington's substance were the Paddington Post Office, built in 1885, and the Courthouse and Police Station, built in 1888.

Other changes appeared in the suburb. After Robert Cooper had run into financial difficulties, the distillery on Glenmore Road was sold in 1860 to John Begg, a property developer; it became a tannery that, according to records, 'stank to high heaven'.[68] Juniper Hall was being used as an orphanage by 1852, and then, as Ormond House, became a college for young ladies.[69] In the 1870s it was occupied by John Begg, and finally, in 1885, it was taken over by the government; part was used as a children's court,[70] while part was eventually used as a dormitory for 'delinquent' girls.[71] (See Chapter 4.)

Further west, Marshall's Paddington Brewery had become an important Sydney business. Its annual Christmas party was often written up in the Sydney newspapers; for example, the *Sydney Morning Herald* reported on 15 March 1898 that 'Over 40 employees and visitors left the brewery in two large drays, and reached their destination at 11 o'clock, where the day's sport was commenced by feats of strength, footraces, etc. A cricket match was then played for trophies.'[72]

Not everyone was impressed with the suburb. Visiting English poet Francis Adams, writing in the 1880s, saw Paddington as a 'hideous suburb':

Places like Newtown and Enmore, Paddington and The Glebe, are simply that congeries of bare brick habitations, which is just as much an arid, desolate waste as the mid-desert. Utterly unrelieved by tree or grass, they oppress the soul and shrivel up every poor little instinct and aspiration towards natural purity and health in man, woman and child.[73]

In spite of this, many Sydney literary figures enjoyed living there. Bertram Stevens, initially a solicitor's clerk but later becoming editor of *The Bulletin's* 'Red Page' and the *Lone Hand,* and co-founding editor of *Art in Australia* and *The Home,* lived at 65 Glenmore Road in 1898 and 1899. Ethel Turner moved to Paddington as an 11-year-old in 1881, living at 465 Oxford Street; she published *Seven Little Australians* 13 years later.[74] And the turn of the 19th century the poet Christopher Brennan lived further down, at 229 Glenmore Road, while some decades later, writer and journalist, Mary Gilmore lived at 96 Glenmore

Road, on its corner with Liverpool Street.[75] (See Chapter 9.)

Public parks

Councils were not just concerned with roads, drains and garbage. Respectable locales required public cultural infrastructure such as libraries and places for proper forms of leisure. Before 1880, for example, only eight parks had been established in the whole Sydney metropolitan area. Public land in Sydney's oldest suburbs had been initially alienated entirely by grants with no provisions for public spaces such as commons or recreational areas. This was the case with Paddington. By 1854, therefore, when the vaguely worded *Public Parks Act* was passed, giving the colonial government power to grant to trustees 'any land for the purpose of recreation, convenience, health and enjoyment of the inhabitants', there was simply no land left to allocate for public purposes in the older parts of Sydney. A new *Public Parks Act* passed in 1884, however, transferred control of these areas to local government by allowing municipal councils to become trustees of public parks.[76]

Down in Rushcutters Valley, land reclamation began in the 1870s, following the *Act* of 1878 that reserved 6 acres (2.4 ha) to be set aside for a park. The park was proclaimed in 1885 and almost immediately encroachments began to occur; in 1892 a tram depot and powerhouse were built to winch the cable trams up the steep ascent to Edgecliff. In 1897 a fountain was erected on the south-western side to commemorate Queen Victoria's Diamond Jubilee.[77]

During 1897, just under 5 per cent of Paddington was transformed into a public park. Like most of the sites chosen for parks and reserves in Sydney, the area had been highly undesirable; both Centennial Park and Moore Park had been sandy wastelands. Higinbotham and Robinson's map of Paddington shows a government reserve of 13.5 acres (5.5 ha) for 'Public Recreation'.[78] Much of this was thick scrubland and bush that had been overtaken by weeds and 'exotic' plants. Adjoining it to the east was a low lying swampy part of around 4.5 acres (1.8 ha) that was to become Hampden Park (later renamed Trumper Oval and Park after the renowned Australian cricketer). Parts of it had to be filled up to four metres to make the oval. Marked as a 'Quarry Reserve for use of the Woollahra Municipality' on the map, it had become a dump for ash and rubbish.[79] The two sites were to form Hampden Park, named in honour of Sir Henry Robert Brand, second Viscount Hampden, the colony's governor between 1895 and 1899.

Figure 3.10: Civic worthies at the opening of Hampden Park, 1897. Sydney City Council Archives SRC 14521 (HP 040/040862).

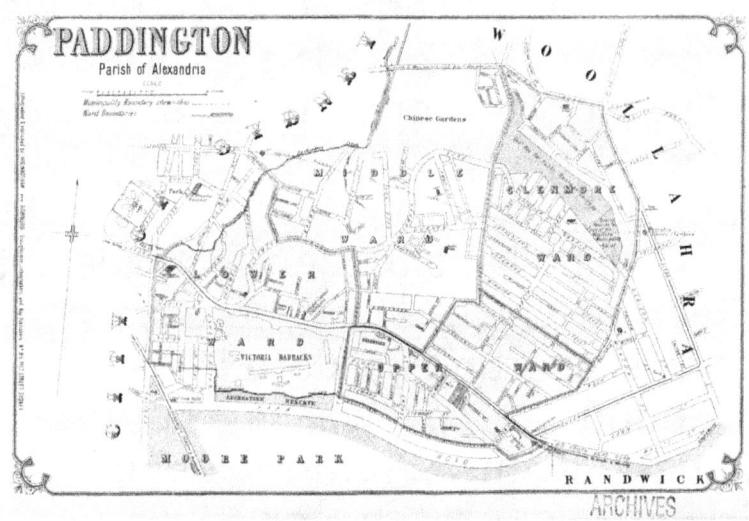

Figure 3.11: Map of Paddington, Atlas of The Suburbs of Sydney, 1886–88, by Higinbotham and Robinson. National Library of Australia.

While schools, churches and neighbourhoods had played their part over the years in fostering a growing sense of community identity, parks and ovals also now had a role. Hampden Park became an important place in the cultural and ceremonial life of Paddington. Cricket was a vital part of the Australian, and especially masculine, cultural identity and a powerful link to British heritage. Competition cricket matches were played on the oval from the formation of the Paddington District Cricket Club (PDCC) in 1893–94. The famous Australian cricketer Victor Trumper (1877–1915) lived in Paddington for some time and played for the PDCC. On 31 January 1903 he made 335 runs during a three-hour display of brilliant batting for Paddington at Redfern Oval, which became part of Sydney's sporting folklore.[80]

Around three weeks before this landmark event, Premier Sir John See officially opened the new, 'picturesque' 250-seat pavilion at Hampden Park. This was a gala affair. Many aldermen from surrounding councils – including the mayors of Paddington, Woollahra and Randwick – attended, along with members of the colonial Legislative Assembly and Legislative Council. The ground was 'decorated with flags, and the Sobraon boys band rendered selections on the lawn'. In his speech, the premier said that he 'regarded parks ... as necessary to the well-being of the people' and that he 'did not think too much money could be spent of these parks'.[81] In his words, and on the ground in Paddington, could be seen the growing influence of the garden city/suburb movement in Australia.

Another development had occurred in 1894, when a local Rugby Union Club was formed, and the 'Paddington Electorate' club remained in the Metropolitan Division First Grade until 1900, when the NSW Rugby Union established a 'district scheme' that divided the city and suburbs along new boundaries. Thus at a meeting at the Paddington Town Hall on 22 March 1900 – chaired by the mayor of Paddington – the Eastern Suburbs District Rugby Union Football Club was formed. The new club even adopted the old Paddington club's red, white and blue colours.

Three years later, indicating the continuing dominance of Australian British inheritance, a game of rugby league was played at Hampden Park; five years before the beginning of the rugby league competition in Australia.

Parks also had political dimensions. Of the 95 parks created between 1863 and 1902 in Sydney, 50 were established in the four-year lead-up to the Centenary, an event that was crowned in Sydney with the grand opening of Centennial Park. To be given a significant park was perhaps the next best thing to a railway line or station platform. Paddington's only park, however, was to be one of the 21 parks gazetted in the 1890s (and one of only two in 1897).[82] A grant of £3000 from the colonial government – which then would have purchased about 10 four-room dwellings in the area[83] – along with the proceeds of a public subscription were used to resume the land.[84] The 1897 opening of the park was tied into the celebrations around Queen Victoria's Diamond Jubilee, thus the vice-regal connection with the name Hampden Park. (See Chapter 10 for more on the changing landscape.)

Into the 20th century

Paddington seemed set for a bright future, having experienced decades of 'progress'. When Samuel Lyons had advertised a land sale there back in 1842, he proudly announced that it was 'a portion of the celebrated estate of Paddington'.[85]

Figure 3.12: Street fronts of 30–32 Oxford Street, Paddington, taken in 1900 during Cleansing Operations after the bubonic plague. State Library of New South Wales, digital ID a147282u.

A generation or so later, it could still be said by many to be a desirable place to live. In 1892, the *Geographical Encyclopedia of New South Wales* characterised the suburb as follows:

PADDINGTON (*Co. Cumberland*), a postal suburb of Sydney, with mail twice daily. Telegraph and money-order offices, and Government savings bank, with delivery by letter-carriers. Situated on the high land to the E. of the city, and on the Old South Head Road ... It is a favourite place of residence for persons having business in Sydney...[86]

But the closing decade of the 19th century was one of social and economic turmoil in the colony. Numerous banks failed, building and construction in the city faltered, unemployment spread, mortgagees could not keep up their payments, and industrial unrest was widespread, with strikes and lockouts disrupting Sydney's waterfront and closing down factories. Paddington's growth thus slowed during this decade, such that it was not fully developed until the end of the first decade of the 20th century.

Nevertheless, it was still a proud suburb. In its Jubilee publication in 1910, the Council of the Municipality congratulated itself:

> There is no suburb around Sydney that is more popular than Paddington. It is easy to access to

the city. Its streets and footpaths are well made and well kept and efficiently lighted at night time. It has three lines of trams, all of which are well patronised. The houses are compact, well designed and, as a rule, possess every modern convenience. The rents are within the reach of the class of persons who desire to live in such a healthy locality, and who consist very largely of well-to-do people, and rarely do they desire to change their residence.[87]

Figure 3.13: Stables at the rear 30–32 Oxford Street, Paddington, 17 July 1900. State Archives

and Records New South Wales, digital ID 12487_a021_a021000014.

Apart from some new shops appearing along the 'high street' – an ongoing process – other major changes occurred in the streetscape of Paddington in the early years of the 20th century. The Paddington Reservoir, closed in 1899, was then used by the Metropolitan Board of Water Supply and Sewerage for storage until 1914.[88] Reflecting an increasing concern for public health, in 1901 the Benevolent Society of NSW purchased Flinton, that 4-acre (1.6-ha) estate in Glenmore Road, for £14,000, and its new use was to be as a 'lying-in hospital' for women. It commenced operations in October 1901. The architect George Sydney Jones was then commissioned to design a modern new hospital wing, which was officially opened as the Royal Hospital for Women in May 1905.[89] And soon after the founding of the hospital, a group of young women, who were aware of 'the difficulties that beset the lives of working mothers and interested in the care and education of young children', established the Sydney Day Nursery. The first such nursery was in Woolloomooloo, but in 1924 the group opened the Eastern Suburbs Day Nursery at 33 Heeley Street in Paddington, in what had been Olive Bank.[90]

Figure 3.14: Paddington street scene, 1917, lower Glenmore Road looking south. Photograph, John Henry Harvey, State Library of Victoria, H2009.100/574/.

More change reflected the development of new technologies. The old reservoir became the Water Board's garage and workshop from 1914 until 1934,[91] and motoring schools and motor and electrical engineers and petrol stations began to appear in the area.[92] Theatres for the 'moving pictures' arrived. Possibly the first in Paddington was West's Olympia Cinema in 1910, on the corner of Oxford and South Dowling streets, on the recently sold site of the old Marshall's Brewery,[93] although open-air cinemas seem to have appeared about the same time or even earlier, often using the old stables of the now defunct horse-bus businesses, as occurred at the old Sydney Omnibus Stables at the top of Sutherland Street and at Donovan's Stables in Hargrave Street.[94] These were followed in 1915 by the Five Ways Picture Palace, named after the five streets intersection upon which it sat. Rebuilt in 1929, it was run by the Hickey family.[95]

Having the military barracks in the neighbourhood meant that Paddington residents were intimately aware of when Australian soldiers went off to war. They witnessed many parades of soldiers leaving the barracks for overseas action, as when soldiers departed to the Sudan War in 1885, the Boer War in 1899–1902, and the Great War of 1914–18. (The latter was a tragedy for

Australia: of 330,000 who served, almost 60,000 died and 226,000 were wounded.) A whole generation disappeared, and Paddington was not unaffected.

Figure 3.15: Victoria Barracks, Paddington, 1902. National Library of Australia, nla. obj-138301045.

Figure 3.16: The Royal Hospital for Women, Paddington, from Glenmore Road, photo c 1910,

looking south-east. Royal Hospital for Women Foundation.

Figure 3.17: The departure of volunteers of the NSW Infantry Contingent for the Sudan, 1885, Oxford Street looking east. Henry King, 1880–1900 photography, Tyrell Collection, Museum of Applied Arts and Sciences.

And the suburb was about to change, and quite dramatically. Patricia Thompson, a founding member of the Paddington Society, noted that after World War 1 'public taste turned away from terrace houses' and 'year by year, Paddington tumbled down the social scale'.[96] Partly due to new ideas about urban living, particularly those associated with the 'Garden Suburb' movement, with suburbs like Dacey Garden Suburb (Daceyville) catching the public imagination, but also partly due to economic factors, Paddington began a 'perceived' decline that was not reversed until the 1960s.[97] Thompson continued:

> The cost of living rose and the owners of terrace houses found it increasingly hard to equate rents with repairs. Some of the terraces were by now fifty years old ... and had antiquated plumbing, backyard toilets, inadequate lighting, damp walls and leaky roofs ... Paddington went downhill fast.[98]

Paddington's population peaked at 26,364 in 1921, at the start of an era famed as a time of cocaine, jazz, and the razor gang wars in inner Sydney. The decade was almost marked by increasing economic instability, culminating in the Depression of the 1930s, and this period saw a continuing deterioration in Paddington, increasingly seen as a slum suburb.[99] Problems were not perceived as merely economic;

the 'vices of the slums' received increasing attention. As the canon of Sydney's St Andrew's Cathedral put it: 'Immorality and crowded areas always go hand in hand.'[100] Even a few positive developments, like the creation of White City as home to the NSW Lawn Tennis Association down at the bottom of Rushcutters Valley in 1921, did little to alter perceptions.[101]

Oxford Street was now a somewhat narrow street for the amount of traffic that constantly passed along it, particularly in those parts that ran beyond the boundaries of the City of Sydney, which by 1914 had already widened the north side from Hyde Park to Taylor Square. In 1925, the recently established Main Roads Board and Paddington Council 'adopted' a scheme for the widening of Oxford Street between Taylor Square and Centennial Park; but nothing seems to have come of this. Then, in 1928, after much discussion, the Councils of Paddington, Woollahra, Randwick and Waverley agreed on a scheme to widen Oxford Street to 100 feet (30 metres). Initially they put this proposal to the Main

Roads Board, but the board was reluctant to go ahead without guaranteed government funding, and instead proposed that some widening could be inexpensively achieved by the simple expedient of realignment, rather than the purchase and demolition of existing buildings. Cutting back the width of existing footpaths and 'shaving off' the frontages of some shops did not however appeal to Paddington Council.[102] But the onset of the Great Depression put an end to all this, with the Paddington Council in particular registering a huge falling off in revenue. All talk of street-widening schemes was quietly dropped.

Figure 3.18: Photograph by Charles Kerry of Burns Johnson boxing match at open-air Sydney Stadium (later covered) at the Rushcutters Bay edge of Paddington, looking south with Paddington uplands in the background. Canadian Tommy Burns and African American

Jack Johnson competed for the World Heavyweight Championship title in front of a crowd of 20,000, 26 December 1908. Johnson won. National Library of Australia.

Figure 3.19: Photograph by Sam Hood shows the Davis Cup at White City, 1934. State Library of New South Wales.

The Great Depression and World War 2

The Great Depression certainly had its impact on Paddington residents. Unemployment, soon a common feature of life in what was now very much a working-class suburb, rose at an alarming rate.[103] Many tenants fell behind in their rental payments, as the generally male breadwinners lost their jobs. Along with the many Paddington residents who still depended on irregular or seasonal employment, they now tramped the streets in search of work that had simply disappeared. And when a job was advertised, queues stretched around the block, full of hopefuls.[104] Tenants were no better off: 'Some owners evicted tenants who could not pay their rent and these houses were soon derelict, with broken windows and swinging doors, vandalized almost beyond rehabilitation.'[105] In times such as these, families and neighbours needed to support each other: 'the local shop and the local pub became very important social centres. The crime rate was up, street gangs did function as did sly grog and two-up.'[106]

Under these circumstances, the local politicians were important in the life of such a close-knit community. Not surprisingly, in what was now an adversely affected suburb, open political agitation occurred. The Town Hall became the focal point, the place where anti-eviction rallies were organised. At a huge public meeting there in 1931, nearly 100,000 people converged on the building to hear Jack Lang (NSW premier), Eddie Ward (member for East Sydney) and other politicians speak against the federal government's economic policies. The crowd blocked Oxford Street for half a mile in each direction.[107] Locally, the Unemployed Workers Movement provided the backbone for resistance and support for the family.[108] Assistance also came from the Sydney City Mission at the corner of William and Underwood streets, and the Salvation Army Depot in Glenmore Road.[109]

It was often women's role to help keep the family together under such dire circumstances,[110] while even the kids did their bit. Some, like Kevin Ryan, remember going to Centennial Park, sitting with their legs in the ponds and then pulling the leeches off and selling them to the chemist in Oxford Street, who would use them for bruises and black eyes.[111]

What also gathered pace in this period was the push for 'slum clearance'. Various plans were put forward for 'pulling down the old and building anew' in line with 'modern' ideas about how a household would best function. And suburbs like Surry Hills, Darlinghurst and Paddington had by now become etched into the popular imagination as slums. But while by general consensus Paddington was ripe for action, it remained largely unaffected by the slum clearance practitioners, interrupted by the Depression, then World War 2.

Many of the kids who lived through the war years remember specific incidents; like the night of 31 May 1942 when three Japanese midget submarines slipped into the harbour and fired their torpedoes at the USS *Chicago.* These missed their target and instead sank the depot ship HMAS *Kuttabul;* the kids hid under the kitchen table.[112] And it wasn't long before Sydney was experiencing the 'American invasion' – 'oversexed, overpaid, and over here' – although the city never became, like Brisbane, an American village. But

Paddington saw some unusual developments. The old Paddington Bakery at 2 Paddington Street became a brothel during the war years.[113]

When the war ended, one joy beat all others, that of seeing some locals coming home.[114] But even though peace was declared and civilian life resumed, things did not instantly return to normal. Hangovers from wartime conditions were to have ongoing effects. Some of the wartime controls were slow to be lifted, and policies of economic and social reconstruction – which included slum clearance – were gradually implemented.

Post-war Paddington and newcomers

Many tenants of Paddington terraces had been protected by wartime rent controls. These were extended into the post-war era with the passing of the *Landlord and Tenant (Amendment) Act* in 1948 and this kept the cost of rental housing low until the mid-1960s. But, while tenants were protected (since their landlords could not extract any rise in rents nor evict certain tenants), no incentive existed to upgrade or even maintain the houses. Thus much of the old housing stock fell even further into disrepair and decay.[115] Life in Paddington, however, continued on. As one boy born in 1933 remembers of the post-war period:

> Paddington was all residential and industrial in those days, it was regarded as fairly low class, fairly cheap. There were a number of farriers around for shoeing horses, lots of nice big grocery shops, a lot of bakeries. One family used to run a movie theatre. Another chap was a postman.[116]

And a variety of light industries now existed in the area:

> There was Hardy [sic] Rubber Company, Tailor's Paints, Zips soft drink factory, a furniture factory, there was a quarry down at the bottom of Cascade Street, and John McGrath's Motors down the bottom. A lot of Paddington people worked locally. A lot of them were wharf labourers, and then the rest of

them were Council workers and tram drivers and guards.[117]

The entire suburb of Paddington, including the areas south of Oxford Street, had been administered since the 1860s by its own council, but a development soon occurred that was to have an impact on Paddington and its independence. Attempts to change the political control of the City of Sydney Council, by bringing into it the working-class suburbs of Alexandria, Darlington, Erskineville, Glebe, Newtown, Redfern, Waterloo and Paddington, were finally successful.[118] The Municipality of Paddington was abolished. In late December 1948 the final meeting of Paddington Municipal Council was held at the Town Hall.[119]

Paddington now became subject to the City of Sydney's planning and zoning arrangements. This meant Paddington was to be extensively remodelled.[120] Many new aldermen supported the ideas of 'slum clearance', to be replaced by high-rise Housing Commission flats.[121] One such site for these flats in Paddington was the Hardie Rubber Company factory, then in an industrial zone, but ripe for re-zoning. Indeed, despite what were referred to as the 'natural advantages' of the area, town planners considered that these were 'hardly discernible under the blight of present development'. The locality was seen as dominated by its 'sub-standard', 'dilapidated' housing.[122] As one resident dryly commented, over the decades, it just kept going downhill:

> The suburb ... having no railway and no wharves, escaped industrialization and simply dozed in its dirt between the two world wars and into the 1950s.[123]

The post-war era brought major changes to Australian society, and from the 1950s Paddington was no exception. It began to shift quite dramatically, and for a variety of reasons. One was the rapid growth in car ownership, financed by the ever-expanding hire purchase sector. And with Oxford Street through Paddington being the major route to the affluent Eastern Suburbs, this would have a major impact on the street and its businesses, as well as on the suburb's old terrace housing. The

Department of Main Roads, which had replaced the Main Roads Board, had Paddington in its sights. This was an added reason for investors not to spend any money on repairs and renovations; the property might well be demolished because it was in a precinct over which the dreaded words 'DMR affected' were in place.

Another impact came from the changes to the law governing the state's drinking hours. After 6 o'clock closing was repealed in 1954, hotels were allowed to stay open till 10pm. Then in 1955, the state government legislated 'to allow sports clubs to sell liquor and then to run poker machines [that] revolutionized suburban facilities'.[124] These led to changes in an evening's socialising in Paddington, particularly for men. And the arrival of television had its negative impact; in 1958 the Five Ways Picture Palace was forced to close. It later became a supermarket.[125]

This was also the start of an era of mass migration schemes. Europeans came in droves and provided the labour to drive Australia's modernisation through new industries and monumental projects such as the Snowy Mountains Hydroelectricity Scheme. Paddington was one such area where many 'New Australians', from Greece, Italy and Eastern Europe, settled. For them, the cheap rents and easy accessibility by public transport to the factories of Redfern, Alexandria and Waterloo made Paddington a desirable locale. Competition arose between newcomers and the older working-class residents for both employment and housing.[126] Australian-born residents who could afford to, moved out to quarter-acre blocks in the new 'sylvan suburbs' on Sydney's expanding fringes, leaving their former homes to the 'New Australians'.

The newcomers began to establish their own communities, recreating aspects of their old world cultures. Soon whole precincts began to bear some resemblance to their places of origin. Neighbours lived close by, recreating the familiar sounds, smells and habits of homelands on the other side of the world. Census figures tell the story. In 1957 in Paddington the proportion of non-British European-born people was only 4 per cent. By 1961 this had risen to 23 per cent and by 1966 it was one-third.[127] Many bought or set up corner shops and other small businesses to cater for their compatriots. In 1967, the *Paddington Journal* advertised:

> GREEK COOKING – at Paddington Fruit Market, 346 Oxford Street: dolma, caviar, páte, cheeses, food for parties ... Good fruit and vegetables too![128]

All this diversity injected Paddington with a livelier and richer ambience.[129] But not everyone welcomed the changes. One long-standing shopkeeper on Oxford Street went so far as to advertise on his windows: 'Shop here before the day goes.'[130] Yet even among this influx of the new, the old lived on. Long-term residents remember listening to the radio or the gramophone – and then watching the TV – in the evening, with the family gathered around,[131] while at the local pub a few old timers would nurse their schooners, reminiscing.

Apart from the influx of immigrants, bringing their cuisine and modes of living, other new arrivals stepped into the scene: 'cultural practitioners'. As author Clive James noted, 'Nobody except a few aesthetes had any idea at the time that Paddington's terrace houses were desirable residences.' Two such 'aesthetes' were from the literary set: Patricia Thompson and her poet husband John, an ABC broadcaster and producer, who also co-edited the first *Penguin Book of Australian Verse* in 1958. They moved into 66 Goodhope Street in the early 1950s.[132] Others to arrive were Dr Philip Parsons, a drama academic at the University of New South Wales, and his wife Katharine Brisbane, the national theatre critic of the *Australian* newspaper. Eventually, in 1971 they set up Currency Press, to publish books and plays that 'reinterpreted the past with a local perspective and gave voice to the rapidly-changing present'.[133]

Figure 3.20: A crowd gathers to see Frank Sinatra at the Sydney Stadium, 2 December 1961. Fairfax Photographs.

Also drawn by the cheap rents were university students and hippies. Over the 1960s and into the 1970s, the hills of Paddington echoed to the sounds of Ravi Shankar and the Rolling Stones, names like Jean-Paul Sartre and Simone de Beauvoir would come up in conversations, kaftans and djellabas became common sights, and the smell of pot permeated the air. Indeed, the narrow passageway between 194 and 196 Glenmore Road was then known locally as 'Marijuana Alley'.[134]

Reflecting the tastes of these new arrivals, from the early 1970s Paddington pubs also hosted some of Sydney's better-known bands. The Unicorn on Oxford Street was a favourite venue for Dogs in Space. It was just one of a string of local pubs featuring live music, and the Greek Community Centre, once West's Olympia Cinema, also hosted some of the more successful performers such as Jeff St John and The Id, Split Enz, and The Reels. Paddington Town Hall boasted some of the most memorable nights, when the young groovers came in their thousands.[135] The Town Hall was a popular venue for a wide variety of events, not only for the locals but also for the wider city, everything from the riotously bohemian Artists and Models Balls to the far more staid and respectable Greek community gatherings,[136] to the anti-eviction rallies of the Depression years, or school children's 'fancy dress' parties, and the first Aboriginal debutante ball in Sydney was held there in 1966 (see Chapter 1).

Gentrification

Gentrification was a process that would alter the face of Paddington dramatically. Indeed, Paddington was the first Sydney suburb to begin this process, which saw many of the city's older suburbs – long regarded as slums and worthy of nothing more than demolition – increasingly bought into by young professionals who turned dingy terrace houses into smart, inner urban residences. Early 1960s Paddington was still overwhelmingly working-class, but this began to change, with an increasing representation of white-collar workers and professionals. In the 1966 census, 11 per cent of Paddington's residents were professionals; by 1971 the proportion had nearly doubled to 21 per cent. It rose to 31 per cent by 1976.[137] When set against the demographic trends of Sydney as a whole, these changes were even more dramatic. Whereas between the censuses of 1966 and 1971 the proportion of professional and white-collar workers in the Sydney workforce rose by only 0.5 per cent, in

Paddington it rose by a remarkable 7 per cent – 14 times the Sydney average.[138]

While gentrification sped up in the following years, 'aesthetes', immigrants, students and gentrifiers weren't the only ones to make Paddington home. Some of Sydney's 'Push' also wended their way to Paddington. Journalist Wendy Bacon and academics Don Anderson and Stephen Knight lived in 14 Olive Street in the 1960s, as did academic Michael Wilding soon after arriving in Australia in 1963. Germaine Greer was a frequent visitor,[139] and was perhaps rather unflatteringly recreated as Gretel, a character in Wilding's novel *Living Together,* set in 79 Windsor Street: 'the strong jaw, the glaring eyes, the thighs like steel handles of a nutcracker'.[140]

Gentrification had its impact on local retailing. Soon a large number of the shops on Oxford Street were selling the antiques that furnished the newly restored terrace houses, or the Australian native plants that went into the newly planted gardens, and all the other accoutrements of gentrification. On Oxford Street between Barcom

Avenue and the about-to-be restored Paddington Post Office – known as 'Paddinghurst' – there were no fewer than 20 antique shops.[141] Clothing retailers also began to take over many of the rundown shops. Snazzi, at 363a Oxford Street, brought a sophisticated, fashionable clientele to the street. In 1974 Paddington acquired its first licensed bottle shop, and its name, the Paddington Grog Shoppe, reflected the mood of the moment.[142] But gentrification had its costs. As the *Paddington Journal* noted in October 1969, 'Paddington is running out of cheap opportunity. Everybody's "on" to it, and prices are high.'[143]

Other entrepreneurs soon made their appearance. Old buildings were converted, some to smart restaurants like the Hungry Horse, while others became the art galleries that were soon a feature of Paddington. Possibly the first was Rudy Komon, who bought in at 124 Jersey Road, at the corner of Paddington Street. He converted the ground floor of the building, formerly a wine saloon, into an art gallery that was opened in November 1959 by Harold

Holt, future prime minister of Australia; the opening exhibition was titled 'Tom Roberts to Jon Molvig'. Then came Barry Stern, who opened his gallery in Glenmore Road in 1961. He was soon followed by others: Kym Bonython opened the Hungry Horse Gallery in Elizabeth Street in 1966 and Gisella Scheinberg's Holdsworth Galleries appeared on the fringes of Paddington in 1969. Clive Evatt's Hogarth Gallery in Walker Lane, off Oxford Street, came later, in the early 1970s. Many of these gallery owners acted for the many artists who lived in the area, and bookshops and art schools soon followed.[144] (See Chapter 6 for more detail on gentrification, and Chapter 9 for the creative flourishing of Paddington.)

Figure 3.21: Lampooning 'The Trendy Gay Gentrifier', Martin Sharp, Oz Magazine, 1964. State Library of New South Wales, ML Z/Q059/80, © The Martin Sharp Estate.

Gay Paddington

Another component in the suburb's changing face was with the increasing appearance of gay men and women. Part of this was simply the 'overflow' from further down Oxford Street in Darlinghurst. Finocchio's wine bar, opposite Paddington Town Hall, became Enzo's, exclusively gay,[145] and Paddington Town Hall hosted many 'gay lib' dances from the early 1970s.[146] Also on Oxford Street came Oddy's coffee shop, just opposite Greens Road at Victoria Barracks,[147] while many local hotels took on a gay tinge. At Five Ways, the Royal Hotel was a favoured haunt of the many actors who lived locally – with figures such as Gordon Chater and Noel Brophy prominent among them; it later established its Elephant Walk bar as openly gay. In April 1976 the Imperial Hotel opened the Apollo Bar,[148] and further down Oxford Street, other Paddington hotels followed suit. The Albury and Unicorn hotels became almost exclusively gay. They were both on the 'Golden Mile', and had 'gone gay' in 1978 and 1980 respectively, as part of what a *National Times* journalist called the 'gayification of the inner-city pubs'.[149] Gay gentrifiers in Paddington who needed assistance could avail themselves of the services of the camply-named local handymen 'Hinge and Bracket'.[150]

The gay component to the gentrification of Paddington had long been noted. An early comment had come from the satirical magazine *Oz* in 1964. Cartoonist Martin Sharp lampooned the trendy 'camp' renovating a terrace in Paddington; this smart 'queen', after telling us what he does and where he shops, goes on:

> and I have an absolutely MAD little terrace house in Paddington ... it's just too too DIVINE ... it was really nothing when I got it ... and so cheap too ... and *Vouge* [sic] are going to do a colour feature on it and I'm just too thrilled for words.[151]

Several factors might help explain this. One is that areas like Paddington, with their more diverse, even bohemian, residents, were less likely to be condemnatory of their more unconventional neighbours. Also, maybe many of the homosexual men moving to these areas were relatively affluent, particularly if they were a gay couple with two incomes, like Max Kelly and Brian Hoad. Some became active members of the Paddington Society.

Two councils, politics and planning

In 1968 Paddington was divided between the City of Sydney Council and Woollahra Council.[152] It once again became the plaything of state politicians with their own agendas. But the greatest threat to Paddington in this period came from the Department of Main Roads (DMR). Under the impact of the increasing ownership and use of the motor car – and particularly with the closing of the city's tram network in 1961 – the DMR renewed its efforts to widen Oxford Street as far as Bondi Junction. It had continued to resume and even demolish properties. By the 1950s it owned all of the private properties on the southern side of Oxford Street in Paddington.[153]

But whereas earlier schemes had been influenced by the 'City Beautiful Movement' and the push had been for the creation of a boulevard for Oxford Street, by the 1960s the main focus had changed dramatically. The DMR planned a system of massive expressways for the city, with a full-scale eastern expressway with six lanes of traffic through Paddington to Bondi Junction and beyond. Such a scheme would clearly have a detrimental effect on both Oxford Street retailers and local residents, but the DMR, along with planners in the City Council, still considered much of Paddington as 'slums'.

Figure 3.22: Pat Thompson speaking at a rally to save Juniper Hall, 1984. Max Kelly is standing second on the left in white trousers. The Paddington Society Archives, PS_574.

So in mid-1964 – primarily in response to the threat of the massive carving up of Paddington (with roads designed to meet the motoring needs of people from outside the area) – at a boisterous and crowded meeting in Paddington Town Hall, the Paddington Society was formed.

A flash point came in 1969 when plans were announced that Jersey Road was to be widened, with many of its grand old Victorian terraces to be demolished. This was the Paddington

Society's first conservation battle. Its founding members were John Thompson, as president, and Patricia Thompson, Don and Marea Gazzard, Viva Murphy and Sheila Rowan as committee members.

People living in Paddington had an appreciation of the suburb's unique historical and aesthetic qualities, and consequently a growing willingness to fight to protect its built environment.[154] From the mid-1960s, the Society became an active force within the politics of urban planning, challenging the plans of road-builders with detailed and expert submissions, and producing from within its ranks some of the finest advocates for the retention and remediation of the built fabric of the city. It was primarily through the efforts of the Paddington Society that an inquiry was set up by the NSW government in 1968 into the suburb's heritage and significance, culminating in the eventual heritage listing by the National Trust, a decade later, of the whole suburb of Paddington.

Public meetings at Paddington Town Hall were a feature of this burgeoning interest in heritage preservation. During the 1970s it was also to Paddington Town Hall that local residents came to meet with the members of the NSW Builders Labourers Federation to make alliances over green bans on proposed expressways.[155] Thus Paddington, which had been marked for destruction and redevelopment in the 1950s and 1960s, was given a new lease of life.

Seismic shifts: 1970s–90s

The 1970s was a decade of dramatic change for Australia, and also for Paddington. They were generally years of ongoing economic prosperity in Sydney; its population grew to 3.2 million in 1981, and major redevelopment projects of parts of the city were undertaken. New ideas were emerging. In 1975 a group of young historians met at Max Kelly's house in Heeley Street and founded the Sydney History Group. Their aim was to promote what was then the 'new' field of urban history. In that same year the

Uniting Church opened the Saturday Paddington Markets in its grounds, catering expressly for artists and craftspeople who 'wish[ed] to express alternative ideas and methods of production and trading'.[156] All this further boosted the suburb, bringing in loads of tourists, many of them from overseas. Retailing boomed on Oxford Street. In the 1970s, amid the old – butchers, boot-makers, greengrocers and grocery shops, and George Warnecke's store selling a mix of junk, memorabilia and bric-a-brac – there were now cafes, boutiques, antique shops and 'vintage clothing' shops. But over time, as Oxford Street became more popular, gradually the old stalwarts closed. Boutique names in fashion increasingly appeared.[157]

The 1980s were good years for Paddington. Retailing boomed, with popular brand names like Country Road, Esprit and General Pants Company opening on Oxford Street,[158] and smart restaurants like Buon Ricordo opening in 1987. Terrace renovations continued apace, turning the suburb into a perhaps somewhat self-satisfied and decorous enclave, so unlike its various past manifestations. Juniper Hall had another transformation: from 1925 it had operated as flats, but in the lead-up to the Bicentenary in 1988 it was taken over and restored by the National Trust, and was, for some years, open to the public.[159] More change came in the 1990s. In 1997 the Royal Hospital moved to new premises at the Prince of Wales Hospital in Randwick, ending its Paddington life of almost 100 years. The hospital's old site (itself one of the original gentry villas Flinton) was sold and developed for housing, becoming known as Paddington Green.[160]

Figure 3.23: Juniper Hall, above in 1895–1915, below in 1983 showing shops to be removed in

the restoration. National Trust of Australia (NSW).

Into the 21st century

In the first decade of the new century along Oxford Street, a process that had been going on for some years, initially slowly and unobtrusively – a retail and restaurant exodus – culminated in this situation: '89 shops along the 4.3km stretch from the city of Sydney to Bondi Junction are vacant, for lease or closing ... Paddington, bearing the brunt of the storm, clocks up 46, a vacancy rate of just over 18 per cent. In the area immediately surrounding Jersey Road, it is as much as 65 per cent.'[161]

What had led to this situation for Paddington's own iconic 'high street'? The slump is often blamed on a range of issues, including unreasonably high rental rates, the opening of Westfield's malls, online retailing and negative gearing. High rents were certainly one cause. Here, the street was a victim of its own success, and owners of commercial properties had been able to keep increasing rents. One fashion retailer who had moved into 'the Siberian end' near Queen Street in 1996, paying an annual $30,000 in rent, found her rent increased to $50,000 in 1999 and then to $70,000 in 2005.[162] As rents crept up with the strip's retail popularity, when other factors kicked in, many tenants simply weren't able to pay these rents. By 2007 many tenants saw themselves as 'working solely for their landlords', and simply left. When online retail became an increasing feature of Sydney consumers' purchasing patterns, now a new competitor faced all retailers. In 2010, when Westfield Mall in the CBD opened, Oxford Street found itself book-ended by two Westfield malls (Westfield Bondi Junction had opened in 2003). Shoppers often found it far more convenient to go to one of these, where designer boutiques, other specialty shops, department stores and cafes and restaurants were all located in one place, and car parking was not a problem.

Figure 3.24: Saturday morning in Paddington in the 1980s. Garry Wotherspoon Collection.

While increasing and diverse competition and high rentals might have been causes, the 'curse of negative gearing' allowed many shops to stay empty for years; landlords could pick up a higher tax break for loss of rental income.[163] So for quite a while, parts of Oxford Street were an array of empty shopfronts, with a hodge-podge of 'For Lease' signs, darkened windows and dog-eared posters. This did little to encourage new businesses to set up. But some improvements have taken place in the last few years, an ongoing process. From 2010, rents started to 'come back' to the new reality,[164] and real estate agents say some rents have halved. One fashion retailer and 30-year tenant on the street reports that a landlord he knows is now looking for 70 per cent less than she was four years ago.[165] And adaptive re-use of buildings has improved the streetscape. Part of the old reservoir, which had been sold to Paddington Municipal Council in 1934 and was then used as a service station until the roof collapsed in 1990, was reopened by the City Council as Paddington Reservoir Gardens in 2009, following major restoration and landscaping.

Nowadays tourists come for the Paddington Markets and the Reservoir Gardens; the University of New South Wales's Art and Design School – formerly the College of Fine Arts –

brings the Millennials to the area; successful Gen Y-ers crowd the rejuvenated pubs and restaurants; and the suburb's two 'art-house' cinemas, the Verona and the Chauvel – the latter in the Paddington Town Hall – draw their aficionados. And activity once again increasingly occurs off Oxford Street. Apart from various walking tours through the streets of terraces,[166] there is 'commercial creep' along Glenmore Road,[167] Five Ways flourishes and William Street houses an eclectic bunch of designers and traders in the tiny shops and terrace houses: its festival has been held every September since 2009.[168]

Paddington today is probably best known for its streets of restored terrace houses with their distinctive cast iron balcony railings, flowing down in waves from the Oxford Street ridge to the harbour shores below. The suburb has a heritage listing, and its terrace housing is highly sought after, and very expensive. Thus a remarkable transformation has taken place, from what was once seen as a working-class slum worthy only of demolition, to a wealthy and self-conscious Victorian precinct. The latter still carries a whiff of that old 'Rushcutters Valley' gentry, whose 'presence' lives on in local street names such as Begg Lane, and Underwood, Flinton, Gurner, Duxford, Broughton and Olive streets.

Chapter 4
Early Paddington

Robert Griffin

When the first Europeans sailed into Port Jackson in January 1788 they found, in the words of Captain Arthur Phillip, a 'very superior ... harbour containing a considerable number of coves, formed by narrow necks of land'.[1] For those on the First Fleet this was an extraordinary and, for some, picturesque landscape 'diversified with gentle ascents, and little winding valleys, covered for the most part with large spreading trees'.[2]

On the southern side of the harbour, in the area that is now Paddington, was a high, heath-covered ridgeline and, below this, a thickly wooded valley with 'splendid specimens of the mahogany, the blackbutt, the blood tree and the red gum'.[3] Several creeks, with small waterfalls, coursed down the slopes and fed into a large, reed and rush-covered wetland before emptying into the shallow, sandy bay of the harbour. For more than 6000 years the Cadigal clan had hunted, fished and gathered food there, their way of life attuned to the natural environment.[4]

In the weeks following the landing at Sydney Cove, the many bays of the harbour were explored in the search for materials to support the new colony. It appears that the first Europeans came to the area at this time, seeking tall rushes from the wetland for thatching the roofs of their huts. Originally known as Blackburn Cove, after the master of the First Fleet ship the *Supply,* the bay was soon renamed Rush Cutting Bay.[5]

Apart from rush-cutting and perhaps some timber-getting on the slopes surrounding the bay, there was little European activity in the area until 1803, when a 15-foot (4.5-metre) wide road was constructed along the ridgeline. This road, really a track, provided access to the signal station on South Head and followed the high terrain from Sydney Cove.[6] The signal station had been established in 1790 and, apart from boat travel, the only access to the station had been via an Aboriginal foot-track, the *maroo,* that ran along the harbour foreshores, past Rushcutters Bay and then the pilot station and fishermen's huts at Watson's Bay (see Chapter 1). After commissary-general John Palmer had received his grant of land at Woolloomooloo in 1793, travellers using the *maroo* track had to go around his land, up to the ridgeline (now Oxford Street) and then back down to the track at Rushcutters Bay. When the road along the ridgeline was improved in 1811, this South Head Road became the main access route to all land east of Sydney Cove, the *Sydney Gazette* correctly predicting that it would become 'a beautiful avenue of recreation, either as a pleasant drive or promenade'.[7]

Figure 4.1: View of the Heads, at the entrance to Port Jackson, detail, from Views in Australia, published 1824, Joseph Lycett. Mitchell Library, State Library of New South Wales.

Early land grants

THOMAS WEST

In 1810 Thomas West, a convict carpenter, petitioned Governor Lachlan Macquarie for permission to establish a watermill in the valley above Rushcutters Bay. West, sentenced to life transportation for burglary, arrived in the colony in 1801. Employed in the government lumber yard, West became overseer of carpenters and demonstrated his entrepreneurial skills by making coffins; it is also said that he hung the bells in St Philip's Church.[8]

Macquarie was apparently impressed by West's industry and agreed to his request for land to construct the mill, although no official land grant or title was issued. The governor took a personal interest in the project, visiting several times during the mill's construction and described it as a 'most useful undertaking'. In January 1812 the governor attended its opening:

> Mrs M & myself attended by Secretary Campbell went to Thos

West's Water Mill (the first ever and now the only one in the Colony) to set going and to grind the first wheat; it only having been completed in these last few days after great labour and industrious exertions on the part of West, the projector and proprietor of it.[9]

Macquarie is said to have named West's land Barcom Glen and the first known use of the name was when West advertised his mill in July 1812, describing it as 'cheaper than the windmills and grinding much finer'.[10]

The boundaries of West's land were vague. It extended from Rushcutters Bay along Rushcutters Creek, in what was known as Lacrozia Valley, and while deputy-surveyor James Meehan's survey in 1816 indicated 40 acres (16 ha), West later extended his claim southwards to the boundary of South Head Road.[11]

West had built a hut near the mill for his family, but little is known of this structure and it was replaced in 1832 by a single-storey stone house at the head of the valley, with commanding views over Rushcutters Bay and down the harbour.[12] West continued to operate his mill until at least 1822 and although he cleared parts of his land for an orchard and grazing dairy cows, the steeper parts remained uncleared and became known as West's Bush.[13]

West had allowed quarrying of stone on his land near South Head Road for government buildings, on the understanding that he would receive further grants of land from Governor Thomas Brisbane. When this quarrying continued in 1830 West prevented further access, claiming ownership of the land. However, West had never received an official grant and as the town of Sydney grew, this became valuable land. In 1831 West's new, powerful neighbours, the colonial secretary, Alexander Macleay, and surveyor general, Thomas Mitchell, brought legal action questioning West's ownership – possibly prompted by Governor Richard Bourke's decision to issue land grants in the area to the colony's senior government officials. After several court cases, regarded by many as emancipist against the exclusives, West won his case although his land holding was slightly reduced.[14] West retained this estate until his death in 1858, when much of it was inherited by his son Obed. Obed had built his own house, Barcom Glen House, opposite his father's mill by 1845 – a single-storey stone house, with attic rooms and a basement level, facing north-east towards Rushcutters Bay.

Figure 4.2: Barcom Glen House, c 1900. Courtesy of West family descendants.

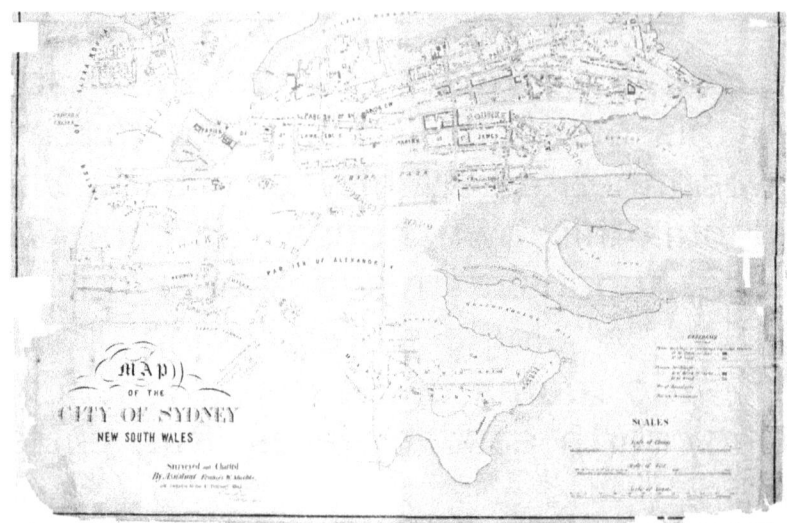

Figure 4.3: Map of the City of Sydney (detail), 1845, Francis Sheilds. This detail shows West's house and mill on the creek line leading to Rushcutters Bay, his second house at the head of the valley and Barcom Glen House close to the mill marked 'O West'. The villas of Woolloomooloo Hill are to the right (north). Sydney City Archives.

While Obed remained living at Barcom Glen House until his death in 1891, he began subdividing parts of the estate in the 1860s and much of it was broken up during the 1870s and 1880s by way of 99-year leases and government resumption for public works.[15]

WILLIAM THOMAS

In the years following the opening of Thomas West's water mill, Governor Macquarie was to make the first official land grants in the area, to two very different individuals. The first was in 1816 to Captain John Piper, naval officer, responsible for the collection of customs duties and harbour dues. The other, in 1817, was to the little-known William Thomas.

Captain Piper was granted 190 acres (77 ha) east of Rushcutters Bay, including Eliza Point (now Point Piper). Here Piper began building Henrietta Villa, described as 'the most superb residence in the colony' and the venue for Piper's sumptuous entertainments.[16] To provide access to his house on the point, Piper built a road along the higher ground from the South Head Road, avoiding the reed swamps of Rushcutters Bay and Double Bay. The upper section of Point Piper Road, later known as Jersey Road, was to define the eastern edge of James Underwood's grant (see below) and in

1860 defined the eastern edge of the Paddington Municipality.

The first official land grant to be made in the Paddington area was to William Thomas in October 1817. Little is known of Thomas and it has been suggested that this grant was made to Thomas by Governor Macquarie after his carriage had accidently run over one of Thomas's children.[17] Thomas was granted 40 acres (16 ha) on the eastern side of West's grant, comprising the flat land near the bay; this included part of present-day Rushcutters Bay Park and the White City tennis complex. (See Figure 2.11 and Figure 4.7.)

Thomas had occupied the land by November 1816 for he warned against trespassing on his 'farm at Rush-cutting Bay Point, by water or land' and threatened to 'detain all boats'.[18] The flats were good farming land and were used for market gardens from the 1830s until the early 20th century.

JAMES UNDERWOOD

The next land grant was not made until 1823 when Governor Brisbane promised 100 acres (40 ha) to the partnership of James Underwood, Robert Cooper and Francis Ewen Forbes for the establishment of Australia's first legal distillery. Underwood, Cooper and Forbes were emancipists[19] – each had been sentenced to 7 or 14 years transportation – and all three had become involved in trading ventures in the colony, although Forbes was not to enjoy the success of the others. Underwood had gained a spirits' licence by 1813 and Cooper had been the proprietor of two public houses in London, so with this background Brisbane was reasonably confident of their success. His decision to establish a local distillery was based on two factors: controlled local production would be better than the potent imports from India; and the dubious quality of the local illicit stills. Brisbane chose the Rushcutters Bay area for the distillery as it was a relatively remote location but still close to the town. The land, which extended from South Head Road down the slope towards the bay – approximately 25 per cent of present-day Paddington – was not to be sold for five years, 20 acres (8 ha) were to be cleared, and fences and buildings constructed to the value of £100.[20]

Construction began almost immediately, on the lower part of the grant near a good stream of fresh water (near present-day Jersey Road) and the Sydney Distillery opened in October 1824. A sample of the first production was sent to the governor and a few days later the opening of the distillery was marked by a large procession with a 300-gallon cask of rum carried by a dray into Sydney Town.[21] However the partnership had been dissolved three months earlier – Forbes, facing bankruptcy, sold his share to Underwood and, after a series of disagreements, Cooper also sold his share but retained 3 acres (1.2 ha) of land on South Head Road where he had begun building his house, Juniper Hall. Cooper went on to establish his own distillery near Blackwattle Bay while by 1825 'Mr Underwood has a 200 and 1,700 Gallon Still and could make 3 to 400 Gallons of Spirits a day'.[22] The distillery produced gin and rum, and perhaps port, brandy and apricot liqueur, which was carried from the distillery by bullock drays using the most level path to the South Head Road. This winding road followed the contour of the hillside and was probably made by the 'mechanics and labourers' employed by Underwood in the construction of the distillery; it became known as Glenmore Distillery Road.

Figure 4.4: A view from the heights of Paddington over Underwood Paddock, with Glenmore Road winding across the slopes. Landscape with view of harbour and houses, 1861, in Views mainly of the Eastern Suburbs of Sydney, 1859–63, George Roberts. Mitchell Library, State Library of New South Wales.

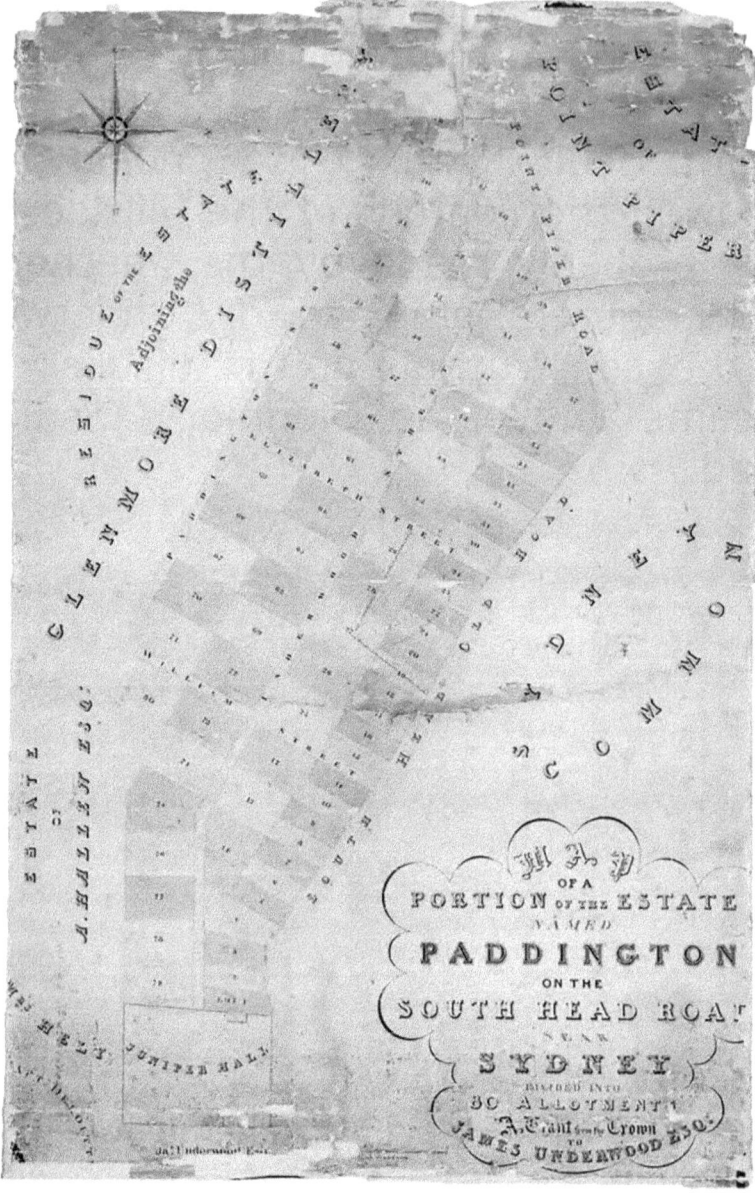

Figure 4.5: Map of a portion of the Estate named Paddington ... 1839, PL Bemi, James Underwood. Mitchell Library, State Library of New South Wales.

Underwood, who had built a residence at Rushcutters Bay by 1830, continued to operate the Sydney Distillery until 1836.[23] He then leased its operation and the name changed to the Glenmore Distillery.[24] While the distillery continued to operate until the mid-1850s, in 1839 Underwood subdivided 50 acres (20 ha) of his land above the distillery, along the South Head Road between Juniper Hall and Point Piper Road (now Jersey Road) and as far down to present-day Paddington Street. Consisting of 80 allotments, this was the first large-scale subdivision and it was advertised as 'that well known estate called Paddington'.[25] The subdivision created four new streets: Underwood, Paddington, Elizabeth (named after Underwood's wife) and William (named after his son).

After the distillery closed the buildings were rented to merchant, developer and local alderman John Begg, who established a tannery there in 1860. Begg then purchased the buildings and surrounding land and subdivided it, creating Cascade Street and selling the tannery as a factory for the Colonial Rubber Company (see Chapter 5).

Villas of Rushcutters Valley

By the early 1830s the once relatively remote location of the West, Thomas and Underwood grants had begun to change. As the town of Sydney grew and its nature shifted from penal colony to free settlement, the development of its surrounding areas steadily increased. One of the first and perhaps greatest changes was at Woolloomooloo Hill (present-day Potts Point, Kings Cross and Darlinghurst) – once a 'piece of barren, rocky and desert [sic] land' – that became the first and most fashionable suburb of Sydney.[26]

During the 1820s and early 1830s the transition of New South Wales from penal colony to free settlement was marked by the appointment an increasing number of government officials. The colony's new official establishment needed housing in or close to Sydney Town so that they could carry out their official duties and in 1828 Governor Ralph Darling provided building allotments on Woolloomooloo Hill for this new elite of senior civil servants. These grants were only confirmed when certain conditions were met – including that the plans were personally approved by the governor and were built to a minimum standard.[27] The result was 'a number of elegant villas ... erected by the more wealthy residents of Sydney, being to that place what the Regent's Park is to London'.[28] In other words, an exclusive suburb with houses that reflected the social standing of its residents.

By 1832 these grants had been taken up and the new governor, Sir Richard Bourke, needed to find land for more recently arrived government officials. Refusing the suggestion to subdivide Hyde Park, which Bourke thought should be 'preserved ... for the People of Sydney', his solution was to extend Darling's exclusive suburb of Woolloomooloo Hill to the south-east, along the South Head Road and on the slopes above Rushcutters Bay. Bourke's intention was clear – he would impose 'the same conditions upon these Grantees as Governor Darling had on dividing Woolloomooloo Hill, conditions which have had the effect of erecting a beautiful suburb at that Place' and would now 'procure the erection of Villas in a beautiful situation near the [Rushcutters] Bay'.[29]

In both England and in the colony, the suburban villa had become the middle-class ideal: a detached house offering picturesque views of the surrounding landscape and set within its own gardens, providing a healthy atmosphere and space for recreation, separate from the increasingly crowded and filthy towns. With picturesque views over the many bays and headlands of the harbour, while also being close to the town, the slopes above Rushcutters Bay were the ideal situation for the building of suburban villas; although Bourke did double the size of the intended grants to 6–8 acres (2.5–3 ha), admitting the site was 'inferior in Situation' to either Hyde Park or Woolloomooloo Hill as it was further from the town. This was the first subdivision of Paddington and was to result in what historian Max Kelly termed 'The Rushcutter Valley gentry'.[30]

The first grants were made during 1831 and 1832 on land to the east of Thomas West's estate: along the South Head Road and on each side of the only other road in the area, that leading to Underwood's distillery. These grants, like those for Woolloomooloo Hill, were issued to senior government officials: Colonel Henry Dumaresq, private secretary and brother-in-law to Governor Darling; William Lithgow, auditor general; John Kinchela, attorney-general; John Edye Manning, registrar of the Supreme Court; John Gurner, clerk of the Supreme Court; Roger Therry, commissioner of Court of Requests; Frederick Hely, principal superintendent of convicts; and Francis Rossi, principal superintendent of police. There was also the surveyor Robert Hoddle; Reverend Richard Hill of St James' Church; the highly regarded educator William T Cape; and the Australian Subscription Library, which Governor Darling had considered 'a Public Institution of great importance'.[31] Like Woolloomooloo Hill, there were no successful emancipists. However, there were already three emancipists living nearby: Thomas West at Barcom Glen; James Underwood near his distillery on the lower slopes; and Robert Cooper at Juniper Hall.

Figure 4.6: Sydney Harbour from Paddington, in Scenes in New South Wales, 1856, Mrs Allan Macpherson. A view from the heights of Paddington showing the setting for the villas of the Rushcutters Valley gentry. Mitchell Library, State Library of New South Wales.

While West completed his new house on the slopes above his watermill in Lacrozia Valley when the grants were being made in 1832, Underwood's house was completed by 1830 while Cooper's Juniper Hall was completed some four years earlier. Situated high on the ridgeline on the South Head Road it was a substantial building, one of the largest houses in the colony at the time. Commenced six years after Cooper had received his conditional pardon, Juniper Hall signified his success and remains as one of the earliest surviving houses of inner Sydney.

Cooper appears to have begun building Juniper Hall shortly before the distillery partnership with Underwood was dissolved in 1824.[32] In the settlement Cooper retained the 3 acres (1.2 ha) of land surrounding the house, which he named after the berry used in distilling gin. The house was probably designed by Cooper himself; it was a large, plain two-storey rendered brick box.[33] It had little architectural refinement and was very similar to houses built 10 or even 20 years before.[34] Its most distinguishing features were its scale and its position high on the ridge on South Head Road, the only road to the east, with views south towards Botany Bay, north to the harbour and over the town.

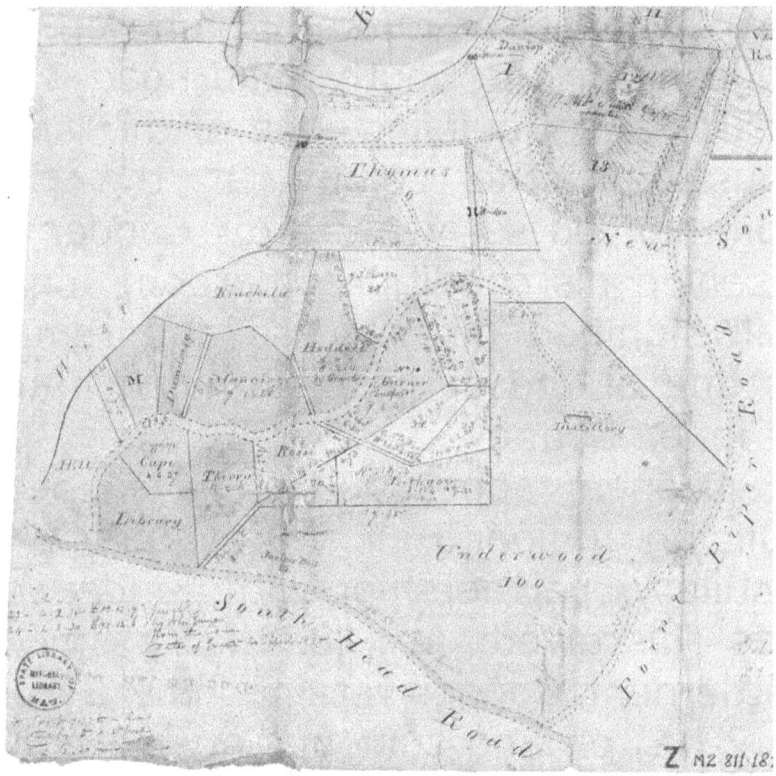

Figure 4.7: Mrs Darling's Point to South Head Road, property map (detail) 1833–37. This map shows the land grants of the Rushcutters Valley gentry, on each side of the Glenmore Distillery Road, and the surrounding earlier grants made to Underwood, Thomas and West. Mitchell Library, State Library of New South Wales.

Figure 4.8: Ormonde House, Paddington, from Views in Victoria, New South Wales and Tasmania, 1853, John W Hardwick. This view shows Juniper Hall high on the ridge of Paddington with its surrounding stone wall. To the right is Ormond Lodge, constructed by the Coopers as their house in c 1850 when Ormonde House was leased. Hardwick was living in the adjoining cottage when he drew this sketch. Only part of the cottage occupied by Hardwick survives at 4 Underwood Street. Mitchell Library, State Library of New South Wales.

The house, orientated towards the road, had a front elevation of five bays, with a central entrance door and oversized semicircular fanlight flanked by French doors.[35] The fanlight and extended eaves of the roof were the only stylistic elements, with the rear elevation similar to the front. The interior arrangement was also straightforward: a central hall running the depth of the house, with a central staircase separating the small front lobby from the rear, and on each side two large rooms. These included the usual dining room, parlour and probably a breakfast room, with characteristic detailing of run plaster work and cedar joinery.

On the upper level were the bedrooms, and what appears to have been a drawing room.[36] Upstairs drawing rooms were more characteristic of townhouses: for a house built outside of the town, such as Juniper Hall, the preference was for a ground floor drawing room that could open onto the garden. Perhaps for the emancipist Cooper, an upstairs drawing room was associated with the more cultured and 'genteel'.[37]

In its prominent position the house was a landmark and was apparently designed with this in mind. The rear elevation, clearly visible from the harbour, is almost identical to the front and with a basement kitchen the house was designed to be seen 'in the round'. As architectural historian James Broadbent has commented, Juniper Hall was 'tentatively following the notion of a suburban villa ... built on the ridgeline to see, and be seen'.[38]

By 1829 Cooper, his third wife Sarah and their children had moved into the house.[39] Nothing is known of the interiors of this time, however the furnishings were likely to have consisted of a mixture of English and local manufacture, a mixture of the simple lines of late 18th century English furniture, with square or turned tapering legs, and Regency designs with sabre legs.[40] The interiors were presumably close to this description of the time:

> The doors and interior fittings-up of the better description of our houses are of colonial cedar, kept polished in the manner of mahogany, the tables and chairs also being usually the same. Rush-bottomed chairs, manufactured here, supply the place of the latter for common purposes. The India cane mat is generally substituted

for the English carpet, on account of its superior coolness...[41]

Figure 4.9: Stair hall, looking to the drawing room, Juniper Hall. Constructed 1824. Although the stair hall was rearranged in an early remodelling of the house, Juniper Hall retains much of its original layout and detailing. Photo: J Whitelock, 1989. National Trust of Australia (NSW), 1988.

Within a few years Cooper, perhaps prompted by the new villas rising on Woolloomooloo Hill, began to remodel his dated house. By 1831, when Juniper Hall was offered for rent, there was a 'verandah and balcony complete' and the house was described as 'a genteel two-storey Residence, with eight elegantly furnished rooms ... a coach house and stabling, kitchen, laundry, and servant's rooms, a good garden, well stocked with fruit trees ... with every necessary convenience for the reception of a Respectable family'.[42]

The respectable family that took up residence was that of John Kinchela, the recently appointed attorney-general and one of the first grantees in the 'Valley of Rushcutters'. It seems Kinchela intended to oversee the building of his own house from Juniper Hall, which he renamed Ormonde House to remove its association with gin distilling.[43] As Kinchela was constantly in debt it appears that he could not afford to build and when he and his family left Ormonde House in 1835, the Coopers decided to retain the name.

One of the first of the villas built in the 'Valley of Rushcutters' was Engehurst, for the principal superintendent of convicts, Frederick Hely, and his wife Georgina. Hely had received a small grant of a little more than one acre and in 1833 he bought the neighbouring grant of 6 acres (2.4 ha) from Captain Rossi, with frontage to Glenmore Distillery Road. Hely then commissioned an initial design from the architect John Verge, described in the *Sydney Gazette* as 'an architect who has done much for the establishment of Sydney and its environs ... To his judicious taste we are indebted for the elegance of most of the villas on Woolloomooloo Hill, some of which are worthy of the suburbs of London'.[44] Verge's elegantly designed villas, with their beautiful detailing, established the architectural standard for the 1830s and works attributed to him include Elizabeth Bay House (1833) for the colonial secretary Alexander Macleay, and on Woolloomooloo Hill: Rockwall (1830) for the civil engineer John Busby; Tusculum (1830) for the successful merchant Alexander B Spark; Goderich Lodge (1831, demolished) for Thomas Macquoid, governor's sheriff; and Barham (1832) for the clerk of the executive council, Edward Deas Thomson.[45] Verge's design for Engehurst was characteristic of his work: a two-storeyed, stuccoed 'very handsome and spacious mansion' consisting of 21 rooms.[46]

It is not clear whether Engehurst was built to Verge's intended design as Verge produced several other designs; Hely died in 1836 and much of the house was demolished in 1878 with only a portion of the house surviving in today's Ormond Street.[47]

However, the original design is remarkably well documented and as the plans carry Governor Bourke's signed approval, the design is indicative of the type of house that Bourke envisaged for the new suburb; a continuation of the villas of Woolloomooloo Hill. The plans for Engehurst, combined with early survey plans showing the villas set within their grounds, provide insight into the lives of 'the Rushcutter Valley gentry'.

Engehurst is characteristic of the villa form, with rooms arranged around a central stair hall (see plan, Figure 4.10). An imposing neo-classical house, the front elevation of five bays had a central breakfront of three bays with pediment, moulded stringcourse, pilasters and a columned entrance porch flanked by arched niches. On each side of the central breakfront were elegant

French doors framed with masonry architraves, frieze and cornice; a characteristic element of Verge's work. The double entrance doors, with decoratively carved panels and a patterned transom light, were similar to those of Elizabeth Bay House, and like that house opened onto an almost cubic vestibule. This space, probably intended to have diagonally patterned stone paving as at Elizabeth Bay, was linked to the central stair hall. As in any house of standing, the principal rooms of the ground floor included a drawing room, dining room, library and breakfast room. Both the drawing and dining rooms had French doors opening onto the surrounding garden with, no doubt, views over the harbour. On the upper level were two larger bedrooms with attached dressing rooms, two smaller bedrooms and a water closet.

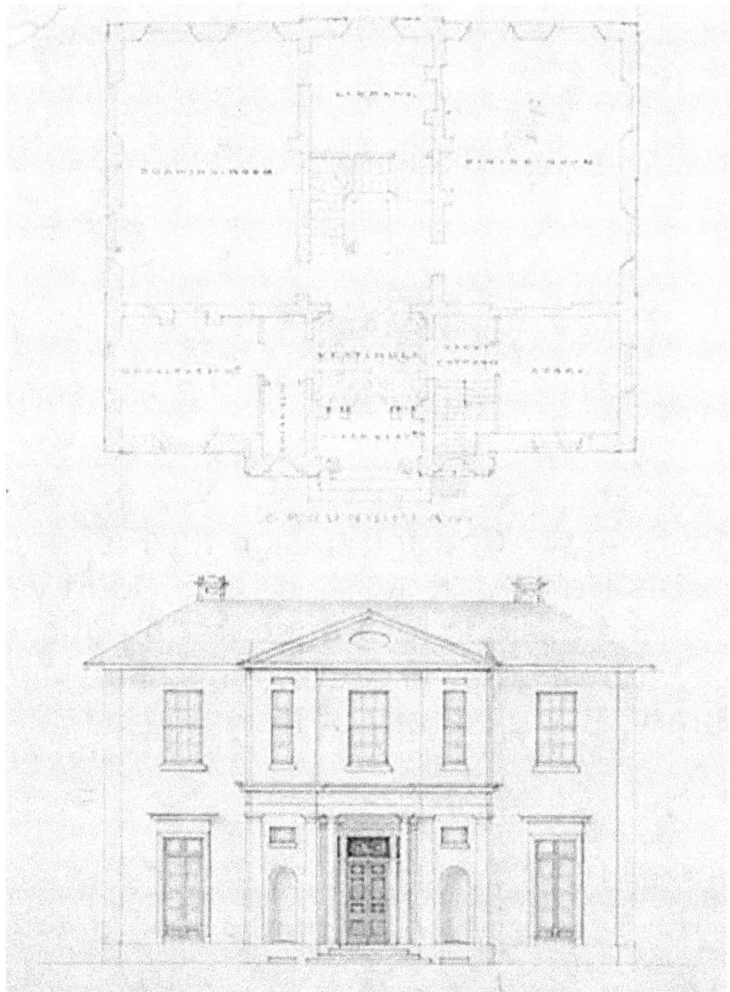

Figure 4.10: Design for a house on Captain Rossi's Allotment at Rushcutters Bay, Engehurst, 1833. Plan and front elevation, John Verge. Mitchell Library, State Library of New South Wales.

Figure 4.11: Cottage design for Frederick Augustus Hely, Engehurst, c 1833, John Verge. One of the designs for Engehurst produced by Verge, showing the breadth of his skill. Mitchell Library, State Library of New South Wales.

Figure 4.12: The surviving section of Engehurst, Ormond Street, Paddington. Built c 1835. Only a portion of the original house survives after subdivision of the estate and a series of demolitions and additions made to the original house (see Chapter 5). Photo: Robert Brown, 2017.

All the ground floor reception rooms were to be finished with decorative plasterwork cornices, beautifully detailed fine cedar joinery as evident in Verge's drawings – so characteristic of his work – and fitted with marble chimneypieces.

While it is uncertain if the completed house followed this plan, an 1846 description of the house indicates a very similar structure: 'a commodious Family residence ... commanding the most beautiful view of the harbour' containing 'a dining room, drawing room, and library, seven bedrooms...'[48] While there is no record of furnishings of these rooms they would have been consistent with other similar documented houses of the period; predominantly Grecian style furniture decorated with scrolls, acanthus leaves, the Greek key motif, columns and pediments and possibly some pieces in Gothic or Louis revival styles. The drawing room would have been the most lavishly furnished of the public reception rooms of the house as it was here that guests were entertained and the ladies withdrew following dinner. This richly decorated room would have included a suite of upholstered chairs and sofas, with sofa tables, circular loo tables and occasional tables, a piano, a fitted carpet with hearth rug, window treatments of muslin and perhaps chintz curtains, a chiffonier displaying ornaments, gilt-framed pictures and overmantel mirror, table lamps and a chandelier.

In contrast to this feminine room was the dining room, more masculine in character with 'somewhat massive and simple' decor.[49] An extendable dining table, 12 chairs (usually upholstered in horsehair), one or two sideboards for displaying silver and for the serving of meals, candelabrum for the table and a rich 'Turkey' carpet. The other, more private rooms of the ground floor and the upper floor would have been furnished more simply, with older furniture or furniture of local manufacture, compared to the 'show' rooms of the house.

Figure 4.13: Drawing room, Elizabeth Bay House, 1833–39. John Verge. The furnishing of the drawing room is based on an 1845 inventory of the room that describes its fittings and furniture. Photo: James Horan 2017. Courtesy Sydney Living Museums.

The house was surrounded by 8 acres (3 ha) of grounds, with two service wings consisting of a coach house and stables and the kitchen and servant's wing. From the entrance gates on Glenmore Road a winding carriage drive, perhaps with glimpses of the harbour through the trees, led to the house, passing at least some of the picturesque garden follies that the Helys had commissioned from Verge; a Gothic lodge, a Chinoiserie privy and a Gothic garden house.[50]

Georgina Hely remained living at Engehurst after her husband's death, apparently completing the work to the house and grounds. In this she may have been assisted by her son-in-law Gother Kerr Mann, a civil engineer and architect who had married her daughter Mary in 1838. The couple were living at Engehurst by 1840 and to maintain a household and grounds such as this required a small retinue of servants – senior servants such as a butler, housekeeper and cook – but also house maids, scullery maids, coachmen/grooms and gardeners.

By the mid-1840s there were other similar 'gentleman's villas', each set deep within their grounds on the slopes above Rushcutters Bay, enjoying 'magnificent views of the waters of our lovely harbour'.[51] These included Roger Therry's Flinton (1833, demolished) and John Gurner's Duxford House (1843, demolished), both possibly designed by Verge;[52] and William T Cape's Elfred House (1843, demolished).

However, as at Woolloomooloo Hill, the exclusivity of the Rushcutters Valley was short-lived. Some, such as John Kinchela, having begun to cultivate and prepare the grounds for their house, found that they could not afford to build and were forced to sell.[53] When these sales did occur they tended to be of the original grant, such as the sale of Reverend Hill's grant in 1836 following his death, or in a few lots of several acres, for those 'desirous of securing a valuable suburban residence'.[54]

The economic depression of the early 1840s also caused some to subdivide their estates, with gardens and grounds broken up for smaller allotments. While the area may have lost its exclusivity, it remained fashionable, its residents a mix of the original grantees and those who could afford a substantial residence. Thomas Broughton, successful merchant and city alderman, purchased part of Gurner's Duxford House estate in 1845 to build Bradley Hall (demolished) and by the mid-1840s there were a series of 'gentlemen's villas' on the slopes above Rushcutters Bay. These were substantial stone buildings, professionally designed and usually with separate servants' quarters, stables and coach house, and other outbuildings, surrounded by gardens and grounds and having picturesque views over the bays and headlands of the harbour.

However, the subdivisions continued. In the late 1840s new 'Villa Allotments' were offered, 'sufficiently large enough to admit of a comfortable family residence to be put upon them and ... for a good sized garden in the front and rear'[55] and then in the 1860s a second phase of villa building occurred as other original grants were sold. John Ely Begg, merchant and Paddington alderman, purchased Engehurst in 1868 and then subdivided the grounds to build his own house, Olive Bank Villa, the last of the Paddington villas and one that was to survive later subdivisions.[56]

From the end of the 1860s, as land values and land speculation increased, the scale of subdivision intensified. Some, such as the Beggs, accumulated land for future subdivision and profit, while others, such as John Gurner (Duxford House), Thomas Broughton

(Bradley Hall) and their families, resisted. Both the Gurner and Broughton families maintained their estates and as late as 1889, when their land was surrounded by terrace house development, it remained 'a neighbourhood which during the day is exceedingly quiet, a pleasant spot with old-fashioned houses shaded by dark trees ... which ... might be called retired'.[57] Within 10 years this had changed, Broughton's estate being the last to be subdivided in 1898.

Figure 4.14: View of Rushcutters Bay, Illustrated Sydney News, 15 September 1865, looking north. Bentley's Bridge and the villas of the Rushcutters Valley can be seen in the distance, this view probably from the lower garden of Bradley Hall. National Library of Australia.

Figure 4.15: Olive Bank Villa, built 1868, Heeley Street Paddington, photographed in 1925 soon after its conversion to the Eastern Suburbs Day Nursery. The density of the surrounding subdivision is clearly evident in the background. Woollahra Libraries Local History Collection.

Victoria Barracks and Paddington village

The village of Paddington began on land granted to the Australian Subscription Library in 1833, part of the 'valley of Rushcutters' land grants.[58] The 8 acres (3 ha) of land was positioned above the valley, on the South Head Road to the east of the road to the distillery (later Glenmore Road). (See Figure 2.12.)

The library had been established in 1826 and had operated from rented premises, being forced to change location several times. Whether Governor Bourke intended the land grant should be used for the library buildings or for financial benefit by its sale is unclear, however with the decision to establish the Victoria Barracks on the South Head Road in 1840, the library decided to sell.

A decision on the location for a new military barracks had been delayed for some years. The existing military barracks was located on a 16-acre (6.5-ha) site in the centre of the town, a site it had occupied since 1792.[59] By the early 1830s the barracks was regarded as an impediment to the growth of the town, occupying a large amount of increasingly valuable land. In 1836 plans and specifications for a new barracks were prepared by the recently appointed commanding royal engineer, Major George Barney, and a new site proposed on the southern edge of the town (now Prince Alfred Park).

This was approved by Governor Bourke however concerns over the ownership of military land in the colony and the way in which the barracks land might be disposed of resulted in delays. In 1840 a committee of the Legislative Council was formed to resolve the issues and its recommendations included that as the proposed new site for the barracks was becoming more developed, another site should be selected. It recommended either Grose Farm (now Sydney University) or the town common on the South Head Road.[60]

The site on the South Head Road was chosen for strategic reasons – it was high on the ridgeline between Sydney Harbour and Botany Bay – but also because its sandy soil was unsuitable for agriculture. It also contained sandstone that could be used for building and there was a water supply from nearby Busby's Bore.[61] Construction began in 1841 under the supervision of Major Barney and was completed in 1848 by his successor, Lieutenant-Colonel James Gordon. The title of Victoria Barracks began to be used in 1844, in honour of the reigning monarch.[62]

The Australian Subscription Library land opposite the barracks site was offered for sale in May 1840. In the subdivision, as historian Max Kelly pointed out, land on the South Head Road, an increasingly busy thoroughfare, fetched very high prices with the lots further back fetching about half the price.[63] On the South Head Road commercial buildings such as hotels and grocery stores were established while the cheaper lots came to house those involved in the construction of the barracks, the beginnings of a distinctive working-class area.

While convicts were employed in quarrying the stone and preparing the ground for the barracks, it was masons, paviors (pavers), carpenters and blacksmiths who carried out all the above ground works. The main contractor was the firm of Hugh Brodie and Archibald Craig, the leading building contractors of the time; they were also involved in the construction of Sydney's most fashionable building, the new Government House. In expectation that they would complete the entire contract for the barracks, Brodie and Craig built 'upwards of thirty houses at great outlay, for the accommodation of the workmen'.[64] These timber and stone cottages were opposite the barracks, on what had been the library's land, near the intersection of South Head Road and Glenmore Distillery road and created Gipps Street and Brodie's Row. It was here that the village of Paddington began.

By 1844 there were at least 30 stonemasons living in the area. In the following year 50 stonemasons and builders and five carpenters were employed at the barracks, with many living nearby. To provide for these workers 'stores, produce merchants, water carriers, wheelwrights, blacksmiths, turnkeys, dairymen, a baker and.... a mid-wife' came to the area and Paddington village grew rapidly.[65] The village not only provided for those involved with the barracks, it also began to provide for the increasing number of 'gentlemen's villas' being established further down the hillside above the Rushcutters Valley.

The establishment of the barracks also saw other land owners in the area profit by selling their land. Between 1840 and 1842 there were a series of land sales by those who had bought in Underwood's Paddington estate. While some such as Sir Charles Nicholson profited by buying and selling quickly, others such as JJ Curtis were forced to sell by the economic depression that began after 1840 – Curtis's land was advertised as 'allotments suitable for the building of respectable tenements for mechanics and tradesmen'.[66] Despite many blocks in the Paddington estate having the attraction of views over the harbour, its development was not as rapid as that of Paddington village. However, the growth of the village also slowed in the years following the initial rush of building activity in response to the barracks. By 1863, three years after the Municipality of Paddington was incorporated, there were only 535 houses in Paddington, its small residential area concentrated in the village near the barracks. Most of the houses in the new municipality were single-storey, two to three-roomed weatherboard cottages. Other cottages were of brick or stone and some were four roomed, 'two up, two down' simple terrace houses (see Figures 5.1 and 5.2). Only 25 per cent of these houses were owner-occupied and most occupants worked in the vicinity of the South Head Road or on the estates of the 'Rushcutter Valley gentry'.[67]

South and West Paddington

To the south of the South Head Road land use was dominated by Governor Macquarie's 1811 dedication of the Sydney Common. Macquarie had closed Hyde Park to the grazing of animals and to replace this town common he dedicated 1000 acres (405 ha) to the south of the South Head Road, in the area that now includes Victoria Barracks, Moore Park and Centennial Park. With sandy soils, low scrub and areas of swampland, in agricultural terms it was unsuitable for anything more than grazing. It also included the Lachlan Swamps, which

Macquarie set aside as the Lachlan Water Reserve in 1820 and were to provide Sydney's water supply from 1830 via Busby's Bore.

Figure 4.16: Victoria Barracks, Paddington, 1871. This view of Victoria Barracks shows some of the commercial premises on South Head Road opposite the barracks, part of the Paddington village and in the foreground sanddunes against the barracks' wall. Mitchell Library, State Library of New South Wales.

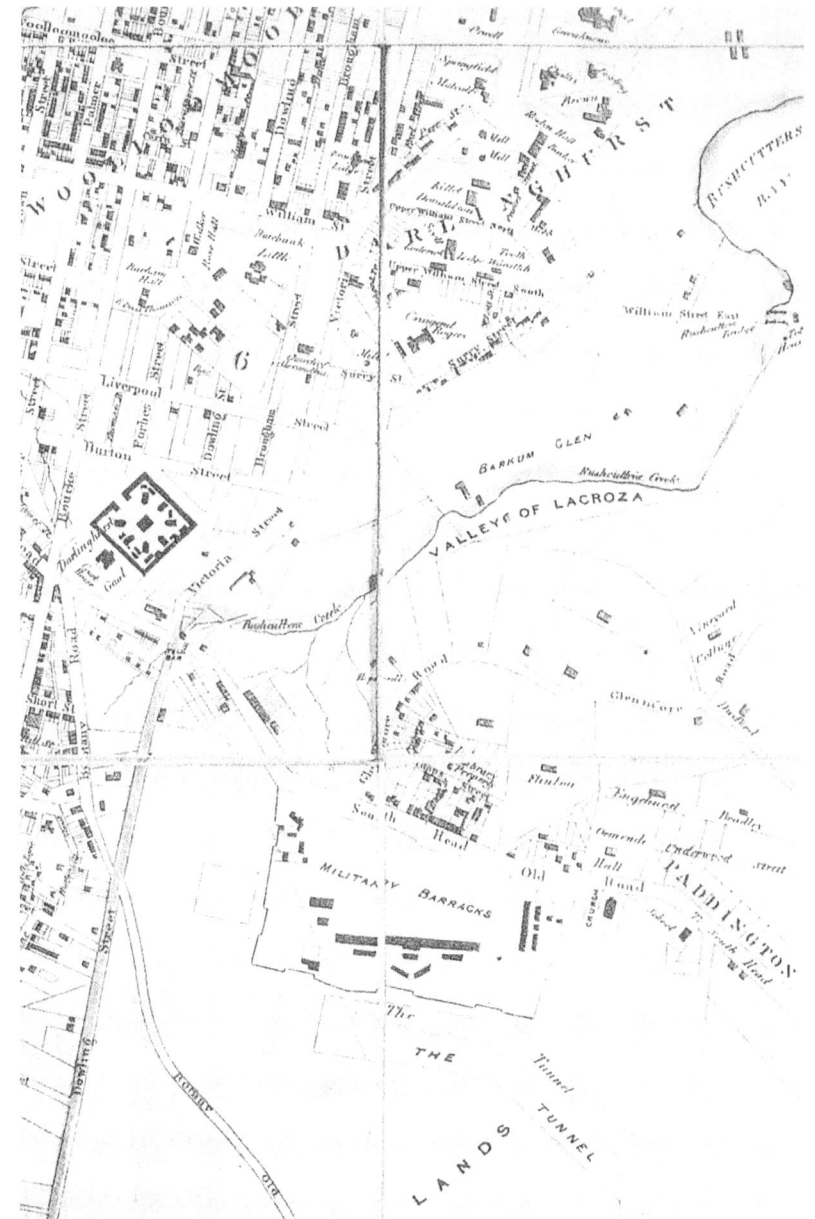

Figure 4.17: Woolcott and Clarke's Map of the City of Sydney (detail), 1854. WH Baron. This map shows the growing subdivisions creating the Paddington village north of Victoria Barracks and that of Underwood's Paddington Estate further to the east. The land grants and villas

of the Rushcutters Bay gentry are also visible along the line of Glenmore Distillery Road. National Library of Australia.

As Paddington developed to the north of the South Head Road, expansion to the south was limited by the Common. It extended to the south and east roughly as far as the furthest boundaries of present-day Centennial Park and on the west to commissary-general John Palmer's land grant, George Farm, on present-day South Dowling Street.[68] Prior to the establishment of Victoria Barracks, the only development in this area had been the commencement of Busby's water supply bore from the Lachlan Swamps to Hyde Park in 1827, and then the construction of Charles Gordon's windmill a few years later. Gordon had been granted 2 acres (0.8 ha) of land south of the South Head Road and here he built a large post mill, on the site of the present 7 and 8 Stewart Place, with his house and a miller's cottage.[69]

It was not until 1840 that a second grant was made in the area south of the South Head Road and this was to

LW (George) Newcombe, who received 2 acres (0.8 ha) near Gordon's grant. Then with the establishment of the Victoria Barracks a series of land grants began to be made on areas of the Sydney Common. In 1850 a grant was made to the Wesleyan Church on what was by then Old South Head Road and this was followed in the 1850s by grants to the Roman Catholic Church, St Mathias School, and land allocated for the State School and the Reservoir. These grants were all related to public purposes, reflecting Macquarie's original intention for public use of the Sydney Common.

Following these early grants of the commons land, from the mid-1850s other sections of the Common began to be sold by the government for private use. While extensive public land was maintained with Centennial Park and Moore Park, there were a series of subdivisions of the northern areas of the Common. The first of these was in 1856, with the West Paddington area of Greens Road and Napier, Albion and Iris streets. Areas were divided into blocks of roughly 15–50 lots and were gradually released from the late 1850s through to the 1870s.

However, the greatest development of Paddington was to take place from the 1870s to the 1890s. The surviving early land grants such as that of Thomas West, the estates of the Rushcutter Valley gentry and the faltering start to housing in the Paddington village and Paddington estate were all to undergo an extraordinary scale of change, as increasing land values and the demand for housing near the city saw the rapid increase in the rate of subdivision. Row upon row and street upon street of working and middle-class housing were created and a newspaper article of 1884 succinctly described the transformation of Paddington:

> A decade has scarcely elapsed since the greater portion was covered with ti-tree, intersected by creeks and rocky eminences and which have now given place to well-constructed streets, business premises and comfortable homes...[71]

Remarkably, the fine streetscapes of terrace housing that were created at this time have survived largely intact. Perhaps more remarkably, despite this period of intense subdivision and transformation, much of the earlier character and evidence of the initial development of the place has survived. This is evident in the fabric of the built and natural environment of Paddington; in street names and street layouts such as Glenmore Road; phases of villa development – from the earliest, Juniper Hall, to the last, Olive Bank Villa – and in the small terrace houses of the Paddington village. It is the quality and extent of this environment that gives Paddington its unique character.

Figure 4.18: Panorama of Paddington, from Views in Victoria, New South Wales and Tasmania, 1853, John W Hardwick. Top: Looking west with Gordon's Mill on the left and Victoria Barracks in the distance on the right. Bottom: Looking west along South Head Road from the corner of Point Piper Road (now Jersey Road) with Juniper Hall in the middle background, above the road. Mitchell Library, State Library of New South Wales.

Figure 4.19: Old mill, Gordon Street Paddington,1862, George Roberts. Gordon, who operated a horse-driven mill in Pitt Street Sydney, had requested a land grant and received this grant in c 1830.70 The mill remained a dominant element of the Paddington landscape until the 1870s and is depicted in various views of the area. Mitchell Library, State Library of New South Wales.

Chapter 5
The Victorian suburb

Robert Griffin and Robert Brown

The most distinctive feature of Paddington is its architecture: an extraordinary concentration of Victorian-era housing, built on an undulating topography. Narrow and turning streets; broad, straight and flat streets; or steeply sloping ones framing harbour views, all are dominated by the rhythmic repetition of terrace houses. There is also an astonishing variety within what is essentially a repetitious form. Verandahs and balconies, projecting party walls, stucco ornament and decorative cast iron work display a remarkable range of detailing and decoration and these houses, arranged in level rows or stepping up and down the steeply sloping streets, create an exceptional built environment.

The majority of these terrace houses were constructed in the Victorian period – Queen Victoria's reign, from 1837 to 1901 – and it is the quality and extent of this Victorian-era terrace housing, in its variety and intactness, that makes Paddington unique. To paraphrase the historian Max Kelly, Paddington is a virtual compendium of the forms of the Sydney terrace house during the 19th century and a superlative example of the diversity of these forms.[1]

This chapter explores the creation of Victorian Paddington: the influence of the topography of the place; the pattern of subdivision of the early rural estates; and the development of its characteristic element, the terrace house. It also explores the way in which the suburb and its housing have evolved, and continue to evolve, to create the unique urban environment that exists today.[2]

Early development: 1800–30s

As previous chapters have described, the early European development of the area that was to become Paddington began with the formation of a series of rough tracks, the principal one of which ran along the ridgeline towards the signal station at South Head (now Old South Head Road). Between 1810 and 1823, three land grants were made on the north-facing slopes and on the valley floor bordering the harbour (see Figure 2.11 and Chapter 4).

The largest of these grants, to James Underwood, Francis E Forbes and Robert Cooper, resulted in two major developments in the mid-1820s: the colony's first legal distillery; and Robert Cooper's Juniper Hall, the first substantial house in the area. While Cooper's house became a local landmark, situated high on the ridgeline on the South Head Road, it was the access road to the distillery (now Glenmore Road) that was to prove the more influential, opening up the north-facing slopes to development.

It was here, in 1831–32, that the first subdivision for housing in Paddington occurred. This was in the form of land grants made to the colony's officials and the result was the establishment of semi-rural estates: substantial villas in a setting of gardens, orchards and fenced paddocks on the north-facing slopes, with picturesque views over Sydney Harbour and the indigenous woodland. These were the villas of the 'Rushcutter Valley gentry' (see Chapter 4).

Early subdivisions and first terraces: 1840–50

In contrast to these large estates were the subdivisions that followed, the first of which focused on the land close to what was now becoming an important road, Old South Head Road. In 1839 James Underwood, having bought out his distillery partners, subdivided 50 acres (20 ha) of the original 100-acre (40 ha) grant. The subdivision extended along Old South Head Road from his former partner Robert Cooper's house, Juniper Hall, to Point Piper Road (now Jersey Road) and down to present-day Paddington Street, which was created as part of the subdivision. (See Figure 4.5.)

Advertised as part of 'that well-known estate called Paddington', 80 allotments were offered for 'the erection of genteel Houses or Cottages ... such a choice spot for health and extensive scenery cannot be outvied, as it has a perfect view of the best parts of Sydney ... Port Jackson Harbour ... [and] Botany Bay'. While 'Merchants or gentlemen with families who hold official appointments or private situations' were encouraged to buy, it was also suggested that 'Capitalists will also do well to bear in mind that Land in all new Colonies is the surest and best speculation for outlay of capital, particularly Suburban spots as these are now termed.'[3]

'Capitalists' such as Sir Charles Nicholson, co-founder of the University of Sydney and a politician and scholar, responded by buying clusters of allotments and then selling quickly for profit, however other speculators were caught by the economic depression of the early 1840s. In the rush to sell, by 1842 the allotments were no longer offered for 'genteel houses or Cottages' but instead for 'respectable tenements for mechanics and tradesmen'.[4]

Land facing the thoroughfare of Old South Head Road had fetched the best prices, with commercial buildings such as inns and stores being constructed, and although the depression slowed the sale of the subdivision, weatherboard houses and several sandstone terrace house rows were built during the 1840s and 1850s. The following advertisement for seven large allotments in Underwood Street and Elizabeth Street gives insight into the nature of development in Paddington in the mid-1840s and following decades:

> This is a bit of that right sort of Building Ground which every tradesman or mechanic knows well enough is becoming scarcer and scarcer every day. For every house he builds in this improving neighbourhood (having no Building Act to bother him), he can bring back his outlay in about three years, knowing that for £30 he can run up a house that will always let, the like of which cost his neighbour £130 a while ago. And where can any poor man get a better bit of ground than one of these lots? That he can put two or three small cottages on, if he like – to let off, reserving one for himself and family. Always plenty of work in this neighbourhood.[5]

The type of terrace houses typically constructed consisted of a single storey with two rooms and sometimes a lean-to kitchen at the rear – some also had two attic bedrooms. These houses had no front yard or verandah and were built to the street alignment.

While the sale of Underwood's 'Paddington Estate' subdivision was slow and extended, more rapid development occurred in the next subdivision, further to the west. This second subdivision resulted in the formation of Paddington village and was the direct result of the colonial government's decision in 1840 to establish a new military barracks. The site of Victoria Barracks, opposite the junction of Old South Head Road and Glenmore Road, was a strategic one: high on the ridgeline between Sydney Harbour and Botany Bay, reflecting the concern for a possible invasion from either point.[6] Construction began in 1841 using locally quarried sandstone and with its defensive walls, ensemble of sandstone buildings and plantings of Moreton Bay Fig trees, this was the first institutional complex on the southern side of Old South Head Road. Its construction also prompted the residential and commercial development of the opposite, northern side of the road, beginning with the subdivision of the Australian Subscription Library land in 1840 (see Figure 4.7 for the extent of this land).

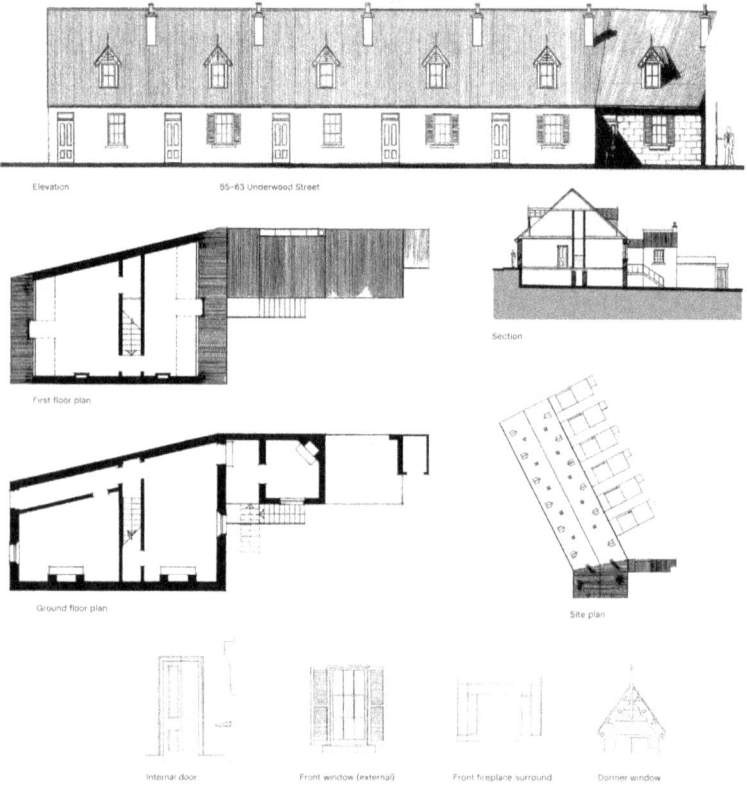

Figure 5.1: Terrace houses, 55–65 Underwood Street Paddington, c 1842. Characteristic of the early terrace housing built in Paddington, this row is relatively simple in form and detailing and built of sandstone with a timber-shingle roof (now corrugated iron). Built to the footpath alignment, each house had a sitting-room/parlour and a dining room, with two attic bedrooms. At the rear was a separate

kitchen and a WC in the yard. © Robert Brown, 1979.

The allotments on Old South Head Road – and closest to the barracks – fetched the highest prices, as in Underwood's subdivision further to the east. These became the focus for commercial development such as shops and inns, while the allotments further back came to house those involved in construction of the barracks – stonemasons and carpenters – as well as others such as military officers and their families.

As the barracks continued building through the early 1840s economic depression, it gave life to the nascent village – builders, carpenters, quarrymen, fencers and blacksmiths working on the barracks needed to be accommodated while retail shops and public houses served these workers, the military, other local inhabitants and the passing trade along Old South Head Road. The nearby estates of the 'Rushcutter Valley gentry' also provided impetus to the village, however the barracks sustained it. Further subdivisions followed, these being part of some of the grants made to the Rushcutter Valley gentry. One example is the late Reverend Hill's Hopewell Estate, located on the western side of Glenmore Road and subdivided in 1842.[7] The attractions of the area were summed up in an advertisement for two large lots in Gipps Street, part of the library grant, described as suitable for the erection of 'four capital houses':

> ...the situation is delightfully elevated for aspect and prospect, and familiar to every one as one of the principle situations for barrack business, and the yet more inseparable convenience of easy access to Sydney for stores and supplies for a general provision and retail dealer.[8]

At first the village consisted of vernacular single-storey cottages of brick and stone, interspersed with timber structures. Some of these were built by the contractors for the barracks, Hugh Brodie and Alexander Craig, for their workmen and created Gipps Street and Brodie's Row. Further development followed, with the surrounding streets of Shadforth, Prospect and Mary Place, and this included some simple terrace house development – houses of two rooms with no front verandah or yard and a lean-to kitchen at the rear.

As the village expanded to the east and west along the alignment of Old South Head Road, the early simple single-storey structures began to give way to larger two-storey buildings of brick or weatherboard – 'two rooms up and two rooms down' with a front verandah and sometimes small front yard and separate kitchen at the rear.

By the early 1850s the largest terrace house development was a row of 10 brick houses in West Street near Old South Head Road (demolished) and nearby were houses in Comber Street and Little Comber Street believed to have been built for soldiers and officers of the barracks.[9]

Mid-Victorian period: 1850–60s

Until 1856, development was limited to the northern side of Old South Head

Road. On the southern side was the Sydney Common, dedicated by Governor Lachlan Macquarie in 1811, which had continued to be used for public purposes – as a common, for the barracks and for churches and schools (see Chapter 4). Two exceptions to this were a grant of 2 acres (0.8 ha) made in 1834 to Charles Gordon for the establishment of a mill and another 2-acre grant made to George William Newcombe in 1840 (see Figure 2.12).

While Newcombe began subdividing his grant in 1849,[10] between 1856 and 1870 a series of subdivisions of sections of the Common were made by the government, creating the areas of South and West Paddington. The first subdivision was that of West Paddington – an area west of the barracks and creating Greens Road and Napier, Albion and Iris streets – the subdivision apparently prompted by the need of accommodation for soldiers' families.[11] This was followed in 1859 by the beginning of subdivisions to the east of the barracks, known as South Paddington, bounded by Old South Head Road and Moore Park Road and abutting the early grants to Gordon and Newcombe. The first subdivision resulted in Stewart Street and, except for 1861-62, annual sales of former common land for residential development took place, with some commercial development along the main road frontage. Institutions such as the Wesleyan Church, the Roman Catholic Church, St Mathias Garrison Church (1859), a Church of England School and National School (1856) were also granted land here, along the Old South Head Road. (See Figure 2.14.)

Elevation

541-547 Glenmore Road

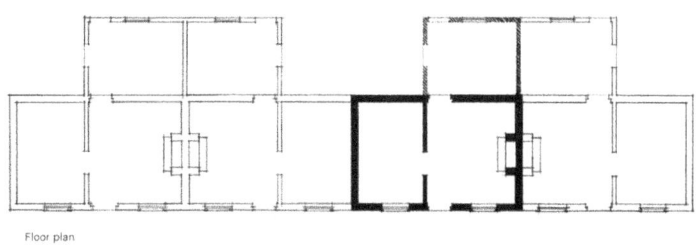

Floor plan

Figure 5.2: Terrace houses, 541-547 Glenmore Road Paddington, c 1856. Although located at the end of Glenmore Road this single-storey terrace is indicative of the first phase of development of the Paddington village, from 1840 to 1860 – small, rudimentary dwellings constructed for workmen. Built of brick with a timber-shingled roof, each house consisted of a parlour/dining room with fireplace and an adjoining bedroom, with a lean-to kitchen at the rear. © Robert Brown, 1979.

Figure 5.3: Terrace houses, 15–19 Gipps Street Paddington, c 1860. The form of this terrace house row – two-storey with ground floor verandah – is typical of the 1850s and 1860s. The ground floor sitting-room and dining room both have fireplaces, as does the principal bedroom upstairs. The bedroom at the rear was usually separated from the stair by a timber wall. A separate kitchen stood at the rear. The larger house on the left was presumably built

for use by the owner/builder. © Robert Brown, 1979.

On the opposite of Old South Head Road, the growth of Underwood's 'Paddington Estate' subdivision had been slow compared to that of Paddington village, probably the result of its greater distance from the town and from the barracks. Its immediate attraction was north-facing views over the rural setting of the slopes to the harbour and by 1860 several large houses had been built here in the better locations such as along Point Piper Road (Jersey Road). These were not as substantial as the villas of the Rushcutter Valley gentry and here, particularly around William and Elizabeth streets, a mix of residential development took place with villas, houses and cottages. There was also some early terrace house development such as Leicester Place in Wentworth Street. Leicester Place appears to mimic the villa development as it was expressed as one large building, with a verandah frontage to the west and a generous carriage circle in front, despite being 9a terrace house row.

When the Paddington Municipality was proclaimed on 17 April 1860, three distinct topographical divisions had emerged. A relatively dense built environment had developed along the ridgeline on each side of Old South Head Road: on the one side was South and West Paddington, dominated by public and institutional buildings; and on the other was Upper Paddington, with its focus of residential and commercial buildings. In contrast to these two areas was Lower Paddington, with more substantial, separate residences erected by the Rushcutter Valley gentry and set in an open rural environment on the north-facing slopes. (See Figure 2.13.)

In the early 1860s New South Wales enjoyed an economic boom and between 1861 and 1871 the population of Paddington rose by 60 per cent to 4250; a higher percentage increase than that for the whole of Sydney.[12] The dense urban environment that had begun to emerge on the ridgeline and upper slopes of Paddington was steadily consolidated and then, during the 1870s and 1880s, this expanded and intensified as the scale of subdivision increased. This was the direct result of an increasing population needing to be close to their place of work, increasing land prices, and, as historian Max Kelly pointed out, increasing costs for the owners of larger estates due to rising rateable values.[13] Approximately 85 per cent of the municipality was owned by a small group of individuals and between 1861 and 1871 Paddington Council raised rateable values of vacant land fourfold. Those estate owners who were owner-occupiers, such as John Gurner of Duxford House and Thomas Broughton of Bradley Hall, resisted the sale of their estates; however most (being absentee owners keen to capitalise on increasing land values) began to subdivide.[14] The development of these land holdings was to create the character of the built environment that Paddington possesses today.

Late-Victorian period: 1870–1900

The 1870s and 1880s was the most active period of subdivision and building in the Paddington Municipality. The first phase, from 1875 to 1880, was a time of intense subdivision and land speculation, with land being bought and sold several times – the prices of land doubled in both 1879 and 1880 – with the resulting allotments generally having a 12–20 feet (3.6–6 metre) frontage with a depth of 80–120 feet (24–36 metres). The usual process was that parts of a large estate would be divided into allotments having a 60-foot (18-metre) frontage to an existing or proposed street; these would again be subdivided into smaller street frontages, usually 30 feet (9 metres); and finally re-subdivided for the construction of two 15-foot (4.5-metre) wide houses. In some instances, an original 60-foot frontage would eventually be occupied by five, six or even seven houses.[15] While some building took place during the 1870s, the second phase from 1880 was to result in the greatest physical change to the Paddington landscape.

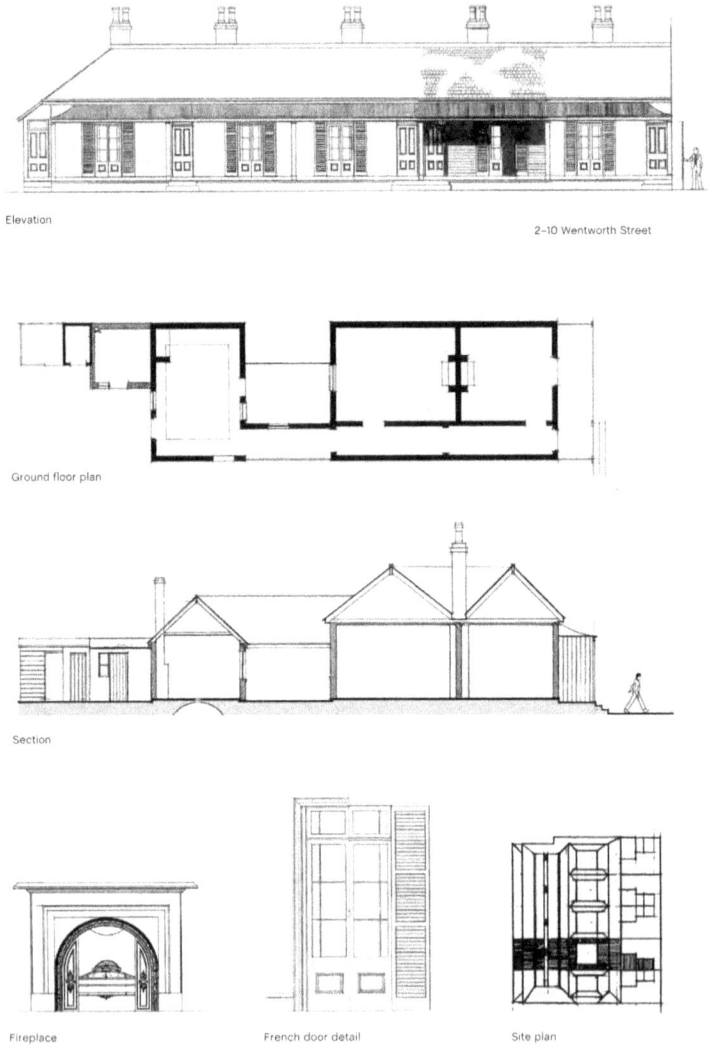

Figure 5.4: Leicester Place, 2–10 Wentworth Street, c 1850s. Although most of the houses in this terrace row originally consisted of only two rooms and a separate kitchen, the overall effect is of a far more substantial dwelling. This is achieved by the continuous line of the slate

roof and verandah, and the French doors with shutters. The courtyard that separated the two main rooms from the kitchen has now been enclosed although the imported English cast iron fire surrounds of the main rooms survive.
© Robert Brown, 1979.

SUBDIVISION OF EARLIER ESTATES

The nature of the subdivision of the earlier estates was haphazard. The length of time taken for the estate's allotments to sell and for buildings to be constructed was extremely variable. According to Kelly, it may have been up to six or seven years before buildings were complete and occupied.[16] It was also rare for a large estate to be subdivided in one phase and the form of the subdivisions were dependent on the nature of the estate, its topography, boundaries and existing access roads. In addition, each subdivision of an estate sought to maximise the return within its usually random boundaries and also sought to create a road system that could be extended for future subdivisions. This meant that later subdivisions had to fit in with the existing pattern; also providing for building requirements and stormwater run-off. The result was an array of street alignments and while lot frontages might be of a regular pattern for a particular subdivision, their depth would vary depending on estate boundaries or neighbouring subdivisions.

One of the early subdivisions of the larger estates was the MacDonald Estate, on part of the land originally granted to Colonel Dumaresq in 1835 on the north-western slopes of Paddington, north of Glenmore Road. This 1874 subdivision consisted of 71 lots, most with a 33-foot (10-metre) frontage, and resulted in the creation of MacDonald Street, Liverpool Street and possibly Brown Street. The form of the subdivision, with long narrow lots having a rear lane service access, established a pattern for later subdivisions. This density of development would have stood in stark contrast to the nearby farm and bushland of Thomas West's Barcom Glen.[17]

Further to the east, two more subdivisions of Underwood's Paddington Estate had been made by 1875. These consisted of a small subdivision of 12 lots in Albert and Underwood streets in 1872 and a much larger subdivision of 606 lots in 1875, creating Paddington, Windsor, Hargrave and Sutherland streets. These four new streets ran parallel to each other, across and down the north-facing slopes between Point Piper Road (now Jersey Road) and Cascade Street. These allotments had 20-foot (6-metre) frontages and rear lane access like the MacDonald Estate, and enjoyed views to the north-east over the valley that was to become Trumper Park.[18]

One of the estates that demonstrates the rapid increase in land prices in Paddington in this period was the Good Hope Estate, offered for sale in 1875 by the trustees of the MacDonald Estate.

Originally a grant to surveyor Robert Hoddle in 1833, on the northern side of Glenmore Road on the lower slopes, the land was purchased by MacDonald, a large estate owner in the area, in

1861 for £200. The subdivision of 1875 created 71 lots with 33-foot (10-metre) frontages along Glenmore Road and the new Good Hope Street. The land was described as having 'one uninterrupted view of unsurpassed grandeur' with views of the harbour and its headlands. It was surrounded by villas and gardens of the Rushcutter Valley gentry and offered sites 'for a Mansion or for a Terrace of first class residences ... within but a comfortable walk to the commercial area of the city' and in 'the most important and rapidly advancing suburb of our city'.[19] While the sale notice may have exaggerated a little, over 70 per cent of the estate was sold on the day of auction and two years later only 9 per cent of the lots remained unsold. The average price at the 1875 auction was £2.10.0 and after the doubling of land prices in 1879 and 1880, land here was selling for at least £9 per foot frontage at the end of 1880. By 1891 there were 67 houses in Good Hope Street, built on the original 45 lots, and each had an estimated rental value of £45 per year.[20]

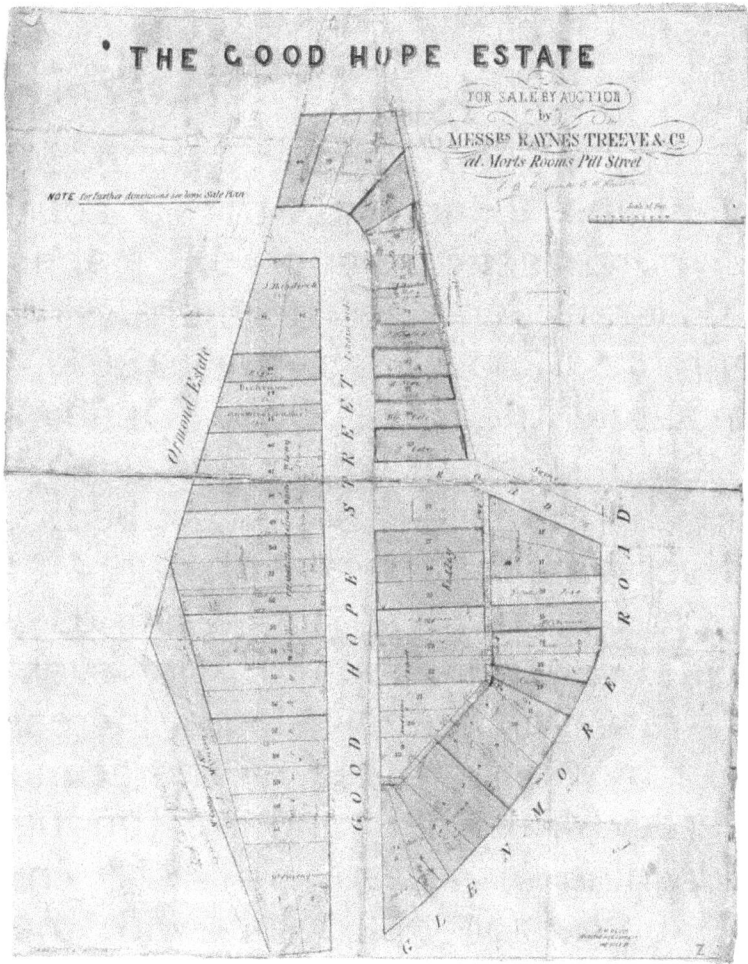

Figure 5.5: Good Hope Estate, Raynes Treeve & Co, 1872. This subdivision plan demonstrates the way in which the maximum number of lots were obtained and streets and lanes laid out within existing irregular boundaries. Mitchell Library, State Library of New South Wales, Z/M2 811.18113/1872/1.

In 1876 there was a further subdivision of 6 acres (2.4 ha) of

Underwood's Paddington Estate and this was followed by the subdivision of two more large estates, that of WG McCarthy's Deep Dene and John Begg's Olive Bank Villa. McCarthy, a solicitor, had purchased part of JE Manning's 1831 grant on the northern side of Glenmore Road and by 1861 had completed the villa Deep Dene. The substantial house, which contained hall, dining and drawing rooms, six bedrooms and servants' quarters, stood in 4 acres (1.6 ha) of gardens and grounds with views over the harbour. However, as the rate of subdivisions increased, McCarthy was tempted by the economic rewards to be had and he too began subdividing his estate. In 1877, in the first subdivision of 33 lots with mostly 33-foot (10-metre) frontages, McCarthy retained the house and a surrounding 1 acre (0.4 ha) of land. Glenmore Road, Glen Street, Stephen Street and Cooper Street all formed part of the subdivision, and a row of substantial three-storey terrace houses that took advantage of the sloping site were built along Glenmore Road.[21] In 1882 the final portion of the estate was subdivided and Deep Dene was subsequently demolished.

The subdivision of these early estates inevitably saw their villa mansions demolished, however two exceptions to this were Juniper Hall and Olive Bank Villa. In 1868 John Elly Begg, a Paddington alderman, purchased Frederick Hely's Engehurst (built 1833–36) and built his Olive Bank Villa in the estate grounds. Begg continued to purchase the surrounding land and in 1877 his son purchased the adjoining Juniper Hall (then known as Ormonde House), built by the emancipist Robert Cooper in 1824. At the time of its construction Juniper Hall was one of the largest private houses in Sydney and now it stood on increasingly valuable land on Old South Head Road. In 1878 Begg subdivided the three estates, resulting in 89 lots of varying frontages. In the following years these lots were transformed by a range terrace house developments, with rows of houses stepping down the slopes of the former estates. The creation of Begg Street (now Ormond Street) saw the partial demolition of Engehurst, however

Juniper Hall/Ormonde House was integrated into the development through the positioning of streets and lanes, while Olive Bank Villa survived with a reduced garden curtilage.

The remaining section of Engehurst was sold and underwent additions and alterations to provide a residence. In 1922 the building was converted to flats and today only a portion of the original house remains after a series of demolitions and adaptations. (See Figure 4.12.)

Juniper Hall/Ormonde House was also sold as part of the subdivision and in 1885 was purchased by the NSW Government for the Children's Relief Board. An extension was made to the eastern side of the house and despite alterations during the 20th century and a series of owners, the house survived until its historic significance was recognised. Similarly, Olive Bank Villa survived by becoming an institution – it remained a residence until 1924 when it was purchased by the Eastern Suburbs Day Nursery, and the house continues to be used for this purpose. (See Figure 4.15.)

By 1880 Paddington had become a patchwork of intensely developed areas with rows of terrace houses interspersed with some larger blocks with free-standing houses and, in contrast to these, a few remaining villa estates with their gardens and grounds. The remaining villas included Roger Therry's Flinton, John Gurner's Duxford House, William Cape's Elfred House, Thomas Broughton's Bradley Hall and Henry Burton Bradley's The Terraces. (See Figure 5.10.)

While Gurner and Bradley refused to subdivide their estates, their properties were eventually sold – Gurner's subdivided after his death while Bradley sold his in only two lots. By 1900 only two of the earlier estates survived: Flinton and The Terraces.

Gurner's Duxford Estate was subdivided in 1885 and the land, situated between Glenmore Road and Cascade Street, formed one of the larger subdivisions, resulting in 140 lots, mainly with 20-foot (6-metre) frontages. The subdivision created Gurner Street, which now provided an important east-west link through the increasingly crowded Victorian suburb, but also Duxford, Suffolk and Norfolk streets which formed a complex interconnection of roadways. As in many of the subdivisions, this was the result of maximising the number of lots available, however Suffolk and Norfolk streets owe their odd alignments to the retention of Duxford House. The house, which stood between the two streets, remained during the first stages of the subdivision, but was eventually demolished in the early 20th century.

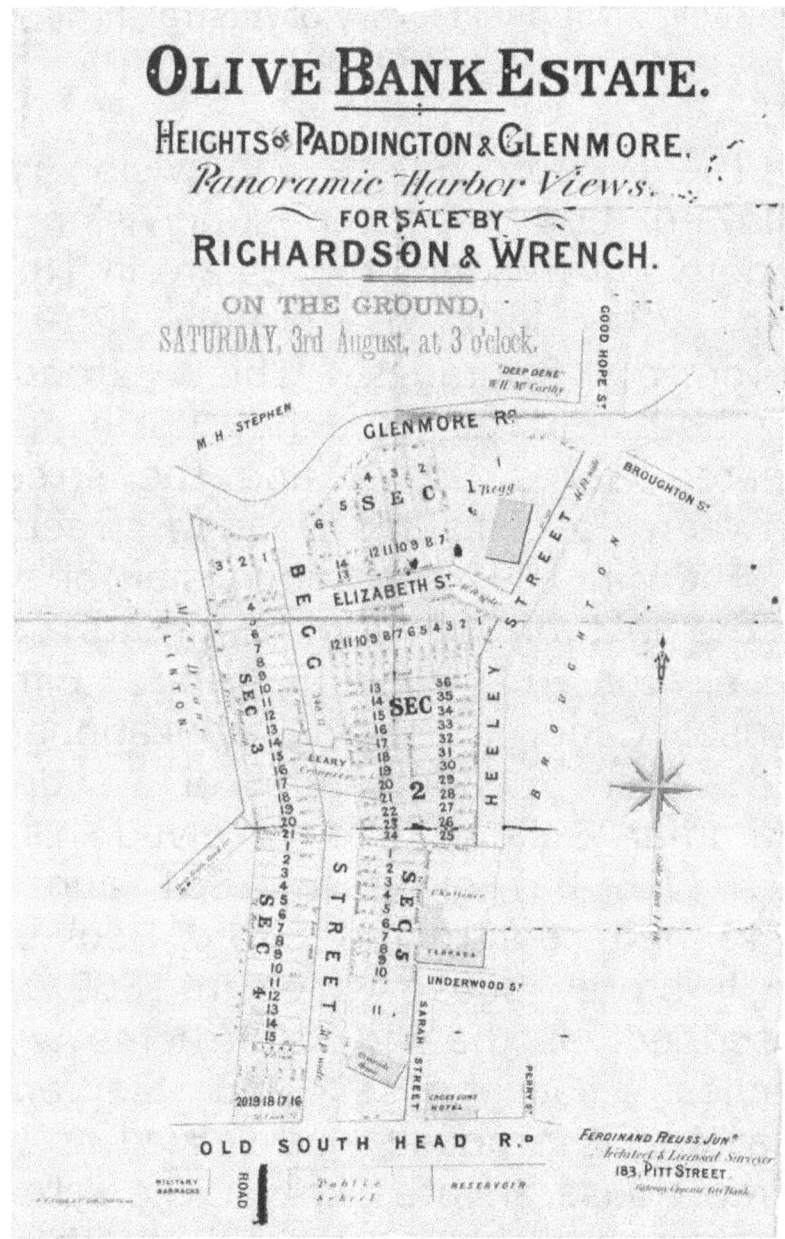

Figure 5.6: Olive Bank Estate, Richardson and Wrench, 1878. This subdivision plan shows the location of Juniper Hall, Engehurst (partially demolished for Begg Street) and J Begg's Olive

Bank Villa. National Library of Australia (nla.obj 230400068).

The Duxford Estate subdivision was followed by a further subdivision of Underwood's Paddington Estate in 1886, with 234 lots of mainly 20-foot (6-metre) frontages. This extended Elizabeth Street to the north and created Harris Street and the streets between Cascade and Soudan streets.

Then in 1891 the subdivision of one of the last of the original grants took place, that of William Cape's Elfred House. Cape, a leading educationalist and first headmaster of Sydney Grammar School, had received his 4 acre (1.6 ha) grant in 1831 and by 1842 had constructed Elfred House, a single-storey house which in 1869 was described as having 10 rooms with stables, coachhouse and servants' quarters. The house also served as the Elfred House Private School. The school, which was highly successful, continued until his retirement in 1856. When Cape travelled to England in 1860 the house was leased and after Cape's death in 1863 his family continued to lease the property, which operated as a ladies' collegiate school during the 1870s and 1880s. The house and school stood in the original grounds of the estate, on the southern side of Glenmore Road, adjoining the Australian Subscription Library's subdivision that had created Paddington village, and by the 1880s the estate stood in stark contrast to the developed village. Finally, in 1891 the 4-acre estate was subdivided in 82 lots, mainly with 20-foot (6-metre) frontages.

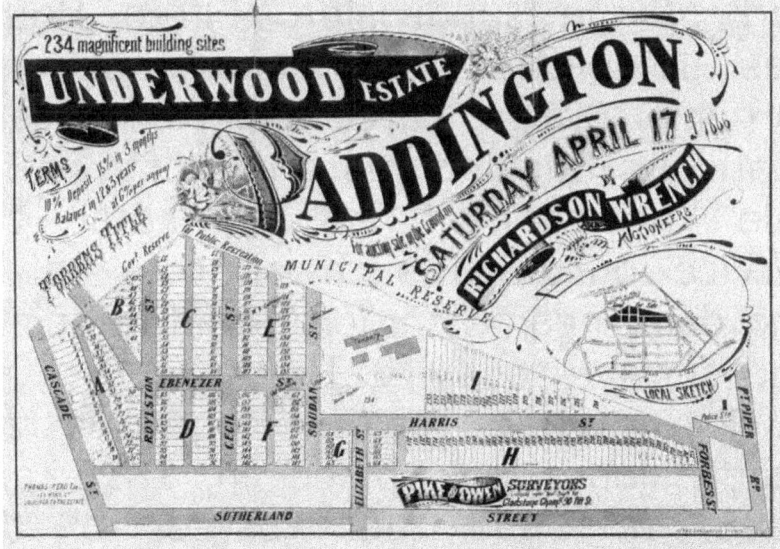

Figure 5.7: Underwood Estate, Paddington, 1886. Richardson and Wrench. This subdivision surrounded the Glenmore Distillery buildings, then being used as a tannery. The buildings were later sold to the Colonial Rubber Company for their factory and eventually demolished –

unit blocks now occupy the site. National Library of Australia (nla.gov.au/and. bib-an24314953).

Cape had purchased land opposite Shadforth Street in the Library's subdivision, ensuring access to his estate from Old South Head Road, so that in the estate subdivision, Shadforth Street was extended into the newly created Liverpool Street. Brown Street and Walker Lane were also created, and Mary Place may have been extended as part of the subdivision. Elfred House was demolished – it stood near the corner of Brown, Elfred and Walker Lane – and its building materials offered for sale, however it appears that the service buildings such as the stables and dairy near Glenmore Road remained and survive today.[22]

The final two large estate subdivisions took place in 1893 and 1898. In 1893 the trustees of the Lawson Estate offered 28 lots of 20 to 26-foot (6–8 metre) frontages 'overlooking Rushcutters Bay Reserve', with frontages to Brown and Lawson streets. The subdivision, which also created Stephen Street, was advertised as deserving of the 'special attention of speculators and builders' as 'The immediate location is densely populated and the demand for houses is practically unlimited.'[23] Despite the effects of the early 1890s economic depression, speculators and builders responded, for only two lots remained unsold a month after the sale day.[24]

The last large estate to be subdivided was that of Thomas Broughton, in 1898. Broughton, grazier and politician, had built Bradley Hall in 1845 and remained living there until the estate was subdivided, three years before his death at the age of 91. As Kelly pointed out, when Broughton first occupied Bradley Hall there were no more than 50 people living nearby but by 1890 there were thousands, his estate surrounded by terrace house development.[25] The subdivision, between Cascade and Heeley streets, contained 189 lots, mainly 20-foot (6-metre) frontages, and its formation was a complex process; it needed to integrate with the surrounding streets of the earlier subdivisions. Stafford Street was created, linked to Heeley

Street, and Duxford Street was extended from the new Broughton Street. To the east, Union and Hopetoun streets joined with the earlier layout of the Paddington Estate. Bradley Hall, which stood in the area east of Duxford Street and north of Stafford Street, was demolished, its building materials and that of the stables, offered as part of the subdivision sale.[26]

Two other early villas that did survive the 19th century subdivisions, along with Juniper Hall and Olive Bank Villa, were Flinton and The Terraces however both estates were to disappear in 20th century redevelopments. Flinton was built for Roger Therry, commissioner of the Court of Requests (small debts), who had received a 6-acre (2.4 ha) grant on the southern side of Glenmore Road, next to Thomas Cape's grant, in 1832. Flinton, apparently designed by the architect John Verge, was described in 1844 as having nine rooms, with a coachhouse, stables and outbuildings. It seems that Therry only occupied the house occasionally and in 1839 it was leased to WS Deloitte.[27] Following Therry's return to England in 1859 it was offered for sale and in following years a series of owners offered the house for lease. In 1863, when it was leased by Paddington's first auctioneer, William Dean, it was described as three storeys with an encircling verandah and 14 rooms.[28]

Dean purchased the house and grounds in 1880 and he and his family remained at Flinton until 1900 when the estate was purchased by an investment and building company that proposed subdividing the site.[29] The estate was then purchased by the Benevolent Society in 1901 as a 'lying-in' hospital, which later became the Royal Hospital for Women. A new wing was added in 1905 and then in 1926 the house was demolished in a redevelopment of the hospital.

Henry Burton Bradley's The Terraces is said to have been constructed in 1849 for the attorney-general John Kinchela however this is unlikely as while Kinchela did receive a grant of 9 acres (3.6 ha) in 1833, he was constantly in debt and died in 1845.[30] It is more likely the house was built for

Bradley, a solicitor and notary, who lived there from 1849 to at least 1875 and, as an ardent horticulturalist, he established an extensive garden of sandstone terraces and 'Magnificent Trees and Rare Shrubs'.

Figure 5.8: Flinton, built 1833; demolished 1926 for the Royal Hospital for Women. A view of the rear of Flinton, taken c 1920 after its purchase by the Benevolent Society. The encircling verandah has been enclosed by this time; part of the grounds with established trees can be seen. Royal Hospital for Women Foundation.

When offered for sale in 1882 the estate was divided into two lots: one with the two-storey stone and brick house, described as containing six principal ground floor rooms and seven bedrooms, on 2 acres (0.8 ha) of land; and another lot 'suitable for the construction of a villa'.[31] The Terraces was purchased in 1901 by Sir Alexander MacCormick, a noted surgeon and academic, and others with the intention of establishing a private hospital. When MacCormick retired in 1926 he donated the hospital to the Presbyterian Church in memory of his son who was killed in World War 1 and the hospital was re-named the Scottish Hospital. As part of its conversion to hospital use, additions were made to the house in 1903, in the Arts and Crafts style, and then further additions were made in 1936, enclosing the original house and rendering it in roughcast, leaving little of the original house evident. The hospital has been recently redeveloped as an aged care facility and during these works a landslip resulted in sections of the building being demolished (to be reconstructed).

THE PROCESS OF BUILDING

The process of building on the subdivided estates was described by

Kelly as transitional owner-occupation. That is, a high proportion of the new landowners were builders of modest means. The builder would complete one terrace house on his land and then live in it while re-financing before completing others in the row. These houses, often of very basic two-storey form, were built in rows of no more than five or six houses and were usually built over a period of several years.[32]

By 1885 approximately 60 per cent of rental houses in Paddington were owned by this type of landlord, whose holding did not exceed four houses. This type of development, by a speculative builder being an owner-occupier, differed from other inner suburbs of Sydney where large rows of terraces were often constructed and financed through building societies. These societies also usually engaged an architect to design the buildings. In Paddington the building societies may have assisted with the financing of some terrace house rows, however the design and construction was generally by the builder/owner-occupier. It was not until the 1890s that larger developers emerged, building terraces of up to eight or nine houses.

Stylistically, the pattern of terrace house development in this period evolved from the plain and relatively simple early terrace house rows described above to larger and more elaborate terraces, exemplified by those of the Victorian Filigree Style, characteristic of the 1870s and 1880s. This style saw the extensive use and embellishment of the verandah and balcony in combination with elaborate classical or Italianate stucco decoration. Terrace houses were usually of two storeys, the front elevation heavily embellished with high, decorative parapets having classical urns, balustrading and often a house name set within a prominent panel. Below this were a series of elaborately moulded cornices while the balconies and verandahs were decorated with intricately patterned cast iron screens and balustrading. This cast iron work, often divided into bays by slender columns, stood proud of the main building mass, shading it and giving it a filigree character.

Each house in the row was separated from its neighbour by a prominent party wall, also with elaborate stucco decoration. The front elevation of each house typically consisted of an asymmetrical arrangement of door and window openings on the ground floor and a symmetrical arrangement on the upper floor, the masonry surfaces embellished with stucco decoration such as window hood mouldings. Opportunities for individual expression within the fabric of these houses were found in the parapet detailing, wall finish, texture and colour; window composition and detailing; roof forms and chimney details; return parapets and party wall ends; the cast iron verandah decoration; and even in the front step risers and front fences. While some of these terraces had narrow front gardens, in some cases these were larger or, depending on the topography, acted as lightwells to a lower ground floor.

Figure 5.9: The Terraces, Freeman Bros & Prout, Sydney, 1866. Mitchell Library, State Library of New South Wales, SPF/427; digital ID a089427.

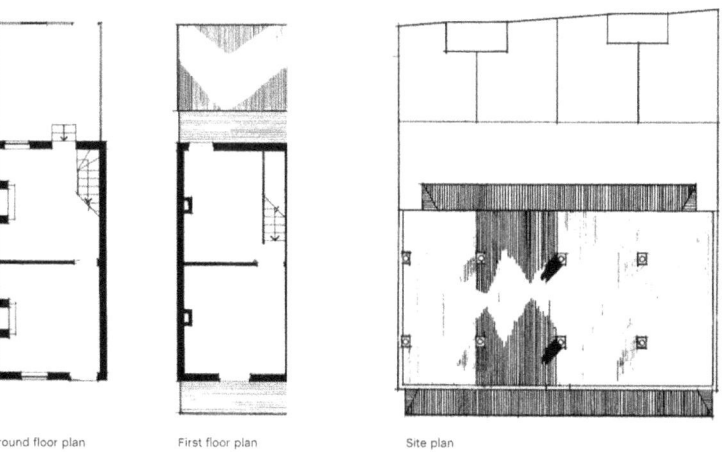

Figure 5.10: Terrace houses, 30–36 Thorne Street, c 1870. The austere form of this terrace house row indicates a 'transitional

owner-occupier' of modest means. A cantilevered balcony type, this terrace row has a characteristic parapet hiding the roofline while the interiors are simply detailed. There are similar terrace house rows in several areas of Paddington, including Hampden Street and Hargrave Street. © Robert Brown, 1979.

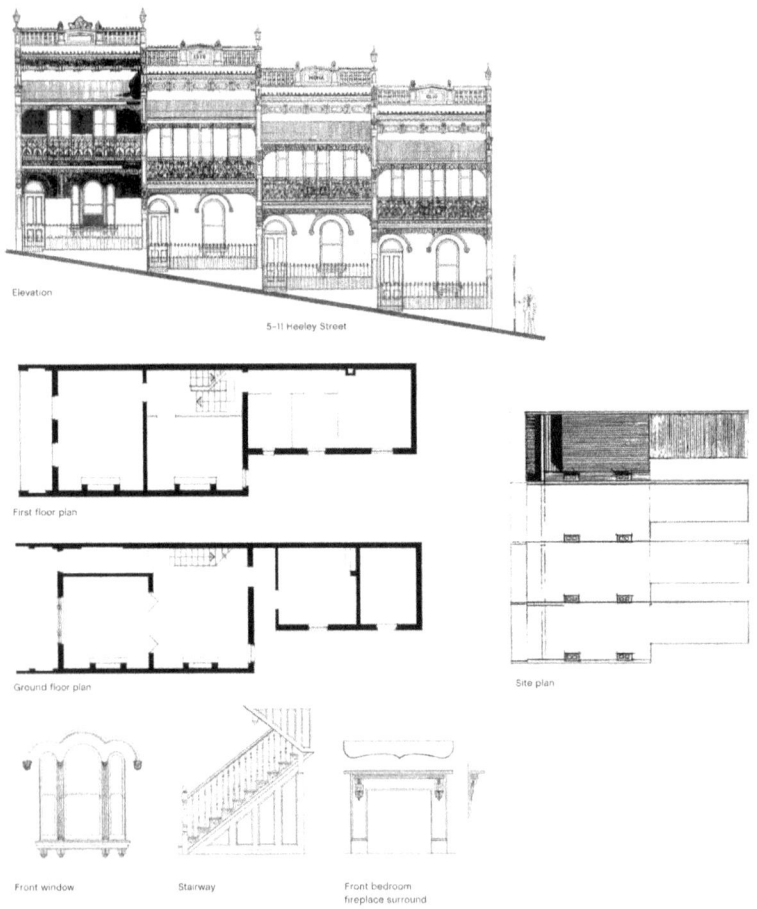

Figure 5.11: Terrace houses, 5–11 Heeley Street, c 1878. The boom years of the 1870s and 1880s saw the development of elaborately

decorated terrace house rows. In this example the houses, named Isis, Mona and Clio, step down the hill in regular succession and feature decorative stucco work with elaborate cast iron on the balconies. The interiors are similarly elaborate, with ornate plasterwork, fine cedar staircases, and large pine folding doors separating the ground floor rooms that have marble fire surrounds. The lord mayor of Paddington in the late 1880s, Charles Hellmrich, occupied the largest house on the left. It later became the home of historian Max Kelly. © Robert Brown, 1979.

The decorative elements of the terrace houses built during this period, in combination with the often-sloping topography which necessitated the stepping of each terrace dwelling, was to result in the creation of Paddington's unique character; streetscapes with a strong visual rhythm of party walls, parapets, chimneys, verandahs, balconies and front fences, all with decorative elements that create an exceptionally rich and picturesque built environment.

The residential density created by this terrace house development also resulted in a structure of local corner shops within walking distance to service the new and growing population. It has been estimated that there was one of these shops for every 45 residents and they were to play a vitally important role in the social life of Paddington beyond the mid-20th century.[33] The characteristic form was a corner entrance door flanked on each side by large display windows facing each street. These display windows were originally given a relatively simple framing of timber pilasters, sometimes quite broad, with elements of classical detailing and supporting a similarly detailed cornice. The shopkeeper's living quarters were upstairs although most had a ground floor kitchen area behind the shop space.

Also during this period, a more intense, linear, commercial development combined with public buildings evolved along Old South Head Road – named Oxford Street from 1875, it extended from Hyde Park to Paddington and then to Bondi Junction. The public structures included school and church buildings and a Post and Telegraph Office (1888) however this development was to slow with the depression of the early 1890s. While commercial and public development revived during the late 1890s and early 20th century, the extent of terrace house building was more limited and it is the pattern of terrace housing established in the 1870s and 1880s that provides the distinctive identity of place that Paddington possesses today.

The terrace houses built following the 1890s depression were much more restrained in style and detailing than those of the previous decades, although larger terrace house rows were now being constructed. There was now limited availability of land for speculation and an increasing change in the nature of ownership – from the individual builder/landlord with a small number of holdings, to wealthier landlords with a larger number of holdings. New terrace house rows now generally consisted of eight or more houses and the 'small landlord builder' began to disappear from the suburb.

In terms of style and detailing, the influence of the Queen Anne Revival and Arts and Crafts styles began to result in more simplified forms, with building materials more 'truthfully' expressed. Elaborate cast iron and stucco decoration gave way to red brickwork; terracotta tiles, copings and chimney pots; painted ornamental timberwork and roughcast finishes.

Although larger terrace house rows were built in areas such as Boundary Street, Duxford Street, Dillon Street and Hopetoun Street, during this period the terrace house began to fall from favour. The combined effects of the outbreak of bubonic plague in The Rocks in 1900 and the rise of the Garden Suburb Movement led to the *Royal Commission for the Improvement of Sydney and its Suburbs* concluding that 'on social or hygienic grounds, workmen should be encouraged to live in separate houses in the suburbs'.[34] As the terrace house became unfashionable, middle-class owners and tenants began to move from what were now regarded as crowded and congested inner suburbs to free-standing houses surrounded by open space in the new 'Garden Suburbs'. In Paddington, between 1900 and 1910 the percentage of owner-occupiers fell from 18 per cent to 11 per cent.[35] Those that remained tended to be those who could not afford to move and increasingly whole rows of terrace houses were bought by the one landlord, with many landlords owning 24 or more houses.[36]

Figure 5.12: Corner shop, Hopewell and Campbell streets, Paddington, c 1970s. Woollahra Libraries Local History Collection.

Figure 5.13: Bowes' Terrace, 44–54 Cameron Street Paddington, 1881. This is perhaps the most characteristic type of Paddington terrace house, modestly detailed but with a rhythmic repetition of forms, in this case stepping down the sloping street. The interior follows the earlier arrangement of two rooms up and two rooms down, but the kitchen is now joined to the main body of the house, positioned on one side to allow light and ventilation to the rear dining room. Behind the kitchen is an open laundry,

with copper and tubs, then a bathroom and WC, all with external access. Although plain, these were well-built terrace houses with the washing and sanitary facilities separated from the living areas of the house, reflecting health concerns of the late 19th and early 20th centuries. © Robert Brown, 1979.

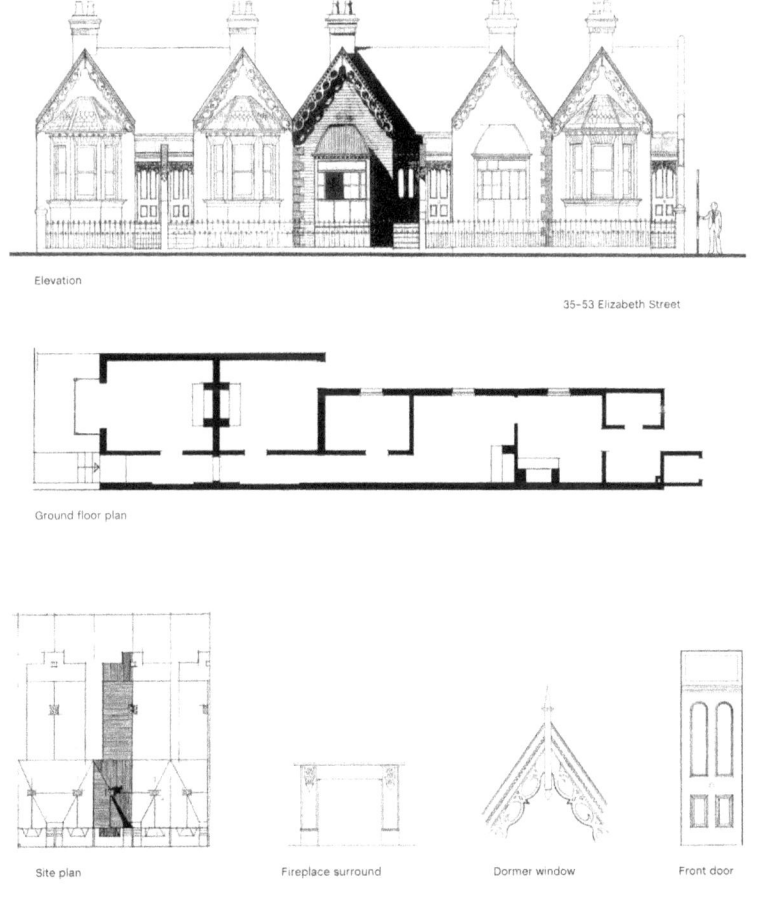

Figure 5.14: Terrace houses, 35–53 Elizabeth Street Paddington, c 1890. Built of exposed red brickwork, with steeply sloping gabled roofs, this terrace house row is arranged in alternating

pairs of houses with bay windows and open verandahs (later enclosed), creating a sense of pairs of semi-detached houses and reflecting an architectural shift from the repetitive Victorian-era terrace house forms. The effect is emphasised by the breaks in the roof line and the stuccoed quoins of some pairs of houses. The interiors now comprise a sitting-room, principal bedroom (both with marble and tile fireplace surrounds), a second bedroom and then a dining room, all with decorative ceiling roses and cornices. Adjoining the dining room is the kitchen with a large cast iron range and beyond this a laundry, bathroom and WC. © Robert Brown, 1979.

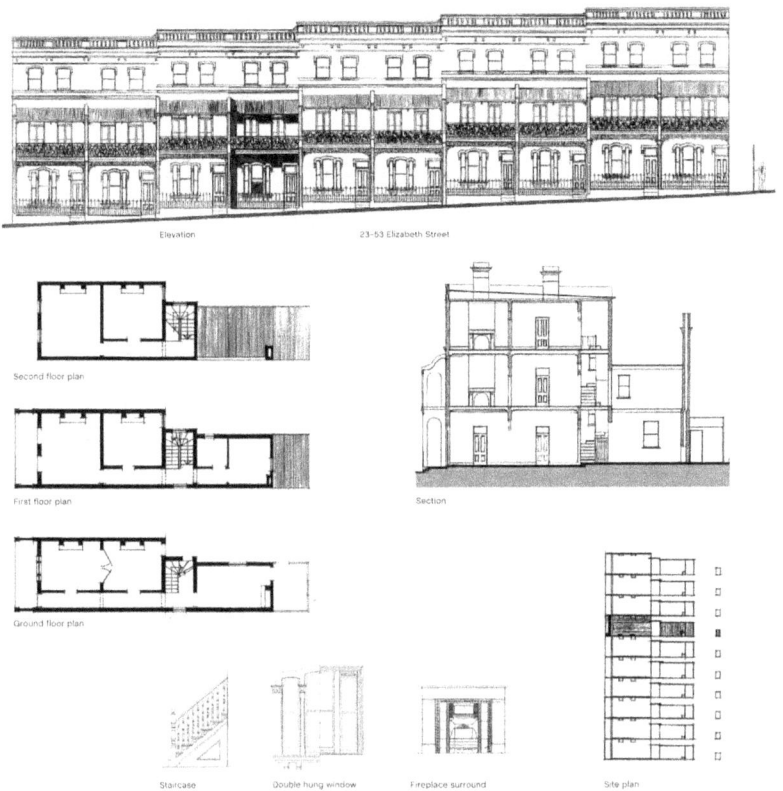

Figure 5.15: Terrace houses, 35–53 Elizabeth Street. This 'townhouse' style terrace house row of 10 three-storey houses, built in conjunction with the Grand National Hotel, is a good example of the larger terrace house rows built in Paddington from the 1890s by wealthier landlords. © Robert Brown, 1979.

Elevation 88-94 Cascade Street

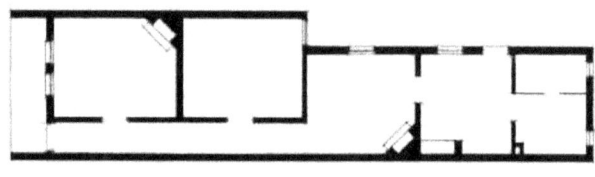

Floor plan

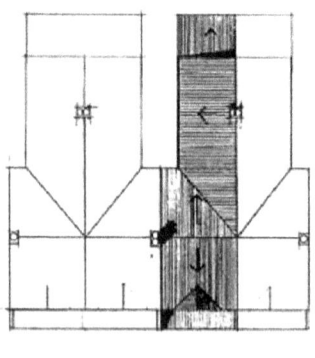

Site plan

Figure 5.16: Terrace houses, 88–94 Cascade Street Paddington, c 1905. A single-storey terrace row demonstrating the influence of the Federation style, with red face brickwork, projecting gables with decorative timberwork and tall, red brick chimneys. The slate roof is capped with decorative terracotta while the verandah has a turned timber frieze with a central glazed panel etched with the house name. The interior arrangement is similar to 1890s terrace houses, although the fireplaces of the main rooms are now positioned in the corner and the decorative plasterwork is more restrained. © Robert Brown, 1979.

Decline and Depression: 1910–50

Between 1910 and the 1920s little further development took place in Paddington; most of the land had been built upon and the population, now mostly tradesmen, unskilled labourers and their families, remained constant at about 24,000.[37] It was now characterised as a working-class suburb and vulnerable to the ravages of the Great Depression of the early 1930s.

As the number of unemployed increased, so too did the number who could not afford to pay their rent. Furniture and personal effects were sold or seized by bailiffs and many were evicted. Those that did manage to keep a job often took in unemployed relatives and friends, while others took in 'boarders' to help pay the rent, often two or more to a room. Many terrace houses became rooming houses, with extra space created by closing in verandahs and balconies. In 1933 60 per cent of Paddington's houses were being shared by two or more families and these houses, now 40 to 60 years old, were becoming shabby and dilapidated.

As the effects of the Depression began to recede, Paddington came to be seen as a slum and was associated with crime. Terrace houses were now regarded as overcrowded, lacking gardens, adequate kitchen and bathroom facilities (despite the majority being sewered) and, to town planners such as NH Dick, they were 'ugly and monotonous'.[38]

A government report in 1935 suggested the solution to the 'slum problem' was demolition and rebuilding, with terrace house rows replaced by two-storey blocks of flats set in gardens and grounds.[39] While this program was delayed by the outbreak of World

War 2, it was revived in the Cumberland County Plan of 1947 and the City of Sydney Council planned the wholesale clearance of Paddington's residential built environment for blocks of flats set in green open space.

Gentrification and conservation: 1950–2000

From 1947 Sydney's population grew dramatically as the federal government encouraged immigration from Britain and then southern Europe to assist economic growth. Between 1947 and 1966 Sydney's foreign-born population grew from 13 per cent to 22 per cent and, as one Paddington resident recalled, the suburb became a 'transit camp for migrants'.[40] The attraction of Paddington for these newly arrived Italians, Maltese and Greek immigrants was that it was affordable, close to the city and to most workplaces. These 'New Australians' were to bring a sense of vitality to Paddington and so begin its revitalisation.

'The poor man's suburb' began to be transformed and by 1960 almost 17 per cent of Paddington houses were owned by immigrants.[41] Landlords were pleased to sell what had become a poor investment – the *Landlord and Tenants Act* meant that tenants on fixed rents could not be evicted – and the pattern of ownership began to change. Instead of one landlord owning a whole terrace row there were now individual owners within the row, and as these owner-occupiers began to renovate their homes, each with an individual expression of approach, the appearance of Paddington began to change.

Figure 5.17: Little Comber Street, Paddington, 1938. Mitchell Library, State Library of New South Wales, digital ID d1_27975.

As one long-time resident recalled: 'Nearly every house ... was brown. The house on the opposite corner was then acquired by Italians ... he even painted the house pink, with white mortar and purple window sills.'[42] One writer suggested in 1970 that 'Mediterranean migrants ... painted the dingy terraces gay colours and made a lot of people see them for the first time.'[43]

Others began to be attracted to Paddington after travelling to England and Europe, where they had lived in terrace houses and discovered the advantages of inner urban living. Some wanted to break the pattern of their middle-class life in garden suburbs, while others realised the benefits of living close to the city. As architect Don Gazzard recalled, he and sculptor/ceramicist Marea Gazzard were drawn to Paddington by the 'architecture and townscape, as well as the egalitarian social environment of post-war immigrants'.[44]

Among the first of this new wave of residents were broadcaster John Thompson and his writer wife Pat Thompson, who moved to Paddington in 1951. They and the Gazzards became active in opposing developments that would change the character of Paddington and in 1964 they were founding members of the Paddington Society. It was the promotion of the whole of Paddington as a significant cultural landscape that contained built fabric of architectural merit that was one of the Society's most significant achievements.

Figure 5.18: Flats at Paddington (rear view), 1956. In 1947 Sydney City Council proposed replacing terrace houses throughout Paddington with this type of apartment building. State Library of New South Wales, digital ID. d2_09140.

The 'landlady brown' terrace houses described by Gazzard began to change as new owners renovated what were often severely rundown properties, guided by publications such as Rob Hillier's *Let's Buy a Terrace House.* Render was stripped from external walls to reveal the original sandstock brick and the advice 'to use as much white paint as possible' was enthusiastically followed.[45]

In 1970, the Paddington Society's *Paddington: A plan for preservation* admitted that the popularity of the area had 'forced the price of houses up to such an extent that only those people who really want to live in a terrace house and "restore" it can afford to buy houses. People no longer come to Paddington simply because the houses are cheap.'[46] The plan's stated aim was to ensure future maintenance of the housing stock and 'eliminate many of the worst sort of "modernisations" which occurred in the past'.

The 'modernisations' of red-textured brick apartment blocks that had begun to appear, particularly along sections of Glenmore Road, were now halted and in the renovation of terrace houses there was now a greater emphasis on retaining or re-instating the original

Victorian form and detailing, at least in the main body of the house. The four rooms in this part of a two-storey terrace house, with the levels linked by a usually well-detailed staircase, generally needed little adaptation to modern living requirements. It was the rear wing, containing the kitchen, laundry, bathroom and a small third bedroom, that became the focus for architectural change, the wing often demolished and rebuilt to take advantage of the open space at the rear.

Figure 5.19: Terrace houses, Liverpool Street Paddington, c 1970. Mitchell Library, State Library of New South Wales, PXE 649 (v.11). Rob Hillier, Let's buy a Terrace House, Ure Smith, Sydney, 1968.

While some terrace house owners continued with the 'do-it-yourself' approach, more affluent owners sought professional advice and assistance. As architects engaged with the terrace house form, some began to explore more radical approaches. Between 1975 and 2015, in a clear indication of the gentrification of the suburb, the list of architects contributing to the Paddington townscape reads like a 'Who's Who' of modern Australian architecture. In 1972 Don Gazzard designed one of the earliest examples of what became known as 'infill development' for small inner city sites: his own house built on a vacant block at the corner of Hargrave and Elizabeth streets. Gazzard's intention was 'to demonstrate that a modern building can fit perfectly with older heritage buildings as long as scale, form and materials are sympathetic'.[47] The house completed a row of terrace houses, with a slate roof of the same pitch as its neighbours. The plan also followed the 19th century form, having a middle floor entry level, one upper level and a lower level to the rear garden. The house's form and materials – 'off-form concrete and semi-industrial details' – alienated many at a time when restoration was the accepted norm and that new work in historic precincts should reproduce the surrounding traditional buildings. However, the house came to be recognised as 'a bold but respectful, modern addition to an old street ... emulation is not essential for good manners'.[48]

Figure 5.20: Exterior, Gazzard House, Elizabeth and Hargrave streets Paddington, completed 1975. Photo: The Paddington Society, 2018.

Figure 5.21: Interior, Gazzard House, c 1975. Don Gazzard, Sydneysider, Watermark Press, 2006. Photo: David Moore.

Figure 5.22: Exterior, 132 Paddington Street Paddington. Allen Jack+Cottier, 1981. The exterior was retained in its original form at Council insistence and apart from 'a swatch of gelato paint colours' it gave no indication of the transformation of the interiors. Courtesy Allen Jack+Cottier Architects.

Figure 5.23: Interior, 132 Paddington Street Paddington. Allen Jack+Cottier, 1981. The new interiors combined vertical open-planning, to counteract the narrow width of the house, with 'high-tech' detailing to create a sense of spaciousness. Photograph: Max Dupain. Courtesy Allen Jack+Cottier Architects.

Other architects, working within the constraints of existing terrace houses, took different approaches to managing the restrictions of long, narrow areas and bringing light into these spaces. In 1980 Peter Stronach of Allen Jack+Cottier, broke with the accepted practice of adapting the existing main rooms of a terrace house by completely gutting the interior of 'a tiny, dark, near derelict terrace' at 132 Paddington Street. The exterior was retained at Council insistence; 'facadism' had become a generally accepted approach to maintaining the character of an historic precinct. In radical contrast to the conserved facade, Stronach created an open plan interior of semi-industrial steelwork that included an additional floor. To create a sense of spaciousness, a series of voids between the levels opened the house vertically, allowing light to spread throughout the interior.[49]

Another architect to break with conservationist practice in Paddington was Alec Tzannes. His classically-inspired design for a terrace house, built on a site occupied by a fibro shed at 159 Windsor Street, was rejected by Woollahra Council on the grounds that its classical facade was inconsistent with the Victorian streetscape.[50]

Tzannes successfully argued that its form reflected the terrace house precedent, the London townhouse, and its scale and proportion complemented the existing streetscape. Tzannes' aim, like Don Gazzard 10 years earlier, was to challenge existing attitudes and in this case planning controls 'to better assist innovative architectural design in the area'.[51] The interiors also demonstrate an innovative approach to planning, with a skylit cross stairwell bringing light throughout the centre of the house and dividing public and private areas. The house, which won several architectural awards, was subsequently regarded by Woollahra Council as setting the standard for infill development.[52]

Figure 5.24: Exterior, Henwood House, centre, Windsor Street Paddington. Alec Tzannes, built 1982–85. Photo: Lindy Kerr, 2017.

Figure 5.25: Living room, 66 Hargrave Street, Paddington, 1980. The interiors of this terrace house, photographed in 1980, reflect an

extraordinary history of occupation, from the Victorian/Edwardian arrangement of objects on the mantelpiece and manner of picture hanging, to the 1930s wallpaper, smoker's stand and light-fitting and the 1960s vinyl-covered lounge, plastic flowers and Aboriginal motif plates on the chimneybreast. Terrace houses demonstrating such a continuity of occupancy are now rare. State Library of New South Wales, GPO 3–05538 (living room).

All of these buildings were considered exceptional for their time in their approach to reinterpreting the terrace house form. In subsequent decades, as the fashionability and demand for real estate in Paddington increased and house prices continued to rise, such levels of intervention were no longer considered remarkable. While many re-workings of the terrace house form consisted of subtle refinements, retaining a sense of the original and the function of interior spaces, particularly in the main body of the house, of greatest concern is the increasing tendency in recent decades for 'removal and insertion'.[53] In this approach only the main street facade of a terrace house is retained while the entire interior is demolished and rebuilt in Modernist form, with a flow of open space and a linking of the interior and (rear) exterior.

Adaptation and amalgamation: 21st century

In recent years the approach of conserving the facade of a Victorian-era terrace house and yet stripping its interior – regarded as balancing the need to preserve the historic character of the streetscape with the need to provide for contemporary living – has been extended to the amalgamation of two or three adjoining terrace houses. The main facades are retained as individual forms yet the interiors are gutted and redesigned in a new amalgamated form, creating a larger physical home with a bigger garden space often containing a swimming pool.

This process of increasing private space, combined with an increase in public space through the adaptation and redevelopment of sites such as the Paddington Reservoir and Royal Hospital for Women, is the result of revitalisation and gentrification of the former slum; of the imposition of suburban values and suburban form to create a sense of greater space within a dense Victorianera built environment. While this process has attempted to maintain the heritage values of the place, in the case of Paddington's housing – its most valued and characteristic element – this adaptation and amalgamation is posing a greater threat to the integrity of the Victorian suburb than the years of neglect during the early 20th century.

The inherent danger of the approach of 'removal and insertion' and amalgamation is that while the historic character of the streetscape is retained, there is the greater loss of authenticity and integrity. As the structure and interior fabric of these terrace houses is destroyed, not only is the individual record of their history and functionality lost, but also the social fibre of Paddington and the history of those who have lived and worked here is diminished.

These houses have the potential to tell us much about their history and the lives of those who lived in them: from the time of their construction during the late 19th century when the earlier estates were subdivided; through the declining years of the early 20th century and Depression; and into the revitalisation of the post-war years. The challenge now is to retain the 'record of evidence' of this history – intrinsic to the Paddington terrace house – in repurposing for contemporary life.

Chapter 6

Gentrification

Sharon Veale and Peter McNeil

In 2017 a newly renovated Paddington Street terrace was put on the market with a rear lane car-stacking elevator. Some terraces in the suburb now have internal lifts, wine cellars and infinity edge swimming pools. Yet this is the suburb where in the 1920s and '30s terraces were cut up into flats for 10 or more people, with one outdoor toilet. Whatever has happened? This is the process of gentrification. It has proceeded in Paddington since the 1950s and comes with benefits and costs.[1]

Gentrification has been one of the more powerful urban shaping forces in Australian cities such as Melbourne and Sydney since the late 1950s and early 1960s. Neither urban planners nor deliberate government policy dictated how this pattern of urbanism would play out in Paddington; instead a complex constellation of social, cultural and economic influences has shaped it.

Paddington's story is about shifting classes and economic investment and the reimagining of a fine-grained historic inner city area from shabby to high-end chic. Today Paddington has become a spectacle of consumption and leisure. In just over 50 years it has metamorphosed from a suburb perceived to have narrow ugly streets, lined with rows of dark terraces, dunny lanes and alleyways used by families, to one of Australia's richest suburbs. Paddington is now widely regarded as a prestige residential suburb where stylish terraces, markets, high-end fashion boutiques, gastropubs, fine dining restaurants, cafes, gourmet providores, wine bars and galleries reflect the money, style and tastes of its residents.

Youthful intellectualism, cosmopolitan style and artistic sensibilities, combined with old timers and post-war migrants from Portugal, Greece, Malta, Italy and the former Yugoslavia (with their colourful terraces and corner shops), characterised the initial wave of gentrification in the late 1950s. By the mid 1960s this movement had become widespread.[2] Yet today, Paddington's gloss of gentrification has lost its gleam. With a median house price of over $2 million, many old timers, migrants, artistic style and eclectic cool have moved out and on. Diversity has been replaced by a wealthy monoculture of high net worth individuals and investors, which could put Paddington on the path to becoming a 'ghost town of the super-rich' much like London's Chelsea and Kensington.[3] In short, as writer Daisy Dumas has observed, 'the area's changed ... it used to be hip, now it's full of investment bankers'.[4]

In the decades immediately following the Depression and post-war period 'no one confessed to living in Paddington'.[5] Paddington's housing stock had languished, as had its image. Cheap lodging houses with boarded up balconies occupied by unemployed and transient people who could barely afford their rent, combined with petty crime, gangs, prostitution and sly grog, saw the image of inner city Paddington descend in the minds of many to a criminal slum.

Wartime rent controls were continued in 1948 when the *Landlord and Tenant (Amendment) Act* passed. Under the statute, landlords had little or no ability to evict tenants or increase rent, which was pegged at the 1939 level.[6] The condition of tenanted properties fell further into disrepair.[7] With investment returns declining, many landlords willingly sold their dilapidated Paddington rental properties. Between 1959 and 1966 around 2000 terraces houses changed hands.[8] This was part of a broader pattern of urban transformation especially notable in Sydney and Melbourne's inner city suburbs where, by the early 1960s, two-thirds of the dwellings had become owner-occupied.[9] Almost 5000 buildings, predominately terraces, were converted from shared houses and rooms in boarding houses to single occupancy dwellings.[10] This shift was dramatic. In 1905 only 10 per cent of terraces were owner-occupied in Paddington; by 1966 just over 60 per cent were in this category.[11]

Figure 6.1: 'Pleasant Paddington', Australian Women's Weekly, 1965 shows John and Patricia Thompson outside their terrace house at 66 Goodhope Street. Typical of the fashionable changes of the period they added a masonry fence in a chic light colour. Australian Women's Weekly, 19 May 1965.

'Sick of living miles away from the city',[12] Patricia Thompson and her husband, John Thompson, purchased a terrace house from a deceased estate in Paddington in 1951 for the 'enormous sum' of £2800. 'No one lived in Paddington'[13] and among their social set they were often asked: 'Weren't you the first people to live in Paddington?' Patricia Thompson's response was: 'Yes, we came with our black guides and our camels and we hacked a way with our machetes.'[14]

Seen as radical and a little eccentric, the Thompsons were early adopters of what would come to epitomise a trendy inner city lifestyle, where corner shops run by 'New Australians' sold cured meats, imported cheese and dolmades instead of devon, white bread and milk. The Thompsons had openly renounced the sprawling sameness of the suburbs where they saw no sense of community and little in the way of activity, infrastructure or amenity. Instead they opted for a location with the city close, lots of places for children to go and a 'marvellously strong community spirit'.[15]

In the late 1960s and 1970s sophisticated, trend setting artists, journalists, writers, actors, architects and young professionals employed in the city, moved into Paddington; attracted by the well-located and affordable housing stock. Many were well travelled and they recognised Paddington to be historically interesting and architecturally charming, ripe for restoration and creative self-expression. So the restorations and renovations The suburb of Paddington occupies a unique place in the history of Australian town planning. As a graduate town planner entering the profession in the mid-1970s, for me, Paddington was not only the place to live, but also the place to observe and engage in community based heritage advocacy first-hand. The success of a newly gentrified community in opposing the state's previously intractable road-widening schemes in the swinging '60s led directly to Paddington becoming one of the first urban conservation areas to receive media recognition and legislative protection. Other towns and suburbs swiftly followed. Paddington's conservation however had begun almost a decade before the statutory processes of the *NSW Heritage Act,* 1977. Nor did the community call for a Green Ban to support its conservation efforts. Paddington's conservation was achieved by dint of engaged local professionals contributing their energy and time to a community in the flux of change and made permanent through the resulting conservation controls implemented by Woollahra Council and the City of Sydney.

Post-war Sydney: 1940s

As wartime austerity eased and there were jobs for all in a booming economy, a garden and a house in the suburbs came within an average family's reach, with a car in the garage, a job in the city and a new public school being built nearby for the kids. The parents of the generation who would become known as the Baby Boomers embraced all that suburbia had to offer and Sydney expanded pell-mell, with the pent-up demand for housing being realised on its fringes. The stellate railway system funnelled workers to the city centre – as did designated County

Roads – but in the inner city, the main arterial roads were the old bullock tracks running along ridgelines, taking easy gradients and inconvenient turns around the idiosyncrasies of early land grants. Sydney's ad hoc settlement patterns were not readily compatible with the needs of mass car ownership. Roads needed straightening and widening, and the Department of Main Roads (DMR) – whose efficient engineers and road builders were not city planners – was in the ascendant. Their reports were sacrosanct, unquestioned remedies to the troubles of Sydney's burgeoning car ownership, traffic jams, and inadequate public transport planning.

In the bright-eyed post-war cities of Australia, the old was under attack. In Sydney, the inner city areas of largely Victorian suburbs and terrace houses such as those of Paddington, Redfern and Surry Hills, were characterised as slums simply by virtue of their age and condition. The *County of Cumberland Planning Scheme* (1948) identified them as 'almost totally substandard areas requiring replacement either immediately or within 25 years'.[1] Similarly, in Hobart, remnant Georgian areas like Battery Point were described as 'old and decadent' in the *1945 City of Hobart Plan*[2] and in need of healthy, progressive redevelopment. In the spirit of the times, the engineers responsible for town planning, considered that such inner areas and old building stock should make way for higher density redevelopment and for road building schemes to improve access from the suburbs to the central business district.

As car ownership increased in post-war Sydney, the arterial roads were increasingly inadequate, and while small widenings of Oxford Street and Old South Head Road eased Eastern Suburbs traffic congestion in Paddington, local residential streets were increasingly used by through traffic. The County of Cumberland Council planners noted also Bonython Gallery in Victoria Street in 1967 cemented Paddington's reputation as a centre for art. During the 1970s Paddington was the breeding ground for radical contemporary art forms with galleries such as Gallery A and Coventry Gallery fostering emerging artists and experimental art forms. During the following decades other galleries opened including major Australian commercial art galleries such as Roslyn Oxley9 in 1982 and Sherman Galleries, from 1988 to 2007. While in 1950 there were only two art galleries in Paddington, by 1983 over 30 had been established.[17]

Figure 6.4: The Hungry Horse Restaurant and Gallery. David Mist exhibited photographs from his Sydney, A Book of Photographs here in 1969. The building was home to Lucio's famed Italian restaurant from 1983 and it became a hub for many corporate, business, media and artistic discussions over the years. Photo: © David Mist. Collection: Museum of Applied Arts and Sciences. Gift of David Mist under the Australian Government Taxation Incentives for the Arts program, 1996.

Figure 6.5: Chef and Diners at The Hungry Horse, from Sydney, A Book of Photographs 1969. A French restaurant that catered for Sydney's increasingly sophisticated palates. © David Mist. Collection: Museum of Applied Arts and Sciences. Gift of David Mist under the

Australian Government Taxation Incentives for the Arts program, 1996.

As part of the evolving pattern of change, 'there was new life pulsing through the old streets'.[18] Galleries were joined by bric-a-brac, antique shops, specialist bookshops and intimate restaurants that would gradually displace the corner shops that had long catered for local domestic needs. A broader network of fashionable people and creatives were attracted to Paddington in the late 1960s and 1970s. One such was the renowned fabric and graphic designer and flamboyant Sydney personality, Florence Broadhurst who relocated her business to Paddington after 1969 capitalising on the growing energy of the area.

People involved in the emerging music, film, theatre, television and advertising industries also found a home in Paddington. Other subcultures established themselves. Gay bars, cafes and clubs were opened with Oxford Street – especially at the neighbouring Darlinghurst end – the symbolic heart of gay culture and a place of political protest and spectacle and from 1978 on the route of the Gay and Lesbian Mardi Gras.

The metamorphosis of Paddington had begun. Between 1959 to 1962 white collar workers comprised 14 per cent of property buyers in Paddington. This more than trebled between 1963 and 1966, reaching 40 per cent.[19] Almost without exception these buyers were young Australia born married couples, some with school age children. They were attracted by the village atmosphere and the quality of the Victorian building stock, which they swiftly set about improving. Of the people that had purchased in Paddington during the 1960s, just under half (43 per cent) of the owner-occupiers had made some form of structural change or improvement to their house by 1966.[20] Many of the migrant families that had initially purchased and improved the housing stock had, by the later years of the 1960s, moved out. This shift transformed the diversity, cultural life, character and composition of Paddington. The new left-leaning, young artistically inclined urbanites and professionals attracted the attention of the burgeoning news and lifestyle media. By now, 'Paddington was looking rather charming'.[21] Images of avant-garde fashion, parties, and glamorous people, living in stylish renovated terrace houses proliferated in glossy lifestyle and interior magazines. Paddington was rebranded as a highly desirable and fashionable historic inner city suburb.

Figure 6.6: Vaike Liibus, Portrait of Florence Broadhurst, Oil on canvas Sydney, 1976. Museum of Applied Arts and Sciences. Gift of Vivien Johnson, 2014. Courtesy Vivien Johnson. Photo: Ryan Hernandez.

Figure 6.7: Page from a wallpaper sample book showing Paddington lacework, titled David Miles Handprinted Wallpaper, Sydney, 1972. David and Cherie Miles also created wallpapers, which were inspired by the area. Museum of Applied Arts and Sciences, Sydney. Gift of David and Cherie Miles, 2003. Photo: Ryan Hernandez.

Early gentrifiers, including the Thompsons, mobilised history and heritage conservation to combat the development and destruction of the urban fabric. The Paddington Society, formed in 1964, became an articulate mouthpiece and energetic forum for promotion of the suburb's history and preservation.

Today, history and heritage in Paddington have come to epitomise class, style and money. Properties in

Paddington are highly desirable commodities. They are bought and sold, renovated – or 'flipped' – for blistering sums and reported enthusiastically by a media obsessed with property values. The *New York Times* captured something of this broader pattern of change in Paddington, in an article titled, 'Their space solution is found next door'. It recounts the story of an investment fund manager and entertainment lawyer, with a growing family, who upsized from a cramped 4-storey 3-bedroom terrace by purchasing the adjacent terrace for $1 million and connecting them internally to create a spacious family home. Their architect-designed $2 million renovation resulted in 'more space than they knew what to do with' while from the architect's perspective the project's biggest obstacle, was the restrictive planning controls for heritage buildings which the architect sensed wanted time to stop in the Victorian period.[22] Yet this same Victorian heritage is marketed for consumption by Paddington real estate agents, retailers, tourism operators and home owners who participate in the collaborative economy hosting visitors to their heritage homes.

Figure 6.8: A Paddington fancy dress terrace party, 1971. Host Charles Manning, wearing knickerbockers and lace up boots, with Miss Libby Thomson, in a vintage lace dress, and Miss Kerry Crowley in a patterned floral midi dress. 'People and Fashion' page, Australian Women's Weekly, 14 April 1971.

Figure 6.9: Ladies' day in Paddington. Walking tours of Paddington led by Viva Murphy, a founding member of the Paddington Society, were a daily occurrence. Rob Hillier, A Place Called Paddington, photoprints, 1970 State Library of New South Wales.

Gentrification was not merely evident in the residential transformation of Paddington. By the 1970s Paddington was a shopping destination for Sydney residents and visitors alike. It was innovative, quirky and dominated by small, sole-traders and eclectic businesses that were part of the appeal of the area. There was Madame Lash's boutique, Game Birds, selling leather corsets at 108 Oxford Street; Treatment, a punk fashion shop; and Peter Moss Interior Design. In a converted terrace house, Paul Jellard's Five Way Fusion promoted imported European and Japanese directional fashion. At 120 Glenmore Road the Maestro Restaurant was serving 'Quails à la Reine', while at Fiveways, the Royal Hotel's Elephant Bar was listed as a 'good cruise bar' in 1980.

Following Angela Child's successful art bookshop in William Street the innovative New Edition opened in 1974. It was owned by William de Winton, who also did much to research and promote Paddington's history. De Winton had arrived from the United Kingdom and found Paddington 'bursting with talent and innovation ... young people were starting up everything from small boutiques to very interesting antique shops'.[23] The colourful interior of the New Edition Tea Rooms was based on the iconic painting by Grace Cossington Smith, The Lacquer Room (1936). Readers could relax on large cushions after perusing the well-stocked shelves of imported and local titles. Live poetry readings were held on the street outside. De Winton also published a series of free, innovative guides to Paddington that included as many as 130 pages of directories, maps, charts and notes on the layered history of Paddington.

Concentrated around the Uniting Church on Oxford Street, the Paddington Markets were the seedbed for local community creativity established to nurture fashion designers, craftspeople, jewellery makers and artists.[24] Commencing in 1973 with around 16 stalls, by 1975 this number had risen to 70. Paddington Markets' success continued. In 1984 it had expanded into the grounds of the adjacent public school and boasted 250 stalls. Icons of Australian fashion and style including Dinosaur Designs, Zimmermann and Collette Dinnigan started selling their designs at Paddington Markets, long before they became established Australian and international brands.

Wanting a piece of the action, other cool fashion retailers and designers clustered nearby to be part of the scene. Robby Ingham established his mecca for carefully curated international brands on Oxford Street in the early 1980s when rents were still 'dirt cheap'.[25] Crowds flocked to the boutiques along the 'Portobello Road of the east' hoping that some of the inner city cool would rub off.[26]

Also, by the 1990s William Street, a small street of terraces at right angles to the Oxford Street thoroughfare, had become a thriving collection of boutique shops located in small terrace houses. It became and remains as iconic as Rowe Street in the city for an earlier inter-war generation. In 1994 a shopper would find there Sweet William Chocolates; Jane Stoddart milliner; Victoria Spring (jewellery); Collette Dinnigan, lingerie and later fashion design; Alison Coates; unconventional floral arrangements; John Normyle interior architecture and antiques; Hamish Clark Antiques, Andrew McDonald (shoemaker); and Ceramic Art Gallery, run by ceramicist Janet Mansfield. The Bonaventura Continental Grocery was at the end of the street and is still trading as Alimentari.

Oxford Street had a distinctive buzz; it epitomised 'hip and happening'. It was the place to be seen on Saturday. But this too was cyclical. Chain retailers wanted in from the 2000s and landlords were offered significant sums for commercial leases, forcing smaller local boutiques and retailers out. The opening of the Westfield Mall in Bondi Junction in 2004 saw the exodus of yet more local retailers. Combined with the rise of online shopping, parking restrictions and the global financial crisis, Oxford Street's energy and buzz eroded further. Many of Oxford Street landlords did not want to budge with rent reductions, stubbornly believing Oxford Street was still worth the price. For lease signs, empty shops, or makeshift stores selling containers of last year's stock popped up. When landlords eventually did drop rents by 30 to 40 per cent still no one really came.

With the rise and fall of Oxford Street over the last several decades the fashion focus of Paddington has shifted. In the attractive refurbished terraces near near the junction of Oxford Street and Glenmore Road, the entrepreneur and property developer Theo Onisforou (son of Cypriot migrants who were greengrocers, and who grew up in Paddington) has created a new fashion precinct known as The Intersection; the names of fashion 'stars' are set in the pavement. Parts of Oxford Street still struggle. This symbolised a broader malaise, as profit seeking abetted by globalisation restructured cities and their economies, often leading to the eclipse of local creativity and distinctiveness. Yet there are encouraging signs of revitalisation in this overripe phase of gentrification, with many fashionable bars, cafes and restaurants springing up. New venues along Oxford Street, including The Paddington opened by the hospitality juggernaut Merivale, have begun to turn around the fortunes of the suburb's premier shopping strip.

Figure 6.10: The Intersection, at the junction of Glenmore Road and Oxford Street,

Paddington. The combination of Victorian streetscapes, Australian designer boutiques, cafes, hair stylists, galleries and a pub has created a chic precinct. Simon Wood Photography 2017.

Figure 6.11: The Recreational Arts Team (RAT): Reno Dal, Billy Yip and Jac Vidgen at the Oceanratting RAT Party, photography by William

Yang, Sydney, 1986. Museum of Applied Arts and Sciences.

Just as fashion contributed to Paddington's cool credibility, so too did music. During the late 1960s, 1970s and 1980s, Oxford Street was a hub for the emerging music industry. Its ebb and flow reflected the suburb's pulse and its appetite for the more independent, expressive and experimental trends of the times. In the 1960s and 1970s, local pubs offered jazz and folk music with beer gardens and barbeques. Warren Fahey opened Folkways music shop on Oxford Street in 1973 with an awning sign boasting 'real music in a sea of shit'.[27] Fahey owned Larrikin Records from 1974–95, an important independent label producing nearly 500 albums and launching groups such as Redgum, Robyn Archer and Indigenous collaborations. Paddington therefore became a hub for Australian folk and other historical music. Fahey also promoted the Paddington Festival, a significant public event held in the park previously located on the current Paddington Reservoir Gardens site.

Local pubs and bars provided venues. Mental as Anything performed at The Unicorn and Died Pretty, Henry Rollins, Jonathan Richman and The Chills played at the Paddington RSL Club. But the heart of it was Paddington Town Hall where in 1977 the cult punk rock band Radio Birdman and its supporting act, The Saints, 'tore the house down'.[28] Experimental subculture returned to the Town Hall during the 1980s and early 1990s with RATizm, RATparade, PRATy, HypeRATive and SupeRATural among others.[29] Attracting drag queens, gays and cool heterosexuals, Recreational Arts Team (RAT) dance parties transformed the party scene and Sydney's night life with an intoxicating mix of illumination, performance art and DJ sets, paving the way for the large-scale dance parties and techno raves of the 1990s. Attended by celebrities and designers, the colour and creative expression captivated the media and once again put Paddington at the vanguard.

Folkways closed in 2009 after almost three decades. The perfect storm had blown through Oxford Street. Dwindling customers, high rent, competition from chain stores and parking restrictions all combined with sharp increases in music downloads which saw turnover plunge. RAT 'ruled the world' for a while too, but by the 1990s, the party concept they pioneered had been exploited and commercialised.[30]

Gentrification continues to be variously defined by planners, urban theorists, geographers and sociologists, among others. The processes, waves and cycles involved have been endlessly described and debated. Paddington has gone from 'scary, to edgy, to trendy to pricey',[31] and in the process become a coveted brand and tourism destination. Paddington's identity, created and fuelled by the talents and desires of its diverse groups, with their complex and shifting interactions, have shaped what we imagine Paddington to be.

As a vital and lively cultural discourse, history and heritage conservation have played a significant role in shaping the image and identity of Paddington. The history and urban fabric that attracted the gentrifiers to Paddington in the late 1950s has evolved but remains amid a pattern of ongoing change and continuity. At the same time, elements of local heritage difference and authenticity have often been displaced, perhaps permanently. With today's economic globalisation and neo liberal urbanism it is perhaps not surprising that the gentle gloss of gentrification is no longer. Instead, one might describe Paddington as a place of productive cultural capital, in which investment and consumption by urban elites and entrepreneurs could remove the heritage gloss even further.

Chapter 7
Conserving Paddington

Sheridan Burke

The suburb of Paddington occupies a unique place in the history of Australian town planning. As a graduate town planner entering the profession in the mid-1970s, for me, Paddington was not only the place to live, but also the place to observe and engage in community based heritage advocacy first-hand. The success of a newly gentrified community in opposing the state's previously intractable road-widening schemes in the swinging '60s led directly to Paddington becoming one of the first urban conservation areas to receive media recognition and legislative protection. Other towns and suburbs swiftly followed. Paddington's conservation however had begun almost a decade before the statutory processes of the *NSW Heritage Act,* 1977. Nor did the community call for a Green Ban to support its conservation efforts. Paddington's conservation was achieved by dint of engaged local professionals contributing their energy and time to a community in the flux of change and made permanent through the resulting conservation controls implemented by

Woollahra Council and the City of Sydney.

Post-war Sydney: 1940s

As wartime austerity eased and there were jobs for all in a booming economy, a garden and a house in the suburbs came within an average family's reach, with a car in the garage, a job in the city and a new public school being built nearby for the kids. The parents of the generation who would become known as the Baby Boomers embraced all that suburbia had to offer and Sydney expanded pell-mell, with the pent-up demand for housing being realised on its fringes. The stellate railway system funnelled workers to the city centre – as did designated County Roads – but in the inner city, the main arterial roads were the old bullock tracks running along ridgelines, taking easy gradients and inconvenient turns around the idiosyncrasies of early land grants. Sydney's ad hoc settlement patterns were not readily compatible with the needs of mass car ownership. Roads needed straightening and widening, and the Department of Main Roads (DMR) – whose efficient engineers and road builders were not city planners – was in the ascendant. Their reports were sacrosanct, unquestioned remedies to the troubles of Sydney's burgeoning car ownership, traffic jams, and inadequate public transport planning.

In the bright-eyed post-war cities of Australia, the old was under attack. In Sydney, the inner city areas of largely Victorian suburbs and terrace houses such as those of Paddington, Redfern and Surry Hills, were characterised as slums simply by virtue of their age and condition. The *County of Cumberland Planning Scheme* (1948) identified them as 'almost totally substandard areas requiring replacement either immediately or within 25 years'.[1] Similarly, in Hobart, remnant Georgian areas like Battery Point were described as 'old and decadent' in the *1945 City of Hobart Plan*[2] and in need of healthy, progressive redevelopment. In the spirit of the times, the engineers responsible for town planning, considered that such inner areas and old building stock should make way for higher density redevelopment and for road building schemes to improve access from the suburbs to the central business district.

As car ownership increased in post-war Sydney, the arterial roads were increasingly inadequate, and while small widenings of Oxford Street and Old South Head Road eased Eastern Suburbs traffic congestion in Paddington, local residential streets were increasingly used by through traffic. The County of Cumberland Council planners noted also that 'Overcrowding is particularly prevalent at present, while space for light and air is obviously inadequate ... in addition to the hazards created by bad living conditions, there are those caused by fast traffic. This danger is enormously increased when the streets are virtually the only form of open space.'

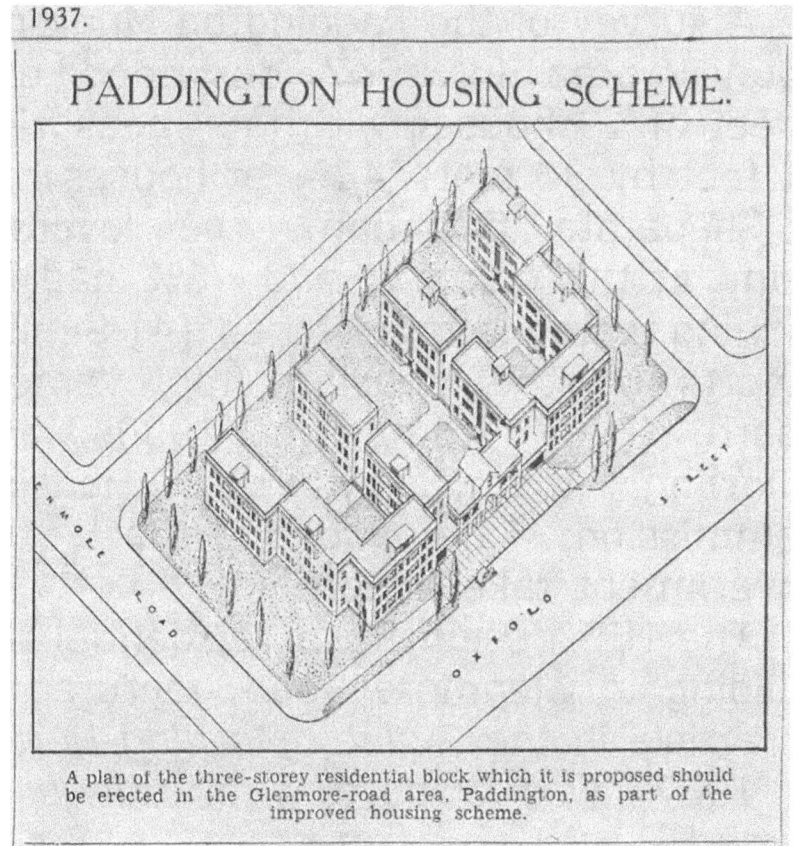

Figure 7.1: As early as 1937 plans for new residential flats in the Glenmore Road area were prepared as part of the Housing Improvement Scheme. Sydney Morning Herald, 4 May 1937. National Library of Australia.

Paddington was described as a 'completely substandard area of old terraces on narrow allotments. Narrow street patterns [with] considerable industrial intrusion.'[3]

A survey of the Paddington Municipal Council area in 1947 described one street of 19 houses with lots measuring 11 feet by 31 feet: '48% of houses had no separate bathroom, the lavatory being in the laundry; and 46% had no running water in the kitchen'.[4] Similar reports by the Housing Improvement Board (HIB) from the 1930s and following them, by the Housing Commission, demanded that the government take action.

The HIB design for a residential flat building in Glenmore Road, featured in an article in the *Sydney Morning Herald* in 1937, was a portent of things to come.[5]

In 1951 Sydney Council's City Planning and Improvement Committee approved a local replanning scheme to demolish virtually all the existing housing of Paddington and replace it with two to three-storey flats.

The Housing Commission wasted no time in commencing construction and in 1954, the Rehousing Scheme for Paddington was opened by Maurice O'Sullivan the minister for Health (and long-term Labor member for Paddington) and Clive Evatt, minister for Housing.

Designed by architects Davey & Brindley, these three blocks of three to four storey walk-ups in Lawson Street provided the type of flats set in open grassy gardens into which Paddington residents from 'substandard dwellings' might be re-housed.

The 1945 *Local Government (Town and Country Planning) Amendment Act* had created the Cumberland County Council which was charged to develop a county-wide plan to regulate and control land use within three years and to oversee the preparation of plans by municipal councils for local government areas. The County Plan took six years to prepare. The *County of Cumberland Planning Scheme* (CCPS) was gazetted in 1951 and designated the following areas as the County Centre: Pyrmont, Ultimo, Surry Hills, East Sydney, Darlinghurst, Woolloomooloo and the central business district. Within the area virtually any commercial development could be carried out 'with consent'. In an era of unprecedented post-war economic investment, the city centre was about to boom, with minimal regard for traffic congestion, environmental planning and social consequences to those living in the inner city areas.

For the Paddington area, the CCPS's land use zoning was mostly 'living area', allowing all forms of residential uses including flat buildings and neighbourhood commercial–industrial uses to continue. Ominously, a broad reservation for a regional road encircled Paddington, one of five expressways that would converge on the County Centre.

Work on the *City of Sydney Planning Scheme* began in 1947, and various draft plans were exhibited several times through the '50s and '60s. Although a basic zoning scheme was adopted by the City Council in 1958, it was not approved by the minister until 1971 and Interim Development Orders and amendments (one-off, site by site development approvals by the minister) flourished. As ad hoc development proliferated in the city, the state government effectively directed planning and development in Sydney through ministerial discretion.

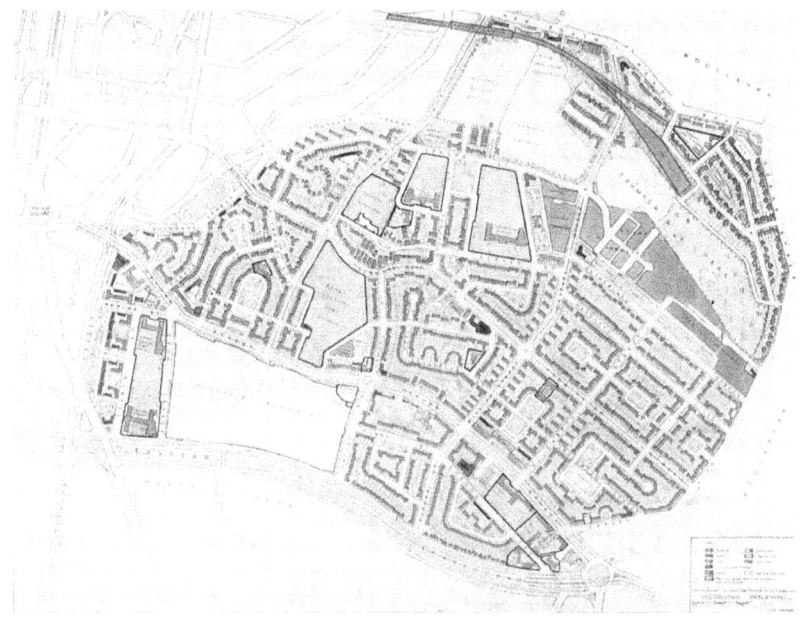

Figure 7.2: A comprehensive re-planning scheme for Paddington from 1951 by Sydney Council's City Planning and Improvement Committee. City of Sydney Archives.

In 1948 the *Local Government (Areas) Act* substantially enlarged the City of Sydney boundaries, taking in large Labor-voting areas, including the former Paddington Municipality, effectively supporting a Labor dominated city council until 1969.

The new urbanites: 1950s

Through the '50s, the loose fit of the CCPS 'living area' zoning was luckily not acted upon in Paddington, as very little redevelopment was financially feasible due to post-war austerity and the effect on land ownership of the *Landlord and Tenant (Amendment) Act, 1948* which continued to keep rents at wartime levels until the late 1950s. Sitting tenants were hard to move, so there was little incentive for landlords to improve their properties and less still to amalgamate allotments for redevelopment. Low rents attracted migrants, students, artists and writers – for whom more communal living spaces held appeal and the quarter-acre block in the 'burbs was neither attractive nor affordable. As Garry Wotherspoon has observed in his history of Oxford Street, 'since landlords could not extract any rise in rents nor evict certain tenants, there was no incentive to upgrade or even maintain the houses. Thus, much of the old housing stock fell even further into disrepair and decay.'[6]

Figure 7.3: Lawson Street Flats, 1954–55. The re-housing scheme for Paddington began with these flats in Lawson Street, built by the NSW Housing Commission. Photo: Lindy Kerr, 2017.

Seminal research undertaken by planner Dr John Roseth[7] into the urban revival of Paddington points also to a public dislike of the terrace house form, and the building life cycle as determining factors. Terrace houses built in the 1860s needed significant repairs to bathrooms and kitchens by the 1920s, yet many landlords had failed to invest, as the Depression deepened in the 1930s, and wartime austerity redirected property investment.

While the cottage in garden concept for suburban development was locally popular, Australia's massive post-war influx of migrants had found the inner suburbs of Sydney more affordable and attractive, with the proximity of friends and family, access to specific foods and the common experience of shared street life. Portuguese migrants found the cheap rents and boarding houses of Paddington appealing, so did Greek and Italian families. In 1947 in Paddington the proportion of European-born population was 4 per cent, but by 1966 it was 32 per cent.[8] Owner occupancy was also increasing in Paddington; from just 10 per cent in 1905, the proportion of owner-occupants was 62 per cent by 1966.

By the late 1960s, the initial influx of migrants was moving west, to the middle ring of Sydney's suburbs – the Italians to Leichhardt and Haberfield, the Greeks to Kensington and the Portuguese to Petersham.

Through the 1950s students, writers and artists had also found Paddington a cheap place to live: among them Margaret Olley, Donald Friend and Colin Lanceley. As few could afford additional studio space many painted from home.

By the end of the 1950s however, artists were being priced out of the suburb, although the art galleries that exhibited their works remained.

By the early 1960s, many of the older protected tenants were passing away, and with local light industries reducing their activity, a new demographic began arriving in Paddington. John Roseth described them as 'new urbanites'.[9] It was an influx of middle class professionals – some fresh from the experience of living in swinging London – who had returned home with positive experiences of terrace house living. They found Paddington to be a version of Chelsea Down Under, appreciating its proximity to the city as much as the bohemian atmosphere and streetscapes of wrought iron lace.

The gentrification process eventually comprehensively displaced the remaining migrant families and the working-class residents and boarders. The rehabilitation movement which began in the early 1960s – when Paddington houses were relatively cheap and ripe for rehabilitation – grew rapidly, and between 1953 and 1966, around 2000 of the 4800 terraces in Paddington were sold[10] to the new urbanites as owner-occupants. There was often significant repair work to be undertaken and sometimes a sitting tenant to deal with, but, Roseth's analysis of council records and Commonwealth census statistics indicates that by the mid-1960s investors and transient owners were also becoming enthusiastic renovators, with terraces in Windsor, Paddington, Hargrave and Sutherland streets particularly popular projects.[11]

With the new urbanites came a gradual change in expectations about neighbourhood development and heritage values. In 1953 one of the first local actions aiming to retain the residential scale and character of Paddington streetscapes was initiated by a relatively new resident, John Thompson, who challenged a long-term Paddington family who wanted to significantly expand their local family garage. Pursuing the case to court, John prevented that proposal, but in doing so became aware of just how vulnerable to unsympathetic change the suburb was.

Swinging Paddington: 1960s

While only occasionally would a larger block or group of houses become available for redevelopment in Paddington, by the 1960s the new urbanites were becoming increasingly concerned about the intrusion of medium and high-density flats. These had the potential to dramatically change the scale and character of Paddington's streetscapes. The first Paddington home of ceramicist Marea Gazzard and architect Don Gazzard had only recently been demolished and replaced with a redbrick walk-up, when in 1964, they chanced to meet with John Thompson, and were alerted to other threats to the suburb. On 11 August 1964, they called a public meeting at Paddington Town Hall to discuss the situation.

The meeting was well attended, and the inaugural Paddington Society (PS) president John Thompson wrote:

> ...we intend to maintain a central publicity campaign and

develop an information source for residents. We plan lectures on practical subjects such as how to make the most of our small plots and how to cope with the structural repairs of old houses. In due course, the architect members will be making available free plans and estimates on how to best improve home facades.[12]

Until urban historian Max Kelly's pioneering *A Paddock Full of Houses* was published in 1978, little had been written to draw attention to the qualities and history of the suburb. There was no established philosophical approach to conservation work. The National Trust of Australia was then still classifying only individual colonial houses and government buildings. The founding of a professional body with a clear conservation philosophy and a more objective approach – the Australian Committee of the International Council on Monuments and Sites (ICOMOS) – was still a decade away (formed, 1976) and its *Charter for the Conservation of Places of Cultural Significance* (the ICOMOS Burra Charter) was not published until 1979. The conservation approach and aims of the Paddington Society were therefore among the first to be publicly expressed and were concerned with preserving the suburb's aesthetic, historical, physical and environmental amenity; essentially its streetscapes of terrace house facades.

The Paddington Society declared itself to be non-political and non-sectarian and had a comprehensive series of aims to conserve and enhance Paddington and its amenity.[13]

Local historian Ron Johnson[14] states that the Paddington Society was the earliest formally constituted urban conservation body in Australia. The Battery Point Progress Association, established in Hobart in 1948 may beg to differ, but the Paddington Society archives record that by 1965 it was definitely an actively operating group. It offered advice to a wide range of resident action groups and amenity societies nationally and supported the formation of trusts and societies with similar ambitions. In addition, the Society maintained an extensive correspondence with professional planners across Australia and internationally as they developed protective mechanisms and guidelines. The combination of local planners, architects and activists that characterised the Society's membership provided strong professional credentials from its establishment. The Society's personal and professional networks were used to great advantage in the battles that lay ahead. The receptivity of the local member John Barraclough, to issues raised by Paddington constituents was instrumental in opening doors and ensuring that the Society's cause was heard by the state government in Macquarie Street throughout the 1970s.

The importance of effective publicity in establishing Paddington's heritage reputation more broadly was also well recognised by Society stalwart Pat Thompson. Enlisting media savvy creatives such as adman, journalist and later festival director Leo Schofield and interior designer and columnist Leslie Walford, local activists created memorable media campaigns to support the conservation strategies in Paddington and Woollahra.

Media fascination with the Paddington lifestyle was visually linked to its heritage values, and such exposure was fundamental to the Society's success in persuading decision-makers of the area's importance. The media access and high profile of its campaigners and spokespersons meant that popular magazines and television programs were always keen to quote the views of local residents such as journalist Ita Buttrose, entertainer Jeannie Little, adman John Singleton, designer Babette Hayes and model Maggie Tabberer. Collectively these high profile residents contributed to the aura of swinging Paddington as the place to live, work and shop through the 1960s and the 1970s.

By October 1964 the Paddington Society had a constitution – modelled on that of the UK Chelsea Society – with assistance from the son of a former chairman of the Chelsea Society who was resident in Paddington at the time. Membership grew steadily, initially with breakfasts and social events, but all too soon the Society had on its hands its first major planning battle.

A new draft *City of Sydney Planning Scheme* (CSPS) was placed on public exhibition in December 1964. It zoned most of Paddington as residential 2 (b), a zoning which although stronger than the previous class C residential zoning (which facilitated wholesale redevelopment), nonetheless permitted flats, and the draft scheme also included the Department of Main Roads (DMR) arterial road reservations. The reservations affected more than 400 properties in Paddington and West Woollahra and ran from Oxford Street to New South Head Road; one along Moore Park Road and Jersey Road and another via Nield Avenue and Liverpool Street. Together these proposals would have fundamentally changed the streetscapes and physically divided Paddington. Under the inaugural presidency of John Thompson, the Paddington Society established a fighting fund and a publicity plan to prepare a submission objecting to the reservations. A subcommittee led by architect Don Gazzard prepared a carefully considered formal objection to the draft planning scheme.

And so it was in April 1965 that the Paddington Society lodged its first official objection to the exhibited draft CSPS, opposing the roadworks and demolitions. The Society's submission also objected to re-zoning proposals which sought to permit opportunities for high-rise flat redevelopment. Significantly, it sought a special zoning to preserve Paddington's character as a special area of architectural and historical interest.

To publicise Paddington's special architectural and historical character, in 1966 the Paddington Walks began, led by Society activist Viva Murphy. The walks were a huge success and introduced thousands of people to the heritage streetscapes of Paddington, interpreting its history and forming a constituency of appreciation and vocal interest far beyond the suburb.

However, the November 1967 re-exhibition of a new version of the draft CSPS proved a severe disappointment to the Society. The road-widening proposals remained – indeed increased – and in spite of the Society's detailed submission objecting to the impacts of increased density, the residential zoning allowing high-rise flats was unchanged. A fresh media campaign was immediately launched and the Society urged that a public inquiry be held. Pamphlets were printed, public meetings held, petitions raised and presented to the Local Government minister, PH Morton. His reaction was to prove a turning point in the conservation of Paddington.

In the words of Don Gazzard:

> The Paddington Society insisted that the issue was a civic and administrative issue, and should not be regarded as an issue of party politics; the Society was concerned solely with the quality of the advice which had been given by an expert department to the Minister of the day; but piquancy was imparted to this attitude by the fact that a State election was imminent and the fate of Mr Askin's government might well depend on what happened in Bligh, traditionally a Labor stronghold, with radical working class and intellectual Paddo

comprising much of the electorate.[15]

Architect planner Walter Bunning was appointed as an independent commissioner by the minister (on the suggestion of Don Gazzard)[16] to review the road reservation proposals. He listened to submissions from 55 objectors, including the QC appointed by the Society to professionally present its case, and he reviewed more than 2000 objections. The evening television news featured Commissioner Bunning walking the streets of Paddington accompanied by John Thompson and other Paddington Society members to see the suburb for himself and to visit houses and talk to residents informally.

Commissioner Bunning's report found the proposed roads unnecessary and (although it was outside his terms of reference) he also recommended that the Paddington area be declared a precinct of architectural and historical merit, thus enabling its existing character and identity to be preserved. He felt that such an approach should ensure 'that Paddington will become to Sydney what Chelsea is to London, the

Left Bank to Paris and Greenwich Village to New York...'[17]

Although Bunning concluded that West Woollahra should also be treated as a conservation zone, he was unable to finalise the issues relating to the widening of Jersey Road, which had to wait until the *Woollahra Planning Scheme* was exhibited. He also recommended the establishment of an expert Paddington Advisory Committee to advise council on all matters relating to the precinct, and a *Development Control Plan* to guide development and change.

Commissioner Bunning's recommendations were swiftly accepted by Minister Morton who agreed that there were many sections of the Paddington area of historic architectural interest that deserved to be retained and rehabilitated with care and skill. Morton confirmed that west of Jersey Road would be zoned as a special residential area 2 (g).[18] This meant that future development would need to conform to development control policies and plans to be prepared by Woollahra Municipal Council. And most importantly he effectively called a moratorium on incompatible development in the interim, stating that 'until such time as the development control policies and plans are finally approved it is intended that development should generally be confined to dwellings and two-storey residential flat buildings'[19] and that a code should be prepared by council to allow the modification of buildings only if it did not adversely affect the general visual and social character of the area.

The Paddington Society breathed a collective sigh of relief that 'practical imagination had triumphed over unimaginative practicality', but celebrations were curtailed when, tragically, John Thompson unexpectedly died.

In May 1968 council provided a report to the State Planning Authority, agreeing with Commissioner Bunning's recommendations, but in August 1969 Paddington was transferred to Woollahra Council as part of a boundary redistribution.

However, when the *City of Sydney Planning Scheme* was yet again re-exhibited for public comment in 1969, the road reservations remained, and the Paddington Society yet again marshalled its forces for the next battle for Paddington. Two subcommittees were formed – the Jersey Road Committee to stop the road widening, and the 2 (g) Committee, which aimed to get the residential zoning right, once and for all.

Figure 7.4: Paddington Society president John Thompson (centre) and Commissioner Walter Bunning walked the streets of Paddington to speak first-hand with local residents during the course of the Jersey Road inquiry. The Paddington Society Archives.

The Jersey Road subcommittee's publicity campaign was without precedent. The slogan 'To widen Jersey Road is to destroy Paddington', encircled by a funeral wreath was produced in Leo Schofield's advertising agency and featured in media releases, local posters and full-page advertisements in the national newspaper of the day, *The Australian.*

Once again, the Society prepared professional, reasoned documentation. A QC was briefed to present its objections and when the public inquiry commenced, all along Jersey Road, balconies were draped with black fabric swathes, ribbons and wreaths. The citizen action march on 2 August 1969 was estimated to attract more than 1000 protesters. It literally stopped the traffic, and successfully attracted extensive media coverage.

In 1969 architect Walter Abraham was appointed as the independent commissioner. Abraham heard from 54 witnesses and again found that Jersey Road should not be widened but that it be extended to Queen Street, a road reservation that remained on the *Woollahra Planning Scheme* maps, never to be implemented, until it was finally removed decades later.

In September 1970, the minister announced that his determination was in accord with Commissioner Abraham's roadways recommendation, and determined the zoning along the western side of Jersey Road to be residential 2 (g). However, since Paddington north of Oxford Street had moved from City of Sydney Local Government Area to Woollahra Council's jurisdiction in 1969, the implementation of appropriate controls had to wait until Woollahra reviewed and considered its position on its new responsibilities for the whole Paddington precinct.

Stepping up the action: 1970s

The Paddington Society was all too aware that the bigger planning battle was not over. Who would prepare the new plan for the conservation of Paddington? The Society had experience in council politics, it had taken on the DMR and won (although the road reservation remained on Jersey Road and the DMR never released its consultant reports). The Society was concerned that Commissioners Bunning and Abraham's recommendations for a special zoning might take forever to be realised, so it was time to deliver the answer itself.

The Special Areas Committee of the Society knew it would need more research and a skilled professional argument to persuade council, staff and committees, as well as related government agencies and the community how conservation planning for Paddington was both possible and practical.

A comprehensive plan of research to identify best-practice conservation area planning in the international and national contexts began. The Society archives reveal much correspondence with planning organisations and consultants in the USA and UK, seeking advice on the management of urban conservation areas, consulting broadly with amenity groups and government agencies. Correspondence with other resident action groups including the Annandale Association, the Carlton

Association and the Hunters Hill Trust provided a national context and stimulated resident action group activity elsewhere.[20]

The Chelsea Society continued to provide input to the new Society and the advice and American contacts of architect and planner George Clarke (Don Gazzard's practice partner at Urban Systems Corporation) proved invaluable. Clarke was working on a similar conservation area planning exercise for Hobart City Council – the *Battery Point Scheme,* approved in 1969. This scheme appears likely to be the first conservation area planning scheme in Australia.[21]

Figure 7.5 and 7.6: The Jersey Road campaign saw protest banners placed across the suburb before the protest march on 2 August 1969. Figure 7.5 shows Jersey Road. The Paddington Society Archives.

Figure 7.7: Aerial photograph taken by the Department of Main Roads in 1968 and used as evidence in the Commission of Inquiry into the widening of Jersey Road, with red line indicating extent of proposed widening. Photograph, gift of Commissioner Walter Abraham to the Paddington Society.

After considerable research and debate, the Special Areas Committee[22] of the Paddington Society determined to prepare a plan to be 'presented to Woollahra Council as a public service, setting out the views of Paddington citizens for consideration when the final DCP is prepared by Council. It was hoped, naturally, that this would speed up the long planning process of eventually getting a plan and regulations to preserve Paddington legally incorporated into the relevant planning scheme'.[23]

Paddington architect Terry Dorrough was commissioned to prepare the research, and George Clarke offered to supervise the work on an honorary basis. Detailed surveys of the whole of Paddington followed, mapping building conditions and uses, building heights and sites of new construction. The analysis of the outcomes was careful and deliberate, and for its era, innovative. The study concluded that the listing of individual buildings within the Paddington area was unnecessary and that the best control would be to adapt the normal town planning controls (such as relating to land use, height, plot ratio etc) with details specific to the area. These could then be easily implemented by council's town planners. Instead of recommending a review of development applications by a special advisory committee for Paddington, the

Society's study recommended public participation, through the advertising of development applications, ensuring that all locals could be involved in the decision-making process.

This approach had a good chance of success in Paddington for two key reasons. Firstly, the threat of major redevelopment in the area was generally low, since the existing subdivision pattern was small scale and the residential zoning capacity was, by and large, appropriately low scale (with some exceptions that would require special attention in the future such as special use and industrial zones). Secondly, since Paddington property had become so much more expensive, most incoming buyers had significant self-interest in doing the right thing in terms of conserving the area in which they were investing.[24] The study concluded 'the popularity of the area has forced the price of houses up to such an extent that now only those people who really want to buy and live in a terrace house and restore it can afford to buy houses'.[25]

After months of study and committee meetings, in October 1970 *Paddington: A plan for preservation* was published, setting out the Society's views on the future planning and management of the whole of Paddington. The document was privately funded in its entirety and the result was a highly professional strategic planning document. The plan incorporated specific planning proposals that the Society advocated for implementation, including a one-way system of traffic circulation and recommendations for revitalising the shopping strip; and car parking as well as a tree planting program.

The plan suggested five key objectives for the residential 2 (g) zone: to prevent demolition of sound houses; regulations to allow rebuilding and filling in of small unused sites; provisions to encourage development of an appropriate kind on larger sites; and regulations to control the appearance of new houses and renovations. The plan also included land use regulations to prohibit undesirable uses.

The Society's proposals were exhibited by Woollahra Council in 1971 and the City of Sydney Council in 1972. However, it was to be many years before these concepts were statutorily enacted to protect the whole precinct. The onus remained with the people of Paddington to remain ever vigilant and persuasive with their neighbours whenever changes were proposed.

At the same time as advising on the development of the preservation plan for Paddington, George Clarke was hard at work on the City of Sydney Strategic Plan – exhibited on 20 July 1971. This plan established for the first time clear environmental conservation objectives for each precinct of the city, along with codes to control their density and character. The Strategic Plan included innovative proposals to permit transfer and sale of unrealised floor space capacity from heritage items in return for guarantees of their conservation; and the establishment of a Preservation Advisory Committee (PAC) as well as control of demolition. The PAC would assist in devising and implementing practical measures to preserve places and structures of architectural and historic significance; the terrace house clusters of Paddington, East Sydney and Surry Hills were specifically identified for such attention.

The state had different objectives and finally gazetted the statutory *City of Sydney Planning Scheme* the following day! The Planning Scheme (controlled by the minister) held all the legal weight. Nevertheless, the 1971 City of Sydney and Woollahra Planning schemes introduced the first positive statutory steps toward achieving urban conservation in Paddington. The scheme provided for the listing of places of scientific or historic interest but more significantly it introduced the 2 (g) (redevelopment) zoning for Paddington North.[26] The city adopted development control codes to implement many of the principles and objectives of the Strategic Plan and numerous subsequent revisions of the codes and updates and revisions of the Strategic Plan followed.

The Paddington Society in its publicity and publications had repeatedly drawn attention to the need to preserve the whole of Paddington as a unit, reinforcing Commissioner Bunning's recommendation to the minister for Local Government that 'the Paddington area ... should be declared a precinct of architectural and historical merit'. The South Paddington area, which had large areas zoned to allow flats, was one of the first sub-areas to be studied by the council. The 1972 South Paddington Precinct Study C4 resolved that future development there should also conform to Paddington North's 2 (g) zone guidelines and by June 1972 the residents and ratepayers were invited to a public exhibition of the South Paddington Action Plan. Fifty-three submissions were received, with a consensus being that the existing environment should be preserved and any future development of the area should be in conformity with a residential 2 (g) zoning. The South Paddington Action Plan was adopted by council in December 1972, and the State Planning Authority was requested to vary the *City of Sydney Planning Scheme* in response.

However, it was not until November 1977 that the relevant statutory document, Interim Development Order

22, was actually gazetted for South Paddington.[27] This was a delay of five years.

The West Woollahra Study also began in 1972,[28] with the preparation of a detailed conservation plan for Oxford Street and the Jersey Road area to change the structure of zonings and to remove the large areas zoned to allow flats and replace them with the Paddington, 2 (g) zoning.[29] At last complementary studies and controls were identified for the whole of the Paddington conservation area.

From zoning to detailed guidance

All too soon it became evident that the 2 (g) zoning needed some fine-tuning to provide specific guidance for new owners and designers restoring Paddington houses. Concrete slabs were replacing timber floors, the removal of original plaster to reveal fashionable chipped brick feature walls and the loss of timber cottages were early problems and controlling these activities was proving difficult within the existing planning provisions. The role of the council building inspector was of critical importance in Paddington, providing continuity and strict pursuit of conservation objectives in implementing the planning controls.

Over time, a range of codes, plans and policies developed smoother, more detailed planning processes, with the initial *Development Control Code for the Paddington Area* being adopted by council in August 1974.[30] This included a building materials guide that stipulated the use of masonry, retention of timber floors and use of vertical design elements.

In 1997 Woollahra Council proposed a heritage DCP to cover the whole municipality, but it lacked specific applicability for Paddington. Once again, intensive input from Paddington Society members on the DCP Working Party (notably Cedric Carle and Bill Morrison) provided detailed advice on specific controls for Paddington, which contributed to the 1999 DCP.

With each iteration of the DCP came further detailed guidance for owners, designers and council officers to influence and monitor the processes of inevitable change in Paddington, culminating in the current 2015 Development Control Plan chapter C1 on the Paddington Heritage Conservation Area, considered to be an exemplar of its type.

Arising from the community desire to preserve the continuity of scale and character of the existing patterns of buildings and streets that made up the unique streetscape of the area, these controls were initially two dimensional and fabric orientated. However, the provisions also allowed some additional 'historic area' uses such as antique sales, book shops and galleries; uses that were considered compatible with the tourism activities permitted in the precinct. But high rent galleries competed with and forced out the corner shops and convenience stores needed by residents. The recognition that more than the facades needed conserving led to controls on the scale and character of rear service wing extensions, and requirements to retain chimneys and rear outbuildings. Nonetheless, Paddington's distinctive back yard dunnies and service lanes all but disappeared.

Throughout these changes the professionalism of the Paddington Society was paramount, with some of Sydney's leading architects and planners providing key voluntary advice from year to year.

A large group of volunteers also provided ideas and worked on studies that were given to council pro bono – maintaining a major civic contribution and creating a national model for conservation area management.

At the councils, building inspectors and town planning officers drafted and honed statutory provisions that eventually became models used across the state for managing development in conservation areas. These included Margaret Harvey-Sutton, Meredith Walker, Stephen Davies, Warren Turner, Caron Mounsey Smith, Ruth Daniels, Libby Maher and Chris Bluett. The old days of planning by faceless bureaucrats were challenged as citizen-participation was demanded and included in the planning process.

The Paddington Society was one of the first community groups to actively engage in influencing town planning decisions, followed by the Balmain Association in 1965, the Glebe Society and Hunters Hill Trust in 1968; such groups drew upon astute local professionals, some of whom could also effectively access decision-makers. The planning academic Leonie Sandercock[31] notes that the approach of these somewhat 'elitist groups' assumed that 'institutions and policies change by persuasion and education'. Letters to aldermen, editors and MPs and associated pressure could work, and initially, such as the battles for Jersey Road, these methods were effective. However, they were geographically specific, and lacked the necessary power to stop large and immediate threats. It was the rise of the larger more politically oriented resident action groups (RAGs) in the late 1960s, and eventually the uniquely Australian Green Ban movement after 1971[32] that eventually convinced a new state Labor government to introduce legislation with conservation provisions; the *Heritage*

Act, 1977 and the *Environmental Planning and Assessment Act,* 1979. At a Commonwealth level *The Report of the National Estate* (the 'Hope Report', 1974) ushered in the Register of the National Estate and established the Australian Heritage Commission in 1975.

Although the Australian National Trust movement had been operating in New South Wales since 1945 it was not initially the area advocacy organisation it is today. Its classification system for identifying significant buildings started to include conservation areas in the early 1970s in NSW; effectively following, not leading, public opinion. Among the first conservation areas to be Trust listed were the Hunters Hill Urban Conservation Area in March 1974, followed by Paddington in June 1974. Like so many listings of the National Trust, these were confirmation of increasing community consciousness of threats to cherished urban streetscapes.

And so it also was with Paddington; following the findings of Commissioners Bunning and Abraham, public action and participation in its future planning were led by the community and monitored by them; it took over a decade for the statutory process to catch up. It was 1984 (following another detailed survey of Paddington's 4500 properties by the National Trust) before Woollahra LEP 24 was gazetted, replacing the 1971 City Planning Scheme and later Interim Development Orders. The finer grain detail of development control had been handled by a range of plans and policies issued in 1974, 1976, 1984 and a series of Development Control Plans (DCPs) in 1999, 2008 and finally DCP 2015. But how did these pressures and changes play out in the real world of daily life in Paddington? One of the biggest changes observable in old photos of Paddington is the opening up of its enclosed balconies.

No building or planning permissions were needed and these simple renovations created refreshed streetscapes, revealing the wealth of architectural detail, often hidden for decades.

When it came to entirely new buildings in Paddington, at first, infill buildings tended to be replicas of their neighbours. Adjacent building height, bulk, scale and materials provided the framework within which the designer worked and the approvals were made, but over time these principles were challenged.

Vacant land was rare in Paddington, and when a site on Hargrave Street came up in 1970, Society President Don Gazzard saw an opportunity to show how good contemporary design could fit into an established streetscape of terraces. Adopting the roof pitch of adjacent houses to tie into its corner position, and a broad verandah at its upper level, Gazzard used his signature Sydney School style and off-form concrete, in an approach very different from the imitative new development then prevalent. Gazzard wrote:

> The planning norm for new houses in Sydney heritage areas in the Sixties required that the design imitate the Victorian style of the surrounding houses. When a site became available in Paddington in 1970 I designed a house to challenge this view and demonstrate that as long as the scale, form and materials are sympathetic,

contemporary modern buildings can blend in with and augment the heritage context.[33]

The house won the 1976 Royal Australian Architects' Merit Award and today it is recognised as a milestone of infill design from Paddington's bohemian phase; it is now individually listed as a heritage item by Woollahra Council.

It is interesting to contemplate whether the Gazzard House would win consent today, or whether its form, scale and off-form concrete would be considered unsympathetic to the proportions of a traditional streetscape and the materials of a Paddington terrace.

Is the battle over yet?: 1980s

The 1970 *Paddington Plan for Preservation* was indeed a great public service. It provided Woollahra Council with the baseline document on which more detailed studies and statutory documents could be built, such as the *Policy for the Control of Changes to Facades of Buildings in Paddington and the Edgecliff Glebe* in November 1976. As further studies were undertaken, statutory processes developed and controls moved from protecting only facades, to conserving buildings in the round. The *Environmental Planning and Assessment Act,* 1979 introduced the current state planning hierarchy of state and regional plans and policies, with Local Environmental Plans (LEPs) regularised across the state and Development Control Plans (DCPs) providing the fine grain controls at local government level.

Through the 1980s, 1990s and into the new century, the planning for Paddington built upon the achievements of the 1970s, with the Paddington Society[34] continuing to lead community interests in advocating for better traffic management, assessing and objecting to major developments and reviewing and suggesting improvements for development control codes and LEPs.

Major battles were fought in the 1980s and 1990s, some won, some lost on specific sites, just as they were on sites throughout Australia as the economy boomed, then went bust.

As house values and client expectations continued to rise, the infill design controls for Paddington were being tested. Architect Alec Tzannes' first Paddington commission in Windsor Street in 1982 did not find favour initially with council assessors. The award-winning Henwood House, completed in 1988 caused debate about the appropriateness of contemporary design approaches in the conservation area. A debate that continues today.

Figure 7.8: Paddington on the cusp of change in 1961. The bright paint schemes and enclosed balconies of post war residents, and a rare vacant block in Windsor Street typify the planning and development issues that prompted

the development of Paddington's streetscape controls. City of Sydney Archives.

Figure 7.9: Paddington gentrified. By 2017, the balconies have been opened, the contrasting paint schemes retired and a polite new infill terrace constructed in Windsor Street, reflecting the guidance of Woollahra Council and the various development control plans, culminating in 2015. Photo: Lindy Kerr.

Refreshing the knowledge: 1990s

In 1995 Woollahra Council commissioned a 20 year review of the area, the *Paddington Conservation Report* from Warwick Mayne-Wilson and others.[35] Together with the

Paddington Townscape Study by Conybeare Morrison and Partners 1997, a new benchmark for detailed survey and analysis for Paddington was set, underpinned by Ron Johnson's field survey work and the *Thematic History of Paddington* completed in 1995.

Using these base documents, the Paddington DCP 1999 was one of the first DCPs in NSW to adopt the conservation philosophy embodied in the Burra Charter. It provided detailed heritage planning and building design guidelines for new development and for alterations and additions to existing development. It was just the sort of guidance applicants needed when proposing development in the Paddington Heritage Conservation Area, under the related parent LEPs (1995) and continuing into the LEP 2014 and DCP 2015.

Figure 7.10: Gazzard House, 88 Hargrave Street. Don Gazzard, a former president of the Paddington Society designed his own home in Paddington in 1970, demonstrating an approach to sympathetic design in the 1970s. Photo: The Paddington Society.

The DCP chapter devoted to Paddington is now a document of more than 100 pages continuing the clear philosophical basis of the 1999 and 2008 documents. It includes detailed guidance on every aspect of development in the conservation area from dormer windows and roof pitch to excavation for underground parking and swimming pools. These latter issues are evidence of the extraordinary increase in value of Paddington real estate, as is site amalgamation. DCP 2015 seeks to ensure that subdivision and amalgamation proposals respond well to the relevant historic character of Paddington and its historical pattern of subdivision and development. Successful site amalgamations are so subtle they are not generally apparent, with rear links established within existing built forms, and no streetscape change.

Not only does the DCP 2015 provide guidelines and controls to protect the significant character of Paddington, it also tackles the thorny problem of encouraging good contemporary design which responds appropriately to that character, with architect Alec Tzannes providing input about the appropriateness of contemporary design approaches. The DCP now requires applicants to demonstrate that contemporary design techniques, materials or idioms and design elements provide an appropriate response to the relevant aspects of the site's historical and physical context.[36]

For the rare larger scale sites in Paddington available for redevelopment, site-specific controls needed to be developed on a case-by-case basis. When the relocation of the Royal Hospital for Women was announced in 1996, the Society was once again swift to anticipate the need for a masterplan compatible with the Paddington context, and presented a plan to the Project Reference Group, which formed the basis for debate and eventually became part of the site master planning process undertaken by Stockland. The final design was evolved through extensive community consultation and included a new public park with frontage to Glenmore Road, constructed by Woollahra Council; and a commercial plaza on Oxford Street as well as through site pedestrian links and car access, but not through traffic, retaining community access without adverse traffic impacts.

A key element of the redevelopment project was placing low-rise residential units on the periphery of the site, protecting the scale and amenity of existing terrace houses on nearby streets and surrounding the proposed park. The concept also required retention of heritage items within the new development, including the gynaecology wing and the chimney stack of the former hospital as well as the gatehouse off Oxford Street. Additional height and floor space was allowed for the central and commercial development to offset the site area dedicated as a public park. The proposal was adopted by the Benevolent Society and forms the basis for the redevelopment seen today with the overall effect of creating amenity and uniting the two sides of Paddington by creating a sensitive connection between Glenmore Road and Oxford Street. The results are generally recognised as having fulfilled the needs of all parties, and again demonstrate the important contribution of the Paddington Society to the fabric of Paddington. A win for all parties.

Top down planning weakens wins: 2000–17

In a neo liberal era, with small government popular and in the ascendancy, the advisory role of the DCP is under threat. The legislated opportunities for certain forms of development considered to be 'exempt or complying', once again threaten the future of Paddington's streetscapes through small, cumulative and unsympathetic changes.

In 2012 the planning minister, Brad Hazzard, set out proposed planning reforms for NSW in a White Paper, and in particular sought to diminish the use of DCPs, which he felt had become overly complex and prescriptive: 'Because of some councils' desire to treat DCPs as statutory rather than guiding, it simply added another level of red tape and bureaucracy, which is acting to strangle getting the housing we need.'[37]

Figure 7.11: Challenging the Paddington development controls, the Henwood House

(1982–88) by architect Alec Tzannes presents the terrace house idiom in the contemporary form of the 1980s. Photo: Lindy Kerr.

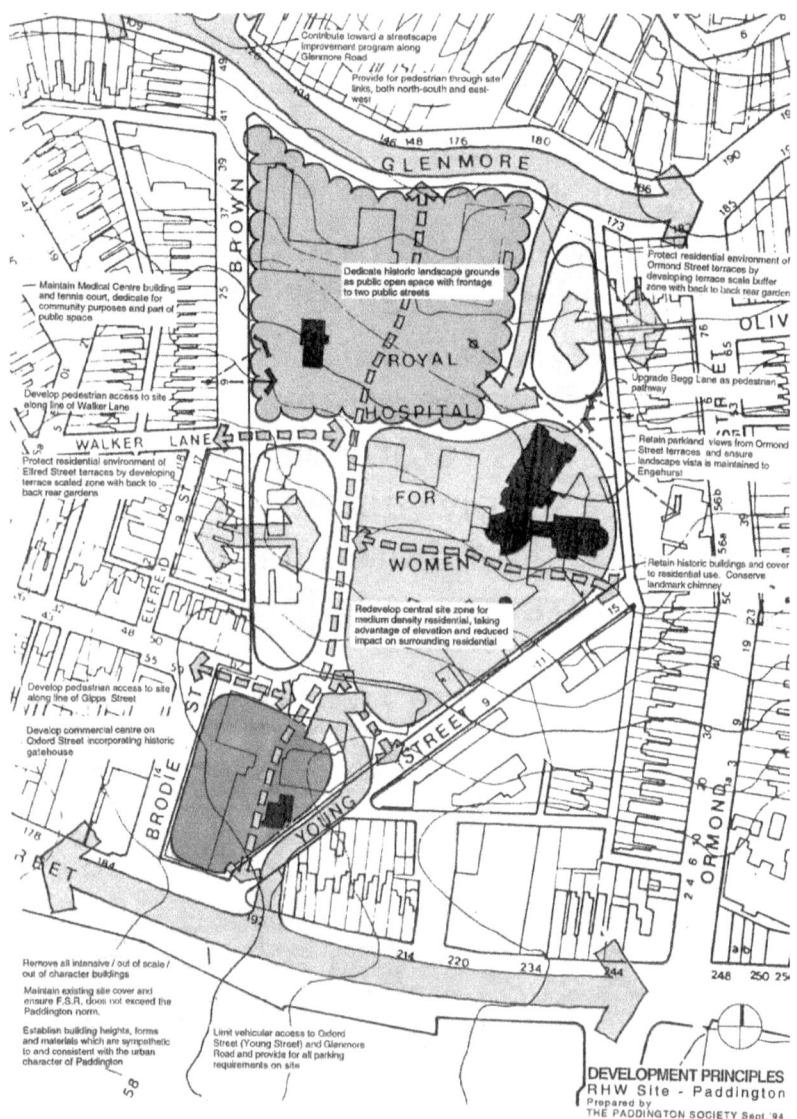

Figure 7.12: Royal Hospital for Women Concept Plan prepared by the Paddington Society in 1994. This established the development

principles adopted by the Benevolent Society for the redevelopment of the site of the former Royal Hospital for Women. The Paddington Society Archives.

The Paddington Society was quick to react, advocating that heritage conservation areas should be exempted, as they would otherwise end up as collateral damage. The Hazzard planning reforms did not proceed, but the reliance of councils and applicants on DCPs had been shaken.

The Paddington Society remains alert and constructive and its successes in earlier battles have not decreased its level of activity or vigilance. The depth of expertise within the Society enables it to continue its contributions to the conservation of a precinct of national heritage significance. Its engagement ranges from large-scale developments like the Royal Hospital for Women site, the St John's Church development in Oxford Street and developments at White City and the Scottish Hospital site, down to the small and increasingly rare timber cottages of Paddington.

Figure 7.13: Securing an exemplary outcome for the redevelopment of the Royal Hospital for Women site was a major campaign for the Paddington Society. The former hospital buildings were adaptively re-used and infill development compatible with surrounding streetscapes was designed by a range of architects. Photo: Lindy Kerr.

The Society has for more than 50 years dedicated itself to the conservation of Paddington for future generations. Through the Society, members have provided to councils professional advice and reports prepared by some of Australia's top heritage and architectural practitioners. This key civic service by numerous members is recorded in the 2003 profile of the

Paddington Society *It Never Stops Does It!* prepared by Ron Johnson. Through specialist subcommittees and technical reports the Society effectively delivered the specialist advice that consultants and heritage advisers later used when employed by councils.

Commissioner Bunning's and Abraham's recommendations have been fulfilled; Paddington is today a celebrated precinct of architectural and historical merit, its existing character and identity preserved. Moreover, the area is subject to planning instruments which recognise that 'Paddington is a living place which will continue to undergo change; appropriate contemporary design is encouraged and necessary if change is to occur in a manner which respects the significant characteristics of Paddington.'[38]

Figure 7.14: Redevelopment of the former Royal Hospital for Women site resulted in a new public park for Paddington. Simon Wood Photography, 2017.

Chapter 8

Bohemian Paddington

Sandra Hall

Sydney's bohemian tribes had a variety of homes before many of them began to converge on Paddington in the early 1960s. In the 1890s, Arthur Streeton, Tom Roberts and other painters of the Heidelberg School settled into Curlew Camp in Little Sirius Cove at Mosman to work *en plein air.* Others preferred the streets and suburbs of the inner city. A disparate band of journalists, cartoonists and illustrators clustered around Circular Quay, where *The Bulletin* had its office, with the Julian Ashton Art School nearby. And in the 1930s and 1940s, a second group formed around *Smith's Weekly,* among them the poet, Kenneth Slessor, who found his inspiration in Kings Cross, Darlinghurst and Sydney Harbour. But unlike the painters, he extracted tragedy from the beauty of the harbour's waters. His greatest poem, *Five Bells* was his response to the death of his friend, the cartoonist, Joe Lynch, who fell from a ferry and drowned.

Slessor and friends, together with the journalists, painters, actors, academics and students who came after them, chose their watering holes from an assortment of inner city pubs and cafes. Some favoured Pakie's, a long-standing club in Elizabeth Street established in 1929 by Augusta, 'Pakie' Macdougall, whose artistic connections were so impressive that she was able to call on Walter Burley Griffin and Roy de Maistre to help her with the decor.[1] And before they discovered the Russian restaurant, Vadim, at Potts Point, a few of the journalists who were later to write for Tom Fitzgerald's *Nation* magazine frequented The Lincoln cafe in Rowe Street or they joined the art students crammed into Elizabeth Street's Lorenzini's, a narrow espresso cafe-cum-wine bar which served a red so potent that it blackened the teeth of those who dared drink it.[2]

Others liked to mix with the businessmen and the wharf labourers at Jim Buckley's Newcastle Hotel in lower George Street. And 'The Push', the Libertarian group that grew out of the teachings of Sydney University philosophy professor, John Anderson, in the 1950s, claimed the Royal George Hotel in Sussex Street as their base.

Edgecliff, too, had its bohemian clan. In the post-war years, it gathered in Merioola, a mansion on the corner of Edgecliff Road and Rosemont Avenue. The house had begun life as a stone Victorian cottage but in 1911, the lawyer and businessman, Arthur Wigram Allen, bought it, transforming it into a grand Edwardian house with vaulted ceilings and an all-white ballroom decorated in an eclectic style combining the neo-Classical with the Oriental. It had Ionic columns, elaborate latticework and potted palms and its dimensions were generous enough to accommodate the reception Allen gave for the Prince of Wales when he visited Sydney in 1920.[3]

Allen and his family lived there until his death in 1941, when it was divided into apartments. Then in the late 1940s, it was taken over by Chica Edgeworth Lowe, who combined a bohemian outlook with an interest in real estate, and she let its rooms to 'paying guests'. Painters Donald Friend, Justin O'Brien and Francis Lymburner and the photographer, Alex Murray, all spent time there, together with Loudon

Sainthill, who would go on to a successful career as a theatre designer in London, and Jocelyn Rickards, the costume designer who would do the same.[4]

By 1951, however, the group had broken up and those who had not gone to Europe began drifting into Paddington, lured by the hope of being able to live there more cheaply than was possible in their old neighbourhoods.

Godfrey Miller was one of the first painters to settle there. In 1956, after being forced to move out of the loft he was renting near Circular Quay, he bought a house in Sutherland Street, surprising his friends, who had always believed that he had very little money. The view of Rushcutters Bay from his window found its way into some of his paintings. But it was the opening of the Rudy Komon Gallery in Paddington Street which established the suburb's status as a magnet for artists.[5]

Sydney's art market had centred on the galleries inside Farmers' and David Jones' stores, together with the inner city Macquarie Galleries run by Treania

Smith and Lucy Swanton. Then came the pair set up in Potts Point by Thelma and Frank Clune and their son, Terry with his business partner, Frank McDonald.

This was the way things stood until Komon's arrival on the scene triggered a radical change to the market's geography. He was a Czech, whose experience on the art market dated back to the war years when he had known many of Prague's painters and cartoonists. Among the etchings he brought with him when he arrived in Australia in 1950 was one by Edvard Munch, which he sold to the Art Gallery of Western Australia.[6]

Figure 8.1: The convivial Rudy Komon outside his Paddington Street gallery. Rob Hillier, A Place Called Paddington, Ure Smith, Sydney, 1970. State Library of New South Wales.

In Sydney, he complemented his career as an art and antique dealer by becoming a wine judge and cellar master for the Wine & Food Society of NSW. And in 1959, he bought an old McWillam's wine bar in Paddington

Street, promptly converting it into a gallery.[7] His stable of artists grew very fast, partly because he adopted the European custom of paying them a retainer in return for the right to sell their work.[8] Fred Williams, Leonard French, Clifton Pugh, John Brack and Peter Powditch were just a few of the names who grew to appreciate his practice of combining his skill as a dealer with his enthusiasms as a bon vivant. Lunching and dining well became an intrinsic part of the gallery's operations.

Figure 8.2: The Hungry Horse's Betty O'Neil with her stable of artists. From left to right: Bill Rose, John Olsen, Robert Klippel, John Coburn,

Stan Rapotec, Colin Lanceley, Betty O'Neil, Emanuel Raft, Robert Hughes, Leonard Hessing, Charles Reddington, Carl Plate. Andrew Starr and Jan Morice, Paddington Stories, Andrew Starr and Associates, Paddington, 2000.

While this was going on, Merioola's Chica Lowe had taken over another former wine bar on the corner of Elizabeth and Windsor streets and let the ground floor to restaurateur Madeleine Thurston for the establishment of a French restaurant, the Hungry Horse; named after an old rocking horse that Lowe had brought from Merioola. It had been placed in the hall and the tenants had used it to leave notes for one another. Now it stood in the restaurant's front window, and soon afterwards came a gallery, set up on the floor above. A wealthy Queensland collector initiated the project before handing it over to his manager, Betty O'Neil, an art lover who had been running a dress shop in the city.[9] She gathered a stable of young Sydney artists, among them Colin Lanceley, Frank Hodgkinson, John Olsen, Clement Meadmore and Bill Rose; the group formed a nice counterpoint to Komon's, which was dominated by Melburnians.

Paddington galleries multiplied and diversified. Senta Taft's Galleries Primitif opened in Jersey Road in 1961. Barry Stern moved out of Kings Cross and into Glenmore Road in 1962 and soon afterwards, Melbourne's Gallery A opened in Sydney under the direction of Max Hutchinson, Ann Lewis and Rua Osborne, who set up in a sandstone cottage in Gipps Street and devoted themselves to the abstract and the avant garde.

In 1967 the scene received another great boost with the arrival of Kym Bonython. Born into the Adelaide establishment, Bonython was a man of many talents and interests. He had been a farmer, a World War 2 bomber pilot, a jazz impresario and a racing driver – of speedboats and motorcycles – but art was a major preoccupation. He had a gallery in Adelaide and in 1965, he took over the Hungry Horse from Betty O'Neil before buying a capacious, light-filled building in Victoria Street, Paddington and opening another Bonython Gallery there. When Brett

Whiteley returned to Sydney from New York and Fiji, he was exhibited here.

Figure 8.3: Senta Taft's Galleries Primitif in Jersey Road was devoted to tribal art from the Pacific. Rob Hillier, A Place Called Paddington, Ure Smith, Sydney, 1970. State Library of New South Wales.

By then, Paddington was benefiting from something much bigger than a shift in the art market. The Vietnam

War had created a climate of protest among young people and with it had come the counterculture; a movement championing feminism and sexual liberation and questioning materialistic values and everything they represented, from the nuclear family to the nine-to-five job. The previous generation, with memories of the Great Depression and World War 2 still fresh in their minds, had seen Paddington as a slum, indelibly linked to the hard times that had marked their youth. When they had felt ready to settle down and raise their families, they had wanted all that was new, bright and spacious. In contrast, many of their children saw brightness as blandness and found monotony in the airy, open streets of the suburbs. If they had experienced the coming-of-age ritual shared by so many young Australians in the 1950s and 1960s, they had lived for a while in Europe, returning with a taste for antique furniture, heritage and houses with 'character'.

Paddington suited them very well and they went to work, shaping the terraces to their needs. They modernised bathrooms and kitchens, opened up the interiors by turning two pokey rooms into one generous space and brought in air and light by adding windows and skylights. All this was possible without compromising the integrity of the architecture that had brought them to the suburb in the first place.

Figure 8.4: Kym Bonython's Victoria Street gallery cemented Paddington's reputation as a place to see the best in contemporary Australian art. Rob Hillier, A Place Called Paddington, Ure Smith, Sydney, 1970. State Library of New South Wales.

Writer Patricia Thompson, and her husband, John, arrived in 1951 from Collaroy, where they had lived for seven years, enjoying the air, the water and the bucolic feel of the place. But John was about to spend six months in London as part of an annual staff exchange and Pat did not fancy staying on with two children in a house that had been threatened by both flood and bushfire.

They wanted a house in the Eastern Suburbs but those they liked were too expensive and they were getting desperate when they spotted an advertisement for one in Paddington. They had reservations. The suburb was still being written off as a no-go zone – the haunt of criminals, razor gangs, prostitutes, drug runners and alcoholic two-up addicts – but they were willing to take a chance, moving in two nights before John was to leave for London. Pat, who was blessed with an engaging sense of humour and a complete lack of pretension, later recalled their housewarming party when the guests tended to stand around in groups muttering to one another about the

Thompsons' bewildering move to a slum.[10]

Figure 8.5: Paddington's terraces and those with an urge to restore them inspired a boom in Victoriana. Rob Hillier, A Place Called Paddington, Ure Smith, Sydney, 1970. State Library of New South Wales.

Theirs was a semi-detached house, for which they paid £2800, realising later that they could have had a row of four or five terraces for just a little more.

Of all their friends, the only optimist was the author, Cyril Pearl. Failing to be put off by the rising damp, the flowered linoleum, the dim overhead lighting, the outdoor lavatory or the stained bath with its terrifying geyser, he remarked that 'Paddington was a natural place for the middleclass to come back to after its panic flight to the outer suburbs between the wars.'[11]

The Thompsons knew very little about the suburb's history until another Paddington resident, the author, Ronald McKie, ignited their interest with some research he had done. McKie had been a war correspondent in India and Burma but he is best remembered for *The Mango Tree,* a novel about his Queensland childhood. He and the Thompsons set about learning all they could about the suburb's first hundred years and a spirit of camaraderie sprang up between like-minded residents intent on restoring their houses in a style in sympathy with their Victorian beginnings. 'We used to compare our luck in finding a match for missing ironwork panels or discovering that under the thick black, pink, or nile-green paint in the parlour the mantelpiece was marble or slate. Regrettably, the painters who had rather liked living or having a studio in Paddo began to move out as our crowd moved in, possibly because rents tended to rise, or perhaps they found the aroma of gentrification a bit stifling.'[12]

A chance meeting with the potter, Marea Gazzard, in 1964 prompted the Thompsons to think of setting up an organisation to campaign for the preservation of the suburb's intrinsic character. Marea's husband, Don, was an architect interested in town planning and together they recruited other residents and held a meeting in a room in Paddington Town Hall. It was packed to overflowing and a residents' action group, the Paddington Society, came into being.[13]

By 1970, it had scored an unprecedented victory, securing the suburb 2 (g) status, shorthand for 'zoning as a special area of outstanding architectural and historical interest'. (See Chapter 7 for more detail.)

The campaigners were delighted while realising that they now had an aesthetic challenge on their hands. In an article headed: 'The crucial problem of not getting twee', *The Bulletin* magazine canvassed the potential pitfalls:

>...in any issue which involves individual tastes, as Paddington's protection and restoration does, it's difficult to decide just how comprehensive controls should be. For instance, a number of restored terraces have been laboriously stripped back to their sandstock brick surfaces, but in the eyes of those with purist views, this is a mistake. Again, many of the European migrants who moved into Paddington in the early 'fifties painted their terrace in colours that would certainly have scandalised the Victorians. So what happens? Do the purists have the right to impose their ideas on people who have paid a great deal of money for their houses and now want to renovate them in the way which suits them best?

Figure 8.6: Potter Marea Gazzard and her architect husband, Don, helped to launch the Paddington Society. Rob Hillier, A Place Called Paddington, Ure Smith, Sydney, 1970. State Library of New South Wales.

The Bulletin concluded that the Society's newly released report on the question was on the right track in opting for consistency 'without forcing a fake "old world" character on to new buildings' but it couldn't resist a final cautionary note: 'Its qualities can be enhanced with care, but they can be spoilt just as easily with self-consciousness. After all, spontaneity has been responsible for all that's best in the Paddington revival.'[14]

Six months later, the Society's policy was put to the test with a contretemps that crystallised the issue; once again, *The Bulletin* was on the case. 'Suburban guerillas' headed an article on the demolition of The Paddington Printshop. Standing on the corner of Gurner and Norfolk streets, it was originally one of the suburb's corner-shop buildings, and so, prized by the Society and its sympathisers.

The news of its destruction flashed around the village at high speed. According to *The Bulletin,* Patricia Thompson's hairdresser had telephoned her at 7.30am with the news, which she found difficult to believe, and a Society meeting was held that night. During the post mortem, it emerged that the building's owner, who was planning to use it as a gallery, had struck trouble during the renovations. He and his architect claimed that the discovery of a multitude of structural weaknesses meant that demolition and rebuilding were the only options. However, during the wrangling that surrounded the incident, it emerged that he had planned to finish the building with a mock-Spanish facade in keeping with the restaurant across the street. Tempers cooled during subsequent talks between owner and Society and the Spanish idea was eventually exchanged for a mock-Victorian facade with a balcony (as the building stands today).

The disgruntled owner complained that time and money could have been saved if the Society had asked him to make the change at the start. 'Pseudo Spanish, pseudo Victorian – what's the difference? It's all pseudo. If it had been a convict building with true, honest convict bricks, then it would have been another story. But that building was no older than the 1910s.'[15]

Patricia Thompson's answer to that resonated with her reluctance to assume the role of tastemaker:

We don't have a hard-and-fast attitude because that would put us in an antiquarian's position. We can't tell people what we want them to do or not do. As for the age of the building, I think that's irrelevant. Most of these corner shops were built in the 1880s or 1890s ... But the point about it was that corner shops are part of what architects call the Paddington streetscape. We think of things being harmonious, not antique.[16]

For a child, Paddington's streets constituted a playground that was fun precisely because it didn't look like a playground. The Gazzards' son, Nick, a teenager in the late 1960s, remembered that much of his spare time was spent dodging around the back lanes with his friends while waging war against rival gangs. Scouts and Police Boys' Club members were their favourite antagonists. And from the age of 14, he managed to persuade the publican at the Windsor Castle to let him in to hear the bands whose music accounted for the pub's popularity. He recalled, too, that motor bike gangs found their way to the Windsor Castle, jamming up the Saturday afternoon traffic by riding six abreast along Windsor Street.

Patricia Thompson had been right about some painters feeling stifled by the suburb's gentrification. In a 1962 *Four Corners* program about the suburb's change of identity, a grumpy Bob Dickerson told the interviewer, Michael Charlton, that he was moving out. The place had become completely bogus – overrun with people 'who don't do anything' and are just interested in 'living off people who paint'.[17]

The Melbourne import, Clifton Pugh bemoaned the constant distractions; too many for him to concentrate on work. Doors were left wide open, people sat outside their houses entertaining their friends. It was altogether too extroverted. Peace and quiet were nowhere to be found. And Frank Hodgkinson had simply decided that it was impossible to buy a house in Paddington for a reasonable price.

Figure 8.7: The Windsor Castle and the bands that played there attracted a diverse and fashionable crowd. Rob Hillier, A Place Called Paddington, Ure Smith, Sydney 1970. State Library of New South Wales.

Margaret Olley, on the other hand, was proving to be an enthusiastic investor in the suburb's property market. One acquisition was a terrace in Paddington Street with an old stable at the end of the back garden and in 1971, Gail and David Earle became her tenants. They were recently married. David was an anaesthetist at the Royal Hospital for Women, Gail was a theatre nurse and they thought that the adventure of moving into a suburb which hadn't entirely shaken off its raffish reputation was worth it for the convenience of living close to work. They found Olley a tolerant if unorthodox landlady, liable to call in at any hour of the day to make a cup of tea or ponder one of the many dried flower arrangements she had left in the house with a view to painting them some time in the future.

One day, Gail arrived home from work to find one of the blinds on the front windows shredded and dried flowers scattered everywhere. Realising that the couple's Labrador, Montego, was the culprit, she was still contemplating the debris when Olley walked in. After hearing what had happened, she told Gail not to worry about the blind. If she'd been cooped up all day, she, too, might have got bored and done the same. The best thing they could do was to have a cup of tea.[18]

For an art student, Paddington was the ideal place. Terraces made good share houses, part-time jobs were to be had in Paddington's cafes and pubs and the burgeoning array of private galleries made it easy for students to keep up with the work of established artists, some of whom were their teachers. Along with East Sydney Technical College – later to become the National Art School – there was the Bakery Art School in Paddington Street, where John Olsen and Bill (William) Rose presided. Juliet Schlunke, who was 18 when she went to study there, re-visited those years in a memoir published in 2016 with drawings and annotations by Olsen. Written in diary form, it gives a picture of a time and place in which drawing lessons, lunches and art openings were all of a piece. Olsen, it seems, was able to switch effortlessly between instructions in life drawing and tips on the art of preparing shellfish for paella.

Figure 8.8: The Windsor Castle, c 1964 with crowd on pavement. Robert Walker Archive, Art Gallery of NSW Archive, Gift of the Robert Walker family 2008, © Estate of Robert Walker/Licensed by Viscopy.

Schlunke also recalls a series of guest appearances by both artists and models, the most memorable being Gretel Pinniger. Then in the early stages of crafting her career as the dominatrix, Madame Lash, she had a sideline as an artists' model. Posing in black leather S&M gear with whip and high-heel boots, she concluded her session by demanding that all the male artists in the room put on a reciprocal display of candour by dropping their trousers.[19]

By this stage, Paddington exerted a gravitational pull for those looking for education as well as entertainment.

Architect Bill Lucas, a key figure in the Paddington Society, was compelled in this direction by a strong entrepreneurial streak. And he and two other arts activists, Mary White, and Lucas's sometime collaborator, the interior designer, Marion Hall Best, tried to start an arts centre in Paddington. It failed to eventuate but Lucas did arrange the purchase of one of Paddington's oldest houses, Sea View Villa, where his wife, Ruth, established Guriganya, a community school run along progressive lines.

Figure 8.9: Bill (William) Rose teaching at the Bakery Art School c 1968–69. Robert Walker Archive, Art Gallery of NSW Archive, Gift of the Robert Walker family 2008, © Estate of Robert Walker/Licensed by Viscopy.

Figure 8.10: For those who like to explore Sydney on foot, one of Paddington's great charms has been its preponderance of narrow streets and lanes. Rob Hillier, A Place Called Paddington, Ure Smith, Sydney, 1970. State Library of New South Wales.

And in the summer of 1968, a group of academic mavericks chose the manse of St John's Presbyterian Church in Paddington as the setting for their Free University. Lectures were scorned in favour of discussion groups on topics ranging from fashion to 'The Problems of Democracy in Australia' and the enrolment fee was a flat $10 with an instalment plan available. Bob Connell, one of the organisers and a postgraduate student in government at Sydney University, explained the policy: 'We're against the distinction between "teacher" and "taught", the feeling that lecturers have particular, god-like access to a body of truth which they dole out.' The examination, system, he added, violated human dignity, not to mention science.[20]

On a more commercial note, the suburb also spawned a fast growing number of boutiques and design studios. In 1969, Florence Broadhurst moved into Roylston Street with her highly distinctive line in wallpapers. Featuring flowers, birds and geometric designs, they were boldly stylised with vibrant colours, metallic finishes and a durable vinyl coating. And they had many Paddington residents reconsidering their conviction that they could exist only within white walls.

By then, the suburb also had a well regarded bookshop. In 1967, on the corner of William and Paddington streets, Angela Child, who was married to ABC radio's jazz man, Eric Child, opened The Paddington Bookshop specialising in books on Japanese gardens, contemporary art and, naturally enough, jazz. And seven years later came William and Nancy de Winton's New Edition in Oxford Street. A Saturday morning shopping trip could segue into an afternoon spent doing one of New Edition's Paddington walking tours or a session at one of the pubs listening to live music.

Figure 8.11: Pioneering bookseller Angela Child. Rob Hillier, A Place Called Paddington, Ure Smith, Sydney, 1970. State Library of New South Wales.

Figure 8.12: Exploring Paddington on foot. Actor Chris Winzar and friends Underwood Street, Paddington, 1966. Robert Walker Archive, Art Gallery of NSW Archive, Gift of the Robert Walker family 2008, © Estate of Robert Walker/Licensed by Viscopy.

Galleries, too, diversified with poetry readings, 'happenings' and performance art. In 1970, the Watters Gallery in Liverpool Street was the setting for a Contemporary Arts Society symposium on censorship in the arts. With an exhibition of Richard Larter's nudes as backdrop, it encapsulated the mood of the times. Paddington's creative community had been at the centre of the campaign against Australia's draconian censorship laws. Now, however, Liberal politician and *Bulletin* columnist Peter Coleman, was arguing that the campaigners had more or less won the day while the 'anticensorship orthodoxy' was carrying on as if nothing had changed, ready to support 'the most absurd nonsense' as being of artistic merit.[21]

Larter was having none of this. People who set themselves up as moral guardians, he said, were frauds for worrying about sex while they should have been worrying about starvation, napalm, pollution and exploitation.

The film editor, critic, filmmaker and generally film-fixated Michael Thornhill just wanted the chance to make up his own mind. Time, he said, was the final arbiter of artistic merit but it couldn't very well do its work if books, films and plays remained in limbo; unread and unseen.[22]

Meanwhile, on art's lighter side, Gallery A's stable of contemporary artists proved they were capable of making a pretty good joke at their own expense when the gallery held its Christmas show at the end of 1971. Billed as the '5c and Up Wonder Xmas

Show', the exhibition included 'Untitled Wall Sausage', a frieze of deep-fried sausages on silver paper, a marble cake studded with real marbles and John Firth-Smith's 'Dying Painting', which was swaddled in a blood-spattered sheet and sustained by an intravenous drip, with a wall chart showing its medical history (sad). The general mood of the event was wryly philosophical. Having realised that people don't buy art at Christmas time, Gallery A had decided to make them laugh instead.[23]

Film people, too, were finding a home in Paddington. In the 1950s, Mervyn Murphy, a Paddington local, bought a paddock in Young Street, site of a thriving two-up school, and in a shed on the land, set up the beginnings of Supreme Films. Sound stages and post-production facilities were developed and a variety of feature films and television productions were made there. *On the Beach,* Stanley Kramer's 1959 adaptation of Nevil Shute's apocalyptic novel, was just one of the international co-productions to be processed there.[24]

Local independent filmmakers also used it. Throughout the 1960s and early 1970s while the film industry was struggling to be re-born, many of those who would eventually make it happen were producing short films and much of their work was going on in Paddington.

One of the most experimental groups was Ubu, an underground film movement which came together in a Paddington share house in the early 1960s. Former Sydney University student Albie Thoms, who had worked in theatre, joined fellow film buffs Aggy Read, David Perry and John Clark to screen American underground films in their front room and went on from there.[25]

Inspired by Ubu, The Filmmakers Co-operative would follow, eventually setting up in a lane in East Sydney and providing a place for future feature film directors such as Phillip Noyce, Peter Weir and Gillian Armstrong to show their early work and in 1970, Thoms and Read worked with Martin Sharp and other artists in establishing The Yellow House in Potts Point as a gallery and forum for all that was innovative in the visual arts. Another stalwart was Roger Foley, alias Ellis D Fogg, whose light shows were part sculptural, part political and spectacular to the point of being hallucinogenic.

All of these events were covered by the independent journal, *Filmnews.* Edited by Tina Kaufman, who had been in on the birth of Ubu, it would go on to find a home in an office in Paddington Town Hall.

Paddington was also the headquarters of T&M Productions, a literary and cinematic union between Paddington and Balmain. Michael Thornhill represented the Paddington end, while Frank Moorhouse was the Balmain component. Their ambition was to interest a TV network in a series of short films based on Moorhouse's stories about Americans in Australia. As it happened, they made only two: *The American Poet's Visit* (1969) and *The Girl from the Family of Man* (1970). The first was inspired by a 1966 visit to Sydney by the American poet, Kenneth Rexroth, when 'a socially disastrous' party was given in his honour.[26] The other, *The Bulletin* reported, was about an American girl who had 'commitment' in the way that other people have children or hobbies that consume their conversation. With a seven-day shoot and a crew of just six people, Thornhill managed to incorporate the first of Sydney's Vietnam Moratorium marches into the action by bluffing Woolworths in George Street into letting him climb on to their awning with his hired Bolex.[27]

By then, the word was out. When Sandra Gross and her husband, Yoram, arrived in Sydney to re-establish the successful animation studio they had been running in Israel, they were told that creative people were gathering in two Sydney suburbs: Balmain and Paddington. Both were relatively close to the city and property was inexpensive. Lured by the possibility of water views, they decided to try Balmain first, but after they got lost while driving there, they settled on Paddington instead.

The terrace that they bought in Caledonia Street was just what they wanted. They set up their studio downstairs and lived upstairs. And to substitute for the art they couldn't afford, they hung their walls with Sandra's tapestries, which she made from offcuts from the carpet factory next door. One of their first pieces of furniture was a piano and during their first Christmas, their Italian neighbours came in to sing along while Yoram played European carols. This household embodied the spirit of bohemian and creative life in Paddington at the end of the '60s.

Figure 8.13: Parties were part of the Paddington streetscape. Rob Hillier, A Place Called Paddington, Ure Smith, Sydney, 1970. State Library of New South Wales.

Chapter 9
Creative Paddington

Peter McNeil

Margaret Olley, one of Australia's favourite artists, died in July 2011. She had become synonymous with the suburb of Paddington. As if to celebrate her art and personal energy, her estate left the downstairs lights of her home blazing, revealing the bright walls as well as her own artworks, including rooms she made famous by including them as subjects. Olley loved the suburb of Paddington. She could paint, garden and, entertain there from her large corner terrace in Duxford Street. She liked the art crowd as well as the young people working in shops and the working-class people who still lived there. She recalled that, as art students at the old Darlinghurst Gaol in the early 1940s, 'Paddington beckoned ... we knew there was something across beyond the Cutler Footway, but initially we dared not go there'.[1] Within a generation Paddington was teeming with artists and galleries. But the suburb had changed by the time of her death. With Olley's passing, had Paddington's place as the arts hub also passed away?

Creativity embraces literature, art, music, design and many aspects of business, and it also encompasses the everyday and the domestic, the ephemeral acts of cooking, gardening and decorating, as well as the actions of workers employed by others.[2] Creative artists have often been associated with bohemianism, which has shifted meaning and emphasis over time. In the 1890s it might have been bohemian just to be a writer or painter; in the 1920s to attend an 'Arts Ball' semi-clad or dressed in masquerade; by the 1970s much of Paddington debated feminism and the Vietnam War and identified with the counter culture. They lived in share houses or bought a small terrace if they could find the money. The 'musos', actors and DJs of the 1980s and '90s nearly always have a Paddington party story. The creatives of Paddington today are more likely to run an art space, architecture or design firm, engage in public relations and media, trade commodities, or be retired doctors or lawyers. In the Paddington–Moore Park area today, nearly 20 per cent of employees work in legal and financial services.[3]

But why have so many culturally influential people lived in Paddington? Located conveniently close to the central business district which could be reached by bus, tram and later the train link at Edgecliff station, its mixture of terraced houses, small factories, workshops and warehouses, provided cultural producers – whether they be artists or advertising executives – a range of multi-functional spaces and interpersonal networks.

The Paddington we view today: well-kept, expensive, well-heeled and with many trees, bears little resemblance to the Paddington of just 50 years ago. Paddington was once poor and shabby. Yet it was precisely the flexibility and charm – as well as the affordability – of this almost intact late Victorian streetscape that appealed to musicians, poets, artists, journalists, anarchists and 'free thinkers'. Much of the accommodation was transient and therefore flexible, which was not typical outside the inner city. Paddington's views towards Sydney Harbour or Botany Bay and its partly hilly environment also cannot be overlooked as a factor in its appeal. Anyone with an eye for beauty liked the vernacular architecture of mixed shops and terraced dwellings, and the sense of a slightly seedy Mediterranean hill town. The terrace house roofs run like the lines of a seashell up and down the Paddington hills and ridges, perfectly captured in a late work by Donald Friend. In an ABC documentary for *Four Corners* in 1962 the artist Clifton Pugh noted the visual excitement of Paddo with its cast iron and steep roads. It was full of life with the doors open and people chatting in the street. He said that Paddington had become so much fun it was hard to get much work done anymore. Other districts in Sydney such as Surry Hills have a mix of terraced housing and former spaces of artisanal work (albeit with a much higher proportion of light factories, which remained in use well into the 1980s). Glebe and Balmain were closer to the University of Sydney, and as they gentrified had large number of academics, writers and other cultural workers, but no other place in Sydney with the exception of Elizabeth Bay–Kings Cross in the inter-war years has such strong artistic associations as the suburb of Paddington.

Figure 9.1: Margaret Olley painting in the rear 'salon' of her Duxford Street terrace, 1987. Michael Amendolia.

Figure 9.2: Donald Friend, Still Life with Paddington Landscape, no date. Watercolour,

ink and gouache on paper, 70x104cm. Image courtesy of Sotheby's Australia. © Donald Friend/Licensed by Viscopy, 2018.

The compact nature of the suburb – it can be crossed by foot in about 30 minutes – the density of the Paddington 'footprint', the regular foot traffic through a maze of streets and 'dunny lanes', and the concentration of pubs, bars, restaurants, bookstores and galleries created a vital mix of people and ideas. From the late 1960s–1970s the artists, poets and writers were joined by architects, planners, journalists and publicists, from the 1980s by antique dealers and celebrity chefs, and in the 1990s by designers and 'start-ups'.

Figure 9.3: Millstone, one of two surviving, made of vesicular basalt with dressed face, from a water-powered flour mill, used at Barcom Glen watermill, erected by Thomas West, Paddington, 1810–1812. Museum of Applied Arts and Sciences. Presented by Mr Edward T West, Mrs EM Loder and Mrs AB Ellis, 1906. Photo: Ryan Hernandez.

Early creatives

Innovation in 19th century Paddington ranged across a wide variety of artisanal and technological feats which often involved the 'do-it-yourself' culture of semi and skilled workers as a result of necessity and at other times the high technical achievements of engineers and builders.

Busby's Bore, named for its engineer John Busby, for example, was an underground tunnel lined in sandstone that carried water from the Lachlan Swamps, now in Centennial Park, to a reservoir in Hyde Park. It was a major piece of colonial engineering some 3.6 kilometres long and 3 metres high in parts. The simply grooved basalt millstones from Barcom Glen watermill, the first such facility in colonial Sydney, developed by transported convict Thomas West between 1810–1812, near present-day St Vincent's Hospital, survive in the Museum of Applied Arts and Sciences.[4]

TS Mort attempted, but failed, to make an ice factory for the meat export industry in present-day Ice Street. The tracts of sandstone worker-housing ('Paddington village') developed to assist in the building of the Victoria Barracks from 1838, included myriad acts of quarry-work, stonemasonry, carpentry and glazing, conducted on a challenging site, mainly by French-Canadian convicts. Many of the famous vernacular men's Sydney cabbage-tree hats and public wastepaper baskets were designed and woven in Paddington by the soldiers' wives posted there.[5]

The wealth of the owners of the group of grand Paddington houses such as Juniper Hall, Engehurst, and Sea View Villa was generated by entrepreneurs working in the brewing, newspaper and other industries in the 1830s and '40s. Glenmore Distillery was the first Australian legal distiller (producing gin, rum, port and liqueurs) from 1823 (the site later became Servis Industries and the Hardie Rubber Factory). Paddington later held a Fosters Cycles factory, a coach works (Gordon Street), Marshall's Brewery and Glenmore Tannery and Soap Works.[6] As a contrast, Asian market gardeners laboured in the 'Chinese Gardens', marshy and increasingly polluted grounds at the bottom of Cascade Street. The land was resumed after 1891, reputedly 'in the interest of public health'.[7]

In the last third of the 19th century, Paddington housed a great many artisanal workshops. A number of professional photographers had their studios in Paddington. The photographer Alexander Brodie (b 1818) was a successful creator of stereoscopic views of Sydney with his studio in Sutherland Street from 1882 to 1891.[8] Well-known professional photographer Francis Whitfield Robinson, who photographed landscapes for the Duke of Edinburgh on his Australian tour in 1867, conducted a studio in Sarah Street in 1883–84.[9] William Francis Roberts ran a photographic studio in Paddington 1884–85 and artist Dorothy Hill, an illustrator, lived in Underwood Street in the 1890s.

Figure 9.4: Violin, wood, detail, made by Alfred Walter Heaps at his 46 Oxford Street Paddington workshop, 1905, printed label inside; 'Alfred

Walter Heaps, maker Sydney NSW Date 1905 No.54'. Museum of Applied Arts and Sciences Collection. H8580.

Dressmakers ran small businesses from their front rooms;[10] and drapers, hosiers, glovers, hatters, mercers, shoemakers and hairdressers engaged in their trades. A musical instrument maker, Alfred Walter Heaps (1854–1906), arriving in Sydney from Leeds in 1876, made some of the finest Australian violin family instruments at his 46 Oxford Street workshop.

In the inter-war years of the 20th century Paddington contained 'a lot of small manufacturing businesses employing people doing repetitive work in presses, lathes and assembly work'.[11] Such skills came in useful in creating billy carts for the annual Centennial Park race, in which the 'Pride of Paddo' c 1940 was many times the winner. Home-made of water pipe and a bicycle handle with a silver-painted tin body, it frequently beat the professional vehicles that also competed; a symbol of working-class ingenuity over the shop-bought toys belonging to the 'toffs' of Centennial Park and the City.[12]

SCIENCE AND LITERATURE

A wide spectrum of creative thinkers and writers were brought up in or lived in Paddington over the years: after all, Paddington was presented by its 19th-century advocates as one of the best laid-out and connected suburbs in Sydney and it had a largely middle-class and comfortable population until the Great Depression.[13] Literacy was supported from an early date. The Australian Subscription Library received a Land Grant from Governor Darling opposite the barracks. Literary events such as readings of William Shakespeare and Edgar Allan Poe were hosted by the Woollahra and Paddington Literary Society in the 1860s.[14] The feminist, social reformer and writer Rose Scott lived at the now demolished Lynton, 294 Jersey Road, between 1880 and 1925, where her Friday night salon included the author Miles Franklin. Emeline Carter, a soprano, lived in Cambridge Street.[15]

Scientists, doctors and psychologists also lived in the area, many with extraordinary lives. Walter Frederick Gale of Paddington discovered seven new comets and promoted the science of astronomy. Norman Haire (1892–1952) an Australian-Jewish doctor and sexologist (who departed Australia 1919–40) grew up opposite Paddington Town Hall at Morepo, 255 Oxford Street. Inspired by the writings of sexologist Havelock Ellis, between the wars he was considered one of Britain's foremost commentators on sex and birth control.[16]

Writers have been very prominent in Paddington. Ethel Turner lived in Erang at 465 Oxford Street, Paddington, where she had moved in 1881 as a child; she and her sister Lilian started the literary magazine *Parthenon* there and she famously published *Seven Little Australians* in 1894.

Literary figure Bertram Stevens, co-founder of the major periodicals *Art in Australia* and *The Home,* lived at 65 Glenmore Road in the late 1890s.[17] Kylie Tennant, famous for her word pictures of Depression life and the contrasts of rich and poor lived at 178 Windsor Street.[18] Novelist Dorothy Hewett lived in a room at 25 Moncur Street Woollahra in 1949 (later described in the poem *In Moncur Street*). Her 1959 novel *Bobbin Up* includes the subject of sisters living in an attic on Oxford Street, surrounded by the allure of nearby modernity but the trappings of a down-at-heel Victorian setting:

> Oxford St lapped them round with promises, lured them with impossible dreams ... the whirl of lights, the purr of cars, the distant, velvety roar of the city, haloed with gold ... old, two-storey semis, scabrous with flaky plaster, dim with paperwork baskets of asparagus fern & baked geraniums. The tattered, rusty lace of an iron balcony curved over the street...

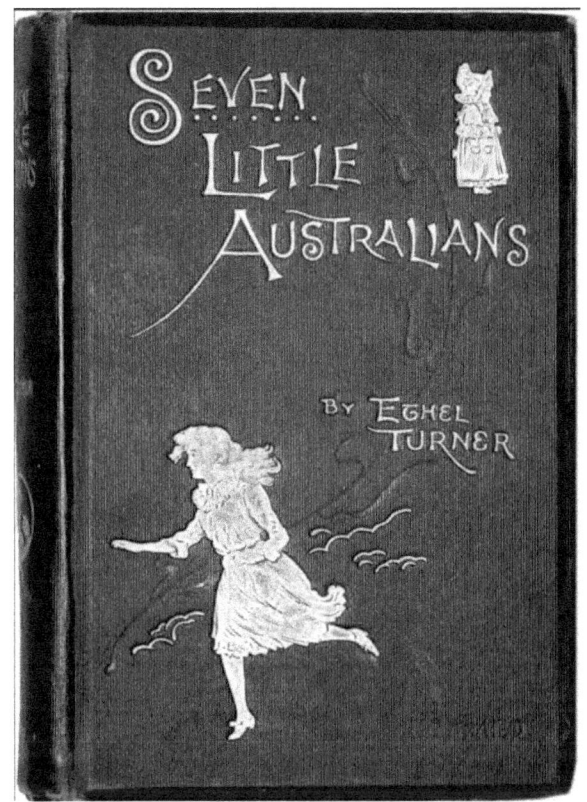

Figure 9.5: Ethel Turner, Seven Little Australians, 1903 edition, cover design. Turner lived in Oxford Street before she published Seven Little Australians in 1894.

Other famous writers including AB Paterson, Dorothea MacKellar and Kenneth Slessor lived in adjacent Woollahra. The poet Mary Gilmore lived at 96 Glenmore Road around 1916.[19] Cyril Pearl (1904–87), who was an editor of the *Daily Telegraph* and then the *Sunday Telegraph* from 1936 to

1941, lived part of his life in Paddington. Well before artists arrived in the area from the mid-1950s, a significant 'back story' of creatives existed in Paddington – people working across visual, literary, journalistic, craft, science and musical industries.

Bohemian culture

Most of the Bohemians of 1920s and 1930s Sydney lived and socialised in lodgings near Central Station, in the flats of Kings Cross or boarding houses of Woolloomoloo. The terrace house was described by many of them in negative terms, as repetitious and ominous.[20] The 'Alps of Darlinghurst', as poet Kenneth Slessor dubbed the area, is visible from parts of Paddington, a reminder of how the quarters of a city are linked to others in both everyday life and also the imagination.

Famous eccentrics grew up in and frequented Paddington. Les Robinson (1886–1968), writer, was born there, later becoming infamous for inhabiting harbour-side caves. The major Australian Symbolist poet Christopher Brennan

(1870–1932) lived at several addresses in Paddington.[21] He was also a University of Sydney lecturer, orator and one of the 'wonders of Sydney', with a strong interest in psychology and sexuality; an alcoholic and complex personality, he died in poverty. One of his poems refers to the contrast between his life and the view down towards the modest Chinese gardens adjacent to Rushcutters Bay, making use of the racist language of the day:

Figure 9.6: Dulcie Deamer, Paddington resident, novelist and bohemian, in her attire for the Artists' Ball, 1923. Photo: Swiss Studios. State Library of New South Wales.

This house of ours is pitch'd upon the utmost spur of Paddington poking its nose among the Chows that till their cabbages in rows where rushes erst were cut and reeds.

Lure of the inner city

Paddington residents always had a strong sense of place, whether they were artists, writers or everyday people. A resident from the 1930s recounted the feel of Paddington thus:

> With gentle slopes leading down to the Harbour foreshores, Paddington was ideally provided with a dress circle setting to view the construction of the Sydney Harbour Bridge. She was fairly nonchalant about it – after all – she had Centennial park for her front garden and Victoria Barracks to defend her against the 'Razor Gang Push' who were making their nasty presence felt in adjoining suburbs – too close for comfort.[22]

Oral histories of Paddington describe a suburb that was once very rough but also enterprising. It included a network of sly grog shops and premises for illegal betting and prostitution including notorious razor gang leader Tilly Devine who ran various brothels in Paddington as well as Surry Hills. Following the Depression, men hawked chokos in billy carts and sold rabbits and self-caught sea-fish door to door.[23] Men and women ran illegal 'SP' booking shops from terrace houses and two-up games were conducted near the rubbish pits of Trumper Park. Many locals walked to work. The low-lying parts of the Paddington basin near Boundary Street held numerous light industries: 'Lustre Hosiery' manufacturing silk stockings, 'Zyp' soft drinks in Roylston Street, the Yellow Cab Company garage and workshop and Advanx Tyres in Neild Avenue (the latter now upmarket apartments). There were many tensions in the Paddington of the day: when in the 1930s a Russian national opened a hairdressing shop in Oxford Street that undercut other traders' prices, a brick was thrown through the window every night until the discounting stopped.[24]

Figure 9.7: Portrait of Christopher Brennan smoking a pipe. Black and white photograph, no date. National Library of Australia. Trove <trove.nla.gov.au/work/20287356>.

Since at least the time of Henry Lawson the Australian inner city had been presented as a melancholy space, with reference to the poverty, repetition and dehumanisation of industrial society.

Christopher Brennan wrote of inner city Sydney thus:

> The yellow gas is fired from street to street past rows of heartless homes and hearths unlit, dead churches, and the unending pavement beat by crowds – say rather haggard shades that flit...[25]

The inner city looked a bit of a mess. In the 1950s–1960s Paddington had few trees, many buildings were poorly maintained, with peeling paint, dilapidated plaster ornaments and enclosed balconies. Patrick White's *The Vivesector* (1970), although not set specifically in Paddington, painted a word picture of the urban condition in his typically acerbic fashion:

> Here the clothes-lines and corrugated iron took over; ladies called to one another over collapsing paling fences. There was a mingled smell of poor washing, sump oil, rotting vegetables, goatish male bodies, soggy female armpits.

Clive James, who went to the Paddington campus of Sydney Technical High School in Albion Street in the

1950s described it in similar terms: 'The only paint (on terrace houses) on show was kack brown and the cast iron balconies looked like scrap metal waiting to be taken away.'[26] Paddington resident, activist and writer Patricia Thompson described the new pastel colours introduced by post-war migrants in the following way:

> I well remember the Lebanese passion for mauve. Other new owners ripped off the ironwork from the balcony and replaced it with asbestos sheeting or plywood ... Such houses looked like respectable old ladies done up as tarts, though the kaleidoscope effect was considerably more cheerful than the previous monotonous brown with black trim.[27]

In photographs of the 1960s and 1970s the area looks stark and quiet, with light or infrequent vehicular traffic. Artists capitalised on these streetscapes with their 'ready-made surrealism', as some of them had done previously in the neglected gold rush towns of the Central Tablelands, often depicting the suburb as unpeopled or populated by shadows. Sali Herman's street scenes of Paddington in the 1940s suggested the quiet solidarity of working-class neighbours.

Paddington was often depicted as fairly empty of people, a complete contrast to today's bustling cafes and shops. The black and white photographs of David Moore from the 1940s focus on the scenographic Paddington streetscape with its abstract contrasts of light and shade. Douglas Dundas, head teacher of painting at nearby East Sydney Technical College from 1938–60 painted a surreal dream-like streetscape around 1960 with a woman walking in her nightgown through empty streets.[28] He may well have been recalling the many local characters, including an old lady in Underwood Street who had not left her home in years and was visited regularly by her son bringing food, and a disabled boy wheeled around the area by his mother in a home-made contraption.[29] This atmosphere with connotations of Jungian psychology (emphasising the unconscious mind) pervaded much of the art of the so-called 'Charm School'.

David Strachan, a painter of surreal and melancholy landscapes and still-lifes had returned from many years of studying Carl Jung in London and Zurich in 1960, and lived at addresses in Paddington Street from 1963 until his untimely death in a car accident in 1970.[30] Photographs of Strachan's terrace depict his collection of art and antiques in the gently restored front rooms and kitchen. Margaret Olley, who greatly mourned his death, was permitted to continue using his terrace as her painting studio and she painted some beautiful still-lifes there. Strachan's residence remains in the family and is relatively intact.

Figure 9.8: Sali Herman, Saturday Morning 1948. Oil on plywood. 38.8x51.4cm. National Gallery of Australia. NGA 72.472. © Sali Herman/Licensed by Viscopy, 2018.

Residents of historic Juniper Hall on Oxford Street (then cut up into 14 flats) included members of the art world including art historian Daniel Thomas, gallerist Kerry Crowley, curator Nicholas Draffin, Asian art specialist Jackie Menzies, environmentalist David Mussared, cartoonist Bruce Petty, architect Francesca Morrison and journalist Julie Rigg. Guy Morrison, journalist, lived nearby.[31] Interviewees recollect the older set of artists, even if they did not know them personally. This sense of the generations interacting is important in Paddington, which is often recollected as a series of layers or palimpsests.

Jackie Menzies, former curator of Asian art at the Art Gallery of New South Wales, notes that the 'artistic' nature of Paddington as well as its flexible and transient housing attracted young people there in the 1960s and 1970s.[32] In many cases artists, writers, activists and journalists moved into the area through their contacts and friendship networks. Paddington provided modest but flexible accommodation with good northern light favoured by artists, cool afternoon breezes in a period before air-conditioning, easy access to inexpensive corner shops, pubs and bars, a short ride to the city, as well as a European sense of foot traffic. TV celebrity Jeannie Little commented that Paddington was surprisingly safe by the 1970s. The trendy inhabitants were mixed up with everyone else including bikers and 'little old ladies'; the suburb 'brings people down to earth', she noted.[33] The flexibility of the shop-front terraces (many owners lived behind or above their shops) saw some artists exhibit their work in their own premises: the Patricia Englund Gallery at 2 Cascade Street in the 1960s showed Patricia and Ivan Englund's important stoneware pottery, bowls, wine jars and blossom jars with their Japanese tenor.[34]

During the first few decades of the 20th century, many creative individuals found the stringent censorship and the minimal arts infrastructure in Australia too challenging. Others such as artist and curator Bill Wright later found Australia 'narrow-minded, passively racist and in compound historic denial' (concerning the plight of Indigenous Australians).[35] Many felt they had to leave the country and become expatriate. They included the writer Patrick White and the artist Roy de Maistre. However, around 1965 many creative practitioners began to return home from centres including London, Paris and New York. A great many artists chose to live in Paddington from the 1950s, and many fortunate enough to have purchased a terrace before the

1990s still do so. Susan Baird, a Hill End artist, resides in George Street. Ceramicist Roswitha Wulff has lived in her Prospect Street terrace for 45 years. She built a gas-fired kiln in the back yard and the noise of her preparing clay prompted her neighbours to enquire if she were a 'female butcher'.[36]

Returning expatriate Australians often chose to live in Paddington. The glamorous Alleyne Clarice Zander (1893–1958), painter and gallerist, had been on painting trips in Europe with Olley and Strachan and lived in Paddington from 1956 after returning from London. Peggy Glanville-Hicks (1912–90) was a leading cosmopolitan notable in world music, artistic collaboration and criticism and one of the first women to compose opera (*Sappho*). She studied folk, Greek and Hindu music among others and returned to Australia in 1975 after living mainly in Greece and the USA. Her Paddington residence at 45 Ormond Street was bequeathed 'as a haven for composers'[37] within the Peggy Glanville-Hicks Composers' Trust.[38]

National Art School students lived nearby in the impressive but dilapidated three part terrace Sobraon (17–21 Ormond Street). The area was vital and not as predictable as other parts of Sydney; energised by the dynamism of the young and the eccentric. The Claremont Theatre Group of Melbourne performed in old churches in Paddington circa 1973[39] and Carnaby Street and 'mod' fashions were de rigueur for many.

Many Paddington artists trained or worked at East Sydney Technical College, later to become the National Art School, behind the old Court House at Taylor Square. Godfrey Miller, who taught life drawing at 'Tech', had a private income and lived as a near recluse in Paddington. Others worked at nearby Alexander Mackie, later College of Fine Arts and now UNSW Art and Design. Paddington as an inner city area with like-minded people created a comfortable zone in which to live and thrive. They generally rebelled against what Kirkpatrick has called the 'Anglophilic suburbanism' that was seen to characterise Australian cities.[40]

Instead they liked the historic architecture, proximity to the city and the visible lives taking place through open doors and windows.

Mid-century art

Between 1959 and 1966 nearly half of Paddington terraces changed hands.[41] Corner shops and stone-built terraces in the area around Gipps Street (some quite large) began to be renovated as a new building type: the art gallery. The 1960s Sydney art scene saw a massive expansion of commercial art dealing following a period in which a few large galleries such as Macquarie and David Jones Gallery dominated the trade. The rise of art dealing, the concept of art as investment, and a shift of private galleries from the city to Paddington created a wholly new atmosphere in the area as an 'arts hub'. By the 1980s 40 private galleries had been established, although some were very small. At the time of writing there are about 20 commercial art galleries in Paddington.

Figure 9.9: Peggy Glanville-Hicks at her Ormond Street home in 1982. Sydney Morning Herald, 3 December 2011.

Viennese-born Rudy Komon, knowing his buyers were in the Eastern Suburbs, opened his famous eponymous gallery on the site of a former wine shop (appropriate as he was also a great wine expert) at the corner of Paddington Street and Jersey Road in 1959. He pioneered in Australia the concept of retainers to keep artists bonded or loyal to one dealer. Founder of the Wine & Food Society of NSW, he provided much of the continental bon vivant image of Paddington and its art scene, which continues to this day in the ambience and art collection of Lucio's restaurant.

Another prominent Paddington gallery was established by Barry Stern in 1961 at 28 Glenmore Road (close to the Oxford Street intersection). Geoffrey Legge of the Watters gallery (run with Frank Watters) was an accountant inspired to enter the profession after living next door to Barry Stern. Nearby at 21 Gipps Street the highly influential Gallery A was established in 1964 by Max Hutchinson, Rua Osborne and Ann Lewis. The gallery specialised in hard-edge, abstract expressionism and related forms and represented emerging forces such as Rosalie Gascoigne, Janet Dawson, John Firth-Smith, Richard

Dunn, Robert Klippel, Frank Hinder, Ralph Balson and Peter Powditch. Hutchinson would later act as an agent for the sale of Jackson Pollock's *Blue Poles* to the National Gallery of Australia.

Arts patron Chandler Coventry opened his avant-garde Coventry Gallery at 38 Hargrave Street in 1970 and moved to purpose-built premises designed by Rollin Schlicht of Allen Jack+Cottier at 56 Sutherland Street in 1974. Described by James Mollison, the inaugural director of the National Gallery of Australia, as one the most important collectors of contemporary Australian Art, Coventry represented the formative periods of artists such as Gunter Christmann, Michael Taylor and Dick Watkins.

Art was also freely taught in Paddington. The Bakery Art School was managed by Bill (William) Rose, Janet Dawson and John Olsen from 1968–1970 as an alternative to 'tech school', the East Sydney Technical College, now the National Art School. It welcomed young students whose studies were subsidised by the fees paid by wealthier women known as the 'Bay Ladies' (referring to Double Bay, Rose Bay etc). Olsen introduced the students to European artists unfamiliar in Sydney such as Egon Schiele, and cooked European dishes for them once a week. The focus was on disciplined abstraction, with artists such as David Aspden and Peter Upward coming in to teach.[42]

Another Austrian émigré was Gisella Scheinberg, who ran the Holdsworth Galleries (1969–96) in a former factory in nearby Woollahra. In the 1970s she exhibited artists associated with the Sydney 'Charm School'[43] and Hill End, including Donald Friend, Margaret Olley and Jean Bellette. Bonython Galleries, which showed the work of Brett Whiteley, opened first upstairs on the site of the Hungry Horse and later in a larger space in Victoria Street, Paddington from 1967–76. The space was then adapted as an advertising agency by John Singleton. As Humphrey McQueen notes, many artists also worked for advertising agencies.[44] Clive Evatt opened Hogarth Galleries in Walker Lane in 1972. Originally showing contemporary international art, it later focused on Aboriginal bark paintings as art, not ethnography, and in the 1990s, significant Indigenous contemporary artists including Destiny Deacon.

Figure 9.10: Opening of Colin Lanceley exhibition, Gallery A, Paddington, 1965. Robert Walker Archive, Art Gallery of New South Wales Archive. AGNSW Gift of the Robert Walker family, 2008. © Robert Walker/Licensed by Viscopy, 2018.

Figure 9.11: William Rose painting at the Bakery life drawing class, Paddington, c 1968–69. Robert Walker Archive, Art Gallery of New South Wales Archive. © Estate of the Robert Walker family, image courtesy of Thames and Hudson. © Robert Walker/Licensed by Viscopy, 2018.

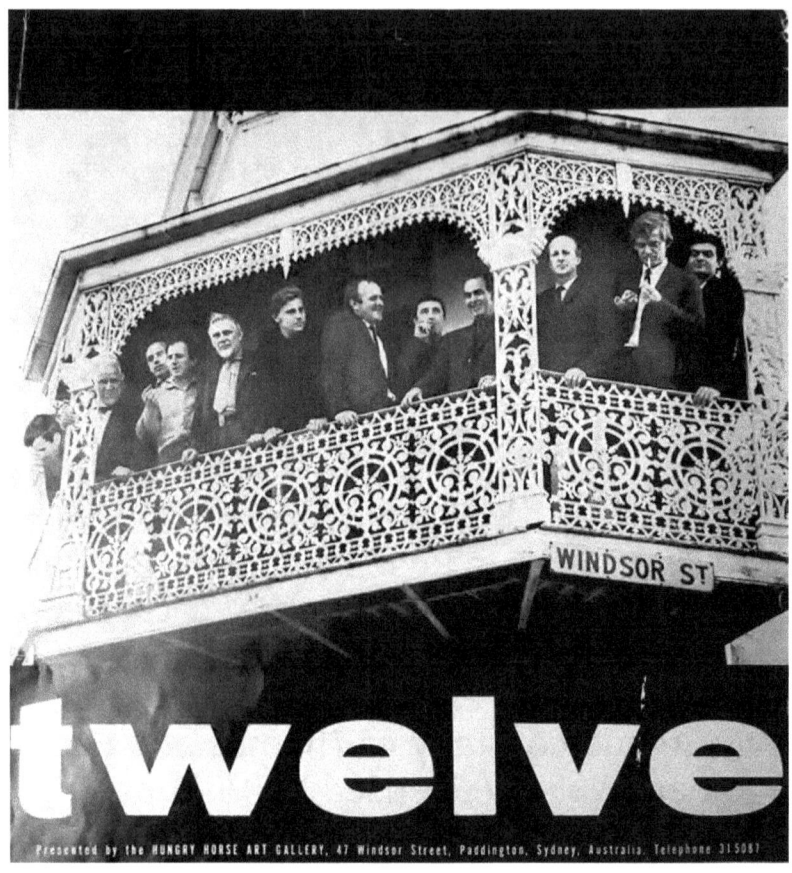

Figure 9.12: From left to right: Painters Frank Hodgkinson, Stanislaus Rapotec, Charles Reddington, William Rose, Karl Plate, Colin Lanceley, John Olsen, Leonard Hessing, sculptor Robert Klippel, John Coburn, artist and author Robert Hughes and Emanuel Raft stand on the upper floor balcony of the Hungry Horse Restaurant and Gallery, 47 Windsor Street at corner of Elizabeth Street (now Lucio's restaurant), Paddington. Hungry Horse Calendar, 1964, The Australian Galleries. Image courtesy of Lucio's Restaurant. © Robert Walker/Licensed by Viscopy, 2018.

The Hungry Horse Gallery and Restaurant was iconic in the 1960s as one of the first French restaurants in Sydney, with an avant-garde gallery upstairs, exhibiting the assemblage work of Colin Lanceley as well as the paintings of John Olsen. A photograph of its young artists standing on the gallery's first-floor lace-work balcony sums up the bohemianism of the time. This was also the ethos at Rudy Komon's gallery – although women were not included (Watters Gallery in East Sydney, showed the new feminist artists such as Vivienne Binns).

At gallery openings, artists mingled with new cultural workers and businessmen such as Harry M Miller, who worked in the rapidly expanding public relations (PR) and promotion industry.[45] Public relations, and its self-promotion, continues to maintain a strong presence in contemporary Paddington.

An amusing but telling article of 1974, describing how to spend a theoretical $10,000 inheritance on art, mentioned the old guard of David Jones and Macquarie Galleries but focused mainly on Paddington. Barry Stern, once a decorator, had made his gallery cosy with 'small tables, exotic chairs, Persian carpets and ... objet's d'art'. At Rudi [sic] Komon's the journalist was served a bottle of good white wine. Stories such as this underscored Paddington's new-found status as chic and smart rather than poor and seedy.

Shirley Wagner's Wagner Gallery traded at 39 Gurner Street from 1978 until the building was sold in 2015; it is now in Hampden Street.[46] It showed the work of an eclectic group of well-known Australian artists such as Arthur Boyd, Charles Blackman and Pro Hart, as well as modern American art such as Andy Warhol. The mix suggests the way in which Paddington business people have responded to very different tastes and market flows.

Galleries Primitif, on the Paddington side of Jersey Road at number 174 was run from 1966 until 2015 by one of Australia's early professional women pilots, Senta Taft-Hendry, who traded in New Guinean and other tribal arts, some of which she acquired on her flights there.[47] John Olsen traced a mind map of the topography of the area in his watercolour 'Walking Down Victoria Street, Paddington, 1963'.

Many prominent architects lived in Paddington attracted by its built environment and arts culture and aspects of their work including innovative infill architecture are covered elsewhere in this volume. They include Don Gazzard, who built a prizewinning modern home with his wife ceramicist Marea Gazzard at 88 Hargrave Street in 1975, Terry Dorrough (architect of Guriganya, a pavilion style house from the late 1970s built on one of the sites of the Progressive School of the same name), Ken Woolley (Woolley House, Cooper Street, 1980 and Stewart Street, 1995), Bill Lucas with Michael Coote (Orange Tree Grove, 8 Bennetts Grove Avenue, an innovative stepped terrace form, 1968) and Andrew Andersons (his own home in Alexander Street, and updates for the Sherman family).

By the 1990s, design firms and start-ups also operated in Paddington. OVO Design (Ruth McDermott and Rina Bernabei), well known for their innovative electric light fittings, was run from the 52 Regent Street front room of McDermott in 1996.[48] The extremely successful Dinosaur Designs (resin jewellery and ornaments designed and sold at first by art school students Louise Olsen, Stephen Ormandy and Liane Rossler at the Paddington Markets from 1982) has been at the same spot in Oxford Street for many years.[49] The 2000 Sydney Olympics torch and the 'Mount Franklin' water bottle (2003) were designed by D3 design from their Paddington office in William Street.

    The Paddington restaurant scene has a long tradition of innovative cooking and smart interior decoration; fine examples have included Claude's restaurant on Oxford Street, established in 1976 and famous for modern French cooking;[50] Lucio's, established in 1983 and notable for fine Italian food and wine (still trading), Oasis Seros (now closed), a 'modern Australian' or French-Asian fusion restaurant opened in 1987 that trained Christine Manfield; Buon Ricordo, modern Italian from 1987 (still trading); and Bistro Lulu, famous for simple French cookery (now closed). Many of the restaurants had their heyday before 1986, when Paul Keating's Labor government introduced a Fringe Benefits Tax covering business dining expenses and the state government imposed Random Breath Testing. These measures brought the long 'boozy' businessman's lunch to something like a conclusion.[51]

Figure 9.13: John Olsen, Sydney Art Opening, no date. Image courtesy of Thames & Hudson. © John Olsen/Licensed by Viscopy, 2018.

Artists in residence

Margaret Olley lived in several properties in Paddington including Gurner Street and her well-known

Duxford Street residence which she renovated mainly between 1965–68. Olley had bought her terraced property with its small hat factory in the garden for £4000. She could walk up or down the hill to see her many friends and ask the 'nice boys' (old-fashioned code for gay men) at the Oxford Street supermarket to save flowers for her to paint.[52] 'I'm always going up to St Vincent de Paul to find if there's an odd ginger jar' she remarked.[53] In some ways this gentle pattern of life still exists for Paddington locals who support their local shops. 'Mixed business' corner shops still operate in the area, although they no longer sell stale cakes half-price to school children or single cigarettes (one penny each) as they did during the Great Depression.[54]

Figure 9.14: John Olsen, Walking Down Victoria Street, Paddington, 1963, watercolour and gouache on paper. Image courtesy of Thames and Hudson. © John Olsen/Licensed by Viscopy, 2018.

Figure 9.15: Sculptor Marea Gazzard at the rear of her residence designed by Don Gazzard, corner Hargrave and Elizabeth streets, 1975. Photo by Bruce Howard, National Library of Australia.

Olley bought Duxford Street as an investment to let as flats in order to finance her travels and painting career; a good example of the fact that living in Paddington did not suggest a sedentary lifestyle. Most creative people in the arts move around, to access friendship networks, to gain new insights and inspiration. Olley moved back into the hat factory in the back garden in 1988 but continued to have lettings.

It was Olley who suggested that romantic modernist painter Donald Friend move to Paddington on his return to Sydney from Bali. Friend lived on three occasions in Paddington. From 1962–66 he resided at 1 Hampden Street, drinking and listening to jazz with the artists, filmmakers and journalists of the 'Paddington Push' at the Windsor Hotel. At the pub he observed marijuana-smoking youth as well as 'the jolly fat beer-sodden Paddington ladies'.[55]

Olley's estate agent later helped Friend find a narrow, detached two-storey house in 1 Belmore Place where he lived from 1984–87. It was selected expressly because it resembled the marooned 19th century townscape of Hill End, the outback artists' colony near Bathurst, where Friend once owned a miner's cottage. Cold and drafty, but surrounded by a patch of vacant land where Friend grew flowers and vegetables, the modest Paddington house projected a surreal profile that resembled the paintings of Giorgio de Chirico, the Italian artist who painted marooned buildings in dream-like landscapes.

Like Olley, Friend found beauty in the everyday, buying cheap objects in the local shops to decorate his house and in turn incorporating representations of them into his art.[56] When he had the money, Friend dressed his houses with kelimrugs, ceramics and tribal art from 'the antique shops, galleries and junkeries of Paddington'. Friend captured in his watercolours of this period the effect of looking out of the classic first-floor projecting balcony into a canopy of vegetation that became characteristic of Paddington. These balconies with their mandatory wall blocking to the neighbours provide the 'semi-secluded' private space that makes the 'permeable public/private interface' and spatial divisions of Paddington so interesting.[57]

As with Herman and Strachan before them, Olley and Friend shared an ability to see hidden beauty in the shabby or discarded past. Victorian taste was generally out of favour with the architectural establishment and other tastemakers from the 1910s to the 1950s who preferred early Georgian, Arts and Crafts or Modern architecture. Moreover, most middle-class Australians could not wait to flee the inner city Victorian 'slums'. However, the interest in mid-to-late Victorian Australia mirrors that of aesthetes abroad, who favoured various revivals of the Baroque and the Rococo. Cecil Beaton had found old Sydney architecture a bit puzzling and reminiscent of New Orleans when he visited in 1968. 'Rococo' was the very term used by Australian poet, broadcaster and heritage activist John Thompson to describe Paddington in the 1960s.[58]

Figure 9.16: Donald Friend, Pears, Avocado and Balcony View, 1984, pen and ink and watercolour, 73.5x54cm. Painted at 1 Belmore Place, Paddington, where Friend resided from 1984–87. Private collection. © Donald Friend/Licensed by Viscopy, 2018.

Counterculture revival: 1960s and 1970s

Paddington held a fair share of hippies and counter-cultural types. Michael Dransfield, who lived in a loft behind 55A Brown St, composed *Drug Poems* (1970–72) and the narrow footway between 194 and 196 Glenmore Road to Cooper Street was known as 'Marijuana Alley'.[59] Seventy-nine Windsor Street was the setting for Michael Wilding's comic novel *Living Together* (1974), which commented on communal living. As the impetus to publish Australian voices grew, Currency Press was established at 87 Jersey Road in the home of Katharine Brisbane and Philip Parsons in 1971, later operating from 330 Oxford Street.

Other artists congregated closer to the northeast borders of Paddington, much of which was demolished by the commissioner of railways in 1971 to make way for the new Eastern Suburbs Railway, a bus interchange and the Edgecliff Centre. This area was known as 'City Fringe' and was home to artists connected in part with the Yellow House in Kings Cross and Gallery A in Gipps Street. They included Vernon Treweeke (1939–2015), an 'abstract eroticist' or psychedelic painter influenced by his time in swinging London of the 1960s, who returned to Sydney from London in 1966 and lived there around 1968.[60] Treweeke made installation and sound art that resembled 'kaleidoscopic mandalas'; he was later founder of the Nimbin Aquarius Festival in 1973. These were the counter-cultural Paddington residents. Friend's diaries record inter-generational tensions about them.

The poet John Tranter lived at 112 Lawson Street in the late 1960s from where he published the poetry magazine *Transit* (1968–69), which included the work of Bob Ellis and Les Murray. Music singer-songwriter Keith Glass (born 1946), who appeared in the 1969 performances of *Hair* as Berger, describes 'tripping' with a friend and wearing make-up at his Gipps Street parties in the 1960s.[61] Radical journalists such as the political activist and anti-Vietnam war campaigner

Wendy Bacon also lived in 'Paddo' in Olive Street, where Germaine Greer and members of the 'Sydney Push' were regular visitors. The anarchist Nestor Grivas ran a type of club in his dug-out cellar in Oxford Street opposite the Rose, Shamrock and Thistle Pub (near present-day UNSW Art + Design). Here Germaine Greer presented an early paper on the clitoral orgasm, communists and social democrats played cards and drank and filmmaker Margaret Fink talked ideas. Frank Moorhouse established the 'Left Club' with strong links to the Builders' Labourers Federation (the BLF) and the Victoria Street protests against the demolition of much of Potts Point. Drugs including marijuana and LSD were sold from the cellar until a police 'bust' ended that period of bohemianism.[62] Paddington therefore was far from being bourgeois or respectable in the 1970s, and encompassed a wide range of bars, clubs and lifestyles.

Charm school

The image of Paddington that we recognise from real estate advertisements and lifestyle blogs today was very much created by artists who were 'mid-career' in the 1950s and 1960s. There was no common aesthetic among their works; however the art of Sali Herman from the 1930s–50s, that of Margaret Olley and Donald Friend and a number of illustrators such as Cedric Flower, Cedric Emanuel, and Unk White was frequently reproduced in the popular media. This did much to promote a certain ideal of the Paddington terrace life involving a gentle renovation with minimal interior rearrangement; in contrast to the large-scale rebuilding and interventions that marked the Sydney property market from the 1990s.

Paddington appealed to its residents and many never moved from their homes. The complete list of artists and writers who lived and socialised in Paddington is remarkable. Robert Walker's photographic archive of residents, social events and street theatre in the suburb includes famous artists such as Keith Looby, Janet Dawson and John Olsen and the poets Oodgeroo Noonuccal and Judith Wright.[63] Polish-born Yoram Jerzy Gross (1926–2015), filmmaker and animator of the Australian classics *Dot and the Kangaroo* (feature film 1977) and *Blinky Bill* (1992) lived much of his adult life in Caledonia Street where he ran his studio. Elwyn Lynn, freethinker and artist, lived nearby in Moncur Street Woollahra from 1964–97, very near the building whose facade was taken to represent the flat building in the famous Australian TV drama *Number 96* (Channel 10, 1972–78). Artist Ruark Lewis who works across Indigenous text, performance and installation lives in Bennetts Grove Avenue.

Post-1980s

By the mid-1980s, two generations of artists were present, although many had left the area as their needs had changed.[64] The older generation of artists living in Paddington included David and Hermia Boyd, Bill Rose,

Margaret Olley, Cedric Flower, Robert Dickerson, Louis James and Donald Friend. Former inhabitants included John Olsen, Charles and Barbara Blackman and Janet Dawson: 'New artists are moving to Paddington, but they often stay only a few years. For most, the area is too expensive.' 'Paddington is still charming', commented Boyd, 'but the old village atmosphere is fading ... Business and University people have supplanted the wharfie and carpenter.'[65] But Boyd did not resent the newcomers, noting that it was 'these newcomers who have preserved much of the village character, saved the terrace houses and prevented the building of units'.[66] 'Art has also become respectable in that time and money has made it so', he concluded. The new buyers who were investors as well as collectors shifted gallery practices. Galleries began to develop 'stables' as well as developing the careers of new artists and sustaining them over time. This created new markets and also the nature of art making, which became professionalised.

Two outstanding gallerists dominated the Sydney art scene in the 1980s and '90s, both in Paddington. They were Roslyn Oxley and Gene Sherman, and Oxley continues to represent artists today. Roslyn Oxley9 Gallery was first established in a light industrial building in MacDonald Street near the Cutler Footway, and later in the lower part of Paddington at Soudan Lane. Oxley has shown some of Australia's most significant contemporary artists, including assemblage artist Rosalie Gascoigne, photographers Bill Henson and Tracey Moffatt, painter Imants Tillers and sculptor Patricia Piccinini. Oxley also has exhibited important international sculpture, installation and mixed media art including the well-known work of queer photographers Robert Mapplethorpe and Pierre et Giles at Mardi Gras time. Her openings were art events in and of themselves, often with live performers (a podium male go-go dancer at Pierre et Giles), music and people spilling on to the streets, reminiscent of the 'old days' of Paddington when Rudy Komon's events flowed over into the streets and on into the wine bars.

Dr Gene Sherman with curatorial director William (Bill) Wright introduced new standards of research and presentation for contemporary art in a commercial setting when she directed the purpose-built Irving (later Sherman) Galleries at 1 Hargrave Street from 1989 until 2007. Wright noted that the area between the city and Double Bay (with Paddington as its centre) was known in the art trade as the 'Silk Road', meaning the cradle of commerce, and that it was challenging to run a gallery elsewhere in Sydney.[67] Sherman Galleries was conducted in a striking new building incorporating a sculpture roof garden (on the site of a former corner shop) designed by architect Victor Berk. Sherman faced challenges in having the contemporary design approved but she was adamant that she 'couldn't use a gallery that used a 19th century model', that is, small rooms and inadequate lighting, nor would she agree to erect a 'mock heritage building' on the site. Although she faced stiff opposition from her neighbour, Mr Xanatides, he quickly became interested in the gallery visitors and proudly welcomed guests to opening night receptions. This is a fine example of the interaction of people from different backgrounds, social classes, places and outlooks that recurs in recollections of 'old' Paddington. In 1992 Sherman opened a second art gallery (Sherman Galleries) in a converted car smash-repair shop in Goodhope Street near the Fiveways, now the location of the Sherman Centre for Culture and Ideas (SCCI), established in 2017.

Figure 9.17: Two women outside shop, Paddington, 1968. Robert Walker Archive, Art Gallery of New South Wales Archive. AGNSW Gift of the Robert Walker family, 2008. © Robert Walker/Licensed by Viscopy, 2018.

The Sherman Family Group is housed in the old bakery and its extension on the corner of William and Paddington streets. That this building was previously the headquarters of Deeta Colvin Public Relations, and before that the Bakery Art School, is a fine example of the successful 'barnacle' effect of the re-use of old dwellings and structures in Paddington. It is also an excellent example of the pattern of transformation of many buildings in Paddington from light industry to atelier/gallery to PR/media and in this case, a return to an artistic and social-justice creative use.[68]

Other prominent contemporary galleries in Paddington of the 1990s–2000s included Australian Galleries, Savill Gallery, Gary Anderson, Kaliman Gallery and the Gitte Weise Gallery.[69] The Australian Centre for Photography, founded in 1974, exhibited and taught photomedia for many years at 72 Oxford Street.

Just because a group of artists moves into an area, it does not mean that they are gentrifiers. Many artists disliked cookie-cutter post-war suburbia. Instead they appreciated patina, or even decay. They enjoyed the contrasts of older white Australians interacting with immigrant communities, their shops and pastimes.

They liked the everyday activities of the housewives, gardeners and handymen of the area. The artists did not necessarily want to see Paddington change. Olley made her views clear in 2001:

> For me it's perfect. It's really a workers' area and close to the city and to transport ... Also it's peaceful and quiet. And there are all these little art galleries around the place ... [it's] central to everything I want to do. Other people want to be central to sports activities: my central is the arts.[70]

Flexible, quirky, inventive, once boisterous, somewhat crude but often open-minded, Paddington has flourished from the 19th century to our own times as a creative haven of arts and skills. Paddington retains its allure as a space of inspiration. As we walk its streets and laneways we sense echoes, scents, smells and shadows of the past, the hidden beauty that many generations of poets, writers and artists have passed down to us today.[71]

Chapter 10
Changing landscapes

Helen Armstrong

Can you imagine walking towards Rushcutters Bay down the Paddington ridge some 20,000 years ago? You would not find the bay – not even the harbour – only a wide valley floor with clumps of reeds marking a scribble of creeks and a sluggish river that headed east. The river passed through a break in a line of cliffs, now North and South Heads, to flow a further 25 kilometres over a floodplain to reach the sea (over 135,000 years ago during the last Glacial Period the sea level was lower as the ocean had frozen over). Around 20,000 years ago, the ocean level again began to rise. This was the landscape where the people of the Eora Nation lived and although probably not noticeable, it was changing. Over the next 10,000 years the sea moved west towards the break in the cliff line at North and South Heads and filled the valley floor behind the cliffs, creating a harbour and landscape that looked much as it would have to Captain Arthur Phillip in 1788 – a wide harbour with open bays and beaches on the south and steeper, more rugged slopes around the narrow inlets to the north. Today, sandstone outcrops in a number of Paddington streets tell some of this story which begins at least 300 million years ago when beds of sand accumulated in vast, shallow prehistoric lakes. The ebbing and flowing of the water created sand banks with ripples that can be seen in the present day as 'current bedding' in exposed sandstone outcrops (see Figure 10.13).

The Cadigal of the Eora Nation lived around the south-east slopes of the harbour, hunting in the grassland and forests and fishing in the bays. This was their mode of life at least until the First Fleet moored near the Tank Stream. The landscape the European settlers found was a heath-covered ridge running east-west that separated the area into steep forested slopes to the north and more gentle slopes of heath and rock outcrops to the south. Springs and creeks flowed north to wetlands behind the tidal flats and to the south the water drained over gentle slopes to the Botany Sands.

The vegetation on the northern slopes below the heath on the ridgeline varied from tall forests with dense undergrowth on sheltered hillsides to open woodlands on the upper exposed slopes, shown in maps in Chapter 2. Forests also grew around the creeks, where the pink branches and trunks of the smooth-barked apple tree twisted out of the impenetrable undergrowth, contrasting with the occasional straight rough-barked red mahogany. On the more exposed slopes, the forest and thick undergrowth were replaced by rocky outcrops where white smooth-barked scribbly gums and spiky grass-trees grew over and around rocks. These gave way to woodlands of grey gums and stringybark trees that emerged out of rough grasslands of kangaroo grass and clumps of spikey mat-rush.[1] Although considered a natural landscape by settlers, it was in fact a highly-managed Indigenous cultural landscape.

Cadigal cultural landscape

Prior to 1788, the Cadigal had created a cultural landscape of forests, grassy slopes and open woodlands, both north and south of the Paddington ridge. The grassy slopes were the product of the Cadigal's selective firing of the vegetation. This was done to manage the land according to distinct areas of vegetation that supplied food and facilitated the capture of game. Using 'cool mosaic burns'[2] as a planned rotation system, they developed specific plant communities, often in the form of alternating bands of grass, shrubs and trees. The historian, Bill Gammage, points out that sketches by early settlers, such as Joseph Lycett's 1824, 'View of the Heads, at the entrance to Port Jackson' (see Figure 4.1) show these strips of grass and trees to be evident on North Head in 1788.[3] An earlier view from Vaucluse looking backwards to the emerging settlement in 1804 shows two patches of cool mosaic burns as part of the Cadigal cultural landscape south of the harbour, see Figure 10.1.

On the upper Paddington slope, hidden in the bands of woodland, the Cadigal hunters were able to capture wallabies grazing on fresh shoots in the grassland strips produced by these 'cool burns'. Gammage suggests this could be considered a form of herding. In the northern lowlands, a lagoon fringed by rushes provided a rich source of birdlife, fish and other fauna. Crustaceans from the edge of the bay were also harvested for large feasts. Midden remnants of such feasts on the lowlands near the bay showed that the 'tucker' was good. Up on the ridgeline, a well-used pathway took the Cadigal to the east and south-east. Some of the Cadigal camped below the ridge by a stream in the shelter of the lower eastern valley, while others camped by a waterfall in an upper valley to the west.

Figure 10.1: Cadigal managed landscape of grass, shrubs and trees. William Westall's watercolour, Port Jackson, 1804, portrays a view from south of the harbour towards the

west showing banded vegetation due to Cadigal cool mosaic burns. State Library of New South Wales.

Lowlands: settlers and land grants

The newly arrived people from Britain quickly changed the lowlands by fencing off areas for farming. This involved clearing all the heath for grazing and felling the trees for construction materials. As a result, the Cadigal lowlands were the earliest to be lost. In 1810 Thomas West, a convict carpenter was promised the western portion of the Rushcutters Bay lowlands to establish a watermill. Seven years later, settler William Thomas was granted a considerable part of the swamp and flatland further to the east near the bay. By the 1830s the Ridley family had leased and converted the flat land north of the William Thomas grant to market gardens, which were the main source of vegetables for the settlement. Later, by the 1860s, the area of the market gardens was leased to Chinese market gardeners, who maintained the landscape in its rural state for over 40 years, despite disdain from some residents on the upper slopes.

Figure 10.2: Chinese Market Gardens looking south towards the upper slopes. Archives Office of New South Wales # 1006.

Today no traces of the diligent husbandry of this landscape exist. Unlike the Cadigal, the European settlers did not have a high regard for these lowlands. As a little-valued landscape, it was the place to locate industry; first a distillery, then a tannery, quarries, factories, warehouses and finally rubbish dumps.

Various industrial uses persisted in the area until the 1970s when larger industries moved to outer Sydney for greater convenience and cheaper land. By the late 1970s, some of the abandoned sites had been redeveloped into high-rise residential blocks and townhouses and one or two art galleries. But some small-scale factories persisted until 2015; including a smash-repair business and the Eastern Suburbs Towing Company. There were also furniture-making factories, wine distributors and industrial garment manufacturers, including Servis Industries who made uniforms for Qantas and for the orderlies at the Royal Prince Alfred Hospital.[4] Hampden Street was a busy mixed residential and industrial precinct through the 1980s and 1990s. Between 2010 and 2013 Servis Industries and Brosalco, an import business, closed and the sites were converted into art galleries. The lowlands area is now designated as a 'gallery precinct'; the galleries occupying romanticised shells of the former industrial buildings and warehouses.

The ridge: public domain

The ridge that separates the north and south slopes of Paddington also changed from a Cadigal track to a contemporary public domain. The new settlers quickly realised that the Cadigal's passage to the east and south-east was the most logical location for a road connecting the settlement to the ocean headland where the first sighting of ships from Britain could be made. The early journeys to the south headland encompassed picturesque landscapes of woodlands and water views, until the construction of Victoria Barracks, which was completed in 1848. Strategically sited with northerly views to the Heads and long southerly views to Botany Bay, this was the beginning of a public domain comprised of distinguished government buildings, many constructed in sandstone from local quarries. It was also the catalyst for a new village on the northern side of the ridge road, known as the South Head Road (now Oxford Street).

Figure 10.3: Hampden Street, part of the lowlands, with warehouses and light industry converted to galleries, now designated a 'gallery precinct'. Helen Armstrong, 2018.

Remaining relatively unchanged, the imposing 19th century public buildings of Victoria Barracks, the Paddington Town Hall, the Post Office, and the former Walter Read Reserve with its sedate park and possible rotunda for bands, formed a distinctive civic precinct. Added to this, a fine row of Moreton Bay figs and jacarandas define the southern edge of Oxford Street as it runs up the slope past Victoria Barracks.

Paddington Town Hall and the Post Office mark the crest of the hill and the civic entrance into Paddington; the Walter Read Reserve being replaced in 2009 by the Paddington Reservoir Gardens within a previously concealed reservoir. The new Reservoir Gardens respect the existing civic character of the precinct by remaining within the structure, or shell, of the former reservoir below street level. The civic entrance gives way to the commercial section of Paddington's Oxford Street, which has maintained its urban qualities as a continuous row of small characterful shops and pubs on the north side of the road and a southern arc of more dignified churches, schools, and small green plazas (dating from the late 19th century to the present).

Figure 10.4: Oxford Street spine of public buildings and avenue planting. Simon Wood Photography, 2017.

With the passage of time, the public domain extended from the ridgeline down the north slope via Glenmore Road, a significant Paddington thoroughfare whose evolving character included a distinctive neighbourhood precinct, known as Fiveways. Further down the slope, Trumper Park Oval added to the importance of Glenmore Road with a stately row of lemon-scented gums marking the grand entrance gates to the oval.

The conservation section of Woollahra's *Development Control Plan 2015*[5] highlights finer grain details in the public domain such as kerbs, gutters, and footpaths. However, the sloping topography of the area has also resulted in many remarkably evocative elements, such as rock outcrops dressed in stone, often intersecting with the original rock face. In one example on upper Cascade Street, layers of landscape can be observed spanning millions of years, through to the late 19th century, up to the present with recent stone walls (see Figure 10.13). The changes to ground levels have also occasioned stone steps leading to elegant walkways, as at upper Cascade Street and nondescript back lanes, such as Windsor Lane and Sutherland Avenue.

Figure 10.5: Entry Gates to Trumper Park Oval, Glenmore Road. Row of lemon-scented gums along Glenmore Road marking the entry gates to Trumper Park Oval. Helen Armstrong, 2017.

Uplands

EARLY ESTATES

The upper slopes, both north and south of the ridge, were important camping sites for the Cadigal until they were displaced by early settlers who introduced a cultural landscape of villas, gardens, orchards and fenced paddocks for grazing. This landscape continued to evolve until the 1870s. The view to the north from these villas was described as '...one uninterrupted view of unsurpassed grandeur ... grassy slopes and oceans of woodlands...'[6] This view however was about to change as the various large estates were subdivided into small lots and streets over the next 20 years.

Figure 10.6: 1870 fig tree over lower Brown Street. Note, building works with temporary fencing beside figs and construction crane emerging from canopy. Simon Wood Photography, 2017.

Unlike the lowlands, remnants of the landscape heritage of the Rushcutter Valley gentry on the upper slopes have endured in the form of huge dark spreading figs, tall narrow araucaria pines, and old gnarled camphor laurels. These trees, mostly 160 years old, are listed in the *Woollahra Significant Tree Register*.[7] The garden of 'The Terraces', considered one of the finest mansions on Paddington Heights, was described in 1882 in the following terms:

> ...An Educated and Judicious Arborescence pervades ... which may be fitly described as one brilliant mass of Magnificent Trees and Rare Shrubs of mature growth, glorious in height, perfect in form, exquisite in symmetry, clumped and clustered together in a most attractive manner ... delightfully secluded as if in the deepest heart of a sequestered wood.[8]

The tree canopy and other elements of this garden persisted as a consistent feature of aerial photos of Paddington, until recently (see Figure 10.9). These impressive trees, their trunks pressing against the fence beside the slope of Brown Street, were a Paddington landmark (see Figure 10.6). Despite their heritage listing, the few trees that are now left compete with a multistorey development in the Scottish Hospital grounds. In general, the built heritage of the large estates and their gardens have not survived. A green link persists, however, from Rushcutters Bay, past the Weigall playing fields, continuing upslope through the Scottish Hospital and the former Royal Hospital for Women grounds, through to Victoria Barracks on the ridge and down to Moore Park.

Figure 10.7: The Terraces villa and gardens, built 1849 for HB Bradley, taken 1866 showing

early garden planting. State Library of New South Wales.

LANDSCAPE OF TERRACES

The subdivision of the large estates into rows of fine-grained terraces from the 1870s to the 1890s resulted in the specific urban landscape of today's Paddington. Sloping streets of stepped terraces created a rhythm of intricate details that were a delight in themselves. Until the 1970s, however, the terrace landscape was mainly treeless. This contrasts with the ridges and valleys of Woollahra, where rainforest trees planted on large estates in the 19th century (spreading figs, tall Norfolk Island and Kauri pines) form a dark green eastern boundary to the Paddington valley.

South Paddington's pattern of generous streets and trees aligned on the contours of the land, connected by narrow sloping lanes, appears more grid-like and hierarchical than those of the north-west, which were largely dictated by the boundaries of early land grants. The continuous avenue of brush box in Regent Street and the majestic row of cabbage tree palms along the centre of Moore Park Road give an added sense of formality to this Paddington precinct.

Another part of the uplands is the precinct west of Victoria Barracks which extends to the avenue of plane trees defining South Dowling Street; bounded in the south by Moore Park Road and to the north by Oxford Street. Within this precinct is a landscape consisting of avenues of Hill's figs, such as those in Napier and Selwyn streets (possibly planted in the 1970s).

Figure 10.8: Sloping streets of stepped terraces created a delightful rhythm of intricate details; roof-lines, chimneys and balconies. But until the 1970s, the terrace landscape was mainly

treeless. Rob Hillier, Let's buy a Terrace House, Ure Smith, Sydney, 1968.

Figure 10.9: Aerial view of treeless streets of Paddington in 1951, compared to Woollahra and Potts Point. Note, Woollahra Quarry to the east and Paddington Quarry to the west of Cascade Street to right of centre, with the Stadium just to the south of New South Head Road. The old Darlinghurst Gaol is on the far left. Land and Property Information New South Wales.

Figure 10.10: Treeless streets and lanes of Paddington, c 1968. Rob Hillier collection, Mitchell Library, State Library of New South Wales. Rob Hillier, Let's buy a Terrace House, Ure Smith, Sydney, 1968.

Waterways

In geological terms, the area's windblown sand deposits – lying above sandstone – provided good drainage and natural freshwater springs. To the south, these springs flowed into the Lachlan Swamps and were redirected through Busby's Bore to become the water supply for Sydney Town. Maps (in Chapter 2) show springs and creeks cascading down the northern slopes to the lowlands, culminating in a lagoon which seeped into the west side of Rushcutters Bay.

Three main creeks flowed down the north slopes. To the west, a natural spring arose near today's Taylor Square and cascaded over rock outcrops to form Rushcutters Creek, flowing on through the Lacrozia Valley (named by Major Thomas Mitchell as it reminded him of Spain). The strength of the flow was sufficient to drive the watermill in Barcom Glen. On the flatter lowlands, Rushcutters Creek flowed into the swampy wetlands and lagoon used to irrigate the Ridley family's market gardens from the 1830s. The waterways were later organised into complex channels by the Chinese market gardeners in the 1860s. This arrangement continued until 1908, when the water was diverted into pipes to provide dry ground for new, predominantly recreational uses of the lowlands.

Figure 10.11: Tannery reservoir 1861, on Glenbrook Brook. Part of George Roberts' sketchbook showing watercolour of Glenmore Tannery (spelt Glanmore), Views mainly of Eastern Suburbs of Sydney, 1859–1863. State Library of New South Wales.

Figure 10.12: Glenmore Brook as irrigation channel for market gardens. Note, Neild Avenue

bridge and view looking south c 1890. City of Sydney Archives.

To the east, within a long narrow valley enclosed by cliffs was a natural spring falling to a creek flowing west, Glenmore Brook. A third upland spring arising near the west end of Paddington Street cascaded over rocky ledges (now Cascade Street) down to Glenmore Brook. The meeting of these creeks proved an appropriate location for a distillery, including two reservoirs for the distilling process, constructed by convicts in 1828.[9] Various industries, including a tannery, used these reservoirs until the 1890s when both creeks and reservoirs disappeared into underground pipes. Rushcutters Creek was similarly piped, emerging in a channel on the western edge of Rushcutters Bay Park. In 1967 a new water feature, the Duck Pond, was created in Trumper Park.

In South Paddington, long views extended over the Sydney Common to the Lachlan Swamps. Although these spring-fed wetlands were the water supply for Sydney Town, they were dominated by a rubbish dump (indicating how little wetlands were valued by the settlers). Later they became the ponds in Centennial Park, while the water used to supply the town was hidden in pipes and a covered reservoir on Oxford Street from 1866 to 1899. The memory of the reservoir has become a public feature in the form of the Paddington Reservoir Gardens (see Figure 10.19).

Quarry landscapes

For much of the 19th century to the mid-20th century, sandstone quarries were a notable feature of Paddington, the stone being used to build villas, houses and public buildings in the area. As with the sandstone outcrops, it is also possible to walk past quarried stone faces in a number of Paddington streets, such as the cliffs at the end of Soudan Lane and Roylston Street. The quarry faces in these streets tell the Triassic story going back 300 million years ago when beds of sand accumulated in vast shallow waters. The current bedding in these exposed quarry faces, similar to those on Paddington's sandstone outcrops (see Figure 10.13), is evocative of the ebbing and flowing of water that rippled the sand banks to ultimately form layers of rock.

F Arnold and Sons was the longest lasting quarry operator, providing yellow and white sandstone. The firm first opened a quarry east of Victoria Barracks in Regent Street in 1879, then later moved to 110 Cascade Street in 1915, and took over the Woollahra quarry in 1925.[10] Early aerial photographs show the Paddington Quarry on the west side of Cascade Street and the Woollahra Quarry east of Hampden Park (see Figure 10.9).

Figure 10.13: Current bedding in Triassic sandstone outcrops in Cascade Street, Paddington. Helen Armstrong, 2017.

Figure 10.14: Avenue of plane trees in Roylston Street, abruptly terminated by quarry face. Helen Armstrong, 2016.

Distinctive quarry faces can be found today along the original unformed western alignment of Harris Street, extending to Cascade Street. This extended quarry face results in an abrupt separation between streets on the valley floor and Elizabeth and Sutherland streets on higher contours. Most of the long quarry face is unkempt except for Roylston Street's dramatic southern end. Shaded by large trees, it forms a sculptural backdrop to the street.

There are also remnant quarry faces in Trumper Reserve. Once dense bush and scrub in the 1860s, the area became severely degraded by industrial activities, including quarrying. In 1967 the quarry was closed, filled with soil five metres deep, and planted with native trees and shrubs. This covered the old quarry tunnels, leaving remnants of the quarry face as a backdrop to a newly formed Duck Pond which was created from the natural spring that once fed Glenmore Brook; a creek which has been long lost to drainage pipes.

Figure 10.15: Former quarry face and the Duck Pond c 1967, Trumper Reserve. Helen Armstrong, 2012.

Recreation landscapes

LOWLANDS

Local government was prompted to consider the community's recreation needs with the growth of Paddington's population, as large estates changed to streets of terraces. In a competitive response to the State's proposed large public park (the future Centennial Park) on the Lachlan Swamps, the local council decided to establish a Paddington recreation area. Once again, the lowlands were seen as easy to appropriate, in this case for recreation.

In the 1870s, a flurry of interest resulted in a proposed recreation reserve at the foot of Cascade Street. In 1878, the eastern lowlands between Glenmore Road and the old distillery site – by then a swampy rubbish dump – were filled and levelled. The resulting Hampden Park opened in 1897. It included a cricket oval with a corner grandstand which was screened by a tall fence, obliging would-be spectators to pay for their entertainment. It appears that a two-up school was located at the base of the quarry wall behind the oval. The 'cockies' sat above the quarry and if the police raided, they would drop a stone into the water beside the two-up school, dispersing the gamblers into the surrounding scrubland.[11]

Figure 10.16: Hampden Park Grandstand at the base of Cascade Street, 1959. Looking south-west across Trumper Park Oval towards the grandstand, later demolished; to the right are the Chevrolet Dealers 'Stacks', 353–357 Glenmore Road. City of Sydney Archives 008/008542, City Planning Department negatives, 1951–1964.

This fenced oval contrasted with the openness of Rushcutters Bay Park which was created at a similar time north of New South Head Road. The park was formed by building a curved seawall 200 metres into the bay and filling behind it to form a large open park of grass and trees, including a swimming pool on the eastern side.

Despite the new recreation facilities, the lowlands continued to be used for industry and by the Chinese for market gardens until, in the era of the White Australia Policy, the Chinese were forced to leave their gardens early in the 1900s. Their gardens were then drained to create open-air pleasure grounds, including the White City Amusement Park which operated from 1913 to 1916. Rushcutters Bay Park, the sports grounds and the tennis courts are all that remain today.

Apart from Rushcutters Bay and Trumper Park, dating from the 1880s and 1890s, most of the open space in Paddington is relatively recent. Some 20 pocket parks with playground equipment are now scattered throughout the area. They were mainly created from the 1970s to the 1980s, when traffic management changed many residential streets; including the introduction of planted roundabouts, traffic calming gardens, and street closures.

Figure 10.17: Trumper Park Oval with new grandstand, 2017. Simon Wood Photography, 2017.

UPLANDS

In recent times, two large parks have been created as important contributions to the public domain: Paddington Reservoir Gardens and the Royal Hospital for Women Park. Paddington Reservoir Gardens replaces the former Walter Read Reserve on the roof of the Paddington Reservoir.

The Reservoir Gardens inhabit a number of levels. The open grass areas evoke the former elevated grassed reserve (see Figure 10.18). At street level there is a simple plaza relating to the civic buildings of the Town Hall and Post Office. Sinking below street level into the old reservoir chambers, there is a labyrinth of courtyard spaces, both open and roofed, around a pond evoking the former water storage. Removed from the traffic noise above, these are spaces for quiet contemplation.

The new Royal Hospital for Women Park contributes to the existing public domain along Glenmore Road, extending the community area around the Fiveways precinct to Brown Street with its historical link to the Scottish Hospital. The park design responds to its history, which includes the early estate of Flinton and the Royal Hospital for Women, marked out by sandstone blocks and stone footprints. The hospital grounds were landscaped between 1907 and 1910 with plants suggested by the director of the Royal Botanic Gardens, Joseph Maiden. They included Moreton Bay and Port Jackson figs as well as camphor laurels, resulting in large figs lining Glenmore Road. They were later felled and replaced by eucalypts which were in their turn cut down. It is fortunate that the camphor laurel trees at the corner of Brown Street and Glenmore Road have been retained and provide strong definition to the historic boundary of the Royal Hospital for Women.[12] The generous area of undulating grassland is enjoyed by the local residents and is shaded by a large remnant camphor laurel tree in the centre.

Figure 10.18: 1964 Paddington Reservoir with park over. Sydney City Archives File 014/014385.

Environmental landscapes

The environment movement of the 1960s changed perceptions and values related to urban bushland. As a result, the creation of Trumper Reserve in 1967, from the rehabilitation of a former quarry, included planting the area with native plants. By the late

1970s the reserve was heavily infested with weeds. At the beginning, people enjoyed the green space without discriminating between weeds and native bush, so weed control was relaxed, however by the second decade of the 21st century, urban bushland management has become more rigorous. Currently, weed management in Trumper Reserve involves bush-care experts, some of whom require that large old celtis trees in nearby private gardens be felled because of their invasive windblown seeds.

Figure 10.19: Paddington Reservoir Gardens today, with Paddington Town Hall and Post Office and restored Juniper Hall and gardens on the right. Simon Wood Photography, 2017.

Trumper Reserve is popular for walking and some of its trees are associated with local folklore. An extremely large Moreton Bay fig up the slope from Trumper Park Oval (evident as a lone tree in many early photos) is known as the Trumpalar Tree – the focus of the novel by Judy Bernard-Waite, published in 1981.[13]

In the 1970s, the environment movement prompted the desire to plant indigenous street trees. As many of the streets were narrow, these were usually small bottlebrush trees in strong contrast to the fine fig and plane avenues in Paddington Street, and similar avenues in Hampden, Cecil and Roylston streets on the valley floor. In the 21st century, the 1970s notion of environment has been revised as sustainability; evident in the large and thriving community gardens created above Trumper Reserve and the whimsical community garden in the Windsor Street closure at the corner of Elizabeth Street.

Streetscapes and gardens

Streets and gardens are layered cultural landscapes that often reflect changing social values. In Paddington, the streets and gardens have ranged from the high Victorian terraces defining streets to marginal slums and more recently various shades of gentrified landscapes, often including street closures in the form of pocket parks.

MARGINAL STREETSCAPES AND GARDENS

Paddington became depressed and run down in the early 20th century. The streets of terraces were treeless and the back gardens were '...a bit of grass, a frangipani tree, clothes lines and some staghorns'.[14] With the advent of migration following World War 2, European migrants moved in and sought to adapt their terraces, often changing the back garden in the process. Greek migrants for example planted olive trees, figs, lemons and herbs and arranged their back gardens for family gatherings with trellises and grapevines over paved areas to provide for dancing.

Figure 10.20: The huge Trumpalar fig (c 1870) within Trumper Reserve and dominating the bush surrounding Trumper Park Oval. Simon Wood Photography, 2017.

Figure 10.21: A 1960s marginal landscape in Paddington. Neglected terraces, some with blocked-in balconies, Bennett's Grove Avenue at rear of Underwood Street. Abandoned car on vacant block, now Bill Lucas' Orange Tree Grove units. National Library Australia Bib. ID 3547812, photo by Lee Pearce.

In their turn, the migrants' shops and vibrant street life attracted bohemian artists to Paddington. They altered their cheap rental properties, forming collectives with shared vegetable gardens. The bohemians also embraced the environment movement of the early 1970s, digging up the concrete laid down for Greek dancing and planting eucalypts and bottlebrush in their small gardens and streets. These plantings were later to outgrow both the gardens and the narrow streets.

GENTRIFIED STREETSCAPES AND GARDENS

The gentrification of Paddington is particularly evident in the changing streetscapes and gardens. Architects often bought rundown terraces restoring them to their Victorian character by removing the additions undertaken by migrants. By the 1980s, early gentrifiers had created an urban landscape of renovated terraces, with occasional large eucalypts in the back garden. The renewed terraces now appealed to more conservative residents who, requiring privacy rather than communal living, erected high walls around their small front gardens, again changing the character of the street. Later the front walls came down to show off diminutive front gardens of formal low box hedges, often around water features or sculptures, enclosed by traditional cast iron palisade fencing. Occasionally an old frangipani was allowed to stay.

Figure 10.22: Gentrified Streetscape, Glebe Street Closure. Note use of clipped buxus hedges. Helen Armstrong, 2018.

STREET TREES

The existing mixed and varied tree plantings in the streets within Paddington are an undocumented mystery, however they appear to be linked to street tree plantings in the Woollahra Municipality and the City of Sydney as a whole. In Woollahra, from 1890 to 1930, avenues in the bays – Rushcutters Bay, Double Bay and Rose

Bay – were planted with Moreton Bay figs and Norfolk Island pines. In 1918, Joseph Maiden, director of the Sydney Botanic Gardens distributed 321 Indian laurel and brush box trees throughout Woollahra Municipality.[15]

Apparently, early plantings of rainforest trees also occurred in Paddington streets as individual examples of these trees are evident in photos of the period; as well, a few poplars remain in Jersey road and some kaffir plum were only recently removed from Suffolk Street. It would seem that apart from avenues of planes, figs and brush box trees in Paddington and Regent streets, and Alma Street with its central row of Canary Island palms,[16] the streets were not planted with formal avenues.

Figure 10.23: Paddington Street with plane trees. Helen Armstrong, 2017.

The streets of Paddington were not graced with avenues of trees until the 1970s–80s. In the streets of South Paddington, such as Renny Street, the street trees form consistent avenues of brush box or Hill's fig. The older streets near Darlinghurst, such as Napier and Selwyn streets also have fine avenues of Hill's figs. The lowland streets, Hampden, Cecil and Roylston streets, are planted with similarly outstanding avenues of Hill's figs and plane trees.

The remaining streets in Paddington tended to be planted with an eclectic mix of older eucalypts and planes mixed with some rainforest trees; such as those of Cambridge or Hargrave streets with blackbean, red cedar and plum pine. Other streets were planted with colourful deciduous trees; such as the Chinese tallow found in Goodhope Street and the golden robinia at the northern end of Glenmore Road. There are no records about the jacarandas in Glenview Street but they were probably planted in the late 1970s. Excessive lopping for overhead powerlines has resulted in a number of streets with disfigured trees which in some cases have been replaced by small blueberry ash.

The street trees in Paddington reflect contested landscape values. To some, the brilliant colour of the jacarandas and the majesty of planes and figs are intrinsic to Paddington's landscape character. To others, older trees disturb the pavement and drop leaves and fruit. In north-facing areas, they are considered to block views and some species cause hay-fever in spring. Despite this, today most Paddington streets have trees. Some are older formal avenues of large trees. Occasionally old large eucalypts, planes, and jacarandas remain in some gardens and streets. In contrast, the street and garden aesthetic associated with the more recent gentrified Paddington is an intricate residential landscape of rows of variously coloured terraces, many stepped to reflect the varying angled and sloping street layouts, planted with small colourful street trees such as the Chinese tallowwood and the golden robinia, replacing the 1970s bottlebrush and paperbarks. More recently, street tree planting tends to be the small blueberry ash.

Figure 10.24: Regent Street with brush box trees. Helen Armstrong, 2017.

Figure 10.25: Selwyn Street with Hill's figs. Helen Armstrong, 2018.

Changing landscape aesthetics

Paddington's landscape aesthetic has come full circle. The highly valued lowlands used by the Cadigal had poor aesthetic value for the European settlers. Seen as marginal landscapes, particularly the eastern valley now known as Trumper Reserve, they were considered only fit for industry and the dumping of rubbish. This attitude persisted until the 1970s when the recreated bushland assumed new value. In contrast, the uplands, highly valued by the 19th century gentry as a location for their villas, became an equally valued urban landscape of row housing until the early 20th century, when a house and garden in the suburbs had more appeal for many. After 50 years, this neglected urban landscape was reinvigorated, this time to include the planting of small native trees, unlike the rainforest giants of the 1880s–1990s, and more recently small colourful exotic trees. The conservation values are similarly divided into upper slopes and parts of the lowlands. The cultural landscape of terraces and avenues are well protected by heritage planning, while parts of the lowlands are now protected as urban bushland under the vigilant management of the local council and volunteer bush-care groups. Street trees are not protected and are consistently damaged by expedient lopping for overhead powerlines.

The future of Paddington's cultural landscape is not secure as evidenced by the redevelopment of the Scottish

Hospital, Paddington's most significant upper Gentry Estate. Unlike the treeless terrace landscapes of the 1960s, some 150 large spreading rainforest trees were already evident in 1950 (see Figures 10.8 & 10.9) and had reached magnificent proportions by the 2000s. Despite concerted efforts by the community and Council, over 130 large trees were felled for bulky buildings of up to 8 storeys covering most of the site.

Paddington now faces the challenge of urban consolidation and its associated destruction of gardens and large trees; particularly threatening lowland recreation areas in private ownership. There is also the ever-present pressure for road widening such as New South Head Road and the inevitable felling of avenues of heritage trees. The richness of Paddington's landscape is that, although it has always been changing, traces of previous landscapes remain. One can still describe Paddington in terms of uplands and lowlands, although the bulk and height of potential developments could mask this topographic delight.

A suburb whose landscape tells a story from 300 million years ago to the present will require vigilant stewardship as a safeguard for future generations. This will involve carefully managing change and anticipating and preventing possible impacts that could erase elements of Paddington's changing landscape story.

Chapter 11
Survival

Peter Spearritt

There are only a few suburbs in Australia where the name commands immediate national recognition. Even fewer where the name also conjures a sense of architectural integrity. Mosman, Double Bay and Toorak are well-known as middle-class havens, but their architecture is varied, and has for some time been under attack from neo-Tuscan mansions, so popular with tax minimisers who have more wealth than taste. Renovating and/or rebuilding gargantuan homes, still free of capital gains tax for self-proclaimed owner-occupiers, has destroyed many historic precincts in near city suburbs.

Carlton, in Melbourne, retains thousands of terrace houses, and tempting Italian restaurants, but the Housing Commission of Victoria knocked down whole streets for high-rise blocks, as they did in nearby Collingwood and Richmond. The architecture of North Adelaide and Parkville (Melbourne) remains relatively intact, well-known by architectural historians, but neither are household names. And as both central Melbourne and central Adelaide are flat, their generous roadways have become arterial roads which bisect their historic precincts.

As the chapters in this book demonstrate, Paddington has retained more of its dominant late 19th century character than anywhere else in Australia, with its combination of grand and modest terrace houses, churches, shops and pubs. The Paddington Town Hall, opened by Lord Jersey in 1891, was undoubtedly 'the finest' suburban municipal hall, with only the Sydney Town Hall a grander edifice.[1] With a static population, between 24,000 and 26,000 at all the censuses from 1911 to 1947, Paddington's character remained fairly stable over that period. Nearby suburbs had noxious trades, while others became so rundown during the Great Depression that manufacturers could readily afford to demolish houses for small-scale factories, in Surry Hills, Redfern, Alexandria and Waterloo. Some of Paddington's larger terraces had already been turned into guest houses, popular with both visitors on a limited budget and country men and women moving to Sydney to find work. Balmain, with its harbour-side setting, had docks, a huge soap factory, and by the 1930s a vast power station. Paddington was not without a handful of small industries, including a small brewery, but the big breweries were in nearby suburbs, along with the large manufacturers of the day, from glassworks to tobacco. Major land-holders protected Paddington from prospective encroachments.

On the ridge the Victoria Barracks, the monumental Town Hall and the reservoir prevented incursions, while on the north both the steep topography, the Women's Hospital and the Scottish Hospital were barriers to redevelopment, along with Trumper Park. The White City tennis courts (1922) were another barrier, though now abandoned they present what will no doubt be a hotly contested redevelopment site. The equivalent of a six-storey building has already been approved on the valley floor.

There have been key moments in the history of urban redevelopment in inner Sydney where manufacturing, retailing and housing developers more or less did whatever they felt like, as did a number of government instrumentalities. Paddington's terraces survived the Depression with just a few demolitions and hundreds of filled-in balconies. Many balconies were turned into bedrooms, and others into tiny kitchens (usually with a gas ring, sometimes with a sink), enabling landlords to rent out to two or more households, if not a boarding house. Paddington survived the manic redevelopment of Sydney in the 1960s better than most, with only the Telstra building on Oxford Street, which began life as a government-owned telephone exchange, a fetching monument to masonry brutalism.

The main reasons Paddington has survived have been teased out in this book: the steep topography of much of the suburb, the relatively high building quality of most of the terrace housing stock, the difficulty in amalgamating sites for different uses, the way in which the tramways muted the destructive potential of the motor car, and the fact that the old money never entirely left, nor were whole streets owned by the Anglican church, as in the case of Glebe. And Glebe had the drawback, as did Darlington, that with the University of Sydney abutting both, on opposite sides of the campus, their terrace stock was always being eyed off by successive university registrars keen to expand their footprint.[2] The Paddington Society, established in 1964, at the apex of the demolition and redevelopment frenzy in Sydney, fought a sterling battle to retain the character of the suburb. Middle-class professionals were at the heart of this battle, as they were with the Balmain Association, set up just a year later. Both groups fought for heritage conservation and streetscape intimacy, knowing full well that many residents were working-class tenants, and that incoming European migrants were among a new influx of terrace purchasers who saw value in both the structures and the community.[3] European migrants often painted the terraces in bright colours, adding a sense of freshness to what many Sydneysiders still thought of at the time as 'slums'.

Figure 11.1: The scale of buildings on the harbour side of Oxford Street has remained unchanged since the Imperial Hotel opened in 1910. Juniper Hall, 1824, survived many attempts to demolish it while the Post and Telegraph Office, 1885, hung on through the 1990s when Australia Post did their best to sell off as many of their valuable sites as they could. Simon Wood Photography, 2017.

Of the two great challenges that face Paddington today – hyper gentrification and motor vehicle saturation – one is inescapable, as with much of the rest of inner Sydney, while the latter can still be tackled. House prices will continue to rise because of proximity to jobs and the city centre and because the suburb has managed to retain so much of its character. Tenants, unless on very high salaries, will continue to pay a considerable proportion of their income on rent. Over-reliance on the car, in a place well served by public transport, could be further reduced.

Streetscape intimacy of the tram

Inserted into Paddington at the end of the horse-drawn era, trams provided streets with a real sense of intimacy. Tramlines favoured relatively narrow shop frontages, small hotels and corner shops, both along the Oxford Street and the picturesque undulations via the Fiveways. Melburnians, familiar with wide tramway reservations, used to marvel at the route. Of course you could go well beyond Paddington on your tram trip, but as you passed through you saw all that the suburb had to offer, from hotels, hospitals, pawn brokers, illegal brothels and cinemas to substantial, if usually run-down terrace houses. Most were tenanted, from long-time residents to a variety of workers wanting to be near Sydney's major centres of employment.

Paddington still had a great deal of local employment in the 1950s, when only a small proportion of households had a car and very few women had licences. You didn't need a car to get to the surf beaches or to the city, and the tram would get you to school or to your workplace, including the myriad of factories to be found in the inner western suburbs. All the major Christian religions of the day offered a nearby church, with a synagogue in neighbouring Woollahra. Most Paddington residents worked within a radius of just a few kilometres, as most jobs remained in the city or in the nearby industrial suburbs. Getting rid of the trams and replacing them with buses, in 1960, along with rapidly rising car ownership, changed how people saw and went about their business in Sydney.

The inner western suburbs, widely denounced as slums since the 1930s by both major political parties, were sites ripe for the NSW Housing Commission to erect high-rise blocks and major institutions to build new structures, including the vast Mail Exchange at Redfern (1965). Sydneysiders were confronted with a frenzy of demolition and rebuilding. The AMP headquarters at Circular Quay (1962) broke the 150-foot height limit and all but one of the city's elegant arcades fell to the demolisher's hammer. Redfern, Waterloo and Alexandria made way for new commercial structures along with Housing Commission walkups and high-rise flats.

Paddington, at the end of the 1960s, is captured by the photographer Rob Hillier in his book *a place called PADDINGTON.* Even the typography of the large-format coffee table book, with PADDINGTON in capital letters, is revealing. The book documents, in an array of black and white photographs, the dramatic changes of the 1960s, as well as what remained of what we might call the old Paddington. We find portraits of well-known writers, most notably Cyril Pearl, artists and art gallery owners, including Cedric Flower, Elwn Lynn, Rudy Komon and Kym Bonython and composer Peter Sculthorpe. 'Miss Julie O'Brien, BA', a research assistant in the Economics Department at the University of Sydney, agreed to pose topless, leaning against a tree, to a backdrop of two terraces, one with a restored balcony, the other with its balcony filled in. She appears again at the end of the book, naked, in full back-lit silhouette, standing on a verandah with the wrought iron balcony lace-work behind her. Two female booksellers are depicted fully clothed, as are the designer Florence Broadhurst and the publisher of the *Paddington Journal,* Jannie Southan. Dorothy Rosewell, 'one of Australia's few women estate auctioneers', who specialised in the buying and selling of terrace houses, wears a mini dress to a backdrop of an auction sign. There is just a hint, in some photographs, that not all residents were mainstream heterosexuals, but no attempt is made to portray the gay culture, already arriving from nearby Kings Cross and Darlinghurst.[4]

Figure 11.2: The picturesque tram route through the Fiveways favoured shops with narrow frontages. Cafes with pavement dining replaced traditional shops a couple of decades after the trams were removed. Simon Wood Photography, 2017.

The old Paddington is portrayed in the book via photos of terraces and commercial premises, some rundown, some done up. The shops that have changed little in appearance and external signage – since both European migrants and incoming white-collar workers started to 'do up' terraces – include antique dealers, corner shops and a tattooing studio, while new restaurants (Hungry Horse, Le Chardon, D'Arcy's) and art dealers (Galleries

Primitif, Komon, Native Art Gallery, Barry Stern) all occupy terrace houses, often on high visibility corner blocks replacing previous businesses. Despite the influx of artists, architects, designers and writers, the old Paddington also survives in photos of patrons of the Windsor Castle and Four in Hand hotels, beer and smokes in hand, even if the Windsor is described as a 'swinging pub', aping the terminology of swinging London. A 30-storey block of flats under construction at Edgecliff is tellingly captioned 'A sight Paddington residents hope to avoid – high-rise development which could destroy the village atmosphere.'

The State Labor government's Landlord and Tenant legislation pegged rents at 1939 prices for some decades. Jannie Southan, editor of the *Paddington Journal,* wrote in her introduction to the Rob Hillier book that the Act 'virtually transferred property control from owners to tenants'. It is certainly true that owners did not want to spend much on the upkeep of rent-controlled properties, so many decided to sell up in the 1960s, at what today would be regarded as cheap prices, even for that time. Of course the new owners had to spend quite a bit on renovations, not least internal bathrooms and modernised kitchens, but they ended up with a solid property that could be readily on-sold.[5] The architects who moved into the area often gave neighbours free advice on both design and materials, creating an understanding of the architectural character and the importance of streetscapes. At Christmas, Southan informs us, 'new residents look to the comfort of the old ones, usually pensioners, at the all-embracing seasonal party put on by the Paddington Society when jewels and haute couture mingle with tidy best dresses'. Southan regretted that 'SP bookmakers', happily tolerated in an earlier era in Paddington, were unlikely to survive. The state government, introducing the TAB, soon finished them off.

    Small block sizes, terraces with shared walls, and rising property prices in the 1960s and 1970s, along with continual lobbying of the Paddington Society, saved Paddington from home unit development in the 1960s, with a few notable exceptions, including a large red-textured brick block in Goodhope Street. The Society's greatest early victory was to subvert the Department of Main Roads' plans to widen Jersey Road. The late 1960s and 1970s high-rise apartment boom that swept the Eastern Suburbs, bypassed Paddington. A developer simply had to buy up too many terrace houses, by now with rising values, to create a suitable site. Strata developers had to provide at least one car space per unit, and Paddington's topography made that very difficult. But in nearby Edgecliff and Darling Point huge old houses with large grounds could be purchased, sufficient to excavate into sandstone for underground parking lots.[6]

Attack from the rear

Over the past 20 years the greatest changes to the appearance of Paddington have been at the rear of the terrace houses, with both demolition and additions at the back of the house itself and dramatic changes at the laneway level. Many terraces have had their rear sections demolished and replaced with much larger rooms, new bathrooms, kitchen and living areas opening on to a back patio, new rear first-storey balconies and other devices. Some of these changes offer the occupant enhanced city views, in a housing style where the front always addressed the street. Large rear extensions dramatically change the streetscape from the laneway, as do the rash of garages built in recent decades. The only terrace houses that had the prospect of catering for the car without altering the dominant appearance of the street, were those few with horse stables at the rear, but only when they had a street or back lane entrance sufficiently wide to accommodate a car. In recent times, with the rise and rise of SUVs, garage entrances are getting wider and wider. Whole laneways have been given over to single or double garages, hardly sympathetic to the landscape of the lane. But at least successive councils have not normally tried to sell off laneways to the abutting property owners, as has happened in some other inner suburbs in Sydney and Melbourne.

Most heritage battles in Paddington have been between individual landowners, their neighbours and the council. Heritage and landscape experts can be readily found to defend the Paddington conservation area, but other qualified professionals – often charging a much higher fee – can also be hired to argue that the rights of the individual, to do more or less whatever they want with their property, should be paramount while paying lip service to conservation issues (primarily the appearance of the terrace from the street). The penchant of the very wealthy to spend whatever they need to get what they want is nicely demonstrated in situations where two terraces have been purchased and turned into one giant living establishment. This is not always obvious from the street, but is blindingly evident from the back lane, unless, as is usually the case, money is also thrown at a gargantuan back wall, turning the back lane into a blank-walled fortress. Fortunately Sydney sandstone prevents many of the wealthy from building underground garages, now so popular in more affluent sections of the Eastern Suburbs and the lower North Shore.

Figure 11.3: The terrace house form has proved remarkably adaptive as in this William Street shop top housing precinct. View looking north. Simon Wood Photography, 2017.

Daytrippers

Paddington got onto the Sydney tourist map in the late 1960s, when 5000 tourists per annum went on non-profit making tours endorsed by the Paddington Society. The town planner John Roseth remarked that 'Paddington has become a "must" on the list of sights for tourists and is on the itinerary of every sightseeing bus.' By 1970 there were four commercial tourist groups bringing their buses through Paddington. Rows of Paddington terraces started to appear on postcards. The Paddington historian Max Kelly, then a lecturer in economics at the University of New South Wales, predicted a notable increase in international tourism to Australia, particularly from North America and Japan, and noted the tourist potential of Paddington as 'a unique historic architectural and topographic area', a 'cohesive whole' just like Montmartre, the Vieux Carré, Trastevere, Williamsburg, Charlestown, and Greenwich Village.[7]

Emerging as the 'in place' for Sydneysiders to visit, the Paddington

Markets opened in the Uniting Church grounds on Oxford Street in 1973, promoting the work of local craftspeople, including fashion designers and jewellers. The market attracted both locals and visitors, and introduced Paddington to a group of younger people who might not have bothered to go to the art galleries and couldn't afford some of the classy restaurants. One of the first of the new generation of markets in Sydney, it still operates but now has many competitors, from Bondi to Kirribilli. Markets have become commonplace, and it is increasingly hard to distinguish one from another. Similarly, Oxford Street continues to face stiff competition, not only from revamped department stores in the city but also from the Westfield shopping complex at Bondi Junction, which has the advantage of 'free' car parking, rail access and the major bus interchange for the Eastern Suburbs.

Figure 11.4: The intersection of Glenmore Road with Hopewell Lane and Gipps Street bristles with high-end female fashion, including bridal wear. Residents, shoppers and diners are always on the lookout for a parking spot. The golden rain trees offer much needed shade. Simon Wood Photography, 2017.

Australia experienced an enormous increase in international tourist arrivals in the 1980s, because Boeing 747s made it quicker and cheaper to get here from the rest of the world. By the time of the Bicentennial Celebrations in 1988, Paddington featured along with Darling Harbour, the Archibald Fountain (in Hyde Park), Pier One (on Sydney Harbour), Chinatown and the Opera House as one of Sydney's key attractions. Since then Paddington has faded somewhat from the tourism hierarchy in Sydney. It doesn't have an iconic activity – like the Bridge Climb – and it is less readily legible to a visitor than the Rocks and the Opera House. It is not all that easy to get to from the fulcrum of tourist Sydney, Circular Quay. Meanwhile Sydney continues to experience intense competition in its shopping, dining and drinking locales, from Darling Harbour – with regular waves of state government investment, especially for the revamped convention centre – to Casino-funded landscape interventions at Barangaroo, with James Packer's gargantuan hotel and carefully manicured sandstone foreshores.

With mean and median terrace house prices hovering around $2 million many of Paddington's current owner-occupiers may prefer that the tourist and daytripper market fades away. Paddington's pubs and cafes remain popular, pavement eating and drinking thrives in Sydney's generally temperate climate, and the local council gets revenue from the outside seating allocation on council property. Paddington may not be well placed to cash in on the growing Chinese tourism market, but plenty of other places in Sydney – especially Darling Harbour, where commerce comes first and residents are secondary – will happily cater to changing demands and tastes.

Confronting the future

Paddington will never regain the sense of local power it enjoyed as a separate municipality until 1948. During that period local business people wielded financial power, both as landlords and as sources of employment. Municipal amalgamations have robbed most suburban communities of any sense of local representation, making community groups – not least the Paddington Society – along with schools, churches, pubs and until recently hospitals (now closed), important places in which to garner local opinion. The state government continues to call the shots on major road and transport issues, while the Woollahra Council of recent years has often favoured local opinion over the demands of outside developers and the major political parties.

Predicting the future of urban places is notoriously unreliable. When television was introduced to the United States in the 1950s some commentators claimed that it would reduce demand for overseas travel, because you would be able to see foreign places in your own lounge room. Decades later some workplace experts confidently predicted that by 2010 most people would work from home on their computers. Neither prediction came to fruition. In the case of Paddington some underlying trends will most probably persist, while others are much less predictable. Real estate will continue to be valuable in a city where real estate speculation has always been a major driver of the economy.

Paddington has avoided the current high-rise apartment boom that is decimating the character of our inner city residential areas, so while it has a shortage of affordable housing to buy or own, it doesn't run the risk of hundreds of empty properties should there be a downturn in the economy. The bulk of the terrace housing stock and the road pattern will remain much as it is today, but the forms of transport may be very different. Almost 60 years after it was ripped up light rail could be reinserted with much less difficulty than the tram line now being rebuilt down George Street in the city. Driverless cars might make the streets safer, but the only way to cut down traffic and traffic congestion would be to create more pedestrian spaces, as has already happened with some road closures. Pedestrian access could be much improved to and from Edgecliff Station, with a more direct pathway and better lighting. Meanwhile Oxford Street, with its buses, trucks and cars, remains an unpleasant arterial road, with successive recommendations to civilise it falling on deaf ears.

Paddington will continue to be protected by abutting crown land, Victoria Barracks and Centennial Park, with smaller barriers, including Trumper Park. With only a handful of large redevelopment sites in the offing, most notably the Scottish Hospital site, residents will need to remain vigilant about the appropriateness of new housing, including its scale. The suburb already has more than enough commercial space – for pubs, cafes, restaurants, food, clothing and art – so allowing infill apartment building with commercial space on the ground floor may not be a good move.

Australian cities have a variable record when it comes to preserving their residential heritage. Melbourne and Sydney both have strong heritage lobbies and reasonably strong state heritage legislation, but this rarely proves enough on very valuable sites. Community pressure still counts for a lot, as does retaining community consciousness about urban character, a continuing task for the Paddington Society. Other threats have also been kept at bay: the widespread use of fire alarms has seen many fewer house fires, always a risk in high-density places, while the generally steep topography makes major flooding unlikely. But climate change and extreme climate events can't be ruled out, especially the prospect of major hail storms. With the exception of balcony enclosures before 1986 – when asbestos was belatedly outlawed – Paddington has little fibro, fortunate given the popularity of do-it-yourself renovations.

If you want to show a visitor to Sydney, from Paris or even Tokyo, examples of places that have managed to retain their residential heritage, you don't have many options. Chief among them are Paddington and Millers Point, both subject to gentrification. In Millers Point, the state government both built the stock, to house maritime workers and their families, and – retaining it for a century – saved the fabric. Now that it is being sold off it will be interesting to see what redevelopment pressures emerge. Paddington continues to be protected by a web of resident-owners sharing a well-developed sense of the locality. While there is very little short-stay accommodation within the suburb, the rise of Airbnb has seen the praises of the terrace sung yet again. This works well when you have resident-owners letting out a room or two, but if investors build up multiple terrace house portfolios to let out room by room, it would create huge price pressures for current tenants and turn more and more of the suburb into short-stay tourism accommodation. The so-called 'sharing economy' will benefit investors, but tenants in both the inner suburbs and coastal resort towns will be priced out of the housing market.

Figure 11.5: Residents and businesses are side by side in this lively, dense urban environment. View looking west from Paddington Street intersection, with William Street to the left and residential Hopetoun Street to the right. Simon Wood Photography, 2017.

Walking around Paddington's streets today you still find relics of the horse-drawn era, including backyard stables. And when you look at commercial premises which have had a dramatic change in land use – like the cinema at the Fiveways which is now a supermarket – you often find photographs of the prior use, as you do at the Paddington Reservoir Gardens, replete with nostalgic images of the former petrol station, built on a concrete platform over the reservoir itself.[8] The partly demolished Royal Women's Hospital (1901–97), now repurposed as fancy apartments, also admits to its history. And if you ascend four floors to the rooftop of the landmark Royal Hotel, the Paddington Fiveways is spread out beneath you – a dominant late 19th century landscape where people jostle with traffic and outdoor diners enjoy the streetscape. To the west, in the setting sun, beer or cocktail in hand, you see the concrete, steel and glass of the modern city, just three kilometres away. What a miracle that Paddington survives.

Figure 11.6: The commanding view of Paddington and the city from atop the Royal Hotel. Beyond the terrace houses apartment blocks dominate the landscape. The elaborate roofline of the cinema at Fiveways, now a supermarket, is clearly visible. The top chord of the Harbour Bridge peeks out in the middle background. Simon Wood Photography, 2017.

Appendix

The Paddington Terrace House: 1840–1910

Robert Griffin

Terrace houses may be defined as a series of three or more dwellings built in a row, sharing dividing walls and the same repeated architectural details, and with identical or mirror-image plan.[1]

The Paddington terrace house, like all Sydney's terrace housing, had its beginnings in Britain. Most of those coming to Sydney – but especially architects, engineers, builders, carpenters and masons – were familiar with the Georgian terrace housing of 18th and 19th century London. An urban form of building, terrace houses maximised the occupation of the available area of land and, in London, were occupied by everyone, 'from earls to artisans'.[2] They became the most common form of Georgian building and were used in cities such as Bath – for example The Royal Crescent, built 1767–74 – and in Bristol and spa towns such as Cheltenham. They were also used to provide accommodation for the military, in the form of barrack housing, and the earliest surviving example of this row housing dates from the 1780s, located in Portsmouth. Terrace houses were occasionally used to house rural workers on large estates and from around the 1780s, with the rise of the Industrial Revolution, terrace housing was increasingly used to house factory workers.[3]

The earliest terrace housing in Sydney appears to date from the late 1820s and 1830s, although the military's Wynyard Barracks (built in 1808–10), contained barrack blocks in the form of terrace housing; a row of individual quarters, which had a ground-floor verandah added circa 1820. However, one of the earliest documented terrace house rows was that built for the trader and business figure Mary Reiby in 1828. This was a row of three houses in George Street, which was described as 'built in a solid and uniform manner'.[4] While no illustration survives of these early civilian terrace house rows, in the following two years seven applications were lodged to build terrace houses in Sydney and from 1830 the numbers of terrace houses constructed in Sydney increased rapidly.[5]

This increase was the result of a period of extraordinary economic growth, with rising immigration and capital imports from Britain. Sydney underwent intense urban consolidation; the increasing number of immigrants, most of whom had no wish to leave Sydney, prompted speculators to invest in terrace housing.

Some of this housing was architect-designed, the result of an increasing number of architects practising in Sydney in response to its economic growth. Examples of architect-designed terrace housing include Queen's Court (demolished), designed in 1832 by John Verge for JE Manning, and terrace houses designed by Edward Hallen for William Hutchinson on the corner of Macquarie and Bent Streets (demolished).[6]

However, the majority were built by those who could not afford the services of an architect. These were terraces designed and built by the 'free immigrant mechanics' of the 1830s and 1840s and by owner-builders of the later decades. Like the architects, these owner-builders copied that which they had known or constructed in Britain or followed designs found in architectural pattern books.

While the terrace house in Sydney initially followed the form of British terrace housing, a distinctive local form soon emerged. Marked by the addition of verandahs and/or balconies, this was to become the characteristic Sydney terrace house.

The growing demand for cheap and permanent housing in Sydney during the 1830s saw the terrace house become a common form; the use of party walls, common chimneys, repeated architectural details and the possibility of erecting two or three terrace houses on a single-house lot attracted many speculators.[7]

The few building regulations in Sydney and the opportunity of good returns for little outlay resulted in many poorly constructed terrace houses. In response to the largely uncontrolled building boom of the 1830s *An Act for Regulating Buildings and Party Walls ...* came into force in 1837. This Act, largely based on the *London Building Act* of 1709 – introduced in response to the Great Fire of London (1666) –

focused on structural stability and fire safety. This was to have a direct impact on terrace house construction for now exterior walls could not be built from combustible materials; walls had to be of specified thickness, depending on the rating of the house (First Rate to Fourth Rate, based on height, floor area, wall thickness and cost); brick party walls had to be used between all adjoining dwellings and be carried up above the roof line; and front and rear walls had to have a parapet. The concern for the prevention of the spread of fire also saw timber-shingle roofs banned; all timber joinery was to be recessed at least half a brick behind the wall face; and verandahs were prohibited unless built of brick or stone. There was much public outcry against the Act and as a result several amendments were made the following two years. Verandahs and balconies were now permitted if built of hardwood and in some instances balconies could overhang the street alignment; in 1839 the boundaries of the Act were reduced to central Sydney. In both the 1837 Act and the 1839 amendment, Paddington lay beyond the boundaries of the Act, enticing many speculators to build in the suburb.[8] While most Paddington terrace houses built in the early subdivisions ignored some aspects of the Act, such as party walls above the roof line (see Figures A.1 to A.4, terrace houses built between 1842 and 1860), from the 1860s the majority were consistent with its provisions.

The result was a consistent form: party walls projecting through the roof line, with verandahs and balconies defined by projecting masonry walls. This emphasised the individual dwelling, resulting in one of the most significant features of the Paddington streetscape; the repetition of form combined with the response to topography, with row upon row of individual terrace houses stepping up or down the slopes or in some cases angled to the street alignment, exposing the side/blade walls in a stepped arrangement.

Perhaps more significantly, Paddington contains an extraordinary diversity of terrace house forms, providing a virtual checklist of the terrace house typology. The following presents the range of terrace house types to be found in Paddington.[9]

Attached cottage

The attached cottage was one of the earliest types of terrace house rows, being similar in form to the individual cottages first built in the colony and based on British examples. This type was single storey and had a symmetrical facade with a centrally placed door flanked by windows. The roof was usually pitched, with a hip at the end of the row. (See Figure A.1, although this example does not have the hipped roof.) Usually built to the street alignment, the earliest forms of this type had no verandah and consisted of two rooms, with the door opening on to one of the rooms, or with a central hallway dividing the rooms. The kitchen was often in a separate building at the rear, sometimes shared with others in the row, while in later examples the kitchen formed part of a rear wing.

Figure A.1: Elevation. 541–547 Glenmore Road. © Robert Brown, 1979.

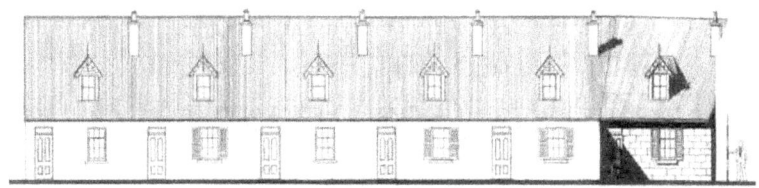

Figure A.2: Elevation. 55–63 Underwood Street. © Robert Brown, 1979.

Figure A.3: Elevation. 30–36 Thorne Street. © Robert Brown, 1979.

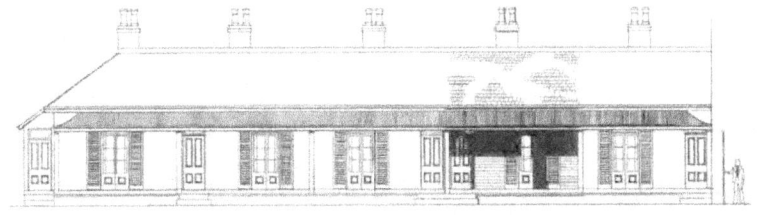

Figure A.4: Elevation. 2–10 Wentworth Street. © Robert Brown, 1979.

Bald face

The bald face type has an asymmetrical elevation, with the front door to one side and no verandah. Early examples were single storey with a pitched roof, but from about the 1830s were built with two storeys. Single-storey examples often had an attic bedroom (see Figure A.2) while early two-storey examples had one large room upstairs; later two rooms became the norm. The ground-floor rooms were arranged one behind the other and, like the attached cottage form, the kitchen was originally a separate building which was sometimes shared with others in the row. Depending on the topography, some had a basement kitchen. Later types had an attached kitchen narrower than the main building to allow some light and ventilation into the rear room of the house. This type of terrace house continued to be built throughout the 19th century, often in brick, and some examples are difficult to date.

Cantilevered balcony

Cantilevered balcony terraces are two-storeyed houses with an upper level balcony projecting over the footpath. Built from the late 1830s, these tended to be larger than the bald faced terraces (see Figure A.3). This type usually had a pitched roof with a shallow, concave curved roof to the balcony, although some early examples were built without a balcony roof. Built with an asymmetrical facade, with the door to one side, early examples had a separate kitchen at the rear. Later examples had a rear service wing, with the kitchen on the ground floor and a small bedroom above. The popularity of verandahs and balconies resulted in a cantilevered balcony often being added to bald face terraces.

Ground-floor verandah

While verandahs had been advocated for use in England from the 1820s, it seems that many thought them inappropriate and instead the balcony became the preferred form.[10] In

Australia, the addition of a verandah to terrace houses marked the beginning of the development of the characteristic Sydney terrace house type: two storeys with verandah and balcony.

The verandah is such a characteristic element of Australian architecture and so commonplace today it is hard to imagine that its adoption was slow. However, as architectural historian Robert Irving pointed out, in John Eyre's 1810 panorama of Sydney, only six free-standing houses have verandahs. While it is uncertain if the adaptation of the verandah to the terrace house form was similarly slow, by the 1830s it had become universally popular, judging by the objections to the 1837 *Building Act.* The 1838 amendments permitted verandahs, provided they were of hardwood or non-combustible materials; stopped two foot from the sides of the house or abutted a nine-inch masonry party wall. In addition, they were not to project beyond a set distance from the building line, depending on the width of the street. These regulations were to directly affect the form of terrace house rows, particularly with the use of projecting masonry walls dividing one verandah from the next, and it was not until the mid-1850s, when corrugated iron roofing sheets became generally available and concerns over fire control were overcome, that verandahs became characteristic of the terrace house form.[11]

While verandahs appear to have been added to single-storey cottage and bald face terraces when space at the front of the building made this possible, single-storey terraces with a ground-floor verandah do not appear to have been built until around 1850; Leicester Place, 2–10 Wentworth Street in Paddington is believed to be the earliest surviving example in Sydney[12] (see Figure A.4). This type of terrace house row was set back from the street, with a small front garden, and had a pitched roof and usually an asymmetrical front elevation with the door to one side. They were built with a rear wing, usually 'back to back' in the row, creating an L-shaped plan for each house. Although two-storey terraces were to become more popular, the single-storey verandah type continued to be built throughout the later 19th century and into the early 20th century, adopting the Federation style (see Figure A.5).

Two-storey terrace houses with a ground-floor verandah were built from around 1830, with the earliest surviving examples dating from 1835 (in Millers Point). In this type the ground-floor verandah was usually built to the street alignment and had an asymmetrical front elevation with the door to one side (see Figure A.6). The roof was pitched, and sometimes behind a parapet, while the verandah roof was usually shallow curved, concave corrugated iron. There were two ground-floor rooms, sometimes without a hall and then later, typically with a side hall. Later examples also had a small front yard and a rear wing housing the kitchen.

Figure A.5: Elevation. 88–94 Cascade Street. © Robert Brown, 1979.

Figure A.6: Elevation. 15–19 Gipps Street. © Robert Brown, 1979.

Figure A.7: Elevation. 5–11 Heeley Street. © Robert Brown, 1979.

Figure A.8: Elevation. 44–54 Cameron Street. © Robert Brown, 1979.

Verandah and balcony

The two-storey terrace house with a verandah and balcony was built from the 1850s and was to become the dominant form of terrace housing in Sydney, and especially in Paddington, in the late 19th century (see Figures A.7 and A.8). This type evolved from the townhouse form (see following) and was set back from the street with a small front garden and an asymmetrical facade. Early examples had a pitched roof and later this was usually behind a parapet and often in a skillion or single pitch form. The parapet and whole facade, including the party walls of the verandah and roof, the verandah and balcony balustrading and even the front fence, became increasingly decorative as the century progressed. Most characteristic of the type were the elaborate cast iron panels, columns and brackets of the verandah and balcony; even plainer forms of this type of terrace house had their decorative cast iron.

The interior layout consisted of a side hall and two rooms on the ground floor with two rooms above, the front room occupying the whole width of the building while the rear room was narrower due to the positioning of the staircase.

Early examples usually had a single storey rear wing but later this was characteristically two storeys, with a small bedroom above the kitchen and built 'back to back' with others in the row, giving an L-shaped plan that allowed light and ventilation into the rear rooms.

Townhouse

Townhouses, substantial masonry buildings of three or more storeys, became a major form of housing in Georgian London (1714–c 1830). This was the result of the London building Acts and subsequent to the publication of architectural pattern books that provided details on the design of fireproof townhouses. Townhouses also became a common building form in cities such as Edinburgh and Dublin, and in fashionable resorts such as Brighton, during the Georgian period and the type was reproduced by architects and speculative builders in the colonies using published designs.[13]

Figure A.9: Elevation. 35–53 Elizabeth Street. © Robert Brown, 1979.

In Sydney the first examples of townhouses appear in the 1830s, copied directly from English publications and commissioned by merchants and others who had made good in the colony. These townhouses were built in pairs or in rows, each house consisting of three or more storeys and often with a basement kitchen.

By the 1840s townhouses had become a common type in Sydney, with many illustrated in Joseph Fowles' *Sydney in 1848* although only a few early examples survive. These early versions were generally bald faced and while some had cantilevered balconies at the second level, later versions almost universally adopted the verandah and balcony (see Figure A.9). The roof, usually pitched, was concealed behind a parapet and the front elevation was asymmetrical with the door to one side.

The interior layout followed the English plans, with a side entrance hall leading to the staircase and two, or sometimes three, principal rooms on the ground floor. On the second level the front room extended the full width of the house, being the principal room of the house, with large windows or French doors. In Sydney in the 1830s and 1840s, the ground-floor front room was often used as an office.[14] In early examples kitchens were housed in a basement level or in a separate rear wing; in later examples, an attached rear wing became the standard design.

Bay window, recessed entry

Terrace houses with bay windows and recessed entries were built from the 1880s in one or two-storeyed versions; some have one feature or a combination of both. In two-storey versions the bay window sometimes extended over the two levels while later versions of the recessed entry type tended to have a recessed partial upper verandah. The addition of the bay window to terrace houses was intended to provide greater light and ventilation, a reflection of the growing concern with healthy living arrangements in the late 19th and early 20th centuries. This type of terrace was usually built without a verandah and with a pitched roof, sometimes with a gable (see Figure A.10). Asymmetrical in plan and elevation, a long side hall gave access to two principal rooms at the front of the house and ran through to the dining room, with an attached rear wing housing the kitchen and other service areas.

Figure A.10: Elevation. 37–45 Stafford Street. © Robert Brown, 1979.

Endnotes by chapter

Paddington: An Introduction

[1] The date was 2 August 1969.
[2] Australian Bureau of Statistics, 2016 Quick Census Stats, 'Paddington (NSW)', <censusdata.abs.gov.au/census_services> (accessed 9/5/18).
[3] Max Kelly, *Paddock Full of Houses: Paddington 1840–1890*, Doak Press, Paddington, 1978, p 4.
[4] Kelly, *Paddock Full of Houses*, p 162.
[5] Kelly, *Paddock Full of Houses*, p 195.
[6] Michael Krockenberger, *Population Growth in Australia*, Australia Institute, Canberra City, 2015, p 14.
[7] Elizabeth Farrelly, 'Cool in the tube: The terrace house stands the test of time', *Sydney Morning Herald*, 14 February 2013, p 13.

[8] *Number 96* (TV series), Wikipedia, <en.wikipedia.org/wiki/Number_96_(TV_series)> (accessed 23/4/18).

[9] Ron Johnson, with Greg Young, *Paddington History and Heritage: A theme history,* Woollahra Municipal Council, Woollahra, 1995, p 11.

[10] Kelly, *Paddock Full of Houses,* p 195.

[11] Johnson, with Young, *Paddington History and Heritage,* p 110.

[12] Kelly, *Paddock Full of Houses,* p 4.

[13] Patricia Thompson, *Accidental Chords,* Penguin Books, Ringwood, 1988, p 237.

[14] See Australian Bureau of Statistics, '5673.0.55.003 – Wage and Salary Earner Statistics for Small Areas, Time Series, 2005-06 to 2010–11', <www.abs.gov.au/ausstats/abs@.nsf/mf/5673.0.55.003> (accessed 23/4/18).

[15] Farrelly, 'Cool in the tube'.

[16] Richard Wollheim, *Art and its Objects,* Penguin, Harmondsworth, 1968, p 139.
[17] Robert Harbison, *Ruins and Fragments: Tales of loss and rediscovery,* Reaktion Books, London, 2015, p 36.
[18] Johnson, with Young, *Paddington History and Heritage,* p 49.
[19] By 1900, 77 per cent of Sydney's Jewish population lived in Paddington, Surry Hills, Darlinghurst or the city, moving further east in the late 1920s and 1930s to Bondi Junction and Waverley. Johnson, with Young, *Paddington History and Heritage,* p 94.
[20] Jill Roe, *History Workshop Journal,* Oxford University Press, 1997, p 290.
[21] Jill Roe, 'The Sydney History Group: From the beginning', *Sydney Journal,* vol 4, no 1, 2013, p 204.
[22] Gregory Young, *Environmental Conservation: Towards a*

philosophy, NSW Heritage Council, Sydney, 1984, p 9.

[23] Louis Nowra, 'Flâneurs: Wanders of the metropolitan world', *The Australian,* 9 June 2017, p 16.

[24] Susan Borham, 'Sale recalls days of dubious dealings', *Sydney Morning Herald,* 19 April 1993, p 2.

[25] Gilles Kryger (b 1928) and Susan Kryger (1929–2017).

[26] Greg Young, *Reshaping Planning with Culture,* Routledge, Abingdon, Oxon, 2016, pp 128–29.

[27] Young, *Environmental Conservation,* p 9.

[28] Robert Shiller, 'How tales of "flippers" led to a housing bubble', *New York Times,* 18 May 2017.

[29] Andrew Starr and Jan Morice, *Paddington Stories,* Andrew Starr and Associates, Paddington, 2000, p 205.

[30] M Barnard Eldershaw, *Tomorrow and Tomorrow and Tomorrow,*

Virago Press, London, 1983, p 10.

Chapter 1: Aboriginal Paddington

[1] Valerie Attenbrow, *Sydney's Aboriginal Past: Investigating the archaeological and historical records,* 2nd ed, UNSW Press, Sydney, 2010, pp 38–39.
[2] Attenbrow, *Sydney's Aboriginal Past,* pp 38–39, 55–56.
[3] Attenbrow, *Sydney's Aboriginal Past,* pp 102–03, 117–19.
[4] Attenbrow, *Sydney's Aboriginal Past* provides the most comprehensive and accessible account of this information.
[5] Attenbrow, *Sydney's Aboriginal Past,* pp 22–30, 57–58. As Attenbrow discusses, while debates exist about clan boundaries, there is no doubt that Paddington was on the estate of the Cadigal. The suffix –'gal' in Cadigal refers to the men of the clan and 'galleon' refers to the women, but the

term Cadigal is commonly used to represent the clan as a whole.

[6] Paul Irish, *Hidden in Plain View: The Aboriginal people of coastal Sydney,* NewSouth Publishing, Sydney, 2017, pp 17–19.

[7] Attenbrow, *Sydney's Aboriginal Past,* p 87; Grace Karskens, *The Colony: A history of early Sydney,* Allen & Unwin, Sydney, 2009, pp 38, 403–06.

[8] Valerie Attenbrow, Pre-colonial Aboriginal land and resource use in Centennial, Moore and Queens Parks – assessment of historical and archaeological evidence for Centennial Park and Moore Park Trust Conservation Management Plan, Report to Conybeare Morrison & Partners, 2002.

[9] Attenbrow, *Sydney's Aboriginal Past,* pp 122–24; Valerie Attenbrow, Ian Graham, Nina Kononenko, Tessa Corkill, John Byrnes, Lawrence Barron and Peter Grave, 'Crossing the Great Divide: A ground-edged hatchet-head from Vaucluse,

Sydney', *Archaeology in Oceania,* vol 47, no 1, 2012, pp 47–52.

[10] For meaning of *muru* see Philip Gidley King in John Hunter, *An Historical Journal of the Transactions at Port Jackson and Norfolk Island,* J Bach (ed), John Stockdale, London, 1793 (Australian Facsimile Editions No 148, Libraries Board of South Australia, Adelaide, 1968), p 409. For Paddington *maroo* see 'Law intelligence: Supreme Court (Civil Side)', *Sydney Morning Herald Supplement,* 18 October 1832, p 1; Edward West Marriott, *Thomas West of Barcom Glen: His life and times and family,* Barcom Press, Sydney, 1982, pp 145–46 and Pl.32.

[11] Andrew Starr and Janet Morice, *Paddington Stories,* Andrew Starr and Associates, Paddington, 2000, p 12; Karskens, *The Colony,* pp 15–16.

[12] David Collins, *An Account of the English Colony in New*

South Wales, vol 1, B Fletcher, (ed), London, Cadell and Davies, AH & AW Reed, in association with the Royal Australian Historical Society, Sydney, 1798 [1975], p 496.

[13] Irish, *Hidden in Plain View*, pp 20–21.

[14] Irish, *Hidden in Plain View*, Ch 1.

[15] Keith Vincent Smith, *King Bungaree: A Sydney Aborigine meets the Great South Pacific explorers, 1799–1830*, Kangaroo Press, Kenthurst, 1992, pp 77–80, 121–22.

[16] Lachlan Macquarie, 'New South Wales. The Governor's Diary and Memorandum book Commencing on Wednesday the 1st of March 1820 and Ending on Thursday 8th of March 1821', in *Journals of his Tours in New South Wales and Van Diemen's Land, 1810–1822*, vol 13, State Library of NSW, A774-2, p 256 (Reel CY301, fr672).

[17] For prior Aboriginal attachment see Edward Hall, 'Mr ES Hall to Sir George Murray 26 November 1828', *Historical Records of Australia,* vol 28, 1828, pp 596–97. For burials see for example Richard Hill and George Thornton, *Notes on the Aborigines of New South Wales: With personal reminiscences of the tribes formerly living the neighbourhood of Sydney and the surrounding districts*, Government Printer, Sydney, 1892, p 7.

[18] Hill and Thornton, *Notes on the Aborigines of New South Wales,* p 7; Obed West, '"Old and New Sydney": To the editor of the Herald', *Sydney Morning Herald,* 24 May 1882, p 3.

[19] Karskens, *The Colony,* pp 526–27.

[20] Smith, *King Bungaree,* pp 143–44, 147.

[21] Irish, *Hidden in Plain View,* Ch 4.

[22] Irish, *Hidden in Plain View*, pp 52–56; Ch 2, Ch 4.

[23] Marriott, *Thomas West of Barcom Glen*, p 194.

[24] Irish, *Hidden in Plain View*, pp 72–73, 123.

[25] 'Native nuisances. A black camp in a church. Old St Mark's, Darling Point', *Evening News*, 22 February 1895, p 3.

[26] 'Death of a well known Sydney character', *Empire*, 11 February 1863, p 4.

[27] Irish, *Hidden in Plain View*, pp 88–91.

[28] Major William Johnston, 'Early days of Waverley', *Eastern Suburbs Daily*, 4 November 1924, np. Plugshell was Johnston's (1869–1948) pseudonym. Johnston refers to 'Massa Hill ... a well-known identity of the city at the time' and this must be Richard Hill as he was then the most active in Aboriginal affairs and both his brothers had died by 1883.

[29] Irish, *Hidden in Plain View*, p 135.

[30] For a good account of these developments see Ann Curthoys, 'Good Christians and useful workers – Aborigines, church and state in NSW 1870–1883', in Sydney Labour History Group (eds), *What Rough Beast?: The state and social order in Australian history,* Sydney, George, Allen & Unwin, 1982, pp 31–56.

[31] 'To the editor of the Herald', *Sydney Morning Herald,* 11 January 1883, p 9.

[32] Irish, *Hidden in Plain View,* pp 111–15.

[33] For Thornton and early board see Irish, *Hidden in Plain View,* pp 115–23.

[34] Irish, *Hidden in Plain View,* p 127.

[35] Irish, *Hidden in Plain View,* pp 127–128. The reference to the use of the coach house (previously a chapel), is most likely what a later resident was referring to when she described Aboriginal people living in 'small stone cottages'. See Violet

Potter, 'Re Old Double Bay Memories', Paddington Society Archives, Woollahra Local History Centre, LH PS 711.4099441 PAD/43 Correspondence File #43.

[36] See for example Esther Wait, *The migration of people of Aboriginal ancestry to the metropolitan area and their assimilation,* BA Honours thesis, University of Sydney, 1950, pp 10, 14–15.

[37] See for example William Ridley, *Kamilaroi and other Australian Languages,* Thomas Richards, Government Printer, Sydney, 1875.

[38] Denis Byrne, 'Deep nation: Australia's acquisition of an Indigenous past', *Aboriginal History,* vol 20, 1996, pp 83, 87–88.

[39] William Dugald Campbell, *Aboriginal Carvings of Port Jackson and Broken Bay,* Government Printer, Sydney, 1899, pp 3–4.

[40] Irish, *Hidden in Plain View*, pp 135–38. See also Haidee Ireland, 'The case of Agnes Jones. Tracing Aboriginal presence in Sydney through criminal justice records', *History Australia,* vol 10, no 3, 2013, pp 245–51.

[41] I have omitted Lucy's surname to preserve anonymity in case she has relatives. 'Inmates Journal entries for 8/4/1882 and 7/9/1882', in *Benevolent Society of NSW Inmates Journal November 1880 to September 1883, State Library of NSW, MSS A7235;* 'Inmates Journal entries for 1/12/1885, 22/1/1886, 15/3/1886 and 22/3/1886', in *Benevolent Society of NSW Inmates Journal October 1883 to December 1886, State Library of NSW, MSS A7236;* Daniel Matthews, *Thirteenth Report of the Maloga Aboriginal Mission School, Murray River, NSW, Mackay & Foyster, Echuca, 1888, pp 12–13.*

[42] 'Missing Friends', *Police Gazette,* 11 January 1888, p 12.

[43] Find&Connect, 'Ormond House (1824–)', <www.findandconnect.gov.u/ref/nsw/biogs/NE01509b.htm> (accessed 30/4/18); Naomi Parry, 'Such a longing': black and white children in welfare in New South Wales and Tasmania, 1880–1940, PhD thesis, UNSW, 2007, pp 118–25.

[44] 'Deserting Wives and Families, Service &c', *Police Gazette,* 11 March 1891, p 83; 'Apprehensions &c.', *Police Gazette,* 18 March 1891, p 97.

[45] Heather Goodall, 'New South Wales', in Ann McGrath (ed) *Contested Ground: Australian Aborigines under the British Crown,* Allen & Unwin, Sydney, 1995, pp 75–80; Inara Walden, '"That was slavery days": Aboriginal domestic servants in New South Wales in the twentieth century', *Labour History,* vol 69, 1995, pp 196–209.

[46] Michael Ingrey, personal communication, 5 August 2015; Death Certificate of Lena Bungary, 12/11/1968, QLD BDM #1968/33007 C7039.

[47] George Morgan, *Unsettled Places: Aboriginal people and urbanisation in New South Wales,* Wakefield Press, Kent Town, 2006.

[48] For example an Aboriginal family recollected by a local resident as having lived in Paddington at some point in the 1930s and 1940s. Dorothy Barnes, Paddington in the '30s & '40s, Interviewed 17 June 2015 by Esther Hayter and Linda Gosling (Paddington Society).

[49] City of Sydney, *Barani Barrabugu. Yesterday Tomorrow. Sydney's Aboriginal Journey,* City of Sydney, Sydney, 2011, p 23; Gary Foley, 'Black Power in Redfern (1968–1972)', The Koori History Website, 2001, <www.kooriweb

.org/foley/essays/essay_1.html> (accessed 26/4/18).

[50] 'Foundation's first ball a colourful affair', *Dawn,* vol 15, no 5, May 1966, pp 4–5.

[51] Jennifer Jones, 'Dancing with the Prime Minister', *The Journal of the European Association of Studies on Australia,* vol 3, no 1, 2012, pp 101–13.

[52] Ann Curthoys, *Freedom Ride: A freedom rider remembers,* Allen & Unwin, Sydney, 2002.

[53] Photos of 'Jenny Bush performing at a Student Action for Aborigines concert, February 1965', in Item 020: Tribune negatives including protests against development in Woolloomooloo, and Student Action for Aborigines fundraising folk concert at Paddington Town Hall, Sydney, New South Wales, 1965, State Library of New South Wales, On 161/Item 020; Winifred Munday, 'The patients see double when they're treated by the nursing twins', *Dawn,* January 1962, p 12.

[54] See Adrian Newstead, *The Dealer is the Devil: An insider's history of the Aboriginal art trade,* Brandl and Schlesinger, Blackheath, 2014, p 295.

[55] id The Population Experts, 'Woollahra Municipal Council'. Breakdown of Woollahra Municipal Council census figures for 2011 and 2016 by suburb <profile.id.com.au/woollahra/population?WebID=140> (accessed 30/4/18).

Chapter 2: Mapping Paddington

[1] Max Kelly, *Paddock Full of Houses: Paddington 1840–1890,* Doak Press, Paddington, 1978, p 140.

[2] Edmund N Bacon, *The Design of Cities,* Thames and Hudson, London, 1967. For map references see: Smith and Gardiner's Map of Sydney and Surrounds (1855), Dixson State Library of New South Wales (SLNSW); City of Sydney (1843),

William Henry Wells, Land Surveyor, Mitchell Map Collection, SLNSW; Map of Alexandria (1840) LPI.png showing early subdivisions from Darlinghurst to Watsons Bay, Mitchell Library, SLNSW; *Plan of the Parish of Alexandria, County of Cumberland*, Mitchell Map Collection, SLNSW; F Sheilds (1890) *Map of the city of Sydney, NSW/surveyed and charted by assistant FW Sheilds*, Mitchell Map Collection, SLNSW; New South Wales, Department of Lands (1928), *Parish of Alexandria, County of Cumberland: Metropolitan Land District, Eastern Division NSW, Sydney* (4th ed, Parish maps of NSW), Mitchell Map Collection, SLNSW; *Z/Parish map – County Cumberland – Parish Alexandria* (1928), Mitchell Map Collection, SLNSW; p Bemi (1842), *Manuscript cadastral map of an area near Rushcutters Bay, Sydney, New South Wales*, Mitchell Map Collection, SLNSW;

Mrs Darling's Point to South Head Road, Property map (1833), Mitchell Map Collection, SLNSW; E Knapp, & Bowden Threlkeld (1856), *34 allotments of land at Yaranabee or Darling Point: For sale by Bowden and Threlkeld 14th Augt 1856,* Mitchell Map Collection, SLNSW; *Australian Subscription Library allotments, as sold by the Australian Auction Co on 11 May 1840* (1840), Mitchell Map Collection, SLNSW; John Armstrong, *Plan of the Paddington Estate, the Property of James Underwood Esq, Being the 150 Acres Promised to Cooper, Underwood and Forbes/J Armstrong,* 1843, Mitchell Map Collection, SLNSW – showing early Paddington Estate subdivision and the Distillery buildings, roads and layout (faintly); W Baron & J Carmichael (1854), *Woolcott & Clarke's map of the City of Sydney: With the environs of Balmain and Glebe, Chippendale*

Redfern, Paddington &c.., 1854, Mitchell Library, SLNSW; G Mann and F Reuss (1863), *Paddington, Alexandria,* Mitchell Map Collection, SLNSW; *Plan of subdivision of the Underwood estate at Paddington/to be sold by public auction by Richardson & Wrench* (1875), National Library of Australia; *Plan of the Municipality of Paddington* (1880), Mitchell Library, SLNSW; Current GIS Information provided by Woollahra Municipal Council and City of Sydney, 2015; W Brownrigg (1846), *This book of maps comprising the various parishes of the County of Cumberland with permission dedicated/by his most obed. servant Wm. Meadows Brownrigg, Land surveyor, estate & land agent,* W Meadows Brownrigg, Sydney, Dixson Library, SLNSW; W Wells & T Mitchell (1850), *This plan of the City of Sydney: Including the environs of Pyrmont, Balmain, Redfern, Chippendale, the Glebe,*

Surry Hills, Paddington & c., Mitchell Map Collection, SLNSW; J Russell & Allan & Wigley (1858), *Sands & Kenny's map of Sydney and its environs,* Dixson Map Collection, SLNSW showing detail of Paddington streets, buildings and holdings. See also Max Kelly and Ruth Crocker, *Sydney Takes Shape,* Doak Press in Association with the Macleay Museum, Sydney, 1977.

[3] Douglas Benson and Jocelyn Howell, *Taken for Granted: The bushland of Sydney and its suburbs,* Kangaroo Press, Kenthurst, 1990.

[4] Edward West Marriott, *Thomas West of Barcom Glen: His life and times and family,* Barcom Press, Bowral, 1982.

Chapter 3: Ever-changing Paddington

[1] Lucy Hughes Turnbull, *Sydney: Biography of a city,* Random House, Sydney, 1999, p 375.

[2] Clive Faro with Garry Wotherspoon, *Street Seen: A history of Oxford Street*, Melbourne University Press, Melbourne, 2000, p 32.
[3] Faro, *Street Seen,* pp 62, 68.
[4] DR Hainsworth, 'Underwood, James (1771–1844)', *Australian Dictionary of Biography,* National Centre of Biography, Australian National University, <adb.anu.edu.au/biography/underwood-james-2751/text3895> (accessed 25/4/18).
[5] Hainsworth, 'Underwood, James'.
[6] *The Australian,* 19 October 1839.
[7] State Library (NSW), George Roberts (c 1800–1865), 'Old mill, Gordon St, Paddington, Sydney, 1862', <acms.sl.nsw.gov.au/item/itemDetailPaged.aspx?itemID=447130> (accessed 25/4/18).
[8] Ron Johnson, with Greg Young, *Paddington History and Heritage: A theme history,* Woollahra Municipal Council, Woollahra, 1995, p 5.
[9] Max Kelly, *Paddock Full of Houses: Paddington 1840–1890,*

Doak Press, Paddington, 1978, p 16.
[10] Kelly, *Paddock Full of Houses,* p 19.
[11] Turnbull, *Sydney,* p 379.
[12] Kelly, *Paddock Full of Houses,* p 16.
[13] *Sydney Morning Herald,* 30 January 1844, p 2.
[14] *Australian Chronicle,* 22 May 1840.
[15] *Sydney Morning Herald,* 30 January 1844, p 2.
[16] Lilith G Norman, *Historical Notes on Paddington,* Council of the City of Sydney, Sydney, 1961, p 5.
[17] Johnson, with Young, *Paddington History and Heritage,* p 5.
[18] *Sydney Morning Herald,* 10 January 1914.
[19] See Chapter 5 for details of these villas and the later subdivision of the properties.
[20] Kelly, *Paddock Full of Houses,* p 42.
[21] Kelly, *Paddock Full of Houses,* p 42.

[22] There is always some confusion about Sydney's population, depending on boundaries and definitions – but see <www.localhistories.org/sydney.html> (accessed 25/4/18).

[23] Kelly, *Paddock Full of Houses,* p 11.

[24] Paul Ashton, 'Suburban Sydney', *Dictionary of Sydney,* 2008, <dictionaryofsydney.org/entry/suburban_sydney> (accessed 16/5/18). These figures excluded inner city residents.

[25] Faro, *Street Seen,* p 82.

[26] City of Sydney, 'History of Rushcutters Bay Park', <www.cityofsydney.nsw.gov.au/learn/sydneys-history/people-and-places/park-histories/rushcutters-bay-park> (accessed 25/4/18).

[27] Johnson, with Young, *Paddington History and Heritage,* pp 49–50.

[28] Kelly, *Paddock Full of Houses,* p 31.

[29] Ronald E Ringer, *The Brickmasters: 1788–2008,* Dry

Press Publishing, Wetherill Park, 2008.

[30] Kelly, *Paddock Full of Houses*, pp 4–5.

[31] Woollahra Municipal Council, 'Local History Facts – G', <www.woollahra.nsw.gov.au/library/local_history/local_history_fast_facts/g> (accessed 25/4/18).

[32] Woollahra Municipal Council, 'Local History Facts – G'.

[33] Paddington Society, *The Paddington Paper,* April Bulletin, 2009, <www.paddingtonsociety.org.au/files/Bulletin_April%2009.pdf> (accessed 25/4/18).

[34] 'St Matthias Anglican church Paddington', *Dictionary of Sydney,* <dictionaryofsydney.org/building/st_matthias_anglican_church_paddington> (accessed 16/5/18).

[35] Paddington Anglican, 'The History of St George's Church', 17 May 2016, <paddington.church/history-stgeorges-church> (accessed 25/4/18).

[36] St Francis of Assisi Catholic Church, Oxford Street,

Paddington, <www.sydneyorgan.com/StFrancisPad.html> (accessed 25/4/18).

[37] 'St Sophia Greek Orthodox Cathedral Paddington', *Dictionary of Sydney,* <dictionaryofsydney.org/building/st_sophia_greek_orthodox_cathedral_paddington> (accessed 25/4/18).

[38] As quoted in Kelly, *Paddock Full of Houses,* p 31.

[39] Warren Fahey's Australian Folklore Unit, 'A portrait of a Sydney suburb', 2008, <www.warrenfahey.com/paddington-born-paddington-bred>, p 11 (accessed 25/4/18).

[40] See, in the Mitchell Library, the drawing by Thomas Balcombe of the *Eclipse* [the Paddington omnibus, 1857] with its load of passengers.

[41] John Askew, *A voyage to Australia and New Zealand ... by a steerage passenger*, Simpkin Marshall, London, 1857, pp 201–02.

[42] Kelly, *Paddock Full of Houses,* p 169, mentions a petition of

1870 that requested, among other things, more omnibus stands in the Glenmore Road–Cascade Street area.
[43] Faro, *Street Seen,* p 84.
[44] Fahey, 'A portrait of a Sydney suburb', p 14.
[45] Fahey, 'A portrait of a Sydney suburb', pp 9–11.
[46] Faro, *Street Seen,* p 88.
[47] Kelly, *Paddock Full of Houses,* pp 115–16.
[48] Frederick Arthur Larcombe, *The Stabilization of Local Government in New South Wales 1858–1906: A history of local government in New South Wales,* vol 2, Sydney University Press, Sydney, 1976, p 141.
[49] Woollahra Municipal Council, 'Local History Facts – G'
[50] Larcombe, *The Stabilization of Local Government,* p 7.
[51] Kelly, *Paddock Full of Houses,* p 59.
[52] Turnbull, *Sydney,* p 380.
[53] Patricia Thompson, 'The corner store', Cambridge Street, 10 August 2012, <cambridgest.blo

[54] gspot.com.au/2012/08/the-corner-store.html> (accessed 25/4/18).
[54] Kelly, *Paddock Full of Houses*, pp 126–29.
[55] Johnson, with Young, *Paddington History and Heritage*, p 81.
[56] *Sydney Morning Herald*, 31 January 1914.
[57] Kelly, *Paddock Full of Houses*, p 40.
[58] Kelly, *Paddock Full of Houses*, p 3.
[59] Brett Lennon and Garry Wotherspoon, 'Sydney's trams, 1861–1914: the rise of an urban mass transport system', in Garry Wotherspoon (ed), *Sydney's Transport: Studies in urban history*, Hale & Iremonger, Sydney, 1983, p 101.
[60] David Keenan, *The Eastern Lines of the Sydney Tramway System*, Transit Press, Sydney, 1989, p 5.
[61] David Keenan, *The Watson's Bay Line of the Sydney*

[62] Keenan, *The Eastern Lines of the Sydney Tramway System*, Transit Press, Sydney, 1990, p 3.

Keenan, *The Eastern Lines of the Sydney Tramway System*, pp 49–50.
[63] Faro, *Street Seen*, p 64.
[64] Council letter to the Colonial Secretary, 7 September 1885, cited in Kelly, *Paddock Full of Houses*, p 129.
[65] *Sydney Morning Herald*, 21 April 1864, in Kelly, *Paddock Full of Houses*, p 149.
[66] *The Australian Star*, 10 November 1890, p 2; for Parkes's speech, see *Sydney Morning Herald*, 10 November 1890, p 5.
[67] 'Paddington Town Hall', *Dictionary of Sydney*, <dictionaryofsydney.org/building/paddington_town_hall> (accessed 25/4/18).
[68] Fahey, 'A portrait of a Sydney suburb', p 4.
[69] Norman, *Historical Notes on Paddington*, p 15.
[70] Turnbull, *Sydney*, p 378.

[71] See Sabine Willis, 'Made to be moral – at the Parramatta Girls' School, 1898–1923', in Jill Roe (ed), *Twentieth Century Sydney: Studies in urban and social history,* Hale & Iremonger, Sydney, 1980, pp 185–86 for details.

[72] *Sydney Morning Herald,* 15 March 1898, p 5.

[73] Francis Adams, *The Australians: A social sketch,* T Fisher Unwin, London, 1893, p 26.

[74] As quoted in Jill Dimond and Peter Kirkpatrick, *Literary SYDNEY: A walking guide,* University of Queensland Press, St Lucia, 2000, p 131.

[75] As quoted in Dimond and Kirkpatrick, *Literary SYDNEY,* pp 118–119, 121.

[76] Larcombe, *The Stabilization of Local Government,* p 57. See also Chris Cunneen, '"Hands off the Parks!": The provisions of parks and playgrounds', in Roe, *Twentieth Century Sydney,* p 106.

[77] City of Sydney, 'Rushcutters Bay Park'.

[78] Andrew Wilson, 'Atlas of the suburbs of Sydney', *Dictionary of Sydney,* 2012, <dictionaryofsydney.org/entry/atlas_of_the_suburbs_of_sydney> (accessed 25/4/18).

[79] Woollahra Municipal Council, *Plan of Management Trumper Park,* The Council, Woollahra, 1996, p 3, <www.woollahra.nsw.gov.au/__data/assets/pdf_file/0017/65114/Trumper_Park_POM_1996.pdf> (accessed 25/4/18). The recreation reserve was originally 14 acres and 22 perches (1 perch equals 25 square metres). The park is currently 6.78 hectares (16.75 acres). See JH Maiden, 'The parks of Sydney: Some problems of control and management', *Journal of the Royal Society of NSW,* vol 36, 1902, cited in Paul Ashton and Kate Blackmore, *Centennial Park: A history,* UNSW Press, Sydney, 1988, p 148. See also

Rob Hillier, *A Place Called Paddington,* Ure Smith, Sydney, 1970.
[80] Bede Nairn, 'Trumper, Victor Thomas (1877–1915)', *Australian Dictionary of Biography,* National Centre of Biography, Australian National University, <adb.anu.edu.au/biography/trumper-victorthomas-8862/text15557> (accessed 25/4/18).
[81] *Sydney Mail,* 14 January 1903, p 89. The *Sobraon* was a reformatory ship used for rehabilitating delinquent and destitute boys.
[82] Ashton and Blackmore, *Centennial Park,* pp 42–43, 148.
[83] Kelly, *Paddock Full of Houses,* p 84.
[84] *Sydney Mail,* 14 January 1903, p 89.
[85] *Sydney Morning Herald,* 3 January and 17 September 1842.
[86] William Hanson, *Geographical Encyclopaedia of New South*

[87] *Wales*, Government Printer, Sydney, 1892, p 305.
[87] Municipal Council of Paddington, *Paddington 1860–1910: Its history, trade and industries,* Local Government Publishing Co, Sydney, 1910, p 13.
[88] City of Sydney, 'Paddington Reservoir Gardens, Paddington', Sydney Parks History, <www.cityofsydney.nsw.gov.au/explore/facilities/parks/major-parks/paddington-reservoir-gardens> (accessed 25/4/18).
[89] 'Royal Hospital for Women', *Dictionary of Sydney,* <dictionaryofsydney.org/organisation/royal_hospital_for_women> (accessed 16/5/18).
[90] 'SDN history', SDN Children's Services, <www.sdn.org.au/about-sdn/sdn-history> (accessed 16/5/18).
[91] City of Sydney, 'Paddington Reservoir Gardens, Paddington'.
[92] Faro, *Street Seen,* p 176.
[93] Faro, *Street Seen,* p 177.
[94] Norman, *Historical Notes on Paddington,* p 27.

[95] Cinema Treasures, 'Five Ways Picture Palace', <cinematreasures.org/theaters/43191> (accessed 26/4/18).

[96] Patricia Thompson, *The Story of Paddington,* Paddington Society, Paddington, 1980, pp 19, 20.

[97] Turnbull, *Sydney,* p 377.

[98] Thompson, *The Story of Paddington,* p 19.

[99] Turnbull, *Sydney,* p 381.

[100] See Maurice Daly, *Sydney Boom, Sydney Bust: The city and its property market, 1850–1981,* Allen & Unwin, Sydney, 1982, p 186.

[101] Elizabeth Farrelly, 'The games people play with history', *Sydney Morning Herald,* 18 March 2003, <www.smh.com.au/articles/2003/03/17/1047749716218.html> (accessed 26/4/18).

[102] See Faro, *Street Seen,* pp 180–81 for more details.

[103] See Roe, *Twentieth Century Sydney,* p 266 for details from the 1933 Census of

unemployment levels in Sydney's suburbs.
[104] Faro, *Street Seen,* p 181.
[105] Thompson, *The Story of Paddington,* p 20.
[106] Johnson, with Young, *Paddington History and Heritage,* p 96.
[107] Faro, *Street Seen,* p 183.
[108] Jocka Burns, in Wendy Lowenstein (ed), *Weevils in the Flour: An oral record of the 1930s depression in Australia,* Scribe, Sydney, 1978, p 209.
[109] Johnson, with Young, *Paddington History and Heritage,* p 96.
[110] See Judy Mackinolty, 'Woman's place...', in Judy Mackinolty (ed), *The Wasted Years? Australia's Great Depression,* Allen & Unwin, Sydney, 1981, p 94.
[111] Kevin Ryan, in Sue Rosen (ed), *We Never Had a Hotbed of Crime! Life in twentieth century South Sydney,* Hale

[112] Ryan, in Rosen, *We Never Had a Hotbed of Crime!*, p 88.
[113] Turnbull, *Sydney,* p 376.
[114] Ryan, in Rosen, *We Never Had a Hotbed of Crime!,* p 102.
[115] Faro, *Street Seen,* p 186.
[116] Bob Slater, in Rosen, *We Never Had a Hotbed of Crime!,* p 138.
[117] Ryan, in Rosen, *We Never Had a Hotbed of Crime!,* p 138.
[118] See Paul Ashton, *The Accidental City: Planning Sydney since 1788,* Hale & Iremonger, Sydney, 1993, p 66.
[119] See Faro, *Street Seen,* pp 169–70 for details of the happenings in Paddington.
[120] Ashton, *The Accidental City,* p 73.
[121] Ashton, *The Accidental City,* p 86.
[122] *The Planning Scheme of the County of Cumberland, NSW,*

Cumberland County Council, Sydney, 1948, pp 33–34.

[123] As quoted in Dimond and Kirkpatrick, *Literary SYDNEY,* pp 117–18.

[124] Peter Spearritt, *Sydney's Century,* UNSW Press, Sydney, 2000, p 229.

[125] Cinema Treasures, 'Five Ways Picture Palace'.

[126] Daly, *Sydney Boom, Sydney Bust,* pp 183–84.

[127] Commonwealth Censuses, 1947, 1961, 1966 as quoted in John Roseth, The revival of an old residential area: A study of the resurgence of Paddington and its implications for Sydney's inner residential suburbs, PhD thesis, University of Sydney, 1969, p 75.

[128] *Paddington Journal,* vol 1, no 1, November 1967.

[129] Turnbull, *Sydney,* p 381.

[130] Interview with Warren Fahey, January 1999, for *Street Seen.* See also Philip Lindsay's contemporary account in his memoir, *I'd Live the Same*

Life Over, Hutchinson, London, 1941, pp 56–57. Greeks and Italians and other 'New Australians' were derisively referred to as 'dagoes', the term originating from the Spanish given name 'Diego'.

[131] Slater, in Rosen, *We Never Had a Hotbed of Crime!,* p 195.

[132] As quoted in Dimond and Kirkpatrick, *Literary SYDNEY,* pp 117, 122.

[133] Currency Press, 'A Brief History of Currency Press', <currency.com.au/currencypressbriefhistory.aspx> (accessed 26/4/18).

[134] As quoted in Dimond and Kirkpatrick, *Literary SYDNEY,* p 121.

[135] See Faro, *Street Seen,* p 223.

[136] Faro, *Street Seen,* pp 211, 262.

[137] *Census of Australia,* 1966, 1971 and 1976.

[138] Peter Spearritt, *Sydney Since the Twenties,* Hale &

Iremonger, Sydney, 1978, p 215.

[139] As quoted in Dimond and Kirkpatrick, *Literary SYDNEY*, p 120.

[140] As quoted in Dimond and Kirkpatrick, Literary SYDNEY, p 124.

[141] For the 'history and romance' of heritage, see *Wentworth Courier,* 26 September 1984; for information regarding antique shops, *Wentworth Courier,* 1 August 1973; for an account of the restoration of Paddington Post Office, see the special booklet, *Paddington Post Office,* published by Australia Post, Sydney, 1979.

[142] *Wentworth Courier,* 4 December 1974.

[143] *Paddington Journal,* vol 2, no 12, October 1969.

[144] Turnbull, *Sydney,* p 381.

[145] For details of the 'gayification' of parts of Paddington, see Faro, *Street Seen,* pp 223–27.

[146] Faro, *Street Seen,* pp 226, 235.

[147] *Campaign,* March 1976, p 7.
[148] *Campaign,* April 1976, p 12.
[149] Philip McCarthy, 'Macho-chic at the pub', *National Times,* 14–20 September 1980, p 19.
[150] *Gay Guide,* Gay Counselling Service of NSW, Sydney, 1984. 151 *OZ,* March 1964, p 6.
[152] Garry Wotherspoon, 'Paddington', *Dictionary of Sydney,* 2012 <dictionaryofsydney.org/entry/paddington> (accessed 26/4/18).
[153] See Faro, *Street Seen,* p 191.
[154] See Zula Nittim, 'The coalition of Resident Action Groups', in Roe, *Twentieth Century Sydney,* p 232, for detail, and what developed.
[155] See Faro, *Street Seen,* pp 218–19.
[156] John Woodward, Report of Commission of Inquiry for the Department of Environment and Planning into a Development Application for the Paddington Retail Markets, October 1987, p 41.

[157] See Turnbull, *Sydney,* pp 376–77 for details.
[158] Turnbull, *Sydney,* p 377.
[159] Turnbull, *Sydney,* p 378.
[160] 'A royal history – 150 years at the Royal Hospital for Women', The Royal Hospital for Women, <www.royalwomen.org.au/news/eventnews/a-royal-history-150-years-atthe-royal-hospital-for-women> (accessed 16/5/18).
[161] Daisy Dumas, 'Oxford Street: A new direction "The Perfect Storm"', <www.smh.com.au/interactive/2014/oxford-street> (accessed 26/4/18).
[162] Daisy Dumas, 'Oxford Street: A new direction "The Owners"', *Sydney Morning Herald,* 2014, <www.smh.com.au/interactive/2014/oxfordstreet/chapter-2-the-owners.html> (accessed 26/4/18).
[163] Dumas, 'Oxford Street: A new direction "The Owners"'.
[164] Dumas, 'Oxford Street: A new direction "The Owners"'.

[165] Dumas, 'Oxford Street: A new direction "The Perfect Storm"'.
[166] Destination NSW, 'Paddington Tours', <www.sydney.com/destinations/sydney/inner-sydney/paddington/tours> (accessed 26/4/18).
[167] Johnson, with Young, *Paddington History and Heritage,* p 109.
[168] William Street Paddington, <williamstreetpaddington.com.au> (accessed 26/4/18).

Chapter 4: Early Paddington

[1] Captain Arthur Phillip to Lord Sydney, 15 May 1788, *Historical Records of Australia,* (HRA) series I, vol I, p 23.
[2] Captain Watkin Tench, quoted in Douglas Howard Benson and Jocelyn Howell, *Sydney Bushland: Two centuries of change,* Royal Botanic Gardens, Sydney, 1988, p 1.
[3] Obed West, quoted in Edward W Marriott, *Thomas West of Barcom*

[4] *Glen,* Barcom Press, Bowral, 1982, p 139.

[4] While Aboriginal people appear to have occupied the Sydney region for tens of thousands of years, it was not until some 6500 years ago, following the end of the Ice Age, that sea levels stabilised and created the harbour foreshores that the Cadigal inhabited and that exist today. See Valerie Attenbrow, *Sydney's Aboriginal Past: Investigating the archaeological and historical records,* 2nd ed, UNSW Press, Sydney, 2010, pp 38–39.

[5] The *Supply* was used by Captain John Hunter for his hydrographic survey of Port Jackson. Contrary to popular belief it was not the place of the murder of two rush cutters in May 1788 (see note by LF Fitzhardinge in Watkin Tench, *Sydney's First Four Years,* Library of Australian History, Sydney, 1979, p 105, note 23).

[6] The road, which followed an Aboriginal pathway, was

constructed by convict labour under a contract won by surgeon John Harris.

[7] Quoted in Garry Wotherspoon, 'Paddington', *Dictionary of Sydney*, <dictionaryofsydney.org/entry/paddington#ref-uuid=e369853df766-fa44-e1ed-0ff613f563bd> (accessed 26/4/18).

[8] Greg Curnow, 'West, Thomas (1773–1858)', *Australian Dictionary of Biography*, <adb.anu.edu.au/biography/west-thomas-13245> (accessed 26/4/18).

[9] Macquarie's journal, quoted in Marriott, *Thomas West of Barcom Glen,* p 87.

[10] Marriott, *Thomas West of Barcom Glen,* p 87. There have been various suggestions for the basis of the name however it may be from the then well-known complex of watermills in Barcombe, Sussex. In 1812, when West water mill commenced, several windmills were operating in Sydney.

[11] Marriott, *Thomas West of Barcom Glen,* p 92.

[12] Marriott, *Thomas West of Barcom Glen,* pp 152, 159. The house appears to have stood near present-day St Vincent's Private Hospital, at the end of Little Barcom Street. It was demolished in 1901.

[13] Marriott, *Thomas West of Barcom Glen,* p 136.

[14] Curnow, 'West, Thomas (1773–1858)'. The 1832 trial reduced West's claim by 5 acres (2 ha) to 71 acres (29 ha). He did not receive the land title until 1844.

[15] For a full description of the house, and of the lives of Thomas and Obed West, see Marriott, *Thomas West of Barcom Glen.*

[16] Joseph Lycett, quoted in James Broadbent, *The Australian Colonial House: Architecture and society in New South Wales, 1788–1842,* Hordern House, Potts Point, 1997, p 98.

[17] Ron Johnson, *Paddington: A theme history,* Woollahra Council, Woollahra, 1997, p 20.

The accident occurred in George Street on 6 October 1814. Macquarie to Under-secretary Goulburn, 15 December 1817, HRA, I, XI, p.733.

[18] *Sydney Gazette,* 16 November 1816, p 2.

[19] An emancipist was a former convict who had received a conditional or absolute pardon.

[20] Johnson, *Paddington,* p 19.

[21] *Sydney Gazette,* 21 October 1824, p 2; 28 October 1824, p 2.

[22] 'Memorandum ... Duties on Spirits', 4 February 1825, HRA I, vol XI, p 488.

[23] Underwood's residence at Rushcutters Bay, *Sydney Gazette,* 1 June 1830, p 3.

[24] The name 'Glenmore Distillery' first appears in the *Sydney Gazette,* 1 June 1837, p 2.

[25] Paddington was named after the London borough. Johnson, *Paddington,* p 16 and Wotherspoon, 'Paddington'.

[26] Memorial [1832]. Colonial Secretary: Allotments and

Construction of houses ... Darlinghurst and Woolloomooloo 1827–46 AONSW 2/1751, quoted in James Broadbent, 'The push east: Woolloomooloo Hill, the first suburb' in Max Kelly, *Sydney: City of suburbs,* UNSW Press, Sydney, 1987, p 16.

[27] The conditions for the grants were that only one 'Villa or residence' was to be built on the land; the plans were to be approved by the governor; the front of the villa must face towards the town; and the building was to be completed within three years at a minimum cost of £1000. See Broadbent, 'The push east' in Kelly, *Sydney,* p 17.

[28] Mrs Charles Meredith, *Notes and Sketches of New South Wales...,* facsimile ed, Ure Smith, Sydney, 1973, p 49.

[29] Bourke to Viscount Goderich, 24 December 1832, HRA I, XVI, p 827.

[30] Bourke to Viscount Goderich, p 826; Max Kelly, *A Paddock Full of Houses: Paddington 1840–1890,* Doak Press, Paddington, 1978.

[31] Statement of the grants made ... at Rushcutters Bay, December 1832; Governor Darling, Minute No 99, 15 October 1831, HRA I, XVI, p 828.

[32] Terry Kass, *The History of Juniper Hall (Ormond House), Paddington,* Department of Environment and Planning, Sydney, 1982, pp 1–2.

[33] James Semple Kerr and Gordon Menzies, *Juniper Hall: An analysis of the existing fabric and documentary evidence...*, np, 1983, p vi.

[34] The houses of William Kent and Simeon Lord, built 1797 and 1803 respectively. See Broadbent, *The Australian Colonial House,* p 127 and pp 8–12.

[35] Broadbent, *The Australian Colonial House,* p 127.

Broadbent quotes Clive Lucas for the sash windows being a later alteration.
[36] This appears to have been at the front south-western corner. See Broadbent, *The Australian Colonial House,* p 129.
[37] Broadbent, *The Australian Colonial House,* p 129.
[38] Broadbent, *The Australian Colonial House,* p 128.
[39] Kass, *The History of Juniper Hall,* p 19.
[40] Terence Lane and Jessie Searle, *Australians at Home: A documentary history of Australian domestic interiors from 1788 to 1914,* Oxford University Press, Melbourne, 1990, p 64.
[41] Peter Cunningham, *Two Years in New South Wales,* facsimile ed, Library Board of South Australia, Adelaide, 1966, p 125.
[42] *Sydney Gazette,* 16 June 1831, p 3; the Coopers returned to their George Street residence prior to travelling to England.

[43] It appears John Kinchela renamed the house after his patron, the Marquis of Ormonde. The 'e' was dropped from the name of the house in the late 19th century.

[44] *Sydney Gazette,* 22 May 1832, p 2.

[45] James Broadbent has noted that only Goderich Lodge can be ascribed to John Verge with certainty, for it appears Elizabeth Bay House involved several designers, Rockwall (Rockwall Crescent, Potts Point) and Tusculum (Manning Street, Potts Point) were begun several years later while Barham (Forbes Street, Darlinghurst) appears to be to Verge's design. See Broadbent, *The Australian Colonial House,* pp 183, 186.

[46] *Sydney Gazette,* 28 June 1834, p 2.

[47] Located at 56A Ormond Street Paddington, only part of one wing survives, beneath a second storey added in the late

19th century and after conversion to a block of flats in the 20th century. See James Broadbent, Ian Evans and Clive Lucas, *The Golden Decade of Australian Architecture: The work of John Verge,* David Ell Press, Sydney, 1978, pp 57–59.

[48] *Sydney Morning Herald,* 29 April 1846, p 4.

[49] Robert Kerr, *The Gentleman's House,* quoted in Peter Thornton, *Authentic Décor: The domestic interior, 1620–1920,* Weidenfeld and Nicolson, London, 1993, p 219.

[50] WG Verge, *John Verge: Early Australian architect,* Wentworth Books, Sydney, 1962, pp 48–50.

[51] Richard and Wrench contract book, A.4531, quoted in Kelly, *A Paddock Full of Houses,* p 52.

[52] *Report of Archaeological excavations at 'Flinton'...,* Austral Archaeology, Sydney, 1999; Verge, *John Verge,* pp 165–66.

[53] Kinchela's estate Ormonde (not to be confused with Robert Cooper's house Juniper Hall that Kinchela had rented and renamed Ormonde House), was offered for sale in 1838. The sale notice includes a detailed description of Kinchela's improvements: *Sydney Gazette,* 30 January 1838, p 3.

[54] Sale notice for Kinchela's Ormonde Estate, *Sydney Gazette,* 30 January 1838, p 3.

[55] *Sydney Morning Herald,* 10 June 1847, p 4.

[56] Olive Bank Villa, at 33 Heeley Street, has been used as an early childhood centre since 1924.

[57] *Daily Telegraph,* 26 June 1889, quoted in Kelly, *A Paddock Full of Houses,* p 60.

[58] Governor Darling had first recommended that the library receive a building allotment in Hyde Park: it 'should take precedence of all private claimants' to ensure that it obtained an important site for

its buildings. Minute No 99, 15 October 1831, HRA I, XVI, p 828.

[59] The site was bounded by present-day George and Clarence streets, and Barrack and Margaret streets.

[60] Rosemary Annable, *The Victoria Barracks, Sydney,* Report prepared for Clive Lucas Pty Ltd and Commonwealth Department of Housing & Construction, 1982, Part 1.

[61] Busby's Bore was a water supply tunnel constructed 1827–37 between the Lachlan Swamp in Centennial Park and the southern end of Hyde Park. It ran directly under the site of Victoria Barracks.

[62] Neil Radford, 'Victoria Barracks', *Dictionary of Sydney,* <dictionaryofsydney.org/place/victoria_barracks> (accessed 26/4/18).

[63] Kelly, *Paddock Full of Houses,* pp 19–21.

[64] Brodie and Craig to Governor Gipps, 8 February 1844, quoted

in Annable, *The Victoria Barracks, Sydney,* p 19.

[65] Kelly, *A Paddock Full of Houses,* p 19.

[66] Johnson, *Paddington,* p 32; Samuel Lyons 1842 advertisement for the sale of the Paddington estate, quoted in Kelly, *A Paddock Full of Houses,* p 22.

[67] Kelly, *A Paddock Full of Houses,* p 30.

[68] John Palmer had been granted 70 acres (28 ha) here in 1793 and soon after acquired Alexander Donaldson's neighbouring grant and named his property George Farm. Palmer sold his land in 1814 in varying sized lots to several owners, resulting in the 'shambolic' development of Surry Hills. Garry Wotherspoon and Chris Keating, 'Surry Hills', *Dictionary of Sydney,* 2009, <dictionaryofsydney.org/entry/surry_hills> (accessed 26/4/18).

[69] In a post mill the whole body of the mill pivots on a post and

can be turned to face the sails into the wind. The foundations of Gordon's Mill remain in Gordon Street.

[70] Ron Johnson, 'Gordon's Mill', *Paddington Society News Bulletin,* September 2007.
[71] *Illustrated Sydney News,* 25 October 1884, p 3.

Chapter 5: The Victorian suburb

[1] Max Kelly, 'The Rocks Conservation Area', in Australian Heritage Commission, *The Heritage of Australia,* Macmillan, Melbourne, 1981, pp 2/67–2/68. Kelly describes the housing of The Rocks and Millers Point in this manner.
[2] Some sections of this chapter draw on material prepared by Craig Burton, landscape architect and heritage consultant.
[3] *Sydney Herald,* 30 September 1839, p 3.
[4] *Sydney Morning Herald,* 26 September 1842, p 3.

[5] *The Australian*, 30 January 1845, p 2. The allotments were in Underwood Street (44-foot –13.5-metre – frontage) and Underwood Street (50-foot –15-metre – frontage).
[6] Patricia Thompson, *The Story of Paddington,* Fiveways Publishing, Paddington, nd, p 3.
[7] *The Australian,* 26 August 1842, p 1.
[8] *The Australian,* 30 January 1845, p 2.
[9] Ron Johnson, *Paddington: A theme history,* Woollahra Council, Woollahra, 1997, p 30. Johnson also records the oral tradition that 2 Comber Street was built for the captain of guard.
[10] George William Newcombe offered two lots for sale, one with a 60-foot (18-metre) frontage to Old South Head Road: *Sydney Morning Herald,* 25 April 1849, p 4.
[11] Johnson, *Paddington,* p 30.
[12] Johnson, *Paddington,* p 48.
[13] Max Kelly, *Paddock Full of Houses: Paddington 1840–1890,*

Doak Press, Paddington, 1978, p 67.
[14] Johnson, *Paddington,* p 62.
[15] Kelly, *Paddock Full of Houses,* p 66.
[16] Kelly, *Paddock Full of Houses,* presents a study of the Paddington Rate Books.
[17] Kelly, *Paddock Full of Houses,* p 68; Bill Morrison, unpublished notes on Paddington subdivisions. These two sources also provided information for the following text on Paddington subdivisions.
[18] Kelly, *Paddock Full of Houses,* p 68.
[19] May 1875.
[20] Kelly, *Paddock Full of Houses,* p 73.
[21] The subdivision provided for two narrow passageways (now removed) between these terraces, providing pedestrian access between Cooper Street and Glenmore Road. This probably also served for the removal of nightsoil.

Information from Bill Morrison, 2018.
[22] *Sydney Morning Herald,* 15 January 1892, p 8; 29 February 1892, p 3.
[23] *Sydney Morning Herald,* 10 May 1893, p 3.
[24] *Sydney Morning Herald,* 26 June 1893, p 2.
[25] Kelly, *Paddock Full of Houses,* p 54.
[26] *Sydney Morning Herald,* 2 April 1898, p 15.
[27] *Sydney Morning Herald,* 16 October 1844, p 1.
[28] *Municipality of Paddington Assessment Book, 1860–63,* quoted in Kelly, *Paddock Full of Houses,* p 56.
[29] *Sydney Morning Herald,* 11 September 1900, p 8.
[30] 'Kinchela, John (1774–1845)', *Australian Dictionary of Biography,* National Centre of Biography, Australian National University, <adb.anu.edu.au/biography/kinchelajohn-2305> (accessed 26/4/18).

[31] *Sydney Morning Herald,* 18 July 1882, p 2.
[32] Kelly, *Paddock Full of Houses,* p 80.
[33] Johnson, *Paddington,* p 73.
[34] Question 2707, quoted in Caroline Butler-Bowden and Charles Pickett, *Homes in the Sky: Apartment living in Australia,* Miegunyah Press, Sydney, 2007, p 4.
[35] Kelly, *Paddock Full of Houses,* p 191; Kelly, quoted in Andrew Starr and Janet Morice, *Paddington Stories,* Starr & Associates, Paddington, 2000, p 72.
[36] Johnson, *Paddington,* p 76.
[37] *Sydney Morning Herald,* 2 January 1930, p 10.
[38] NH Dick, *Housing Problems: Better planning called for,* quoted in Peter Spearritt, *Sydney's Century: A history,* UNSW Press, Sydney, 2000, p 71.
[39] One group of these flats was built in Erskineville in 1938–39.

See Spearritt, *Sydney's Century,* p 71.
[40] Dr Lerner, quoted in Starr and Morice, *Paddington Stories,* p 139.
[41] Research by Paddy Pearl, quoted in Starr and Morice, *Paddington Stories,* p 143.
[42] Max, quoted in Starr and Morice, *Paddington Stories,* p 143.
[43] Jannie Southan, in Rob Hillier, *A Place called Paddington,* Ure Smith, Sydney, 1970, p 9.
[44] Donald Gazzard, *Sydneysider: An optimistic life in architecture,* Watermark Press, Boorowa, 2006, p 59.
[45] Rob Hillier, *Let's Buy a Terrace House,* Ure Smith, Sydney, 1968, p 8.
[46] *Paddington: A plan for preservation,* Paddington Society, Paddington, 1970, quoted in *Architecture in Australia,* vol 60, no 1, February 1971, p 73.
[47] Gazzard, *Sydneysider,* p 88.

[48] Jennifer Taylor, *Australian Architecture since 1960,* RAIA, Red Hill, 1990, p 150. The house has since been listed as a heritage item by Woollahra Council.

[49] *Architecture in Australia,* vol 70, no 6, December 1981, p 24.

[50] The original design for the house was in 1982.

[51] Alec Tzannes, 'First House: Tzannes Associates', *Architectureau,* Issue 89, December 2012, <architectureau.com/articles/henwood-house-bytzannes-associates> (accessed 26/4/18).

[52] Jury report in *Architecture Australia Awards,* December 1988; *Sydney Morning Herald,* 2 September 1989, p 79.

[53] Cameron Bruhn and Katelin Butler (eds), *The Terrace House,* Thames & Hudson, Port Melbourne, 2015, p 21.

Chapter 6: Gentrification

[1] Patricia Thompson, *Accidental Chords,* Penguin Books, Ringwood, 1988, p 225.

[2] Hal Kendig, *New Life For Old Suburbs,* George Allen & Unwin, Sydney, 1979, pp 126–27.

[3] Joshi Herrmann, 'The ghost town of the super-rich: Kensington and Chelsea's "buy-to-leave" phenomenon', *Evening Standard,* 21 March 2014, <www.standard.co.uk/lifestyle/london-life/the-ghost-townof-the-super-rich-kensington-andchelseas-buy-to-leavephenomenon-9207306.html> (accessed 26/4/18).

[4] Daisy Dumas, 'The perfect storm', *Sydney Morning Herald,* 2014 <www.smh.com.au/interactive/2014/oxford-street> (accessed 26/4/18).

[5] Ron Johnson, *It Never Stops Does It! A profile of the Paddington Society: Pioneer in heritage activism 1964–2004,* Paddington Society, Sydney, 2003, p 8.

[6] Rob Hillier, *A Place Called Paddington,* Ure Smith, Sydney, 1970, p 5.

[7] Johnson, *It Never Stops Does It!,* p 8.

[8] Ron Johnson, with Greg Young, *Paddington History and Heritage: A theme history,* Woollahra Municipal Council, Woollahra, 1997, p 97.

[9] Hal Kendig, 'Gentrification in Australia', in J John Palen and Bruce London (eds), *Gentrification, Displacement, and Neighborhood Revitalisation,* State University of New York Press, New York, 1984, pp 235–53.

[10] Kendig, 'Gentrification in Australia'.

[11] Johnson, with Young, *Paddington History and Heritage,* p 97.

[12] Patricia Kent, 'Pleasant Paddington', *Australian Women's Weekly,* 19 May 1963, p 10.

[13] Thompson, *Accidental Chords,* p 222.

[14] Thompson, *Accidental Chords,* p 221.
[15] Kent, 'Pleasant Paddington'.
[16] Lesley Cameron and Michael Craig, 'A decade of change in inner Sydney', *Urban Policy and Research,* vol 3, no 4, 1985, p 25.
[17] Johnson, with Young, *Paddington History and Heritage,* p 106.
[18] Kent, 'Pleasant Paddington'.
[19] Kendig, 'Gentrification in Australia'.
[20] Kendig, *New Life for Old Suburbs,* pp 127–28.
[21] Thompson, *Accidental Chords,* p 244.
[22] Matt Siegel, 'Their space solution is found next door', *New York Times,* 16 June 2011, p D7, <www.nytimes.com/2011/06/16/greathomesanddestinations/their-space-solution-is-found-nextdoor-on-location.html> (accessed 26/4/18).
[23] Interview, Peter McNeil, Margaret Smyth and William de

[24] Winton, East Sydney, 7 April 2017.
[24] Paddington Markets <www.paddingtonmarkets.com.au/about-paddington-markets-sydney> (accessed 26/4/18).
[25] Miranda Rout, 'Revival plans for iconic fashion strips on Oxford St and Chapel St', *The Australian,* 3 October 2014.
[26] Daisy Dumas, 'Oxford Street: A new direction', *Sydney Morning Herald,* 2014, <www.smh.com.au/interactive/2014/oxford-street/index_m.html> (accessed 26/4/18).
[27] Richard Jinman, 'Folkways hits the fade button on an era of silencing pop pap', *Sydney Morning Herald,* 25 April 2009.
[28] Hugh Liney and Frank Cotterell, *Rock 'n' Roll Walk of Fame 'n' Shame: Oxford Street in the late 60s, 70s and 80s,* research by Frank Cotterell, produced by Hugh Liney and Ashley Russell for Gti Media, City of Sydney.
[29] Recreational Arts Team (RAT) parities archive, 1984–1989,

Powerhouse Museum Collection Search 2.53, <ma.as/319660> (accessed 26/4/18).
[30] Hannah Brooks, 'When Rat ruled the world', *Vice,* 2 March 2009, <www.vice.com/en_us/article/when-ratruled-world-747-v16n3> (accessed 26/4/18).
[31] Luci Ellis, 'Property Markets and Financial Stability: What We Know So Far', University of New South Wales Real Estate Symposium, 8 September 2015, <www.rba.gov.au/speeches/2015/sp-so-2015-09-08.html> (accessed 26/4/18).

Chapter 7: Conserving Paddington

[1] *County of Cumberland Council Report on the Planning Scheme for the County of Cumberland* (CCCR), NSW County of Cumberland Council, 1948, p 70.
[2] FC Cook, 1945 *City of Hobart Plan.*
[3] CCCR.
[4] CCCR.

[5] *Sydney Morning Herald,* 4 May 1937, p 16.
[6] Clive Faro with Garry Wotherspoon, *Street Seen: A history of Oxford Street,* Melbourne University Press, Melbourne, 2000, p 186.
[7] John Roseth, The revival of an old residential area: A study of the resurgence of Paddington and its implications for Sydney's inner residential suburbs, PhD thesis, University of Sydney, 1969.
[8] Commonwealth Censuses of 1947, 1966 quoted in Roseth, The revival of an old residential area, p 75.
[9] John Roseth (Planning Research Centre), *Extent Progress and Location of Rehabilitation Activity In Paddington,* Sydney University, Sydney, 1967.
[10] Ron Johnson, *It Never Stops Does it! A profile of the Paddington Society: Pioneer in heritage activism 1964–2004,* Paddington Society, Paddington, 2004.

[11] Roseth, The revival of an old residential area, p 116.

[12] Don Gazzard, The Victory of Paddo Manuscript, ud, Paddington Society Archives.

[13] 'To maintain all features of Paddington, having beauty, architectural and/or historical value; to preserve existing open spaces and increase open spaces for the health and enjoyment of the community; to maintain harmony with existing architectural patterns when new buildings are constructed; to prevent the disfigurement of premises, streets and open spaces by ugly advertisements, poles, wires and unseemly structures; to protect residents from smoke, noise and other nuisances detrimental to the quiet enjoyment of their houses; to protect and add to the amenities of Paddington; to ensure the safety and convenience of pedestrians and vehicles using the streets; to

encourage the development of cultural activities and to compile and record the history of the area.' The Paddington Society, *Paddington: A plan for preservation,* 1970, pp 43–44.

[14] Ron Johnson, *A Peek at Paddington's Past,* Paddington Society, Sydney, 2011.

[15] Gazzard, The Victory of Paddo Manuscript.

[16] Andrew Starr and Janet Morice, *Paddington Stories,* Andrew Starr & Assoc, Paddington, 2000, p 187.

[17] *Report On The Exhibited Proposals Under The City Of Sydney Planning Scheme Affecting The Paddington Area Following A Public Inquiry (The Bunning Report),* Walter Bunning, March 1968.

[18] Although the principle of a new zoning to conserve Paddington was confirmed, a 2 (g) residential zoning was not applied to North Paddington until 14 July 1971 (under the *City of Sydney Planning*

Scheme, Woollahra Scheme Plan).

[19] Paddington Society, *Paddington: A plan for preservation,* October 1970.

[20] Research findings were summarised in the appendices of the Society's seminal 1970 publication *A Plan for Paddington.*

[21] The synergy between Clarke's work in Tasmania and the development of the 2 (g) zoning approach in Sydney is yet to be documented.

[22] The Special Areas subcommittee was chaired by Don Gazzard with Keith Cottier as vice chair, and members include Elias Duek-Cohen, Brian Cassidy, Charles Moess and John Luscombe and Stephen Oquist, assisted by George Clarke.

[23] Paddington Society, *Paddington: A plan for preservation.*

[24] Starr and Morice, *Paddington Stories,* p 185. By the 1976 Census, Paddington had one of the highest concentrations of

graduates in Sydney. Incomes were above average, and Paddington residents were paying above average mortgages.

[25] Starr and Morice, *Paddington Stories,* p 15.
[26] Clause 57, CSPSO.
[27] Chris Bluett, *Attitudes and Urban Conservation Thesis,* BTP, UNSW, 1980, p 75.
[28] Co-authors R Coull, Steven Davies, p de Fibe, Gary Shiels, D Wilkie.
[29] Paddington Control Code adopted 19 August 1974.
[30] A *Policy for the Control of Changes to Facades of Buildings in Paddington and the Edgecliff Glebe* was adopted in November 1976. This was later revised and expanded to include Bondi Junction and West Woollahra and was adopted in February 1984. The Paddington Action Plan, incorporating a strategy and objectives put forward by the Society was adopted by council in July 1977

and land use, height and density zones were adopted in principle in March 1978. A specific *Development Control Code for the Glebe Lands at Edgecliff* was adopted in July 1978.

[31] Leonie Sandercock, Property, politics and power: A history of city planning in Adelaide Melbourne and Sydney since 1900, PhD thesis, ANU, quoted in Bluett, *Attitudes and Urban Conservation Thesis,* 1980.

[32] Forty-three Green Bans were placed by the Builders Labourers Federation for local community groups by 1974, none were in Paddington.

[33] Architect and Writer: Don Gazzard, 'The special place of houses', February 2016, <www.dongazzard.com/publications/articles/the-special-place-of-houses.aspx> (accessed 2/5/18).

[34] For example, submissions such as *Towards a Developmental Control Plan for the Paddington Conservation Area,* Paddington

Society Submission to Woollahra Municipal Council, February 1993, and *Towards an Integrated Traffic Management Plan for the Paddington Conservation Area* 1993.

[35] Co-authors Mandy Jean, Greg Young, Ron Johnson, Margaret DesGrand, L Goldstein.

[36] Alec Tzannes, 'First House: Tzannes Associates', *ArchitectureAU,* Issue 89, December 2012, <architectureau.com/articles/henwood-house-bytzannes-associates> (accessed 2/5/18).

[37] Leesha McKenny, 'Terraces under threat from changes to planning controls', *Sydney Morning Herald,* 12 November 2012.

[38] *Woollahra Development Control Plan, 2015.*

Chapter 8: Bohemian Paddington

[1] Peter Kirkpatrick, 'Macdougall, *Augusta ("Pakie") and* Duncan',

Australian Dictionary of Biography, vol 15, Melbourne University Press, Carlton South, 2000.

[2] Geoffrey Dutton, *The Innovators: The Sydney alternatives in the rise of modern art, literature and ideas,* Macmillan, Melbourne, 1986, p 200.

[3] Dutton, *The Innovators,* pp 100–0l. Judith Ainge, Alan Davies, Howard Tanner, *An Edwardian Summer: Sydney and beyond through the lens of Arthur Wigram Allen,* Historic Houses Trust of NSW, Sydney, 2010, p 54.

[4] Dutton, *The Innovators,* pp 100–03.

[5] Dutton, *The Innovators,* pp 206–08.

[6] Lenore Nicklin, 'Komon, Rudolph John (Rudy)', *Australian Dictionary of Biography,* vol 17, Melbourne University Press, Carlton South, 2007.

[7] Dutton, *The Innovators,* pp 206–08.

[8] Nicklin, 'Komon, Rudolph John (Rudy)'.
[9] Introduction by Jannie Southan to Rob Hillier's *A Place Called Paddington,* Ure Smith, Sydney, 1970, p 10.
[10] Patricia Thompson, *Accidental Chords,* Penguin, Ringwood, 1988, p 221.
[11] 'But, shrewder than most, Cyril Pearl said that Paddington was the natural place for the middle class to come back to after its panic flight to the outer suburbs between the wars.' Thompson, *Accidental Chords,* p 224.
[12] Thompson, *Accidental Chords,* pp 226–227.
[13] Thompson, *Accidental Chords,* pp 236–40.
[14] *The Bulletin,* 14 November 1970, pp 51–52.
[15] *The Bulletin,* 22 May 1971, pp 54–55.
[16] *The Bulletin,* 22 May 1971, pp 54–55.
[17] ABC, *Four Corners,* interview with Michael Charlton, 1962.

[18] Interview with Gail Earle, 25 December 2017.
[19] Juliet Schlunke, *Buns in the Oven: John Olsen's Bakery Art School,* Thames & Hudson, Sydney, 2016, pp 173–77.
[20] *The Bulletin,* 1 August 1970, pp 31–32.
[21] Sandra Hall, *The Bulletin,* 1 August 1970, pp 6, 9
[22] Hall, *The Bulletin,* 1 August 1970, pp 6, 9.
[23] Hall, *The Bulletin,* 2 January 1971, pp 36, 37.
[24] Hillier, *A Place Called Paddington,* p 9.
[25] Tina Kaufman, 'Albie – A well directed life', *Senses of Cinema,* Issue 66, 17 March 2013, <sensesofcinema.com> (accessed 7/5/18).
[26] *The Bulletin,* 24 May 1969, p 15.
[27] Hall, *The Bulletin,* 29 August 1970, p 48.

Chapter 9: Creative Paddington

[1] Paddington Papers, November 2011, from Margaret Olley's speech at the 2006 Paddington Society Annual Dinner.

[2] On an expanded field of skills and creativity see Chantel Carr and Chris Gibson, 'Geographies of making: Rethinking material and skills for volatile futures', *Progress in Human Geography*, 2016, pp 1–19.

[3] For 2011 the major industry employers were: legal and accounting services (7 per cent), auxiliary finance and investment services (6 per cent) and depository financial intermediation (3.9 per cent). See Australian Bureau of Statistics, 'Wage and salary earner statistics for small areas, 2010–2011', <www.abs.gov.au/ausstats/abs@.nsf/mf/5673.0.55.003> (accessed 8/5/18).

[4] Mill stones, 2, vesicular basalt with 'French furrow' dressed faces, possibly overshot water-wheel, used at Barcom Glen Watermill, made by Thomas West, Paddington, 1810–12. MAAS C4011.
[5] Ron Johnson, with Greg Young, *Paddington History and Heritage: A theme history,* Woollahra Municipal Council, Woollahra, 1995, p 30.
[6] Johnson, with Young, *Paddington History and Heritage,* p 7.
[7] Hansard, *Gazette,* no 421, 1891–92 <www.parliament.nsw.gov.au/hansard/Documents/1891-92.pdf> (accessed 8/5/18).
[8] 'Alexander Brodie', Design&Art Australia Online (DAAO) <www.daao.org.au/bio/alexander-brodie/biography> (accessed 8/5/18).
[9] 'Francis Whitfield Robinson', DAAO <www.daao.org.au/bio/franciswhitfield-robinson/biography/> (accessed 8/5/18).
[10] 'DRESSMAKING – Wanted, IMPROVERS, neat workers. Mrs C.S. Rush, 17 Regent St,

Paddington', *Sydney Morning Herald,* 15 April 1890.

[11] J McIntyre, 'Remembering pre-war Paddo lifestyles', Oral History, undated, c 1980s(?), Paddington Society, Sydney.

[12] McIntyre, 'Remembering pre-war Paddo lifestyles'.

[13] In 1891 they were described as 'a good class of people', benefiting from well-built homes, tarred roads, clean footpaths, sewers, garbage collection and tram services. *Paddington: Its history and progress 1860–1910,* Local Government Publishing Company, Sydney, 1910, p 56.

[14] *Sydney Morning Herald,* 3 September 1867, p 8.

[15] 'Gil Docking', Cambridge Street, 18 November 2016, <cambridgest.blogspot.com.au/search/label/Notable%20residents> (accessed 8/5/18).

[16] 'Norman Haire', Wikipedia, <en.wikipedia.org/wiki/Norman_Haire> (accessed 8/5/18).

[17] Jill Dimond and Peter Kirkpatrick, *Literary Sydney: A walking guide,* University of Queensland Press, St Lucia, 2000, p 118.
[18] Dimond and Kirkpatrick, *Literary Sydney,* p 130.
[19] Dimond and Kirkpatrick, *Literary Sydney,* p 119.
[20] Kenneth Slessor described his view from William Street thus: 'cast up in dreary ribbons ... as if by a wave of evil-minded builders, each with its balconies of cast iron grill-work and its narrow, slot-like windows of poison-bottle purple'.
[21] See Dimond and Kirkpatrick, *Literary Sydney,* pp 120–23.
[22] Rosemary Shipway, Oral History, Paddington Society.
[23] Chokos are an easily grown, watery vegetable originating in South America.
[24] McIntyre, 'Remembering pre-war Paddo lifestyles'.
[25] *Poems,* published 1913, but composed in 1895. Christopher Brennan, 'The yellow gas is

fired from street to street', Australian Poetry Library, <www.poetrylibrary.edu.au/poets/brennan-christopher/the-yellow-gas-is-fired-from-streetto-street-0020010> (accessed 8/5/18).

[26] *Unreliable Memoirs,* Cape, London, 1980.

[27] Patricia Thompson, *Accidental Chords,* Penguin, Ringwood, 1988, p 226.

[28] 'Paddington Morning, 1965', sold Leonard Joel, Melbourne, 29 November 3026, Lot 40.

[29] Oral History, Paddington Society.

[30] 'David Edgar Strachan', DAAO, <www.daao.org.au/bio/david-edgarstrachan/biography/> (accessed 8/5/18).

[31] Other well-known residents included critic Grazia Gunn, curators John McPhee, Frances McCarthy and Katrina Rumley, filmmaker Jane Campion, artist John Lethbridge and architect Fran Morrison.

[32] Peter McNeil, phone interview, Sydney, 7 February 2017.

[33] Andrea Dixon, 'Little beginnings', *Sydney Morning Herald,* 28 September 1997, p 117.

[34] *Sydney Morning Herald* advertisement, 14 December 1968, p 33.

[35] William Wright in Conversation with Tony Bond, in Laura Murray Cree (ed), *Twenty,* Sherman Galleries 1986–2006, Fishermens Bend, Craftsman House, 2006, p 40.

[36] Peter McNeil interview with Roswitha Wulff, Bathurst, 10 February 2017.

[37] James Murdoch, *Peggy Glanville-Hicks: A transposed life,* Pendragon, Hillsdale, NY, p 266

[38] Suzanne Robinson, 'Glanville Hicks, Peggy Winsome (1912–1990)', *Australian Dictionary of Biography,* <adb.anu.edu.au/biography/glanville-hicks-peggywinsome-12545> (accessed 8/5/18).

[39] Information courtesy of Andrew Montana, Sydney, Peter McNeil,

informal interview, November 2016.

[40] Kirkpatrick writes a compelling account of the snobbism inherent in this anti-suburban view, which continued in the writings of Robin Boyd in the 1960s and the humour of Barry Humphries in the 1970s–80s. Peter Kirkpatrick, *The Sea Coast of Bohemia: Literary life in Sydney's roaring twenties,* API, Perth, pp 51–52.

[41] Johnson, with Young, *Paddington History and Heritage,* p 97.

[42] Juliet Schlunke, *Buns in the Oven,* Thames and Hudson, Melbourne, 2016; interview, ABC Radio National, 'Books and Arts', 17 November 2016.

[43] Christine France, 'Jean Bellette: Early life and times', in *Jean Bellette: Retrospective,* Bathurst Regional Art Gallery and SH Ervin Gallery, Bathurst, 2004, p 23.

[44] Humphrey McQueen, *Suburbs of the Sacred,* Penguin, Ringwood, 1988, p 162.

[45] Lenore Nicklin, 'How to spend a $10,000 art bequest', *Sydney Morning Herald,* 26 January 1974, p 11.

[46] 'Paddington's Wagner Gallery listed for November auction', *Property Observer,* 20 October 2015, <www.propertyobserver.com.au/finding/residential-investment/sales-andauctions/46660-paddington-swagner-gallery-listed-for-novemberauction.html> (accessed 8/5/18).

[47] Jen Melocco, 'Adventurer gives away $5 million in property sale', *Daily Telegraph,* 27 August 2015, <www.dailytelegraph.com.au/newslocal/city-east/adventurer-gives-away-5-million-in-property-sale/news-story/79526ddf166f5bf4df392ce22bae01ac> (accessed 8/5/18).

[48] Email communication with Peter McNeil, Ruth McDermott, Sydney, 31 January 2017.

[49] Established by Liane Rossler, Louise Olsen and Stephen Ormandy.

[50] Claude Corne, then Damien and Josephine Pignolet from 1981–93. The iconic restaurant closed in 2013. See Scott Bolles, 'Claude's: Another one bites the dust', Good Food, 27 July 2013 <www.goodfood.com.au/eat-out/claudes-another-onebites-the-dust-20130726-2qpui> (accessed 17/5/2018).

[51] 'Twenty defining moments that shaped Sydney's way of eating', *Sydney Morning Herald*, 26 June 2002, <www.smh.com.au/articles/2002/06/25/1023864572930.html> (accessed 8/5/18).

[52] *Sydney Morning Herald*, 20 October 1995, p 16

[53] *Sydney Morning Herald*, 20 October 1995, p 16

[54] McIntyre, 'Remembering pre-war Paddington', Paddington Society oral history, transcript, 'Paddington lifestyles'.

[55] Friend noted the 'art crowd' shifted to the popular Martin's

bar, Oxford Street, around this point. Paul Hetherington (ed), *The Diaries of Donald Friend,* vol 4, National Library of Australia, Canberra, p 587.

[56] Loose cast iron components were included in the Margaret Olley auction, suggesting that she had collected them to make into garden ornaments, possibly from the street. Donald Friend did the same in Hill End. *Margaret Olley AC (1923–2011): An Artist's Life,* Sydney, Sunday 30 June 2013, South Yarra, Mossgreen Auctions, 2013.

[57] 'Semi-secluded' – see G Stewart, *Terrace House Elements Typologies,* Paddington Society, Sydney.

[58] Cited in McQueen, *Suburbs of the Sacred,* p 148.

[59] Dimond and Kirkpatrick, *Literary Sydney,* p 119.

[60] Interview: ABC broadcast, Sarah Schofield with Christine Dean and the artist, Stateline, 2003. See also C Dean, 'Vernon

Treweeke: The secret paintings', Penrith Regional Gallery, Penrith, 2003.

[61] Keith Glass, 'Hair: 'The tribal rock musical', in Iain McIntyre (ed), *Tomorrow is Today: Australia in the psychedelic era, 1966–1970,* Wakefield Press, Kent Town (SA), 2006, p 151.

[62] Anne Coombs, *Sex & Anarchy, The life & death of the Sydney Push,* Viking, Ringwood, 1996, pp 178, 184, 200, 293.

[63] The complete list is as follows: Charles Bannon (printmaker) 1966–68; Charles Blackman (painter) 1968; Tony Bonner (actor) 1966; Peter 'Charlie' Brown (art critic) 1966–1968; Janet Dawson (painter: photographed extensively in the neighbourhood) 1966; Chris Gentle (painter) 1981; Leonard Hessing (painter) 1965; Keith Looby (painter) circa 1984; Chris McCullough (filmmaker) 1966–68; John Olsen (painter) 1977; Oodgeroo Noonuccal [Kath Walker] (poet) (possibly

taken at John Thompson's house) circa 1964; David Perry (painter and filmmaker) 1968; Ken Reinhard (painter) 1981; William Rose (painter) 1966–68; Raimonds Rumba (sculptor) 1968; Owen Shaw (sculptor) 1967; Tim Storrier (painter) 1981; Joe Szabo (painter) 1966–68; Ann Thomson (painter) 1965–c 1970; Chris Winzar (actor), photographed with 'friends' wearing Frankie (Frank) Mitchell Carnaby Street and mode fashions in Underwood Street 1966 and Judith Wright (poet), possibly at John and Patricia Thompson's house, circa 1964. Courtesy Eric Riddler and the Art Gallery of New South Wales Research Library catalogues.

[64] Carol Dance, 'The art of living in Paddington', *Sydney Morning Herald,* 8 August 1985, p 82.

[65] Dance, 'The art of living in Paddington', p 82.

[66] Dance, 'The art of living in Paddington', p 82.

[67] Wright in Conversation with Bond, p 57.

[68] The 'barnacle' analogy is that of architect Jason Fraser and is to be found in the thesis of Lian Williamsz, *Terrace Housing: Past, present and future of the urban form,* UNSW, Sydney.

[69] 'Gitte Weise: Angels at her table', Art Collector, Issue 27, January–March 2004 <www.artcollector.net.au/GitteWeiseAngelsathertable> (accessed 8/5/18).

[70] 'The street where you live', *Sydney Morning Herald,* 8 February 2001, p 50.

[71] The author wishes to thank for their kind assistance the staff of the Museum of Applied Arts and Sciences particularly Roger Leong, Anne-Marie Van de Ven, Glynis Jones and Kathy Hackett as well as Margot Riley (State Library) and Eric Riddler (Art Gallery of New South Wales). Dr Gene Sherman, Bronwyn Clark-Coolee, Dr Virginia Wright, Dr Jesse Adams Stein

and Dr Christine Dean kindly commented on drafts.

Chapter 10: Changing landscapes

[1] Doug Benson and Jocelyn Howell, *Taken for Granted: The bushland of Sydney and its suburbs,* Kangaroo Press, Sydney, 1990; Apple tree; undergrowth hakea, banksia and kunzea; red mahogany; scribbly gums; grass-trees; grey gums; stringybarks; kangaroo grass; mat-rush.

[2] Firesticks <www.firesticks.org.au> (accessed 2/5/18).

[3] Bill Gammage, *The Biggest Estate on Earth: How Aborigines made Australia,* Allen & Unwin, Sydney, 2012.

[4] Ron Johnson, 'Hampden Street, Paddington's Industrial Precinct' unpublished article, Woollahra Municipal Library, nd.

[5] Woollahra Development Control Plan 2015, Conservation Plan

Part C, Heritage Conservation Areas CI, Paddington.

[6] Richardson and Wrench, *Contract Book,* A.4530 as cited in Max Kelly, *Paddock Full of Houses Paddington 1840–1890,* Doak Press, Paddington, 1978, p 55.

[7] Woollahra Municipal Council, Register of Significant Trees, <www.trove.nla.gov.au/version/29506106> (accessed 17/5/18).

[8] Richardson and Wrench, *Contract Book* (Old Firm), May, 1875, as cited in Kelly, *Paddock Full of Houses,* p 71.

[9] Johnson, 'Hampden Street, Paddington's Industrial Precinct'.

[10] Ruth Keir, 'Stones of remembrance: 1879–1977; Stonemasons F Arnold and Sons', Woollahra Library Local History, #MUMSS7711.

[11] Paddington Municipal Council, 'Paddington: Its history and progress, 1860–1910', Paddington Municipal Council, Woollahra Library Local History, 1910.

[12] Royal Hospital for Women Park Plan of Management, Woollahra Municipal Council, March 2005.
[13] Judy Bernard-Waite, *The Riddle of the Trumpalar Tree,* Scholastic Australia, Sydney, 1981 <www.booksandbeyond.com.au/the-riddleof-the-trumpalar/> (accessed 2/5/18).
[14] Unk White and Patricia Thompson, *Paddington Sketch Book,* Rigby Ltd, Sydney, 1971, p 50.
[15] Woollahra Street Tree Masterplan, Woollahra Municipal Council, 2014.
[16] Woollahra Municipal Council, Register of Significant Trees, <www.trove.nla.gov.au/version/29506106> (accessed 17/5/18).

Chapter 11: Survival

[1] Entry on Paddington in *The Australian Handbook,* Gordon and Gotch, Sydney, 1903.
[2] See discussion of Sydney University's expansion plans and

purchasing of terrace houses in PN Troy (ed), *Urban Redevelopment in Australia,* Urban Research Unit, ANU, Canberra, 1968.

[3] This chapter draws on all previous chapters in the book. Readers wanting the general Sydney context for the 20th century are directed to Peter Spearritt, *Sydney's Century: A history,* UNSW Press, Sydney, 2000. A bevy of social/urban histories were published in the 1990s on Sydney's inner suburbs, including Surry Hills (Christopher Keating, *Surry Hills: The city's backyard,* Hale & Iremonger, Sydney, 1991), Chippendale (Shirley Fitzgerald, *Chippendale: Beneath the factory wall,* Hale & Iremonger, Sydney, 1992), Pyrmont and Ultimo (Shirley Fitzgerald and Hilary Golder, *Pyrmont & Ultimo under Siege,* Hale & Iremonger, Sydney, 1994), Millers Point (Shirley Fitzgerald and Christopher Keating, *Millers*

Point: The urban village, Halstead Press, Ultimo, 1991), Leichhardt (Max Solling and Peter Reynolds, *Leichhardt: On the margins of the city,* Allen & Unwin, St Leonards, 1997). There is still only one major book on the Sydney property market, Maurice Daly's *Sydney Boom, Sydney Bust,* Allen & Unwin, Sydney, 1982. Price and demographic data is now readily available, free of charge, from real estate websites, while data on ownership, renting and demography is provided by the national census, held at five-yearly cycles since 1961. The 1933 census is of particular utility because Paddington was still a separate municipality and it contains information on income and the number of rooms in houses, including 'sleep outs', a major concern during the Great Depression.

[4] Rob Hillier, *A Place Called Paddington,* Ure Smith, Sydney,

1970. Southan's introduction is pp 5–13.

[5] Seventy per cent of new owner-occupiers rebuilt their bathrooms c 1961–66. See John Roseth, Revival of an Old Residential Area, PhD thesis, Faculty of Architecture, University of Sydney, Sydney, 1969.

[6] For housing stock and early comments about gentrification see Rob Hillier, *Let's Buy a Terrace House,* Ure Smith, Sydney, 1968; John Wong, *The Houses of Balmain,* Horwitz, North Sydney, 1969; and Bernard and Kate Smith, *The Architectural Character of Glebe,* Sydney, University Co-op bookshop, Sydney, 1973. John Power, a Melburnian then teaching at the University of Sydney, and the founding president of the Balmain Association, was one of the first scholars to recognise the importance of gentrification, in his 'The new politics in the old suburbs', *Quadrant,* vol 13, issue

6, December 1969. Since then there has been a vast scholarly literature on gentrification, though often nowist in orientation, from Hal Kendig's *New Life in the Old Suburbs: Past-war land use and housing in the Australian inner city,* Allen & Unwin, Sydney, 1979 to Renate Howe, David Nichols and Graeme Davison, *Trendyville: The battle for Australia's inner cities,* Monash University Publishing, Clayton, 2014. Despite the Australia in the subtitle, Paddington rates just two brief mentions, while the Carlton Association gets over a dozen pages in all. Melburnians could never be accused of not taking their city seriously.

[7] Paddington Society, *Paddington: A plan for preservation,* Paddington Society, Paddington, October 1970, a 57-page submission to the mayor of Woollahra, published in a roneo format, with maps and diagrams.

[8] See Elizabeth Farrelly, 'Babylonian fantasy land emerges from reservoir', *Sydney Morning Herald,* 13 August 2009.

Appendix: The Paddington Terrace House:1840–1910

[1] Jean Rice, *Terrace Houses in The Rocks: A comparative analysis and assessment of significance,* Sydney Harbour Foreshore Authority, Sydney, 2014, p 8.
[2] John Summerson, 'Georgian London', quoted in Robert Brown and Annette Green, *Type Profiles: Terrace housing in New South Wales,* Australian Heritage Commission, Yarralumla, 1987, p 6.
[3] Rice, *Terrace Houses in The Rocks,* p 9.
[4] *The Australian,* 23 July 1828.
[5] Town Surveyor's notebook, 1827–1832, NSW State Records.
[6] Robert Griffin, The Sydney Terrace House, Master of the Built Environment thesis, UNSW, 1995, p 6.

[7] Brown and Green, *Type Profiles,* p 17.

[8] The Act was amended in 1845 to re-instate the original boundaries, however no further review of building regulations took place until 1879.

[9] This is based on the typology provided by Rice, *Terrace Houses in The Rocks.*

[10] John Papworth, *Hints on Ornamental Gardening,* R Ackermann, London, 1823, quoted in James Broadbent, *The Australian Colonial House,* Hordern House, Potts Point, 1992, pp 10–11; Stephan Muthesius, *The English Terraced House,* Yale University Press, London, 1982, p 174.

[11] Griffin, *The Sydney Terrace House,* p 15.

[12] Rice, *Terrace Houses in The Rocks,* p 84.

[13] Robinson and Hindmarsh Architects Pty Ltd, *Conservation Management Plan, 11–13 Dalgety Terrace, Millers Point,* 2018, p 118.

[14] Robinson and Hindmarsh, *Conservation Management Plan*, pp 118–22.

Select bibliography

Helen Armstrong, *Migrant Place-making in Australia,* Lambert Academic Publishing, Saarbrücken, 2016

Paul Ashton, *The Accidental City: Planning Sydney since 1788,* Hale and Iremonger, Sydney, 1995

Rowland Atkinson, Maryann Wulff, Margaret Reynolds and Angela Spinney, *Gentrification and Displacement: The household impacts of neighbourhood change,* for the Australian Housing and Urban Research Institute, Southern Research Centre, Swinburne-Monash Research Centre, 2011

Val Attenbrow, *Sydney's Aboriginal Past: Investigating the archaeological and historical records,* 2nd ed, UNSW Press, Sydney, 2010

Edmund N Bacon, *The Design of Cities,* Thames and Hudson, London, 1967

Doug Benson and Jocelyn Howell, *Taken for Granted: The bushland of Sydney and its suburbs,* Kangaroo Press, Sydney, 1990

Robert Brown, The development of terrace style housing in Paddington 1840–1980, Bachelor of Architecture Historical Research Thesis, UNSW, Sydney, 1979

Robert Brown and Annette Green, *Terrace Housing in New South Wales,* Australian Heritage Commission, Canberra, 1987

Walter Bunning, *Report on The Exhibited Proposals Under the City of Sydney Planning Scheme Affecting the Paddington Area Following a Public Inquiry,* March 1968

City of Sydney, *Barani Barrabugu. Yesterday Tomorrow. Sydney's Aboriginal Journey,* 3rd ed, City of Sydney, Sydney, 2015

Anne Coombs, *Sex & Anarchy: The life & death of the Sydney Push,* Viking, Ringwood, 1996

County of Cumberland Council, *Report on the Planning Scheme for the County of Cumberland, NSW,* County of Cumberland Council, Sydney, 1948

Carol Dance, 'The art of living in Paddington', *Sydney Morning Herald,* 8 August 1985

Jill Dimond and Peter Kirkpatrick, *Literary Sydney: A walking guide,* University of Queensland Press, St Lucia, 2000

Geoffrey Dutton, *The Innovators: The Sydney alternatives in the rise of modern art, literature and ideas,* Macmillan, South Melbourne, 1986

M Barnard Eldershaw, *Tomorrow and Tomorrow and Tomorrow,* Virago Press, London, 1983

Clive Faro with Garry Witherspoon, *Street Seen: A history of Oxford Street,*

Melbourne University Press, Carlton South, 2000

Bill Gammage, *The Biggest Estate on Earth: How Aborigines made Australia,* Allen & Unwin, Sydney, 2015

Robert Griffin, The Sydney terrace house, Master of the Built Environment thesis, UNSW, Sydney, 1995

Robert Harbison, *Ruins and Fragments: Tales of loss and rediscovery,* Reaktion Books, London, 2015

Rob Hillier, *A Place Called Paddington,* Ure Smith, Sydney, 1970

Renate Howe, David Nichols and Graeme Davison, *Trendyville: The battle for Australia's inner cities,* Monash University Publishing, Clayton, 2014

Paul Irish, *Hidden in Plain View: The Aboriginal people of coastal Sydney,* NewSouth Publishing, Sydney, 2017

Ron Johnson, *It Never Stops Does it! A profile of the Paddington Society:*

Pioneer in heritage activism 1964–2004, Paddington Society, Sydney, 2004

Ron Johnson, with Greg Young, *Paddington History and Heritage: A theme history,* Woollahra Municipal Council, Woollahra, 1995

Grace Karskens, *The Colony: A history of early Sydney,* Allen & Unwin, Sydney, 2009

Tina Kaufman, *Senses of Cinema,* Issue 66, 2018, <sensesofcinema.com> (accessed 9/5/18)

Max Kelly, *Paddock Full of Houses: Paddington 1840–1890,* Doak Press, Paddington, 1978

Max Kelly and Ruth Crocker, *Sydney Takes Shape,* Doak Press in Association with the Macleay Museum, Sydney, 1977

Hal Kendig, *New Life for Old Suburbs,* Allen & Unwin, Sydney, 1979

Hal L Kendig, 'Gentrification in Australia', in J John Palen and Bruce London, *Gentrification, Displacement, and Neighborhood Revitalisation,* State University of New York Press, New York, 1984

Peter Kirkpatrick, *The Sea Coast of Bohemia: Literary life in Sydney's roaring twenties,* API, Perth, 2007

Michael Krockenberger, *Population Growth in Australia,* Australia Institute, Canberra City, 2015

Frederick Arthur Larcombe, *The Stabilization of Local Government in New South Wales 1858–1906: A history of local government in New South Wales,* vol 2, Sydney University Press, Sydney, 1976

Edward West Marriott, *Thomas West of Barcom Glen: His life and times and family,* Barcom Press, Sydney, 1982

Lenore Nicklin, *The Australian Dictionary of Biography,* vol 17, Melbourne University Press, Carlton South, 2007

Lilith G Norman, *Historical Notes on Paddington,* Council of the City of Sydney, Sydney, 1961

Municipal Council of Paddington, *Paddington 1860–1910: Its history, trade and industries,* Local Government Publishing Co, Sydney, 1910

Jill Roe, 'The Sydney History Group: From the beginning', *Sydney Journal,* vol 4, no 1, 2013

Sue Rosen, *We Never Had a Hotbed of Crime! Life in twentieth century South Sydney,* Hale and Iremonger, Sydney, 2000

John Roseth, *Extent, progress and location of rehabilitation activity in Paddington,* University of Sydney Planning Research Centre, Sydney, 1967

Juliet Schlunke, *Buns in the Oven: John Olsen's Bakery Art School,* Thames and Hudson, Sydney, 2016

Jannie Southan, Foreword to Rob Hillier's *A Place Called Paddington,* Ure Smith, Sydney, 1970

Peter Spearritt, *Sydney's Century: A history,* UNSW Press, Sydney, 2000

Andrew Starr and Jan Morice, *Paddington Stories,* Andrew Starr and Associates, Paddington, 2000

Sydney City Council, *Action Plan No 26 South Paddington Precinct C,* Sydney City Council, Sydney, adopted 18 December 1972

Patricia Thompson, *Accidental Chords,* Penguin Books, Ringwood, 1988

Patricia Thompson, *The Story of Paddington,* Paddington Society, Paddington, 1980

Lucy Hughes Turnbull, *Sydney: Biography of a city,* Random House, Sydney, 1999

Inara Walden, '"That was slavery days": Aboriginal domestic servants in New

South Wales in the twentieth century', *Labour History,* vol 69, 1995, pp 196–209

Unk White and Patricia Thompson, *Paddington Sketch Book,* Rigby Ltd, Sydney, 1971

Richard Wollheim, *Art and its Objects,* Penguin, Harmondsworth, 1968

Greg Young, *Reshaping Planning with Culture,* Routledge, Abingdon, Oxon, 2016

Gregory Young, *Environmental Conservation: Towards a philosophy,* NSW Heritage Council, Sydney, 1984

Index

A

ABC Four Corners program 'Paddington Gentrification', *411, 435*

Aboriginal people, see Indigenous people,

Aborigines Protection Association, *22*

Aborigines Protection Board, *28, 31*

Abraham, Walter, *357, 373, 387*

Adams, Francis, *110*

Albury Hotel, *147*

Alexandria,
 map of parish of, *56*
 suburb, *133, 136, 543, 554*

Andersons, Andrew, *473*

Armstrong, Helen, photographs, *502, 506, 519, 521, 535, 536, 539*

art galleries, *146, 306, 369, 394, 399, 401, 416, 426, 459, 466, 470, 473, 484, 488, 489, 492, 502, 554, 558*

 Bonython Gallery, *306, 401, 466*

 Cooee Art Gallery, *37*

 Galleries Primitif, *306, 399*

 Gallery A, *399, 426, 466, 484*

 Hogarth Galleries, *37, 470*

 Holdsworth Galleries, *146, 466*

 Hungry Horse Gallery and Restaurant, *146, 306, 399, 401, 470*

Roslyn Oxley, *306, 488*
Rudy Komon Gallery, *146, 306, 394, 466, 470, 489*
Sherman Galleries, *306, 489, 492*
Wagner Gallery, *473*
Watters Gallery, *426, 466, 470*

art schools,
- Bakery Art School, *416, 466, 492*
- East Sydney Technical College, *416, 461, 466*
- Julian Ashton Art School, *393*
- National Art School (formerly East Sydney Technical College), *416, 461*
- UNSW Art and Design (formerly Alexander Mackie, and College of Fine Arts), *160, 461*

Australian Subscription Library, *64, 82, 184, 208, 232, 257, 444*

B

Bacon, Wendy, *141, 484*
Baker, Harriet, *28*
Bakery Art School, *416, 466, 492*
Balmain, *548*
Balmain Association, *373, 549, 554*
Barcom Glen, *52, 87, 171, 184, 244, 383*
- Aboriginal settlement on, *17*
- house, *21, 171, 176*
- maps, *64, 171*
- watermill at, *171, 383, 439, 515*

Barney, George, *82, 87, 208*
Beard, Jane, *88, 94*
Begg, John Ely, *101, 106, 180, 184, 204, 248, 250*

Bernard-Waite, Judy, *531*
Bonython, Kym, *146, 306, 399, 401*
bookshops, *318, 420*
Bourke, Richard, *81, 176, 184, 194, 208*
Bradley Hall, *56, 64, 204, 208, 240, 250, 257*
Bradley, Henry Burton, *250, 260*
Bradley, William, *46, 56, 250*
Brennan, Christopher, *110, 447, 450, 455*
Brisbane, Katharine, *140, 484*
Broadbent, James, *190*
Broadhurst, Florence, *311, 420, 554*
Brodie, Hugh, *212, 232*
Broughton, Thomas, *56, 204, 208, 240, 250, 257*
Brown, Robert, drawings, *228, 233, 240, 262, 269*
Bungaree, *11, 16*
Bunning, Walter, *350, 352, 357, 366, 373, 387*
Burra Charter, see ICOMOS Burra Charter,
Busby's Bore, *106, 208, 212, 439, 515*

C

Cadi, *7*
Cadigal people, *7, 8, 11*
   landscape management of, *497, 498*
   neighbouring clans, *8*
   pre-European lifestyle, *8, 11, 164, 497, 498, 500, 510*
   see also Indigenous people,
cafes, *152, 318, 393, 416, 567*
Campbell, William, *28, 171*

Cape, William T, *64, 184, 204, 250, 253, 257*
Centennial Park, *110, 114, 217, 444, 518, 523, 571*
Child, Angela, *318, 420*
child welfare, *31*
　see also Ormond House,
Chinese market gardens, Rushcutters Bay, *88, 176, 440, 500, 502, 515, 518*
churches,
　Garrison Anglican Church, *89*
　land grants to, *217*
　St Francis of Assisi Catholic Church, *89*
　St George's Anglican Church, *89*
　St John's Presbyterian Church, *89, 385, 387, 420*
　St Matthias' Anglican Church, *89, 240*
　St Sophia's Greek Orthodox Church, *89*
　Wesleyan Church, *217, 240*
cinemas, *121, 136, 160*
City of Sydney Council, *133, 136, 147, 278*
Clarke, George, *357, 366*
colonial drawings and paintings, *3, 7, 11, 16, 21, 48, 50, 81, 82, 88, 164, 167, 177, 184, 186, 204, 217, 498, 515*
colonisation,
　British colonists, *11*
　early land grants, *46, 52, 56, 60, 64, 171, 176, 177, 180, 184, 500, 502*
　effect of on Sydney Aboriginal people, *11, 16, 17, 21, 22*
　and violence, *11*
　see also Cadigal people;

Indigenous people,
Connell, Bob, *420*
convicts, *11, 81, 212, 439*
Cooee Art Gallery, *37*
Cooper, Robert, *31, 52, 56, 77, 106, 176, 184, 186, 190, 194, 224, 228, 248*
corner shops, *140, 269, 303, 311, 369, 403, 411, 479, 489*
County of Cumberland Planning Scheme 1948, *330, 334*
Craig, Alexander/Archibald, *212*
cricket, *114, 523, 525*
Curtis, JJ, *212*

D
Darlinghurst Gaol, *48, 50, 435, 512*
Deamer, Dulcie, *447*
Department of Main Roads, *330*
expressway proposals 1960s, *136, 147, 152, 346, 357, 558*
road widening, *543*
depressions, economic,
of 1890s, *257, 269*
of 1840s, *81, 204, 212, 228, 232*
of 1930s (Great Depression), *127, 129, 278, 340, 401, 444, 450, 548*
development control plans, *352, 369, 373, 376, 506*
Devine, Tilly, *450*
de Winton, William, *318, 420*
Dickerson, Robert, *411, 488*
Dinosaur Designs, *318, 473*
distillery,
see Sydney Distillery,
DMR,
see Department of Main Roads,

Dorrough, Terry, *362, 473*

Dransfield, Michael, *484*

Dumaresq, Henry, *82, 184, 244*

Dundas, Douglas, *455*

Duxford House, *64, 204, 240, 250, 253*

E

Earle, Gail and David, *414, 416*

Eastern Suburbs Day Nursery (formerly Olive Bank), *121, 204, 250*

East Sydney Technical College, *416, 461, 466*

Elfred House, *64, 204, 250, 253, 257*

Elfred House Private School, *253, 257*

Elizabeth Bay, *11, 16*
   Aboriginal village at, *16*

Elizabeth Bay House, *194, 199*

Engehurst, *64, 194, 199, 204, 248, 250*

Englund, Patricia and Ivan, *459*

Environmental Planning and Assessment Act 1979, *373, 376*

Eora Nation, *497*

Evatt, Clive, *146, 334, 470*

F

Fahey, Warren, *325*

Federation style, *269*

filmmakers, *426, 428*

Filmmakers Co-operative, *426*

Five Ways Picture Palace, *121, 136*

Flinton, *64, 121, 157, 204, 250, 257, 260, 528*

Forbes, Francis E, *52, 56, 224*

Friend, Donald, *435, 479, 484, 488*
   paintings, *435, 479*

G

Galleries Primitif, *306, 399*

Gallery A, *399, 426, 466, 484*

Gammage, Bill, *497, 498*

garden suburbs, *127, 269, 278*

Garling, Frederick, paintings, *48, 81*

Garrison Anglican Church, *89*

gay culture, *146, 147, 311, 325, 558*

Gazzard, Don, *152, 280, 282, 284, 344, 346, 350, 376, 406, 473*

Gazzard House, *284, 376, 378*

Gazzard, Marea, *152, 344, 406, 474*

Gazzard, Nick, *411*

gentrification, *36, 141, 146, 278, 280, 282, 284, 289, 294, 299, 303, 306, 311, 314, 318, 320, 325, 340, 344, 535, 536*

  hyper-gentrification, *554*

gentry estates and villas, *52, 56, 60, 64, 87, 96, 184, 186, 190, 194, 199, 204, 208, 240*

  see also Engehurst; Juniper Hall; Olive Bank; Terraces, The,

Gilmore, Mary, *110, 447*

Glanville-Hicks, Peggy, *459, 461*

Glebe, *549*

Glenmore Brook, *515, 518*

Glenmore Distillery, see Sydney Distillery,

Glenmore Road Public School, *89, 330*

gold rushes, *82*

Gordon, Charles, *52, 64, 82, 88, 217, 233*

Gordon family, *77*

Gordon, James, *82, 208*

green bans, *152, 330, 373*

Greer, Germaine, *141, 484*
Grivas, Nestor, *484*
Gross, Sandra, *428*
Gross, Yoram, *428, 488*
Guriganya Progressive School, *420, 473*
Gurner, John, *64, 160, 184, 250*
Gurrajin, see Elizabeth Bay,

H

Hampden Park, *114, 523*
Hardie Rubber Company, *133, 136, 184, 440*
Hardwick, John W, paintings, *186, 217*
Harris, Jack, *17*
Hazzard, Brad, *383, 385*
Heaps, Alfred Walter, *444*
   violin made by, *440*
Hely, Frederick, *64, 184, 194, 204, 248*

Henrietta Villa, *176*
Henwood House, *289, 376, 383*
heritage, *561, 563, 571*
  see also Heritage Act 1977; Paddington Society,
Heritage Act 1977, *330, 373*
Herman, Sali, *455, 484*
  paintings, *455*
Hewett, Dorothy, *444*
Hill, Richard, *22, 64, 184, 232*
Hillier, Rob, *280, 554, 558*
Hoddle, Robert, *64, 184, 244*
Hodgkinson, Frank, *414, 470*
Hogarth Galleries, *37, 470*
Holdsworth Galleries, *146, 466*
horse-buses, *94, 104, 121*

Housing Commission (NSW), *136, 334, 336, 554*
hotels,
  Albury Hotel, *147*
  Paddington Inn, *88, 94, 96*
  Royal Hotel, Fiveways, *104, 147, 318, 572*
  Unicorn Hotel, *141, 147, 325*
  Windsor Castle Hotel, *411, 414*
Hughes, Robert, *306, 399, 470*
Hungry Horse Gallery and Restaurant, *146, 306, 399, 401, 470*
Hunter, John, *46, 77*
Hyde Park, *50, 184, 212*
Hyde Park Barracks, *81, 82*

I

ice age, *3, 7, 497*
ICOMOS Burra Charter, *344, 378*
Indigenous Paddington, *7, 8, 11, 497, 498, 500*
Indigenous people,
  art, *37*
  Aboriginal debutantes 1966, *36, 37, 141*
  as domestic servants, *31, 36*
  child removal, *31*
  Europeanising of, *11*
  government and religious intervention in affairs of, *22, 27, 28, 31*
  hidden history of, *28, 37*
  impact of the colony on, *11, 16, 17, 21, 22, 27, 28*
  in 19th century, *7, 11, 16, 17, 21, 22, 27, 28, 31, 36, 164, 167*
  pathways of across Sydney, *8, 11, 479*

see also maroo,
in post-war years, *36, 37*
rock engravings, *28*
settlements around 19th century Sydney, *11, 16, 17, 21, 22, 27, 28, 31*
see also Cadigal people; Eora Nation,

J

James, Clive, *140, 455*
Johnson, Ron, *344, 378, 387*
Julian Ashton Art School, *393*
Juniper Hall, *64, 77, 101, 106, 152, 157, 180, 184, 186, 190, 194, 217, 224, 228, 248, 250, 257, 440, 459, 528, 549*
   see also Ormond House,

K

Kelly, Max, *147, 152*
   and history of Paddington, *42, 89, 152, 208, 224, 240, 244, 257, 260, 344, 563*
   home of, *262*
   see also Sydney History Group,
Kinchela, John, *64, 184, 194, 204, 260*
King, PG, painting, *11*
Kogerah, *7*
   see also Rushcutters Bay,
Komon, Rudy, *146, 306, 394, 466, 470, 489*

L

Lachlan Swamps, *64, 106, 212, 217, 439, 515, 518, 523*
Lacrozia Valley, *3, 171, 515*
   see also Rushcutters Bay,
Landlord and Tenant (Amendment) Act 1948, *133, 278, 299, 336, 340, 558*

La Perouse Aboriginal settlement, *27, 28, 36*
Legge, Geoffrey, *466*
Lewis, Ruark, *488*
Lithgow, William, *64, 184*
Little, Jeannie, *346, 459*
Lowe, Chica Edgeworth, *393, 399*
Lucas, Bill, *416, 420, 473*
Lycett, Joseph, paintings, *3, 164, 167, 497, 498*
Lynn, Elwyn, *488, 554*
Lyons, Samuel, *118*

M

MacCormick, Alexander, *260*
Macleay, Alexander, *16, 176, 194*
Macpherson, Mrs Allan, painting, *177*
Macquarie, Lachlan, *11, 52, 171, 176, 232*
Manning, John Edye, *64, 184, 248*

mapping,
  early maps of Sydney, *36, 37, 41, 42, 46, 77, 164, 171, 212*
  retro-mapping, *60, 64*
  see also Paddington maps,
market gardens, *88, 176, 500, 502, 515, 518, 525*
maroo, *11, 64, 77, 171*
Marshall, Joseph, *94*
Marshall's Brewery, *94, 96, 110, 121, 440*
Mason, E, drawing, *16*
McCarthy, WG, *248*
McKie, Ronald, *406*
Miller, Godfrey, *394, 461*
missionaries, *22*
Mitchell, Thomas, *46, 64, 176, 515*
Moore, David, *455*
Moore Park, *110, 217*
  Aboriginal camp at, *22*
Moorhouse, Frank, *428, 484*

Morcombe's grocery store, *101*
Morrison, Bill, *369*
 maps, *60, 64*
Mort, TS, *439*
Morton, PH, *350, 352*
motor vehicles, *554*
 see also Department of Main Roads,
Murphy, Mervyn, *426*
Murphy, Viva, *152, 314, 350*

N
National Art School (formerly East Sydney Technical College), *416, 461*
National Trust of Australia, *152, 157, 190, 344, 373*
Newcombe, LW (George), *64, 217, 233, 240*
Nicholson, Charles, *212, 228*

O
O'Brien, Julie, *554*
Olive Bank, *64, 101, 121, 204, 217, 248, 250, 257*
Olley, Margaret, *340, 414, 416, 435, 459, 466, 474, 479, 484, 488, 492*
Olsen, John, *416, 426, 428, 430, 435, 439, 440, 444, 447, 450, 455, 459, 461, 466, 470, 473, 488*
 paintings, *473, 474*
O'Neil, Betty, *399, 401*
Ormond (Ormonde) House, *31, 36, 106, 186, 248, 250*
 see also Juniper Hall,
OVO Design, *473*
Oxley, Roslyn, *306, 488, 489*

P
Paddington architecture, *224, 548, 549, 554, 558, 561, 563*
 see also terrace housing,
Paddington Council, *96, 101, 129, 133, 240*

see also City of Sydney Council; Woollahra Council,
Paddington, evolution of suburb,
   apartment blocks, *136, 280, 282, 331, 334, 336, 558*
   bohemian suburb, *306, 311, 314, 340, 393, 394, 399, 401, 403, 406, 411, 414, 416, 420, 426, 428, 435*
   creative suburb, *435, 439, 440, 444, 447, 450, 455, 459, 461, 466, 470, 473, 474, 479, 484, 488, 489, 492*
   early 20th century, *118, 121, 127, 129*
   early 21st century, *157, 160*
   early land grants, *46, 52, 56, 60, 64, 171, 176, 177, 180, 184, 500, 502*
   early settlement, *50, 52, 77, 81, 82, 164, 167, 171*
   early subdivisions, *224, 228, 232*
   European migrants 1950s, *136, 140, 278, 314, 340, 535, 554*
   future of suburb, *567, 571, 572*
   gay culture, *146, 147, 311, 325, 558*
   gentrification, *36, 141, 146, 278, 280, 282, 284, 289, 294, 299, 303, 306, 311, 314, 318, 320, 325, 340, 344, 535, 536, 554*
   gentry estates and villas, *52, 56, 60, 64, 87, 96, 184, 186, 190, 194, 199, 204, 208, 240*
   Great Depression, *127, 129, 133*
   hyper-gentrification, *554*
   late-Victorian period, *232, 233, 240*
   marginal landscapes, *531*

middle-class suburb, *340*
mid-Victorian period, *240, 244, 248, 250, 253, 257, 260, 262, 269, 278*
naming of suburb, *77*
pre-European landscape, *64, 497, 498, 500, 502*
prosperity of 1970s–90s, *152, 157, 314, 318, 320, 325*
semi-industrial suburb, *52, 89, 133, 548*
shopping destination, *318, 320, 325, 403, 563, 571, 572*
slum suburb, *127, 129, 133, 136, 160, 269, 278, 299, 330, 334, 401, 548*
terrace housing, see main entry,
town planning, *330, 331, 334, 336, 340, 344, 346, 350, 352, 357, 362, 366, 369, 373, 376, 378, 382, 383, 385, 387*
village to suburb, *82, 87, 88, 89, 94, 96*
working-class suburb, *133, 136, 217, 278*
World War 2, *129, 133*
see also Paddington residents; Paddington streets; Paddington subdivisions,
Paddington Festival, *325*
Paddington on film, Number, *163, 488*
'Paddington Gentrification', ABC Four Corners, *411, 435*
Paddington Green, see Royal Hospital for Women Park,
Paddington Inn, *88, 94, 96*
Paddington landscape,

before European settlement, *3, 7, 8, 164, 497, 498, 500*
during early settlement period, *184, 500, 502, 510, 515*
urban landscape, *502, 504, 506, 512, 515, 518, 519, 521, 523, 525, 527, 528, 531, 535, 536, 539, 543*
Paddington maps, *46, 114, 171*
  aerial views, *64, 357, 510, 512, 519, 521*
  early maps of municipality, *56, 186*
  retro-mapping, *60, 64*
  subdivisions, *56, 177, 244, 250, 253*
Paddington Markets, *152, 160, 318, 473, 563, 567*
Paddington parks, *110, 114, 118, 523, 525, 527, 528, 531*
  Centennial Park, *110, 114, 217, 444, 518, 523, 571*
  community gardens, *531*
  Hampden Park, *114, 523*
  Hyde Park, *50, 184, 212*
  Moore Park, *110, 217*
  pocket parks, *525, 531*
  Paddington Reservoir Gardens, *160, 325, 504, 518, 527, 528*
  Royal Hospital for Women Park (Paddington Green), *383, 385, 387, 527, 528*
  Rushcutters Bay Park, *17, 176, 525*
  Trumper Oval and Park, *114, 244, 450, 506, 518, 521, 523, 525*
  Trumper Reserve, *528, 531*
Paddington Post Office, *106, 146, 504, 527, 549*

Paddington Public School, *89, 318*
Paddington Reservoir, *89, 106, 121, 160, 518, 527, 528*
Paddington Reservoir Gardens, *160, 325, 504, 518, 527, 528*
Paddington residents,
  bohemians, *306, 311, 314, 340, 393, 394, 399, 401, 403, 406, 411, 414, 416, 420, 426, 428, 435*
  creatives, *435, 439, 440, 444, 447, 450, 455, 459, 461, 466, 470, 473, 474, 479, 484, 488, 489, 492*
  gay residents, *146, 147, 311, 325, 558*
  university students, *141, 416, 461, 484*
  see also Cadigal people,
Paddington Society, *280, 314, 382, 387, 549, 554, 558, 563, 571*

'Battle for Paddington', *344, 346, 350, 352, 357, 362, 366, 369, 549, 558*
  formation of, *152, 344, 406*
  preservation plans, *282, 357, 362, 366, 369, 373, 376, 383, 385*
Paddington streets, *42, 94, 217, 416, 531, 535, 536, 539, 543*
  Bennett's Grove Avenue, *531*
  Cameron Street, *269*
  Cascade Street, *269, 519*
  Duxford Street, *435, 474, 479*
  Elizabeth Street, *269*
  Fiveways, *104, 506, 554, 572*
  Gipps Street, *233*
  Glebe Street, *535*
  Glenmore Road, *56, 60, 64, 121, 177, 233, 320, 331, 563*

Hampden Street, *502*
Heeley Street, *262*
Hopetoun Street, *571, 572*
Jersey Road, *176, 357*
Little Comber Street, *278*
Liverpool Street, *282*
New South Head Road, *22, 77*
Old South Head Road, *81, 87, 224* see also maroo,
Olive Street, *141*
Oxford Street (previously Old South Head Road), *94, 96, 118, 121, 127, 129, 269, 320, 504, 549* see also maroo, Paddington Street, *284*
Regent Street, *539*
Roylston Street, *519*
Selwyn Street, *539*
South Head Road, *164, 171*
Thorne Street, *262*
Underwood Street, *228, 420*
Wentworth Street, *240*
William Street, *318, 320, 561, 571, 572*
Windsor Street, *289, 376*
see also Paddington maps, Paddington subdivisions, *56, 60, 82, 101, 176, 184, 204, 212, 224, 228, 232, 233, 240, 244, 248, 250, 253, 257, 260, 512*
    Duxford Estate, *64, 250, 253*
    Good Hope Estate, *244*
    Lawson Estate, *257*
    MacDonald Estate, *64, 244, 248*
    Olive Bank Estate, *64, 250*

Paddington Estate (Underwood Estate), *64, 77, 177, 180, 228, 240, 244, 248, 253*

Paddington Town Hall, *36, 37, 106, 129, 133, 141, 147, 152, 160, 325, 504, 527, 528, 548*

Paddington Village, *82, 87, 88, 89, 94, 96, 208, 212, 217, 232, 439*

Palmer, John, *171, 217*

Parkes, Henry, *106*

Parsons, Philip, *140, 484*

Pearl, Cyril, *406, 447, 554*

Phillip, Arthur, *46, 164*

photographic studios, *440*

Pinniger, Gretel, *416*

Piper, John, *56, 176*

Post Mill, Paddington, *77, 217*

public transport, *94, 136, 330, 435, 554, 571*
  see also horse-buses; trams,

pubs,
  see hotels,

Pugh, Clifton, *411, 439*

Q

quarries, *50, 82, 114, 171, 212, 228, 512, 519, 521, 523, 528*

R

Rae, John, paintings, *50*

real estate speculation, *294, 382, 571*

Recreational Arts Team, *320, 325*

restaurants, *311, 318, 393, 470, 473, 474*

retailing, *152, 157, 160, 563*

Richardson and Wrench, *250, 253*

Ridley family, *88, 502, 515*

Ridley, William, *28*

Riley, Edward, *52, 64*

Roberts, George, paintings, *7, 82, 88, 177, 217, 515*

Robinson, Les, *447*

Rodius, Charles, painting, *11*
Rose, William, *399, 416, 488*
Roseth, John, *340, 563*
Rosewell, Dorothy, *554, 558*
Rossi, Francis, *64, 184, 194*
Rowan, Sheila, *152*
Royal Hospital for Women, *121, 127, 157, 260, 382*
Royal Hospital for Women Park (Paddington Green), *383, 385, 387, 527, 528*
Royal Hotel, Fiveways, *104, 147, 318, 572*
rugby, *114*
Rushcutters Bay, *204*
   Aboriginal settlement on, *17, 21, 28, 31, 60*
   creeks, *3, 7, 27*
   flats, *88, 500, 502, 515, 518, 523, 525*
   see also market gardens,
   maps, *56, 64*
   name, *11, 164*
Rushcutters Bay Park, *17, 176, 525*
Rushcutter Valley gentry estates, see gentry estates and villas,

S

Sandercock, Leonie, *373*
Scheinberg, Gisella, *146, 466*
Schlunke, Juliet, *416*
Schofield, Leo, *346, 357*
schools,
   Elfred House Private School, *253, 257*
   Glenmore Road Public School, *89, 330*
   Guriganya Progressive School, *420, 473*

Paddington Public School, *89, 318*
Sydney Technical High School, *455*
see also art schools,
Scott, Rose, *444*
Scottish Hospital, *260, 387, 510, 527, 543, 571*
Sea View Villa, *420, 440*
settlers,
  see colonisation,
Sharp, Martin, *146, 147, 426*
Sherman, Gene, *488, 489, 492*
Slessor, Kenneth, *393, 447*
Southan, Jannie, *554, 558*
speculative builders, *101, 257, 260, 262*
sport, *114, 127, 129, 176, 523, 525*
stables, *121, 257, 561, 572*
Stern, Barry, *146, 306, 399, 466, 470*

Stevens, Bertram, *110, 444*
St Francis of Assisi Catholic Church, *89*
St George's Anglican Church, *89*
St John's Presbyterian Church, *89, 385, 387, 420*
St Matthias' Anglican Church, *89, 240*
Strachan, David, *455, 459*
street trees and plants, *504, 506, 510, 512, 536, 539, 543, 563, 571, 572*
Stronach, Peter, *284, 289*
St Sophia's Greek Orthodox Church, *89*
subdivisions,
  see Paddington subdivisions,
Sydney,
  early maps of, *36, 37, 41, 42, 46, 77, 164, 171, 212*
  population, *82, 87*

post-war, *330, 334, 336*
redevelopment of, *549, 554*
subdivision of early estates, *176, 204, 212, 224, 228, 244, 248, 250, 253, 257, 260*
Sydney Common, *52, 64, 212, 217, 232*
Sydney Distillery (later Glenmore Distillery), *31, 52, 56, 64, 77, 88, 106, 176, 177, 180, 184, 186, 194, 208, 212, 224, 253, 440, 502, 518, 523*
  see also Cooper, Robert; Underwood, James,
Sydney Harbour, *7, 8, 11*
Sydney History Group, *152*
Sydney 'Push', *141, 484*
Sydney Stadium, *129, 140, 141*

Sydney Technical High School, *455*

T

T&M Productions, *428*
Taft, Senta, *306, 399, 473*
Taylor Square, *48, 129, 461, 515*
Tennant, Kylie, *444*
tennis, *127, 129, 176, 525*
terrace housing, *60, 101, 127*
  amalgamation development, *294, 382, 563*
  balconies, *373, 376, 548, 554*
  building of, *101, 260, 262, 269*
  decorative cast iron and, *163, 224, 262, 311*
  diagrams and plans of, *228, 233, 240, 262, 269*

infill development, *284, 289, 294, 373, 376, 378, 385, 473*
see also Gazzard House; Henwood House,
interiors, *289, 306, 435, 479*
paintings of, *88, 435, 455, 479*
party walls, *224, 262, 269*
photographs of, *278, 282, 284, 289, 306, 314, 357, 376, 416, 428, 474, 512, 531, 535*
rear demolitions and additions, *561, 563*
removal and insertion development, *284, 289, 294*
renovating of, *152, 160, 280, 282, 344, 401, 403, 406, 488*
single storey, *228, 269*
Victorian, *224, 228, 232, 233, 240, 244, 248, 250, 253, 257, 260, 262, 269, 278*
Terraces, The, *64, 101, 250, 257, 260, 262, 510*
Therry, Roger, *64, 184, 204, 250, 257*
Thomas, William, *52, 64, 176, 502*
Thompson, John, *140, 303, 352, 403, 406*
Thompson, Patricia, *121, 127, 140, 152, 303, 403, 406, 411, 455*
Thornhill, Michael, *426, 428*
Thornton, George, *22, 27, 28*
Thurston, Madeleine, *399*
tourism, *563, 567, 572*
walking tours, *160, 314, 420, 563*
town planning, *330, 331, 334, 336, 340, 344, 346, 350, 352, 357, 362, 366, 369, 373, 376, 378, 382, 383, 385, 387*
trams, *94, 101, 104, 110, 118, 147, 549, 554, 571*

Tranter, John, *484*
Treweeke, Vernon, *484*
Trumpalar Tree, *531*
Trumper Oval and Park (formerly Hampden Park), *114, 244, 450, 506, 518, 521, 523, 525*
Trumper Reserve, *528, 531*
Turner, Ethel, *110, 444, 447*
Tzannes, Alexander, *289, 376, 382, 383*

U

Ubu, underground film movement, *426*
Underwood, James, *52, 56, 77, 176, 177, 180, 184, 224*
Unicorn Hotel, *141, 147, 325*
UNSW Art and Design (formerly Alexander Mackie, and College of Fine Arts), *160, 461*

urban history, *152, 344*

V

vegetation,
   native to Paddington area, *497, 498*
   street trees and plants, *504, 506, 510, 512, 536, 539, 543, 563, 571, 572*
Verge, John, *194, 199, 204, 257*
Vestor, Michael, *89*
Victoria Barracks, *48, 64, 77, 89, 121, 208, 212, 217, 228, 232, 439, 504, 510*
   illustrations of, *94, 127, 212, 217, 548, 571*
Victorian terrace housing,
   see terrace housing,
villas,
   see gentry estates and villas,

W

Wagner, Shirley, *473*
Walker, Robert, *488*

photographs, *414, 416, 420, 466, 470, 489*
Walter Read Reserve, *504, 527*
Warrell, William, *17*
water supply, *88, 89, 121, 208, 212, 217, 515, 518*
   see also Busby's Bore; Lachlan Swamps; Paddington Reservoir,
waterways, *515, 518*
   see also Lachlan Swamps; Rushcutters Bay, creeks,
Watters Gallery, *426, 466, 470*
Wesleyan Church, *217, 240*
West, Obed, *11, 17, 22, 176*
West, Thomas, *17, 52, 56, 64, 171, 176, 184, 186, 217, 244, 439, 500, 502*
Westall, William, painting, *498*

White City, *127, 129, 176, 387, 525, 548*
White, Patrick, *455, 459*
Wilding, Michael, *141, 484*
Windsor Castle Hotel, *411, 414*
Winzar, Chris, *420*
Wood, Simon, photographs, *320, 387, 504, 510, 525, 528, 531, 549, 554, 561, 563, 571, 572*
Woollahra Council, *147, 289, 294, 330, 352, 357, 362, 369, 376, 378, 567*
Woollahra Significant Tree Register, *510*
Woolley, Ken, *473*
Woolloomooloo Hill, *171, 176, 177, 180, 184, 186, 190, 194, 204*
   see also gentry estates and villas,
Wotherspoon, Garry, *340*

Z

Zander, Alleyne Clarice, *459*

www.ingramcontent.com/pod-product-compliance
Lightning Source LLC
Chambersburg PA
CBHW071229300426
44116CB00008B/964